W9-AMX-774

WITHDRAWN

DALE H. GRAMLEY LIBRARY
SALEM COLLEGE
WINSTON-SALEM, N. C.

The
Diary
of
Anaïs Nin

Works by Anaïs Nin

The
Diary
of
Anaïs Nin

1955–1966

[V.6]

Edited and with a Preface by Gunther Stuhlmann

Harcourt Brace Jovanovich

New York and London

DALE H. GRAMLEY LIBRARY
SALEM COLLEGE
WINSTON-SALEM, N. C.

PS
3527
I865
Z5
V.6

Copyright © 1966, 1976 by Anaïs Nin
Preface copyright
© 1976 by Gunther Stuhlmann

All rights reserved.
No part of this publication may be
reproduced or transmitted in any form
or by any means, electronic or mechanical,
including photocopy, recording,
or any information storage and
retrieval system, without permission in
writing from the publisher.

Printed in the United States of America

The author wishes to thank the following
for their permission to reprint the material
listed: the *Los Angeles Times* for "Wail of
Tortured Electrons Provides Eerie Film
Score," by Philip K. Scheuer, copyright
© 1956, Los Angeles Times, and for
"Journal of a Troubled Journey," by
Robert Kirsch, copyright © 1966, Los
Angeles Times; The New York Times
Company for "The Playwright's Role," by
Eugene Ionesco, copyright © 1958 by the
New York Times Company; the *San Francisco
Examiner* for "Paradise Lost by Mexico
LSD Colony," by George Dusheck, *San
Francisco News-Call Bulletin,* July 2, 1963.

Library of Congress Cataloging
in Publication Data
Nin, Anaïs, date
The diary of Anaïs Nin.
Vol. 3 has imprint:
New York, Harcourt, Brace & World;
v. 4- : New York, Harcourt Brace Jovanovich.
CONTENTS: V. 1 1931–1934.—
v. 2 1934–1939.—[3]1939–1944.—[4] 1944–1947.—
[5]1947–1955.—[6] 1955–1966.
1. Nin, Anaïs, date—Biography.
I. Stuhlmann, Gunther, ed. II. Title.
PS3527.I865Z5   818'.5'203   [B]   66-12917
ISBN 0-15-125594-6

First edition
B C D E

*This volume is dedicated to Doctors
Raymond Weston, Maclyn Wade,
Leon Morgenstern and Edward Stadler,
who saved my life in January, 1975.
And to nurse Mary Maxwell, who
gave me her own courage and energy.*

Preface

During the summer of 1965, while plans for the publication of her diaries were taking definite shape, Anaïs Nin had a dream which, in symbolic shorthand, seemed to project her ambivalence about finally exposing her great undertaking to the world. When, in her dream, she opened the door of her house, she was struck by a blinding flash of light—by "mortal radiation," as she recorded it. Apparently, stepping out of the lifelong shelter of the Diary, her true home, posed many potential dangers.

Since their inception, Anaïs Nin's journals had flourished in a climate of secrecy. Protection from prying eyes, from outside judgment, had been a precondition of their growth, their continued existence. Once the original *cri de coeur* of the child, conceived as an open letter to the lost father, had become the opium pipe of a young woman's reflections, the warm comfort of confidentiality alone had insured the uncensored spontaneity which provided the impetus, the basic strength, for this ongoing dialogue with a nascent self. Since the 1920s, when Anaïs Nin, in the wake of her early marriage, had begun to secrete the growing pile of slim, handwritten volumes, they had remained in hiding for most of their existence.

Occasionally, in a grand gesture of affection—and at times perhaps to evoke an echo from her solitary enterprise—Anaïs Nin had shown portions of her diaries to a few trusted friends. In France, in the 1930s, she had offered up sections to June and Henry Miller, to psychoanalyst Dr. Otto Rank, to the young Lawrence Durrell. In New York, in the 1940s, she had shared such confidences with some of the "children of the albatross." Undoubtedly, such exposure had contributed, by word of mouth, sometimes in print, to the growing reputation and the quasi-legendary status of her diaries. Enthusiastic friends, economic pressures, anger and frustration at being ignored as a writer, at times had propelled Anaïs Nin into considering publication of her diaries. Indeed, with some reluctance she had prepared edited versions for potential publishers. But all such partial revelation, such breaking of the seals, had been momentary, confidential, always based on trust and friendship.

Anaïs Nin, in her own phrase, had regarded the Diary mostly as "a work of love." As such, her journals had always been handled with the protective care accorded to love itself. This was only natural as long as the Diary served as a confidante, a trusted friend, as an island retreat in a hostile, hurtful, indifferent world. But even as its functions changed, enlarged, as it grew into a more consciously applied tool, the laboratory, the instrument, of her own creation, as it became a magic wand against forgetfulness, against the passage of time, the Diary had been nourished as a private document. To expose such a work to the public, to casual scrutiny, obviously was fraught with mortal danger, as her dream so strongly implied, both for the Diary itself and for its author.

The sudden flash of exposure could easily burn forever the delicate fabric of her relationships with all those who had been captured in the labyrinth of these diaries. It could blister those nearest her, whose lives had been so closely intertwined with hers but whose "portraits" she felt did not properly belong to her alone. It could hurt those who, in moments of personal intimacy, in the confessional of psychoanalytical consultation, had entrusted her with their confidences.

Moreover, exposing the unguarded thoughts, reactions, evaluations, that she had committed to paper without the intent of ultimate disclosure, without the safeguard of artistic rearrangement, would reveal the uncertain woman, unveil the person behind the public persona, lay her open to "the maliciousness of the world." Perhaps most ominously, opening up the Diary might easily jeopardize this final refuge of her self-esteem, the stronghold of her reputation as a writer, as an artist. Exposed to the cold light of the same critics who in the past had ignored, misunderstood, or casually dismissed her deliberate creations, her sometimes self-published novels and stories, would the much-whispered-about diaries, the submerged body of what Anaïs Nin had so industriously, so carefully accreted over a lifetime, crumble into the dust of neglect and hostility?

Although her personal faith in the value of the diaries was unshakable, alerted by her dream, Anaïs Nin grew anxious and fearful. In New York, she consulted her analyst, Dr. Inge Bogner. Perhaps it would be best never to reveal the diaries. Throughout the years she had been urged, advised, to give up what she herself had sometimes regarded as her "neurotic" and "narcissistic" preoccupation. The fate of the diaries—their existence, their continuation—more than once had hung in a precarious balance. Suffering from "guilt and concern" about their content, about the effect they might have on others, she had resolved, once more, in 1955 to burn the diaries. Yet, as so often in the past, she had neither burned the diaries nor stopped keeping them.

Ten years later, Anaïs Nin was still hesitant, apprehensive about the consequences of revelation: "How do you tell the truth without injuring the lives of others? How do you define injury when this damage varies with each person portrayed, with each situation, with each period of time?" But she has come to an inexorable conclusion: "I have to venture, not with a work of art, separate from myself, but with myself, my body, my voice, my thoughts, all exposed."

While the blinding flash of her dream spelled danger, obviously it also symbolized release of an enormous reservoir of pent-up energy, a powerfully liberating explosion. For the slim notebooks of Anaïs Nin's youth had become, by 1965, a massive accumulation. Assembled over half a century, shifted from Louveciennes to Greenwich Village, to storage bins in San Francisco, in Los Angeles, almost lost in Europe in the turmoil of World War II, they now filled two five-drawer file cabinets in a Brooklyn bank vault. The sheer bulk of material, with its burdensome secrecy, the emotional weight of its content, the overwhelming significance of the diaries in shaping and creating her own life, undoubtedly had begun to exert increasing pressures on Anaïs Nin.

Here in these pages, after all, was contained what she regarded as her true lifework, her "most natural, most truthful" writing. The world, hitherto, had seen only a few outcroppings from this mountain of material, consciously created, in the fragmented form of her published novels and stories. The key to her fiction (and to her standing as an artist) was hidden in its essential source, the Diary.

As Anaïs Nin confesses here, she has had, since her childhood, "a fear of imagining and inventing." The "imaginative work of man" for her "had become equated with a separation from human life." To invent a fully developed character, to work up a "proper" story line, to carry an artistic message, to provide a balanced structure—as the critics of her fiction so often demanded—was anathema to her. It meant to impose a plan, a concept, a finite quality, to something that, to her, was forever in flux, that retained its vitality only by being infinite in its prospects.

The heartbeat, the elusive propellant, of Anaïs Nin's Diary was its continuous flow, the constant progression of the day-to-day adventure of living, spontaneously recorded. As long as people were alive, vitally changing and shifting with the light under which they were seen, they retained their possibilities of growth, and no finite quality could be ascribed to them. When they became stationary, fully outlined in imagination by the writer, embalmed, as it were, in a static dimension, when they were no longer nascent, they dropped out of life, they disappeared from the Diary. In her journals, Anaïs Nin could not foresee the next event, the subsequent development, she could only be reactive. To plan ahead, to impose a logical order, to project into the future—that is, to imagine and invent—was not possible. She could only observe, analyze, listen to the secret signals of the self, tune in to the "dream" and its poetic creations that transcended the conscious efforts of the mind. "I am an explorer," Anaïs Nin had written in 1941. "I must visit the lands I am to describe."

While her published fiction had used elements drawn from actual experiences and real people recorded in the diaries, it had always avoided the final stasis of reproduced reality. Taken from an ongoing flow, thus by necessity fragmentary, inconclusive, it had adopted as its method the same principles that had evolved in the shaping of the diaries. Anaïs Nin's fiction, like her Diary, had sidestepped mere verbal photography, documentation, the accumulation of plain facts, the piling-up of anecdotes. "My only discipline has been to cut out the unessential," she had written back in 1942. Against what she considered the perversions of objectivity, Anaïs Nin had pitted her own reflective sensibilities, her openness towards experience.

When she tapped into a strong emotional flow, she could delve into a person's story at great length, with infinite care. On the other hand, where there was no intense crosscurrent of sympathetic response, she could with a few words dismiss an encounter with someone like Charlie Chaplin, which to another person might have yielded a substantial anecdote. Sometimes Anaïs Nin is baffled by the contrast between the factual, the outside world, and her own perceptions. "When I meet these same people in reality, accidentally, I cannot understand or reconstruct the love, the friendship, the exchange and bonds between us. The encounters are deprived of the luminous incandescence I presented in the Diary." The magic, it seems, is often derived from the reflection of the encounter, the intensity of her perceptions, rather than from the facts themselves.

"I wage a constant war against reality," Anaïs Nin admits. The Diary is her only bridge to "earthly life," her sole connection to a world not of her making. ("I am living in the wrong world for the sake of protection, the protection which the conventional life offers with its rules, strictures, legalities.") Only the Diary offers her an arena in which she can be free, where she can pursue her true life. But as long as the Diary must remain a secret, her published fiction is the sole "dynamite" that can blast her "out of isolation."

Faced with the continuing frustrations of her uncertain publishing career, Anaïs Nin, by 1965, had reached the point where her submerged feelings surfaced forcefully and fully articulated: "I felt the need to publish the Diary as strongly as the snake pushing out of its old skin, grown too tight, too small." She was ready to break through. Indeed, as we now can see in retrospect, her subconscious striving to relieve the pressure, to reveal her essential lifework, had been gathering momentum all along. Throughout the 1950s, we find Anaïs Nin increasingly concerned about the form and shape of what once had been an almost instinctive vehicle. While she is typing up the original diaries, volume by volume, she is also imposing new critical standards upon her once spontaneous undertaking. With a more relaxed self-appraisal, with a new sense of maturity ("I feel installed in the present," she is able to write in 1955. "My anger against America is gone") also comes a new craftsmanlike assessment of her diaries. Had her perception of the truth indeed captured the essential reality of those she had portrayed? Was her version of what had transpired at the "heightened moments" of awareness—which had served as the benchmark of her reflections, her selective criterion—accurate and fair? Had her own self-preoccupation fostered distortions, crucial omissions? "It took me a lifetime to learn that happiness is in quiet things, not in the peaks of ecstasy," she writes. Is she then also able to step back, to look at her diaries as something outside of herself, outside of her "personal intuition"?

"I felt suddenly that the very personal quality of the Diary was incomplete," Anaïs Nin notes in the spring of 1962. "I had sacrificed objective knowledge. . . . I suddenly wanted to see people from all angles." With a firming sense of self her emotional dependence on her secret "vice" obviously was waning: "I stopped writing in the Diary." Free of her old "hypersensitivity," she feels capable of approaching the earlier diaries with "the care, the patience, the craftsmanship, the thoroughness" she had lacked previously, which in fact had not been called for as long as no disclosure of the diaries had been contemplated.

While Anaïs Nin is shaping her Mexican experiences into *Seduction of the Minotaur* (published in 1961 by her new publisher, Alan Swallow), while she is collating some of her West Coast and New York encounters into "Count Laundromat" (published as *Collages* in 1964) by using sections culled from the diaries, she is preoccupied on another level with the prospect of the Diary's publication. Retyping the original volumes, filling out, updating some of her "portraits," she is striving not for impersonality, distance, but for a "new objectivity," as she put it. Late in 1962, she writes: "I am starting now as a diary-writer and realist." The emotional intensity of the earlier notebooks has given way to a cooler—if as yet largely unspoken—concern over how to make their eventual publication feasible.

By early 1963, Anaïs Nin had decided "to retire as the major character of the Diary." The old diaries are dead, a major shift has taken place, from now on "the Diary will be called the Diary of Others." Obviously, it is to be not only given over to others as the subjects of her concern, but also offered to others, to us, the outside world, as a gift, the signal of a final liberation that no longer requires secrecy, by a woman at last able to shed her protective veils, to step out into the light and stand alone.

"I became deeply interested in the problem of editing, how to avoid hurting or damaging people. How to reveal in such a subtle way that no explicit statement could be deduced, no facts." No longer in need of protecting herself, Anaïs Nin now worries about others, about the frankness of her portraits, about how to "reveal without the destructive aspects of revelation. How to extract the essence of life without damage." Full disclosure, publication of the entire Diary, in its raw form, is impossible but, she argues, "there was plenty of material so that what could not be published would not be missed." Spurred by the strong desire to publish, a way to publish could surely be found.

Anaïs Nin's concern was not so much with conventional indiscretion, not with the increasingly fashionable biographical and auto-biographical revelation of the permissive sixties, of the sexual revolution. "It was not in my nature," Anaïs Nin confesses, "to be explicit in sexual matters." The taboo she imposed, by her own admission, on "sensual matters," though fostered perhaps by her Spanish-Catholic upbringing, by the damaging effects her father's indiscretions had had upon her life as a child, originated primarily in her romantic, poetic sensibilities, which made even her attempts at writing pornography, as we have seen, a fanciful erotic adventure.

Since any intimate relationship involved other persons, their right to privacy, to protection, was an essential factor to Anaïs Nin. While she could reveal her own highly charged experience of childbirth in minute detail in the first volume of the Diary and in her earlier story "Birth," she respected the privacy, the silence, imposed on her by others, who had requested not to be included in the published work. Though she explored the laborious process of the self-creation of the woman in its endless facets, she remained by choice silent about some relationships.

"Today we live by a savage code; that the life of one man is always to be sacrificed for the benefit of the many, that a public figure belongs to history, that we have a right to know all," Anaïs Nin wrote shortly after the first volume of her Diary had been published in 1966. "We must draw a boundary line indicating where respect for the life of a human being is more important than the satisfaction of sensation-seekers. Writers have given an example of ruthless invasion instead of a lesson in the creative possibilities of intimate portraits. This becomes very crucial in an age which is repudiating the disguises of the novel because it lives through television and films, closer to actuality and the realities of personalities. If our age is noted for alienation it is largely because, in general, we treat each other without tact or sensitivity."

To cover these problems of exposure, certain protective measures could be taken. A character could be veiled in anonymity, given a pseudonym, or eliminated altogether, based on the person's own choice. But perhaps the most important method evolved in Anaïs Nin's effort to employ the writer's craft so thoroughly, so skillfully, "that all sides are heard, all aspects considered . . . in such organic development lies a possibility of balance." The inherent dangers of publication perhaps could not be eliminated altogether, but the potential damage could be modified. "The destructive element of truth is neutralized by a deep probing into motivation which makes you understand a character beyond appearances. What is understood is not judged."

Over the past ten years, five volumes drawn from the original diaries have been published. Each one a separate entity, each one part of a larger whole, covering a quarter of a century, from the winter of 1931–32, to the fall of 1955. Today we know that the brilliant flash so anxiously projected by Anaïs Nin in her dream has not produced a hurtful explosion, a singeing exposure of personal relationships, a gossipy exploitation of the now-famous. The blinding radiance has served instead to fully illuminate Anaïs Nin's major creation. It has given us new insight into her fiction, her "artistic" work. It has revealed a woman at last able to face the world, to face herself, liberated from the need to find comfort and security in her hidden notebooks, freed from her multiple disguises, masks and role projections. It has opened up to a vast readership a singular document accessible to a caring personal identification, a compassionate sharing that exceeds in intensity any expectations, any hopes of final recognition, that Anaïs Nin may have projected into that radiant explosion in her dream in 1965.

GUNTHER STUHLMANN

New York
January, 1976

List of Illustrations

The
Diary
of
Anaïs Nin

[Fall, 1955]

After my experience with LSD, a whole day and a whole night of overstimulation, restlessness and the most extreme fatigue, I felt as if my body had received near electrocution by too great a current of vibrations. It was not humanly bearable, the concentration of a thousand dreams into one, the total separation from one's center, the total voyage into an atmosphere, a rhythm, a space not in harmony with one's physical body. Yes, too strong a current. I think our dreams, reveries were meant to be absorbed organically and gradually, tempered by daylight, cushioned by humble occupations and drab interruptions. We have to have time to absorb these great charges of metaphysical energies, mix them with daily living, live them out, in a human gradation and human cellular development. A chemistry adapted to our human body: a dream, then awakening, then action, then contact with other human beings, then return to the earth, contact with the earth, with our own body. My fatigue reminded me of Artaud's complaint: *Une fatigue de fin du monde* (A weariness like the end of the world). I was empty and listless for a long time. I did not write. For the first time the search for the dream was not a beautiful and natural interweaving of night and day, but a total wrench into space, a nonhuman orbiting. I felt something wrong. My self-propelling apparatus was damaged. Forced. Too much and too much violence, and it took many days of passivity to absorb all I had seen and heard.

Finally I did write about it, from notes, from vivid memory, from Gil Henderson telling me what I had done and said. I still felt that our bodies were not adapted to such intensive reverie.

It frightened me that I stopped writing for a long while (except in the diary). A short circuit. Burnt wires and nerves. Burnt energy.

New York.
Riis Park. One inch between each person. All except the Negroes, who are beautiful, look as if they eat nothing but hot dogs, millions of them. But the sea was warmer than the sea in Los Angeles.

I bought a beautiful book on Japanese architecture, so beautiful

I cannot bear to send it to Lloyd Wright, I cannot part with it just yet.

Ruth Witt Diamant is here collecting poets for her Poetry Center at San Francisco State College. She has done so much for poetry and poets.

I write to Felix Pollak about the Grecian life of California and he asks me an embarrassing question: "Do you mean devoted to physical culture only, body-centered, without the Grecian balance and harmony of body and mind that produced so much of the beautiful and good, the typically Greek sensuous mentality?"

I am afraid that so far I have seen only the cult of the beach, swimming, suntanning.

So far the majority of the people seem colorless and mentally inert.

Felix Pollak writes me: "I have been thinking about, and repeating in my mind, your marvelous sentence, 'The sea of death carries away a little fragment of our soul's island, with each person we loved or admired.' "

Henry is working on the story of Moricand. He remembers that he was born in Paris January 12, 1890.

He writes me that he wrote some revelatory pages about Capricorn, which was also Moricand's sign, all intuitive, "about the fundamental essence of Capricorn." I cannot remember where this passage occurs. Henry wonders what astrologers would say.

"Am about in the middle of the Moricand chapter now. It will be very long. And—like the last word on the subject." [Book later titled *A Devil in Paradise*.]

From diary, age eleven: "I have transposed the war in my heart to the war a hundred times more bloody taking place across the ocean."

Letter to Jim Herlihy:

I am very proud of my private dedication. The fascinating problem of the irresponsible life. That has been the theme of our month. Just as we discussed it more clearly and openly I realized that we live our irresponsible life in secret. The occasional danger of exposure creates our violent attacks of guilt. Our desire to live everything out will always meet with the obstacle of guilt. The unwillingness to cause pain as well as the unwillingness to accept the judgment of others. One of the most inspiring things about our friendship is that we never pass judgment. I should not even state it as negatively as that: we accepted each other's unconscious self, the hidden one. This gives an elating sense of freedom. Now I solved the problem of not hurting anyone, or hurting with amnesia and chloroform. But I never solved the problem of guilt, which is proved by masochism. I can only get rid of the guilt by atonement. Analysis only helped me to shorten the periods of atonement. When you wrote to me about your restlessness and the guilt you feel for even wishing to be free, I wanted to help you. For that is the real drama, the real tragedy. It might account for all the masochism in the world, the sacrifices, the self-destruction. Guilt is at the core, the toxic effect of Christianity. I have often referred to the history of the Caesars. That is even a greater mystery as they were not religious. They felt all-powerful. They were convinced of their omnipotence and godlessness. They considered themselves the only gods. They all committed abominations. And each one of them died of guilt, not from sensual excesses, not from war, not from illness but of a madness brought on by guilt. So guilt is even older than Christianity. In your case guilt presents itself in a more subtle form. When success grows near you begin to feel uneasy. You see a more obvious form of atoning for success in Bill and his destructive drinking. You are too clever, people like you too much for you to ruin anything, but you can spoil your enjoyment, and that is more subtle to detect and to cure. Watch for it. It is the real enemy, the real incubus, succubus, the only demon and the only voodoo.

Letter from Jim:

Your letter was a very special event. One doesn't expect the average letter to be so well written. Your description of Reginald as Hamlet in your house was lovely, and your comments on our lives. I needed hearing the things you said, as it has been a great preoccupation lately—the business of living completely. I think that what has caused me pause in this particular period is the fact that, superficially, I have everything I can rationally expect: the basics, like food, etc., relief temporarily from economic pressures, a handsome lover, new short novel appearing, play in preparation for Broadway, etc., and I think that the living out of these events as contrasted with what I had imagined such an ideal condition to be like, is perhaps a little alarming. The great and beautiful high moments of my life have not been realizations of dreams so much as spontaneous wonder and surprise at certain unexpected events; my relationship with you has been constantly punctuated with such moments, and there are others that would seem less spectacular when I enumerate them: the pigeons in Venice, when they landed on my head and hands and shoulders, I felt like they had flown away with me; and certain encounters with strangers and strange places, and certain lines of prose (many of yours), or a moment in a play, etc. I think that what I am discovering is that the great things are not those we plan on but those which simply happen; and so I feel, at times like this, that my life is arranged too rigidly, as if I were living according to some subconscious and partly conscious plan that ruled out certain realms of wonder and magnificence. I think that I have not really said what I set out to say, but that you may be able to get from this the feeling of what I mean. But these feelings are all definitely related to our splendid talk at the Coffee Mill, about freedom from the ordinary, calendars, planned events, responsibilities of a certain order, etc. I would not like to give you the impression that I am unhappy—only that I am doing a lot of thinking about the way my current existence is structured. It is pleasant and exciting but not extraordinary. I think I yearn for the extraordinary, like a true child of the Albatross.

You put your finger on one of the many inspiring elements of our relationship; but your letter itself was another of the elements—extracting such a beautiful thing from a simple little mailbox is really quite astounding. I think that in my life you are an example of the marvelous; and perhaps you make me less content with those elements in it which are not. You keep me on the beam. You keep my target on the clouds. You keep me from selling short. You are mediocrity's executioner. I am constantly stunned by the fact that when you give the command, life jumps through the hoop as if it were your servant.

Your paragraph on guilt, ironically enough, arrived the very morning after I dreamed that I had been guillotined.

Our fear of not being punished seems to plague us even more than the fear of suffering. Which is a shame, because we seem to have built-in crucifixes anyway.

Let me know if you want me to send you my portable guillotine. Or, are you mowing the lawn instead? It's so strange, so funny, that you and I suffer so at our own hands when our greatest flaw is probably that we are too careful of others, too considerate.

One of the recent sessions with Dr. Bogner seemed unimportant yet was enormously effective. It dealt with my calling her up and asking her if she would mind seeing my friend X instead of me because she was in the midst of a crisis whereas I was well. Bogner said she did not mind, but that she had an extra free hour she could give to X and so I could keep my own hour if I wanted to.

When I came we explored this simple incident. It was true that X had greater problems at the moment. It was also true that I had reached a comfortable stage in the analysis and that in the last sessions we always avoided going too deeply into new realms. Bogner did not doubt my goodwill towards X, nor the naturalness of my desire to help her.

"The two are true. I am only wondering why you could not tell me directly what was in your mind. You did not say: 'I feel I don't need analysis, so I would rather not come.' Or else: 'Do you happen to have a free hour for X, who is having difficulties?' "

"Even if I felt that I wanted to keep my light mood and not see you today, wouldn't it be irresponsible to let you know at the last moment when you had reserved an hour for me? I would not have done that anyway. I don't want to be irresponsible, particularly when you inconvenience yourself to fit in my erratic schedule, trips, etc."

"All this sounds true, and is true. But it is this rigid kind of responsibility which makes you feel, as you put it the other day, as if you were 'living in a cast' and which causes your negative rebellions. You could have said: 'Today I don't feel that I need analysis. If it is not inconvenient to you and if you can use the hour for someone else, would you mind if I did not come?' You, in a way, concealed your true feelings—that you did not want analysis —behind X's need and tried to reach in a devious way, by covering your true wish with an altruistic one, your basic desire not to come. That is why I made you come, because I felt this was a perfect example of evasion. You create the trap: a responsibility. You didn't think that I might be glad to have a free hour. You felt the commitment as inflexible. Then you felt the pressure. But not knowing how to extricate yourself without *displeasing* me or annoying me, you caught on X's need, which was, in reality, a separate issue."

This small issue nevertheless clarified the truth that freedom is an inner attitude, habit, easier to acquire than one imagines. It was like the issue about *time*. Bogner says the reason that I am always too early (an additional anxiety and stress) is to conceal my rebellion against appointments, organization, discipline. So that the feeling of constriction does not come so much from the duties I have to perform as from the clash between these duties and my anarchic self whom I have to hold in check. The constriction is caused by my own destructive rebellions which I have to control like a pair of wild horses.

Recognizing this was evidently important because since I returned to Sierra Madre I have had a feeling of ease. I have had no destructive, negative rebellions (against housework, loud radios). They do not affect me. And because I do not fight them I work more easily. Also because I do not fight them (they are the price for my life here), I can be more humorous and relaxed.

To sum up an extraordinary change caused by analysis. A month without depressions, anxieties or nervousness. I feel installed in the present. I give myself to it. I no longer feel angers, walls, hostilities in relation to the world. My criticalness has lessened. I enjoy what comes. I am not nervous beforehand. I am gay and free. The fears have decreased, the fears of being unable to earn a living, the fears of losing love. There is less rebellion, more smoothness and lightness in living. There is an ability to throw off anxiety. There is no bitterness, no friction, and my anger against America for not accepting my work has gone. Having fewer conflicts I get less tired and accomplish more. I can do housework half a day, write half a day and still go out at night. Lightness and a feeling of strength. It all consolidated this month. It is true I may die without seeing Bali but then I have other things to make up for that. I can make one human being happy. I am close to one human being and closer than before to others. My genuine gentleness is coming back. I do not expect others to love or understand my work. I am not bitter or hurt. So much accomplished. I went to a party; in the past a part of me would hold back because the people were not interesting; this time I entered uncritically, accepting it on its own level. Contentment. It took me a lifetime to learn that happiness is in quiet things, not the peaks of ecstasy. I am grateful for what I have. I feel reintegrated into the human family. I see Americans as people in trouble, not happy on a deep level. I want to help, to teach. To share and impart the wholeness I feel and the strength. I feel strength from my effort to learn first aid. I have overcome the neurosis at last.

[Winter, 1955–1956]

The New York Times:

Moon is on sale only $1 an acre. Long Islander doing land office business in deeds to crater bottomland. For one dollar this is what the lunar buyer gets: A general quit claim to an acre of good crater bottomland. The fine print disposes of the mineral rights (including uranium). It gives the buyer fishing and winter sports rights near the site he purchased. A brochure describing the wonders of the moon as they are at present envisioned by the developer of the area. The brochure waxes enthusiastic in the time-honored manner of real estate promoters. A map that shows the purchaser how he can see his land through a powerful telescope. The scheme is the invention of Robert R. Cole, a former chairman of the Hayden Planetarium. Mr. Cole is now doing business as Robert R. Cole, President of the Interplanetary Development Corporation with an office at the Little Museum, Seven The Place, Glen Cove, Long Island. Copernicus, the crater staked out by Mr. Cole, contains about 2,000,000 acres. More than 3,000 craters have been observed by astronomers on the side of the moon facing the earth. Mr. Cole has made no claims to the other side.

Naturally I responded. It was a scientist's prank to arouse interest in the moon. I received a pamphlet full of information and a deed!

In New York I went to the opening of Michael Field's ice cream parlor across the way from the Plaza Hotel. It was decorated in the old-fashioned way, all in ice-cream colors, very fresh and icy, and filled with celebrities. Some press agent thought it would be amusing to invite both Marilyn Monroe and Jayne Mansfield. It was to the detriment of Jayne Mansfield. Marilyn arrived without make-up, looking fresh and glowing, and instead of posing to be admired, she looked at everyone there with genuine interest, and when I was introduced she turned her full warm attention on me. Whereas Jayne Mansfield was entirely concerned with her appearance, was heavily made up, self-conscious, full of mannerisms and poses, with an artificial smile and a blank expression. If there was a cruel intention in having them both there, it was defeated by the genuineness of Marilyn Monroe and her natural beauty.

Max Gordon and Michael are in this project together. They felt it would be an intimate place for people to come and would satisfy

9

the nostalgic longings for the twenties. I sat and talked with Frances. I had not seen her very often after her marriage to Michael because of my travels. I had seen her newborn child. I knew that when Michael had difficulties with his hearing he gave up concertizing (he was a marvelous pianist) and took up his hobby, cooking, as a way to earn a living. He was such a fabulous cook that the hobby became a full-blown profession. He became famous. People not only appreciated his knowledge, his skill, but his culture in other realms, his writing, his talk, his dynamic presence, and he became more of a Renaissance man than anyone else I knew in New York. The civilization of his cooking extended to his way of life, his choice of friends. But he worked with so much intensity, so tense a will, so concentrated an energy that it concerned me. And it concerned Frances.

Los Angeles.
I saw a woman dressed in the clothes you see in thrift shops. A faded rose lace dress from the twenties, with faded roses on her shoulder, a faded scarf and a torn, faded parasol. She wore satin high-heeled shoes and a hat with a veil and carried an evening bag. This was in the bus, in the morning, and I could see her following the trail of long-past garden parties, preferring echoes of festivities to the present drabness, preferring a faded rose, a faded past to a plain present. Seeing her was like seeing a faded pressed flower in a book. But her fantasy satisfied her. She sat not like a ghost but like one on her way to a party, and her memories, at least from the expectant expression on her face and the lightness of her steps as she left the bus, had not faded as much as the clothes.

Found a passage in Giraudoux's *Choix des Élus* about a woman who went to the Luxembourg Gardens and to lighten a heavy mood would buy all the balloons. So last night when I could not sleep, I imagined balloons tied to my hands and feet, and in this state of lightness I fell asleep.

Bogner is slightly skeptical of the sudden change in my mood. Am I truly well? I do not say I have no problems, because the obsession with an expanded life is still there, and the obstacles to expansion are still there. The duties are there. But my feeling has changed so I can do them lightly and quickly, I can minimize them, and the anxiety has gone.

But why suddenly?

Am I accelerating the cure, the effort to stand on my own feet? But surely one cannot pretend lightness. Before, when I experienced ecstasies from my loves, it was always with an undertone of anxiety, fear, sadness. As if aware of the ecstasy's short life, its fragility. I feel well, Dr. Bogner. I feel I can now earn my living. I look for pleasure in small events. For example, I now enjoy the foghorns in New York. Years ago I thought of the foghorns as signaling all my frustrated dreams of travel, they seemed like wistful sounds of ships leaving without me aboard. Now I think of them as joyous proofs that the ships are there, sailing back and forth, and that any day I will be on one of them. Isn't the miracle in the interpretation of events, in this transformation of nostalgia, regret, longing into hope and faith?

I wrote for Jim a series of small letters to cure the blues:

"If my lover is irritating I will think what a beautiful alibi he gives me for going on a journey."

"If my lover talks too much I will look out of the window and listen to the rain and think how well they synchronize."

Not being published does not make me feel buried, dead. It bears no relation to my love of writing, like a singer's love of singing.

I feel stronger and more certain. One cannot deceive others. Jim feels it. I said to Alice Rahon: "Borrow my courage. I have an ample supply." She laughed.

I am convalescent. Anxiety is like a fulgurant, decimating fever. It is gone. The ordinary rebel thinks: I am in revolt against housework. And engages in a destructive revolt. The housework has to be done. When one is helped by analysis, destructive rebellions end. The housework is there. But I have found ways to lighten, minimize, accelerate it. And I have more energy for it since I do not spend this energy in fretting over it.

I don't feel I can be crushed, suffocated, restricted any more. I do not want the impossible: to be published, to live in Paris, to see other countries.

"Dr. Bogner, I understand what you are trying to say. Even if I

DALE H. GRAMLEY LIBRARY
SALEM COLLEGE
WINSTON-SALEM, N. C.

feel better, even if I have overcome anxiety, tension, the problems are unsolved. But at least now when I hear the foghorns they do not sound like death knells. When the buses are full and pass me by, I do not sit on the curb and almost weep at the inhumanity of the world, the overwhelming struggle even to get home. But now that I feel better I will be better able to solve the problems. Part of getting well is the desire to get well. You have given me the desire and the energy. The energy was wasted on anxiety. If I can shake off depressions, anxieties and angers I can be more effective."

There is nothing stranger than life without anxiety. Why is it we cannot acquire such precious states as complete relaxation and irresponsibility from others, by contagion? I do remember enjoying this quality in Henry. He never strained. He took everything as it came. He made no efforts. He did not feel responsible. When I was with him, it was communicated to me. I remember one day saying: "I have to visit my mother."

He asked: "Why?"

I had never questioned why I imposed this visit on myself three times a week.

The study of Simenon revealed an interesting truth. Because I consider him the best of the realists, better than Zola or Balzac, I made the following discovery. Realism focuses on the observation of the physical details, but mostly of the ugly detail. Simenon is fertile in noting the homely, the plain, the ugly, the mannerisms, the tics, the weaknesses, the bad smells, the drab clothes, the warts, the weak eyes, the animal instinct for the "cave." He stands at the opposite pole from me. But this is not the surprise. The surprise is that I see all this, but I chose to ignore it, because there is another aspect to all our lives, which is beautiful. My repugnance for the ugly, my turning away, is not to say it is not there, but that the realist does not take notice of its opposite. He wallows in the ugly as Henry did, to prove life is ugly. The beauty is ignored. The same people have beautiful moments, beautiful aspects. But we have come to associate reality with ugliness. Why? Mine was a deliberate choice. Every moment you can choose what you wish to see, observe or record. It is your choice. So you create the total aspect according to your vision. We have a right to select our vision of the world.

In my life this choice has been deliberately present. This is the choice of the lover determined to love. If you are determined to hate, then you select obsessionally what is hateful around you, in people, in yourself.

This year when, after meteoric expeditions, I have come closer to the earth, I want to concentrate on physical details. I was connecting with earth only by way of sensuality, by way of sexuality. I wrote this in my surrealist period. It is still true, by way of love; the physical world I evoke is the one deserving love and which the hater overlooks. Henry did this in his early period when he was angry with the world, when he had not attained what he wanted and was intent on revenge. This angry period ceased abruptly when the world gave him his wish, to be loved by the world, admired, respected.

But why does external reality express our character? Why does the reality of some characters look like the Collier brothers, who all their lives amassed junk which finally suffocated them: empty envelopes, rusty paper clips, used pipecleaners, empty beer cans, old newspapers, useless broken objects everyone else would throw away?

Letter from Jim:

I flipped over your letter. The idea of the notes in the little envelopes and the purpose of them was enough to keep me elated for an hour, but then I was too anxious to wait for the blues before I looked inside. I opened one, and it was so beautiful ("If my lover talks too much I will look out of the window and listen to the rain and think how well they synchronize.") and appropriate and poetic and wise that, like a child, I couldn't resist opening all of the others immediately. I have put them back in the envelopes and will use them in the way you suggested—when I need them. But I can't tell you what they meant to me, each one of them; except that I have a feeling that they are in a way of warning—that if I can't learn a lesson through beauty (like these notes) then I damn well deserve the pain I invite. Because I recognized instantly the wisdom and rightness of them. And I know, as you said in your big letter on the Xmas paper, that the pain is often desired; and the implication that one can make a selection for himself. You always amaze me, Anaïs. I should have learned by this time to expect anything from you, but I continue to be freshened and touched in a very special way by the things you do. I often do wonder how very differently my life would have progressed without these touches of Anaïs sorcery. But there is this bad effect you have had: I have a constant quarrel with the concept of a God who would create a world with only one of you—and so many others! I'm glad your mood is still "lined with cork." I think this is a wonderful way of putting it. As for myself, I am more like the solar machine; completely static in the dark—and dark and light interchange like day and night in me.

You ask me to tell you later which of the messages was the *secret formula*; and although I think that they are all important, I think that the fundamental one is the one I quoted in the first paragraph of this letter. Because it's the one that indicates most strongly that one is saved by his own imagination; and this is, and has always been, the Manifesto of our lives, yours and mine. Am I right? Taken altogether, I think these tiny notes will change my life. Is that surprising? I have been elated ever since I opened them! I want to close this with something about your tiny envelopes and the white magic in them. I don't know what to say except that this is never wasted on me. I'm a sucker for magic!

Something tragic happened to Jim. His friend stole the closet keys while he was asleep, found his diary, read it, and as the diary contained, like all diaries, the pain and conflict of the relationship, there was an explosion, and it traumatized Jim. He feels he can no longer continue it. I suggested he write it and mail it to me and I would keep it sealed in separate envelopes. I am so afraid he will destroy it.

Dream: I am in a carriage, dressed in a fantasy costume, a veil around my head similar to that of the woman in the Japanese movie *Gate of Hell*. The men in the carriage are intrigued and want to unveil me. I get angry, get off the carriage and take another. I am on my way to a Festival at which I have to play a part. On the way I stop at a village. My mother and Joaquin are there. Joaquin is weeping gently at being imprisoned in this out-of-the-way place.

I examine some recordings I am carrying. I take them out of their envelopes and find I have broken them, all of them are shattered. They are records of my father's music.

What I most wanted was an artist's life—that is, few possessions, simple surroundings, a simple way of life which would require very little money and very little compromise.

But then a woman's life is always derivative in the sense that the man's profession creates the initial place, frame, atmosphere, design of the life.

———

If you have claustrophobia of the soul you have to maintain a vast switchboard with an expanded universe, the international life, Paris, Mexico, New York, the United Nations, the artists. The African jungle seems far less dangerous than the mediocrity of Sierra Madre.

For a neurosis such as mine, to take roots means to be rooted to a situation of pain. So that even when I would like to have a beautiful home, a fireplace to sit by, a view, they are dangerous (concealing as they do the bars of a cage). My interpretation of the phrase "to take root" is negative; for me it means cutting off avenues of escape, of communication with the rest of the world. So that against the wish for repose, there is an impulse to remain mobile, fluid, to change surroundings.

In New York I had bronchitis. I got out of bed to see Dr. Bogner, to face for the last time, I hope, that *"chute verticale"* (like the characters of Simenon, the downward pull). I became aware the night before of the anxiety grafted onto the bronchitis, which increased the illness, of the weight that oppressed and sank me. I wanted to catch myself in the act, and I did.

I did have a congested chest, throat, nose. It hampered my breathing. But upon this was grafted a multitude of old anxieties. (I am helpless, weak, suffocating. I cannot sleep. Will I die? I need oxygen.) Then I had the dream of locking myself in a room and of someone breaking down the door. All this a dramatization of the initial illness at age nine, of the fatalism, the sinking.

But—my mother was very kind and tender when I was ill. It was the only time she was tender and warm. The only maternal solicitude.

No voice left at Bogner's but I'm determined to exorcise this downward pull. At the slightest incline I shove myself all the way down. I make exaggerated associations: this is like the night at the hospital. No analogy between bronchitis and a major operation, insomnia after surgery, etc. I do remember the overwhelming gratitude for the quiet, silent night nurse, watching. Midnight. Two o'clock. Four o'clock. Dawn at last. When I went to the bathroom I could look out of the window and see people beginning their day. It seemed as if having lived through the night all would be well (as if one couldn't die in the morning or at noon as well!). No. The night, the solitary creates ghosts and voodoos.

I was uneasy, fearful of being deserted. Particularly when ill. My father left when I was at my lowest ebb, after three months in the hospital with a ruptured appendix.

I felt less congested while talking with Bogner. It was on my way out of her office that this phrase came very clearly to my mind: "My mother was very nice to me when I was ill."

But when I'm ill I'm locked in, dependent, and I rebel against this. It stifles me. A conflict sets in. Reading about Proust last night disturbed me. It is the last thing in the world I wish to do, to lock myself in and be ill.

When I realized how much weight I had added to an ordinary bronchitis, the bronchitis improved in twenty-four hours and I was out the third day.

The inner music started again. I reread what I had done on *Solar Barque* and liked it. Tonight I hear the music and all my feelings are awake.

My greatest problem is one inherent in the experiment itself. Because I follow the pattern of free association the design is sometimes chaotic even to me.

The attempt to construct a novel in this way is difficult. One image suggests another, one feeling calls forth another, one incident evokes another memory, none chronological but linked by one's memory, feelings, unconscious associations.

I wanted to show that the adventurer does not forget his past or escape it when he goes to the paradises of the earth. The doctor gives the drug of remembrance and refuses the drug of forgetfulness. He is killed for that because people want to forget. Lillian does not escape, so she returns to remember and liquidate the past.

According to Bogner, we project onto someone our ideal figure and then expect perfection from this figure. With others there is no idealization at the base. Henry did not create any illusion about being an ideal figure. Neither did Gonzalo. So one did not expect anything of them.

Bogner makes this subjective projection very clear. It makes work upon one's self very difficult. Everything is transposed to the *others*. The projection, once examined, is found to be within the self. It originates in the self, in one's needs. But when she seemed to imply that I used this subjective vision in my work too, I became very disturbed. I'm willing to admit errors in living, but not in my work. Bogner did not mean that. She once told me I maintained, in spite of neurosis, an extraordinary connection with objective reality. I took her first statement on subjective vision as a threat to the integrity of my work. She did not mean that. She meant that all truth lies in the *relationship* between subjectivity and objectivity, not in one or the other. But "subjective" has been used as a judgment against my work. Although I defend the validity and value of subjective art, when she says something that sounds like a *doubt* I feel she is implying psychological blindness. But she is not. All she said was that truth was an interplay between them. Hemingway is not an objective writer, as he is said to be. It is Hemingway's vision of war, bullfights, hunting. Bogner said there was no objective writer. The only other time I misunderstood Bogner was again in reference to writing. To remain objective she has not read my books. She relies on my own attitude and reporting on them. She seemed to disagree when I said I used the psychoanalytic way of approaching the truth about character. She meant that psychoanalysis could not contain or describe the whole character because it focused only on the neurotic area. But I felt that since this was the key to the self, it was a way of reaching the secret or nonrational self in which motivation for our acts was contained. I felt that she, of all people, should understand what I was doing. But she questions all extremes, all separations. Nothing is separate. Everything is inter-related. Outside and inside. Body and psyche. In my writing I meant to start with subjectivity, the subconscious, and arrive at objectivity, to unite them.

My image of others has gone through a thousand transformations, from idealization to total rejection, to re-creation and rescue of a totally new self. As I changed, my perspective changed. The theme of images. How one must struggle against this creation and invention of others, listen to them attentively, let them state their own case, weigh and balance the impressions. Otherwise this invention takes over, or projection. We are like sculptors, constantly carving out of others the image we long for, need, love or desire. Often against reality, against their benefit, and always, in the end, a disappointment because it does not fit them.

Economics in my childhood were very tangled (I was ill when my father left the family and Mother brought us from Europe to New York City) and caused me much anxiety. My mother had been trained only in singing, and when her efforts to establish herself as a music teacher failed, her wealthy sisters bought a brownstone house on Seventy-fifth Street. This would assure us a place to live on the first floor, once a dining room, sitting room and pantry. The rental of the rooms in the rest of the house would give my mother a small income. But this became a most uncertain income. When the rooms were unrented we could barely live. (But what games we played in the empty rooms, particularly on the second floor with its carpeted bedrooms, mirrored dressing rooms and what seemed to us luxurious bathrooms.)

So my mother decided to become a purchasing agent for her wealthy sisters and wealthy Cuban friends. The idea came from the fact that they did write to her constantly to purchase this or that from the department stores, long lists which took much time and effort to fulfill. My mother opened a charge account and was to be given ten per cent of all purchases. The plan was clever, and might have worked. I always remember my mother coming home and announcing with characteristic optimism: "Today I made one hundred dollars!" But the hundred dollars was in part mythical, for many of the purchases were never paid for, or so late that our debts increased and accumulated.

As my mother had to go out and work all day, it was up to me to cope with the bills, to separate the items according to the letters received, to type out a list of purchases for each customer and mail the bills. It was also up to me to pay for the charge accounts as much as we were able to, but each month we fell further behind, and the amount we owed far exceeded what we earned. My mother was kind-hearted and when someone wrote to her they wanted to buy a fur coat and would pay a little every month, my mother consented, and I remember this particular fur coat because after the first payment my mother received nothing at all. So that each evening, when she came in to report the amount she had "earned," with a glowing satisfaction, I already knew at fifteen that it was an illusion, that creditors were at the door, that the department stores were calling up during the day, that the carelessness and thoughtlessness of my mother's wealthy family and friends were causing us once more to eat cornmeal omelets, the cheapest way to satisfy my brothers' youthful appetites.

In my talks with Bogner it is apparent that this experience damaged me. I dreamed of a simple, uncomplicated economic life.

Later, when the situation reached a crisis and my mother's credit was cut off, and we again resorted to renting rooms in our house in Richmond Hill, I went out and became a model.

After talking about this I had a dream: "My mother was driving a car. I displaced her and took over the wheel."

Bogner was trying to tell me that independence was a *feeling,* not a thing to be taken literally and dependent on a job, but I argued that I felt far less anxiety as a girl when I did take a job, and that my dream was that finances should be in the background, not in the foreground of one's life, a mere functional necessity, not the cause for anxiety as it was in my girlhood. I do not want to feel helpless or overwhelmed by destructive forces again.

I am baffled, because when analysis seems to be arousing self-sufficiency then it seems to accuse one of aggressivity, of wanting power (I displace my mother who is driving badly).

The money subject is so painful that I wept. An unsolved mystery. I have worked very hard, yet I earn so little. I feel trapped. When I want to treat independence realistically, Bogner examines the motivation to make certain there is no aggression.

Looking at hideous masks from Peru, I wondered. They were made to frighten the enemy. In us, in some of us, the mask we wear for defense is also ugly. I have seen changes in the faces of friends. The mouth grows thinner, the furrows of anxiety deeper, the eyes more veiled, the smile forced. Some acquire a severity they did not have, others a superciliousness, others arrogance. It saddens me. I wonder how we can grow without these masks.

Is it the same with writing? Does writing wear a mask? Jim does his best writing in darkness and secrecy. What we give the world is different.

Neurosis is a "possession." You are possessed by a demon of self-destruction. You are compulsive. You destroy. It is not your voice, your body, your true self. A demon inhabits your body. It is the spirit of the past. It is the past selves superimposing themselves over the present, blurring it, choking it. An Anaïs of fifteen sees her mother working so hard, work accumulating faster and debts even faster. Baffled by the bookkeeping, feeling helpless. Later, working for immediate needs, a model's small salary for four persons.

I did not mind working all day for a dress shop, and all evening for painters and illustrators; I did not mind going without lunch so I could write in my diary, returning home by the last train. But one night when I arrived my mother told me she had signed a contract for a "sidewalk," six hundred dollars. My salary would never cover that. And it was a superfluous luxury. We did not have a proper heating furnace. It took hours to get it going, and I was continually breaking up orange crates to warm up the house in winter. My mother could not see the unreasonableness of her action. I shook her, and the guilt for taking her by the shoulders and shaking her, saying: "Mother, *can't you see,* can't you see how foolish this is?" has weighed on me all my life. The irrationality of my mother, that was the terror in childhood. The impossibility to reason, and the memory of my father saying: "You can't reason with your mother." My father's obsession was "logic." The word had enormous importance for him. I then began to believe that man was logical, and woman illogical. My first illusion about logic, *man's logic.* And when I met my father many years later, in Paris, the shock of realizing he was a mythomane, and, later still, the shock of realizing with Bogner that he died a schizophrenic.

What confusion in my own nature. I wanted to be the woman one could reason with. My most frequent question was: Do you feel I can be reasoned with? Bogner won me the first day when she said that in spite of the neurosis, I maintained an extraordinary hold on reality (objectivity).

For the first time I understand the ancient fear of madness and the treatment of madmen as criminals. Because even in mild neurosis one can detect the destructive spirit and this must have given rise to the idea of possession by a demon.

A dinner with a French man of business is quite unlike a dinner with an American businessman. Charles Heurté sells ovens to factories, but he paints, has an art collection, is socially charming, witty, flirtatious, gallant and never talks business. He is refined, cultured, well traveled, well read, quotes Valéry, writes a book on art criticism. There was talk of Yucatán culture, of China, of Saint Phalle's History of the World being written, there was hand kissing, and a walk along Fifth Avenue, and an invitation to visit the house he designed himself outside of Paris. In looks and dress he reminded me of the world of Marcel Proust because of the art of conversation, which is disappearing, conversation made to please, to entertain, to enchant, to surprise, to impart experience. France has a way of refining face and body and speech so that the economic necessities and occupations are hidden away, as they should be (as you hide a furnace, an air conditioner, a stove, other functional necessities), and focus is only on the beauty attained through them.

The other couple (an Italian banker) charming, and with them an intelligent discussion of Giraudoux. Interchange, exchange, richness.

Dr. Bogner explains what she means by separating pure from impure motivations. "It is the impure motivations which create guilt. In the case of your taking a job to help your mother, it was seemingly a pure motivation, but you felt guilt not because you stepped in to help in a crisis, but because originally you had wanted to take your mother's place in your father's affection, because originally (original sin!) you were angry with her for driving away your father, angry with her for bringing you to America when you were so happy in Spain. So these hidden angers, covered as they are by good reasons for taking a job, became in your dream your moving into your mother's place when she drove badly. This may even explain why you refused to study music (your father's prerogative), why you never participated in politics (Gonzalo's prerogative)." But writing? Henry's writing did not arrest my own. We incited each other. By that time I had overcome the guilt for moving forward and asserting my own gifts.

The pure and the impure are mixed. But the inexorable conscience is aware of every hostile thought and is ever ready to punish.

It is true that I set out to encourage, to publish, to make Henry known as a writer, and that I lagged behind, and that the recognition of his superiority as a writer enabled me to accept his advice, his help and encouragement.

This talk came after my revolution dream: men, many men, in a place like Mexico. They have just finished a revolution and are surreptitiously returning to work. The leader does not want me to hear the details, but I say with an exaggerated detachment: "Oh, don't be concerned over me. I understand revolutions require violence and terrible acts. But the end justifies the means."

My revolution?

And before that: the lake which cures everything. I am swimming in it. Other people are in boats, which are like carnival floats. The boats ride over me and endanger my life. I get angry at them and bang on them very hard.

It was after the talk about my father's disdain for money that we cleared up why I could never solve economic problems. During the last years of his life, in Cuba, when the gas man or a tradesman came to claim payment, he handed over his wallet and said: "Take what I owe you. I won't handle the filthy stuff."

In our family the word "commercial" was a condemnation. No wonder I could not confront the problem directly and simply; I was always hampered by distaste.

Blow after blow after blow. Strongly tempted to burn the diary. Unless I go to Paris and live the life of a Genêt, openly, criminal and monster, I will die. The atmosphere of America, puritan, middle-class, hypocritical, afraid of reality, is like a total absence of oxygen.

Maxwell Geismar writes me:

What bothers me most in this whole thing is your conviction that you are "through" as a writer, at least in this country, and that it is useless to go on writing; if that is what you feel . . . This is death for a writer, and you must not accept this statement except as a momentary revulsion . . . If you are really convinced of this, why not get the diaries published in Paris or Italy, go over there yourself, try to get the right arrangement, or print them yourself as Lawrence did with *Lady Chatterley* and *Pansies*, and you can even possibly make money from them; this may be a desperate recourse, but valid if you feel it is the only thing left . . . (And then of course they will print a censored American version!) Otherwise why not try to write the novel based on a cycle of the diaries; which would still not impair the final worth of the diaries, but might be halfway between what you have published and what you haven't. I think this is the way you should move; but do anything rather than give up!

I have paid the price for not breaking away from the bourgeois world and living altogether as an artist. Why, why didn't I have the ultimate courage to live beyond the reach of all laws and taboos, to be what I am, as Genêt is what he is, committed to no one, subjected to no restrictions, *"Le poète maudit,"* and live with those who obey no taboos, and not as I am doing, living in the wrong world for the sake of protection, as my father did, a protection for which you pay with your life. The protection which conventional life offers, with its rules, structure, legalities, etc., is also a total loss of freedom.

Jim and I talked about this, dared each other. "How your diary helped me to grow," said Jim. "Helped me to deepen. But I still cannot put everything down. I think I may die, and others will read it."

He is intensely active, because his play is being produced, rewriting, attending castings, conferences over incorporating. But the strange fact he proved once more is that he is doing his best writing in his diary.

Bella and Sam Spewack say over the telephone (about *Under a Glass Bell*): "Beautiful writing, as beautiful as it can be, but a word painting. No story. You must tell a story. It has to move. You could have written *Bonjour Tristesse*. Take the Mouse story. You write a sketch. You do not tell enough. We should have known more from the point of view of the maid. You should not have been there."

"How could I not be there if it was the story of the Mouse as discovered in our relationship to each other?"

And the two of them in misery, suffering blindly and desperately in their marriage, she saying: "Only death will free me." Because their *objective* life brought them no knowledge of themselves, or understanding of each other. Thinking that you can blot out the self, and then possess wisdom. Simenon, they say, is not in his books. But of course he is, in his choice of characters, in his obsession with the "downfall," in his constant retelling of the same story: the man who awakens one morning and finds himself alienated from his wife, children, partners, friends, the whole world. He is there all the time, in his somberness, in the absence of euphoria, in the absence of love. All the stories are perfectly told, but they are the same story, the story of Simenon's vision of the world.

It is very strange that when I talk with Jim we agree on something essential, which we call oxygen, so it is not something inexistent. Jim wants freedom in life. He seems able to achieve it. If his play is a success he will achieve it.

But Jim convinces me that the world cannot be trusted with the truth. That the world is a jungle, full of dangers, fierceness, malice.

America hates the artist. He is proved in the wrong when he dies of madness or grief. America will not admit: the artist is my soul and I want to kill my soul because it stands in the way of my achieving power, fortune.

Did the collective life of the Incas ever lead to this absence of self which American collective life has achieved? Blot out the self, say the Spewacks, and when I traveled through America and looked down on its natural beauty I could remember not one figure of distinction. It looked empty, or inhabited by anonymous automatons. Masses. No identities. The canyons and rivers, as beautiful as India or Tibet, but the people living there are so alike, so colorless, you retain a feeling of empty spaces. I looked at them, listened to them, in cafés, buses, in other cars, all along the four thousand miles of travel. They seemed like extras in a film from which the main characters were absent.

I remember Richard Wright saying he could not expand as a writer because the race problem festered in him. I am in danger of the same constant irritants and it will poison my work because I need to love the object of my writing. That is why I am writing about Mexico.

A nightmare also clarified what is making me ill: I was condemned to die by means of an injection in the head administered by a Negro. I had sympathy for my executioner and kept promising I would not make it difficult for him. I was making arrangements for the diary. Then came time for the injection. As its effects began, I started to suffocate slowly. My mother was there. I suddenly realized that if I died she would read the diary. My dying words were: "Swear you won't read it. Promise you won't read it." Then as the suffocation increased I awakened.

I am suffering from guilt and concern about the contents of the diaries and their effect on others. I must burn the diaries.

Lloyd [Wright] was cheated of his due by the stature of his father, an overwhelming shadow, and also by America's hostility to imagination, to poetic architecture. Instead of having to deal with the Borgias, he has to suffer Huntington Hartford, millionaire, who buys a whole page in *The New York Times* to attack modern painting. As a Christmas present for Lloyd (who designed a beautiful theatre center for Wilshire Boulevard in Los Angeles and a fabulous night club for the top of the Hollywood Hills—either of which, if erected, would have made Hartford world famous), he sends a basket of A & P cling peaches and other canned food.

When someone is wounded, as Lloyd is, first give sympathy, then first aid, then combat negativity and loss of hope with assertions of creativity.

The idea of death too is connected with the feeling of guilt. Guilt is punishable by death. And I know what my crimes are. What other human beings only dream of I acted out. I obeyed the dream. But I am unable to free myself of guilt. And Dr. Bogner is unable to give me absolution.

This is the truth which human beings cannot bear, the truth revealed in their dreams. You can fall in love with your father and brother. You can rebel against your mother. You can kill your rivals. You can steal others' loves. You can betray all your loves . . . in dreams. You can be amorous and orgiastic, you can be a thousand women, in your dreams. But enact *one* of them and you are a criminal, in your own eyes, in the world's eyes, and *you are condemned to death*. This was the meaning of my nightmare, I was condemned to death with an injection in my head (the site of dreams).

More striking than this is the factor that it is my mother who must not read the diary.

The untransfigured lives all around me. Most of my rebellions are against mediocrity. But what I want is a life in depth, which is hard to find.

So I study the style of Simenon. He is a master in the physical world. But in an interview he comments that he feels he is a poet, the one thing I believe he is not. He is a realist, a recorder, a psychologist, accurate and profound. But not a poet, because a poet transfigures all he touches and he discards the appearance to penetrate beyond, to the essence. Simenon is like a camera, a tape recorder. He has always selected people who submit to the fatality shaped by their childhood, characters who could not change, who had no power except to slide into destruction, or self-destruction. Not one of them had passion, or heroism, or the power to transform or to escape or to break through the isolation between human beings. It is a vast record of failure. The tone is always fatalistic, joyless. All possible variations on destruction and self-destruction.

Strange. All my recent preoccupations have been with the other aspects of human character: the power to transform, overcome, change, to struggle, if nothing else, against negativity, neurosis, obsessions. I always begin with the heightened moment, the living moment. If there is a descent, a backsliding, it is portrayed regretfully. The story of Henry Miller begins with my total faith in his work, with his joyous visit to Louveciennes. It could have begun with his spending the night in an empty moving-picture theatre, with the detritus, and having to get up and move out when the cleaning woman arrived and prodded him with her broom. It could have begun with Henry not believing and I believing, with Henry angry and I not angry. But always my story would be different from Simenon's, even using the same characters.

Now I do realize that my physical world is subjected to such an intense emotional lighting that it is for most people invisible or abstract. And it is in the realm of emphasis on the physical world that I want to round out my work. I worked too much like an X-ray, taking photographs of the psychic self. That is not the work of the poet, Mr. Simenon. The poet lives in a transfigured night— the night of symbols. Even when he mentions the dreams and interweaves them, he reveals very little of the blind unconscious pattern and compulsions they betray.

Flashes of the inner structure (references to childhood—as when Mallard seeks a certain sordid café because it smelled the same way as his early home) acknowledge the influence of the past. All the fatalities but none of the victories or rebellions against the invisible forces. And none of the escapes through art and fantasy, only escapes to Tahiti, to Africa, ending in disaster.

My ideal is to weed the home of all nonessentials. I seek the Japanese house, with only the beautiful, the essential. I even admire their storage house outside somewhere in the garden where they keep objects which would clutter the bare rooms.

Last night we were at the Campions', eating a barbecue dinner on the patio. The three little ones were in their nightgowns and kimonos, fresh out of the bath, with their hair parted and tied on each side of the ears like wings. They sat as for a formal photograph so they would be allowed to eat with us. Because of their presence, life seemed simple and sweet.

A day of meditation. To organize and reconstruct myself. The novel is difficult. The theme I like is once again too subtle and symbolic and difficult to dramatize. It is disheartening to find everybody extolling *Bonjour Tristesse,* a trite and superficial story. There is no doubt people want to remain on the surface.

After a day of concentration I got up ready for an act I have long postponed, a flight to San Francisco to collect the diary originals and have them nearby to copy. The librarian at Evanston offered to photostat them to save myself typing, but it was at the cost of giving him a copy of the diary. So I refused.

I always like to write by the cold, clear light of airplane cloudscapes. It is a special light, not golden as I imagine the light of Greece, not blue like the light of snowy mountains. It is intensely white, sharp. But if I see everything clearly in this light it is not because of the light itself but the altitude and separation from those I love.

No amount of analysis has made me drain-proof. All my relationships drain me. I allow this. My love for others never seems to wane, to lie fallow, to hibernate, to be listless, negative, in repose. I am never indifferent, lazy or inert. My love is intensely attentive and I can only reach indifference by weariness. The last month frightened me. I felt without resources of energy. Most of it went into the house and garden. I did not care as much about my natural discipline. At four o'clock, after writing all day, I usually bathe, exercise, dress afresh. I did all this with listlessness. Not because I do not feel like writing but because nobody cares. I think Jim is the only one actively in love with what I write. Nobody else. Loneliness. It is difficult to write to an empty hall, to know I will have to struggle to get the book published, struggle to sell it and struggle against hostility.

When I extended friendship to Bella Spewack I never imagined such a sudden turn against me in a destructive letter: "Take yourself out of it. Stop writing minor poems. Tell a story. Dylan Thomas tells a story, and Alain Fournier, and *Bonjour Tristesse.* They tell a story."

Malraux writes about the hero. He is right; the hero in man is there and is revealed in war (Saint-Exupéry, Malraux) or in art. I wonder whether I can be a hero in art—pursue my solitary way, fighting and not minding war, not minding being attacked. Keep my aim in sight. I have a very big, impersonal aim. I have to impart the discoveries I have made about character. But today is the age of the common man and I write about uncommon characters. How can I use this knowledge? Proust solved this even though none of his characters had his personal depth. The characters swim in his consciousness. They are ordinary people, as ordinary as those I know. But Proust looks beyond them and at a kind of collective depth and makes profound deductions. Because I write about uncommon characters, particularly in America, where the artist is considered among the freaks, the bearded lady, the tangled twins, the fat man, I cannot, as Simenon does, write about little people or people such as those who appear in *Bonjour Tristesse.* When I wrote about Henry, who was born a common man, it was to discover all his uncommon qualities and characteristics. Perhaps it is a matter of exoticism. I like foreign countries, uncommon characters, uncommon experience. Nobody understands that the common is but a façade, a persona, and that the rest is hidden and has to be uncovered.

Another thing I cannot write about: those who have fixated their lives and chosen to live on the surface, to remain faithful to the ideas, the music, the books they knew at age twenty, who have a waxed surface of humor, an enameled, painted surface which excludes the recognition of tragedy even when it strikes them, who are intent on neutralizing deep disturbances, crises, unfulfilled wishes. These walls I do not wish to scale. They are erected by fear and what was buried is already deteriorated. The orbit of such people is small, defined. I may like them as human beings, but to me they are like the untouchables. Untouched by life's great mysteries or storms, or high moments. I cannot write about them.

I invented a beautiful Christmas package. I use ice-blue foil, on top of which I spread open a Japanese paper bird. I use the string attached to the bird (intended as a mobile to be hung from the ceiling) as a single string to hold the package. So the silver bird is reflected on the mirror-like blue foil and looks beautiful, about to take off. On that day I was happy, to have created one single beautiful object.

New Year's was gay. Renate is hostessing at Holiday House, which is run by Dudley Murphy. Dudley was once a film producer, produced *Ballet Mécanique* with Fernand Léger, and *Emperor Jones*. It is a modern restaurant and hotel at Malibu overlooking the sea. The background sound of the sea gives it a special character, a constant washing which gives the impression that everything is erased as soon as it is said and your slate is clean. The Murphys gave me a royal welcome because of the books, and treated me to a large bottle of champagne. I danced all evening, kissed strangers for the New Year thinking of the friends I could not kiss.

A clear day of wholeness. There are days which shatter into a thousand pieces, which one cannot put together, hopelessly shredded by small details of living. Some days lack the catalyzer that makes a day whole, abstract and free of small irritants.

I would love to finish the 1955 diary properly. Being also a novelist, I love to wind up with some sort of climax, as in a novel. To point up a climax and make prophecies. I sometimes have the feeling that the diary is not a finished work and needs filling in. When I feel my time growing shorter, I wonder.

Ingrid has short reddish-brown hair, like a fox's, and fox-colored eyes. She has a boy's face, small round nose, and a few freckles. Her skin is very white. She wears no make-up and her eyebrows are unplucked. Her face shines with health. She laughs continuously in an explosive way. She is spontaneous and lively. At Renate and Paul's Arabian Nights party she exposed beautiful, large and heavy breasts. Katy's husband said cruelly: "You had to prove openly you are a woman, for otherwise . . ." Otherwise everything is masculine. Her active self, her direct glance, her bawdy jokes, her open sensuality and finally her marriage to a gentle, passive, self-effacing young man who accepts her leadership. Ingrid's wit and humor are fairly constant. She is alert, pert, lively. I have just read her novel. It is written through the eyes of a child. The style is lively, but the characters are small, petty, negligible, ordinary. An aunt and an uncle one will never remember. Characters one does not wish to know.

A subtle duel began between us. She began to telephone me every day. She wanted my admiration, and I could not give it. So she began to tell me that it was my lack of interest in ordinary people which was missing in my work. "They are not real."

We had a failed party after Ingrid's marriage. The huge log brought by a friend smoked so violently in Renate's fireplace that we all began to cry and to cough. We had to open doors and windows. It was cold and damp. We all shivered with tears in our eyes. Renate came out in the rain as if the sun were shining and said: "I always wanted a garden party in the rain!" From that moment on the gathering became lighthearted.

The other day I went alone to visit Paul and Renate. A friend who always asserted that he never dreamed had at last dreamed, and we thought this called for a celebration. The birth of a dreamer!

The dream was that he and I were watching a horse pursuing an antelope. I observed they were mismated. Finally the horse made love to the antelope. Paul said that horse and antelope were not mismated in mythology. In mythology they gave birth to the unicorn.

Renate told the story of her mad uncle. He refused to go to school and locked himself up in a closet with books. He only came out to get food and more books. At the end of seven years of seclusion he came out and passed his examination brilliantly and became a professor.

His madness was localized in his bones. He insisted that he had no marrow in his bones. Aside from this assertion, his thinking was sound and scholarly. Renate's family decided she should be tutored by this uncle but strongly impressed on her that no mention of bone marrow should be made. Renate, of course, was strongly tempted to discuss this very theme. She had a keen interest in the marrow problem and wanted to find an indirect approach to the subject. She discovered that birds had no marrow in their bones. So she brought this information to her uncle and added: "If you have no marrow in your bones that means you can fly." Her uncle was impressed but did not put this idea to the test. Later Renate extended her research and discovered that this uncle's mother became pregnant while still nursing the uncle. That somehow he found this out and became convinced that this other child, his brother, had sucked all the nourishment from the mother (marrow) and away from him, thus leaving him deficient in marrow. Was the withdrawing into the closet a return to the womb and the feeding on books an attempt to acquire a substitute nourishment? Renate's family knew Freud, and Renate was raised on psychological interpretations. She deciphers symbolic behavior very naturally. We have long talks about this.

There is always inside of Renate this high voltage which propels her into action. Her face expresses intensity and tension. She moves all of her body in harmony with her alert and active mind. There are no pauses or reposes in her. Ingrid laughs all the time, as if all that happened to us were a slapstick comedy. Bones without marrow are as comical as the square-domed heads of Miró's clowns. It is strange how events which, at the time of our experiencing them, seemed tragic, can reveal, with time, their comic side. I can laugh now at how seriously I took the preservation of my virginity while posing for artists at a time when I did not know precisely what this virginity consisted of and the exact nature of what I was escaping from. My mother had given me no information, counting on woman's natural instinct. And obviously woman's natural instinct did function properly, for I remember at age sixteen appearing at nine A.M. at an address given to me by the Model's Club, in one of the loft buildings downtown. The artist who opened the door appeared in his pajamas, half asleep, his opened bed in the background, and somehow his welcome determined my speedy disappearance. The painter who offered to pay my trip to Woodstock because I had no work in the summer (all the painters left New York) assumed I knew what the invitation included, and was so bitterly disappointed at my not moving into his studio as a concubine, that he told all the other painters I had failed in my side of the bargain, clearly made, and they refused to give me work. I was stranded in Woodstock, without work or enough money to return to New York. The most comical aspect of this period is that I was very timid and reserved, and that I appeared at the mountain pool, where all the artists and models swam, in long black stockings, added to the traditional bathing suit, while they had discarded all their clothes. I would be the first to laugh today at the way I must have looked and the way they received me. At the time I felt victimized and the whole episode a tragedy. My mother had to send me money for the fare back.

Paul always looks like a man who, like his Danish forefathers, has seen the midnight sun. He has the look of a blond angel who has just come from a black mass. The midnight sun does not tan one. He smiles innocently although I am always certain he has undressed the angels and the choirboys and made love to them. He never excludes the chief orchestral baton in erotic drawings. He has the small secretive smile of Pan, a love of flowers, butterflies, birds on paper, tender colors and fragile textures in decoration.

I have only seen him angry and fierce once. Renate cannot bear secrets; she is born to open Pandora's box. Paul's soul is like those secret Japanese boxes one can only open with infinite patience and gradually, and even then there is always a section of the box which remains closed. Renate violates this Japanese secret box life of Paul's and Paul, who knows that she will find each time a pagan with the face of an angel, said: "You know, what I give is nothing taken away from you, nothing which belongs to our love."

But Renate is anxious. She never knows when Paul will leave her alone in Malibu, without a car, without warning and without the facility to retaliate for his pagan unfaithfulness with a Christian attempt at unfaithfulness, the one done without pleasure. Only the pagan can enjoy his sensual life like a fruit.

Renate looks anguished, her sea-petal eyes float on a dubious pond, unable to float to the open sea, to the tumultuous universal ocean. When will Paul emerge from his airy houses and bend over to console her for not being a pagan? Consolation is a Christian act. And Paul's only Christian act is the love of angels.

Ingrid has the American suspicion of art and charm. "Paul exploits his unconscious."

"That is where creation comes from. You talk as if the unconscious were an oil well."

Surrealists drew from the unconscious. Occasionally it was self-conscious and they produced artificial works. But that is no reason for feeling that all adornment, all improvisations are artifice. Paul prefers to call on magic, to use costumes and ritual. He studies mythology while I insist we have to delve within for our mythology and find our own, not depend on the classical. For example, why crown the friend who remembered his dream for the first time with the same laurels used by the Caesars? We have to find our own symbols.

Renate's painting is the largest in the room. It faces us as we sit around the table at the end of the afternoon. It is a luminous naked woman reclining beside a panther sitting on its haunches. The face of the panther and the face of the woman are the same size. The eyes of the panther are larger than the woman's. The panther holds all the dark powers of the night and can see into the night. The woman holds all the light of the flesh and the beauty of the sun. They are Beauty and the Beast after a long marriage from which they emerged at peace and equally beautiful. But later, as it grew darker, it was the body of the woman which began to shine with all the phosphorescence of the animal, and the panther disappeared into the darkness. One could see only its eyes. She has absorbed the beast and turned it into illumined flesh, but the beast is the one who has vision into the alchemy.

Renate has forgotten about the artifice in art, and was telling of an experience she had while listening to music. Her body was compressed into a column. At the top of the column was an antenna of science-fiction design that threw lassoes of blue electric lights in circles, which rotated and in their centrifugal motions captured other waves, the waves of the brain seeking contact with other vibrations. The radiations from our brains not only draw fever charts on paper, but they are neon-lighted too, and they throw off sparks like electric short circuits, according to the latest scientific experiments.

Was Renate's dream prophetic?

Mark said gently: "I wish I had dreams like that."

"You will," I said. "It's highly contagious. Look at our friend here, who has remembered his dream for the first time."

"Anaïs, have you finished *Solar Barque*?"

"Not yet."

The neighbors trust me with their children every time they need to go out. The idea of trusting your children to a surrealist must be encouraged.

At times, I must confess, these expeditions into the subconscious realms bring me no riches. There are times when I float into this unconscious ocean where there is no light and no luminous fish, and no visions.

It was equally dangerous to dig for coal, gold, oil, yet men were willing to lose their lives for it. And so the writer dares to dig into hidden worlds, dares perilous explorations in which he might lose, first of all, his contact with human life and possibly his sanity. But he is looking for treasures of another kind. All the treasures of our character lie far below the surface. Freud gave the wrong impression that only the dregs, the nightmares, the perversions lay at the bottom.

I bought paper, let the house go, and settled into the diary world. I copied volume 68. I was happy. I was in a rich world. The Press. Gonzalo. Frances Field (then Brown). Analysis with Martha Jaeger.

Is it distance which makes these people more interesting? I once made a decision that I would never describe anything I was not in love with. Never to write about what I hate. I have broken this promise.

Jim's enthusiasm has incited me to copy more diaries. I couldn't finish *Solar Barque*.

Dream: I was talking over the telephone with my mother. I could hear myself saying: "Mommy." But after a while her voice grew faint and she was silent. I kept calling her in vain. Then I tried to find her. She had shrunk. She was so small, so small, and like a long, thin cat. I felt a terrible sorrow.

When Renate's cat died of a snake bite I told her what I had heard from the Haitians: "Be glad, as it takes the curse off the house and family. They say that cats often deflect misfortune."

In the diary every month, like every novel, has a title. When I nursed Peggy it was my Florence Nightingale month. This one is the Mea Culpa month. I examined all my friendships and judged myself at fault in all of them. I wage a constant war against reality, even the reality of my friends, loves, and persist in attributing to them roles in my dreams, and it is my fault if they cannot always fulfill them. Mea Culpa is heavy to bear.

At Bekins Storage on Huntington Drive, Arcadia, there are three big metal files with all the diaries. As soon as I copy one I return the original to the file and send one copy to Jim.

Jim's letter on organization was accurate and as I copy I think about that. I must fill in, round out the portraits. Each character I live with for a few days I see in both lights, the human light of the diary and the essence or abstraction in the novel. In the diary I follow the life line, in the novel the fantasy. Where to begin?

Tavi, my cocker spaniel, lies at the foot of the bed. He is fourteen years old, the equivalent of eighty years in a man. He is deaf. He does not see very well. He sleeps most of the day. I once thought we would grow old together and that when we were very old I would go off with him like the old Eskimo parents and disappear. But I don't change. I get up at seven, make breakfast, clean the house, do errands, go to the post office, carry the laundry to Count Laundromat, cook lunch, rest a few minutes and then type all afternoon.

Working on the diaries gives me more energy. The interesting development in Frances' life, from poverty in childhood, tuberculosis and a bad marriage, from poverty to health, a good marriage, a child and a glamorous life, and the creation of many good paintings, is remarkable. But the subtle element I would like to capture is that the secret inner world which sustained her was concealed, expressed in the early days only through dancing, sculpture, or in talks with me. This world provided the reveries she is now painting.

Before, she pictured the outer world as brutal and cruel (in her childhood recollections); now she is exposing her sensitivity, vulnerability, her fragile view of imaginative constructions; she is loved, praised, her paintings bought. In spite of not getting the best of psychological help from Jaeger or Staff, knowing their errors, she flowered through her own courage.

The visibility of this secret world before it became painting is what I would like to describe, even though on the surface Frances manifested an intellectual toughness, an analytical sharpness by which she defended her sensibilities and fantasies.

She recognized the imagery I used in my writing but participated in the evening when her friends questioned the "reality" of Stella because of the symbolic abstraction, the absence of story framework. At the same time she is the one who urged me to print the *Under a Glass Bell* stories.

We lost sight of each other for a few years, while she was in the sanatorium, when she went to Europe with a sculptor, when she married Michael, when she bore her child. I was away from New York so much. It was the self which she pictured in her painting that brought us together again, reminding us of our long talks on dreams.

In the world created by Frances illumination prevails; it is a world with a center of gravity in which brilliant fragments are held in the light of maximum intensity. Here the dark realms of the heart are illumined by points of concentrated intuition, tensions produce showers of sparks, color has the soft glow of tenderness and the transparency of insight. Light, shed over experience, becomes a major theme in her work; lines, fragile yet strong, evoke the antennae of intuition itself relating and connecting the many dimensions of feeling.

Experiences this month grouped themselves under the theme of belonging or not belonging: A Hollywood party, baby sitting, my refusal to write an article on Simone de Beauvoir and Mary McCarthy for *The Nation* (I am not deeply interested in either of them, and I know they expect a political essay). In Bogner's deft hand they acquire a synthesis. To belong to a community on a human level only. They all raise the problem of loneliness and the efforts I make to belong to the "family of man" by service, devotion. Among artists I feel at home.

I read the lives of Erik Satie and Paul Klee. Satie is one of my favorite musicians, and his life moves me. His innovations. His humor. His influence and contribution unrecognized. His complexity and imagination. The fact that because of his playfulness with titles to his composition, he was not taken seriously. His hunger. The little room in the workmen's quarter. His long walks back from wealthy homes where he went for the sake of the dinner and always had to play. The fact that after his death, they found so many of his compositions behind the piano, used to save the piano from the dampness of the wall. The fact that many of his compositions lie buried in the Bibliothèque Nationale. Paul Klee's Diary enchanting, also full of playfulness.

It is sad to read Romain Gary's *Colors of the Day* and find that the French war orphans, surrounded by disaster, began to see the American movie gangster as an ideal hero who alone can win in a mad world.

Theodore, a German Jew who gives a Grand Guignol show all by himself. At midnight, to add to the atmosphere of horror and humor straight out of the tradition of Dr. Caligari. But the fine Jewish humor predominates. He ends up with a caricature of madness *à la* Lon Chaney, and his exit line is: "I am mad . . . mad . . . mad . . . And after all it is lucky for me. If it were not for my madness I would have gone crazy long ago."

I ran into an old friend at the Museum of Modern Art. She looked like an enormous bonbon from Schrafft's, all in pale blue satin, head topped by a white fluffy hat like a meringue, a necklace of hard candy. Her latest love appeared. He was once a Hollywood actor. Very suave and, according to her whispered asides, not very virile. He must like big feather quilts and well-stuffed pillows. "I don't dare marry him because I'm afraid he really prefers little boys, and he is a Christian Scientist and takes me to church on Sundays, and I would rather take him to Dr. Jacobson to improve his masculinity with hormones."

Peggy Glanville-Hicks has such interesting theories about classical art and folklore, how they cross-fertilize each other.

She said: "This is an age of spectators. Only they are hostile spectators."

I heard that *Gate of Hell* cost so much—to be color-perfect. The photographers worked with each frame until it was perfect. So few prints could be made to their standard of perfection that it is considered a failure commercially. Very sad for us. I hope it does not mean we will never again see such a beautiful film.

It was very simple. I let Dr. Grath in Sierra Madre diagnose without laboratory tests that I had rheumatic fever and that my heart would get worse with time, and accepted limitations to my activities. I allowed the physical symptoms to overwhelm me. I wanted to have a bad heart and to die. But last week I wanted certitude. I wrote down the symptoms and went to see a heart specialist who tested me for an hour and a half. I have no disease of the heart. He could not say what caused the symptoms. But Dr. Bogner reminded me that anxiety can create all the symptoms of every illness on earth. I used this certitude to get well, climbed back to health and a severe confrontation of my death wishes. Images of my fatal heart disease were accompanied by images of my mother running to the door impulsively to talk to the milkman (while my brother Joaquin and I sat at lunch on our last day together) and how Joaquin and I looked at each other with the same fear of the possibly fatal consequences of her rapid, impulsive, violent physical exertion (she had had a stroke a year or so before).

The power of the spirit is frightening, for miracles, for creation, and for destruction.

Dr. Bogner's final summary was that I was trying to say: "I am going to die. Before I die please give me what I want."

In my dream, the House by the Sea (one of my wishes) was in a storm. The waves swept over it, dragged it out to sea.

Jim said: "I know I had to get away from my people. But now that I'm not trapped, nor condemned to live their life forever, I feel I can go back and describe them. I feel close to them. I do understand them. I want to travel all over America. I do understand it's different with you. You had no country. You were dragged along from one to the other. The artists are your country. You don't have any other. They are your people. But my people are those people who lived on the same street."

Knowing how he feels about art in general, and knowing that art is my native country, the country of the artist, it is a miracle that we can talk to each other. Our meeting ground is not art but life. He reads me because my writing is alive. He will not read Proust. But the modern tempo of my writing he reads. We talk in jazz language, not the classics.

Jim's very typical desire to stay American, to write about home and the familiar. Like Henry Miller remaining thoroughly American after ten years in France.

———

I only use analysis to combat illness or confusion. As soon as I see clearly again, I turn away from it and from over-analytical people. Analysis is only to be used when needed. The rest of the time one should live passionately and impulsively, create and test one's strength.

Submarine Dream: I am traveling in a submarine. Not inside but holding onto it by a long strap when it surfaces, like the strap on an airplane seat. I glide along the surface as water skiers do. Other people are traveling the same way in the opposite direction. Some on horseback. The sea is dotted with travelers and all the ships are under the surface. But I feel that my submarine is now traveling too deep and if it goes any deeper it will pull me down below where I cannot breathe. I contemplate letting go of the strap. But someone tells me that if I do the submarine will sink to the bottom. I have a feeling of responsibility towards the submarine. So I hold on. It is strenuous but I manage to hold on.

Jim is the one who is alive by my definition of aliveness. He is alive in every cell.

After a talk with Dr. Bogner: The primitives were so wise when they enacted rituals of possession by the dead. It proves they knew it happened. And they also knew how to prepare rituals for dispossession. The same thing takes place in us, in the so-called civilized man, but as it is not externalized (we have rituals to bury the dead and then we believe that the relationship is terminated) we are not made aware of the time and place when they re-enter our being, and install themselves in our souls. I did not experience the death of my mother completely when it happened. I suffered a natural, human, physical pain, a natural sorrow. But it was only years later that I developed a heart illness (she died of heart failure) and prepared myself to die as she had, to die with her. I took on some of her negative characteristics: irritability and rebellion. I took on the traits in her from which I suffered and her illness. (Why not take on her cheerfulness, her courage? But that would have added to the pain of her loss.)

I fought against identification with her death by going to a heart specialist and finding I had no heart illness, and on that day I ceased experiencing heart symptoms (which had deceived the doctor in Sierra Madre).

"It is a natural, a common mechanism," said Dr. Bogner. And I understood also how the feeling of disorganization, of inner breakdown was born of the *possession* and not of the LSD experience. It may have started by my nursing several persons through difficult moments, and nursing was my mother's attribute. Thus we live by a sequence of associations, moods, feelings, which it is constantly necessary to separate from our *unpossessed* self, a self free of intrusions by others, of amalgamations with others.

That is why during these months of Mea Culpa I have been so ashamed of myself. I was not being myself but taking on the traits of my mother, traits I did not like, mingled with the quality I once liked so well and felt deprived of in moments of physical weakness, her vigorous taking over in times of stress, her dynamic way of nursing one back to health.

Proust had a great deal to say about possession by the dead, but nothing about the act of dispossession, which is the role of the analyst.

I wonder how the primitives were able to time these crises, this need of exorcism, so mathematically (this is the age of puberty, this of marriage, this is the time for the ceremony to chase away the haunting dead), because all of these have an individual rhythm and have no relation to calendric time.

The spirit of my mother imbedded in her sewing machine and in her gold thimble did not make me love housework. It may have been that my mother's irritation was a clue to her rebellion against the supremacy of the mother role in her, and that what I identified with was a deeper truth I had never seen consciously: a mother who did not want to be a mother all the time, who had to mother a husband, and three young children, who at one time had wanted to be a concert singer.

I never understood the pursuit of wealth instead of the pursuit of love. The anxiety of the businessman is inexplicable to me, as well as his enjoyments. Of course someone may say I showed more anxiety than joy in my concern with love, but it was a world of deep enrichment and the profit a treasure house of memories. If the pursuit of wealth takes your whole life like one difficult mistress and grants your wishes only when you are old, or erratically erases them altogether at any time, she is certainly more often a cheat than the lover who always leaves his wealth within you.

A betrayed businessman has nothing left if the money disappears, as in gambling. The betrayed lover is not empty-handed.

The extraordinary Swedish film *The Naked Night,* directed by Ingmar Bergman. A trite story was heightened into a deep tragedy by an art as great as Goya, or Brueghel. The camera handled by him is a transformer, and sees more than the physical eyes. It encompasses the atmosphere of dreams and nightmares. And because it photographs the darkest and deepest recesses of our being, it imprints on us images which do not erase themselves as soon as you leave the theatre.

Two discoveries, then. The other a fragment from a novel, *Miss MacIntosh, My Darling,* not yet published, by Marguerite Young in *New World Writing.* An astonishing way of dealing with illusion and reality. An immediate entry into the world of the unconscious.

She solved the conflict with the realists by establishing that her mother, the dreamer, was mad and then she was free to install herself within this subconscious world and expose the reveries, the fantasies, the illusions. Labeled as madness for the fearful American public (fearful of all that issues from the night of our being), the wild animals born of fantasy are like the animals in the zoo. There is a cage between the rare specimens and the spectator. My mistake in public relations was to disregard the cage.

But for me who loves to touch the dreamer, and be taken into his dream, the writing of Marguerite Young was instantly the most beautiful expression of our night life I have read since *Nightwood.*

We met once, at John Kennedy's, but I had not read her then, and her monologue overwhelmed me, it was like reading *Ulysses* in one gulp. We tried nonetheless to see each other. Her lilting, singing voice came caressingly over the telephone. "I'm on my way to Italy. Can we meet? It was I who accepted your fragment from a novel for *The Tiger's Eye."*

We did not meet. But as soon as I read her I knew she was probably our very best writer.

I write this diary on the bus, on my way to Jacobson and his vitamins, on my way to Bogner and her clarifications, on my way to see Frances' new paintings.

Max Jacobson's expression when he heals someone, when he hears the words "I feel better," reveals the doctor who cares, who is involved heart and soul in this struggle against illness. The greatest pride and delight appear in his eyes, he is illumined by it. He has once more triumphed over his enemies: illness and death.

Eyes have a definite landscape. Renate's evoke the sea. They are marine eyes. One is aware of the fluid life, the flickering dots of light, the seascape animation of green, blue and gold interplay. Paul's eyes are icicles upon which a winter sun is reflected. The icicles form a stalactite. They never melt. In the friend who remembered his dream for the first time, the green and the gold are warm. They sparkle. They melt. They are Venice eyes, canals of reflections, all the gold of Venice lies in them; one expects them to shine at night.

Then there are the earth eyes. They are without horizons or depths. They have all the browns of the earth, of fox, dog, gazelle, rabbit, doe. They do not reflect water or sky but maintain their earth-cave brown. Black eyes are coals from the mines. They can catch fire. They smolder. The black can burn.

Then there are the neon-lighted eyes. A bulb and a wire, Mazda eyes. One does not fall into their depths but is faced with their emptiness. One is neither warmed nor frozen by them.

There are eyes like those of the Japanese, which seem like the interstices of a Venetian blind, or a shutter, permitting no access to the person. Others have the flickering quality of candles. Others seem like those shop windows on which one sees reflections of the streets, traffic, passers-by. There are the eyes of the American beauty queen, which are carried like precious stones to be admired. They are like the eyes of cats. One can almost see where the round jewels end, the little marbles planted in the flesh. There are eyes which are like a miniature aquarium and one catches flecks of marine life one cannot identify.

Wrote pages on Annette Nancarrow. Rewrote the entire *Solar Barque,* which has come to life. Everything falls into place. Everything I touch expands.

Read Huxley's book, *Heaven and Hell.*

"What we called the mystic or the artist was the one who through art or some departure from the conscious mind achieved by genius or hunger, by madness or by rituals, and today by drugs, man reached what he calls the antipodes."

Huxley left out one of the surest means to depart from the conscious mind: psychoanalysis.

Letter from Jim:

I returned to volume of the diary called *Fire,* finished it, and am now halfway through *Fatamorgana.* My great fear is that I will catch up with you and have no more to read. In *Fatamorgana* the section: "I am at home with the marvelous," moved me deeply. And the section on the changing mirrors of adolescence, childhood. And the sentence: "That the world should have brought itself to such a foolish incongruous impasse! I laugh." —this following a long confession of your vision of the world that seems like perversity to those without this vision. At times you scold yourself for your lack of courage. This amazes me and yet I understand it. Courage is a relative thing. The courage of living fully has become a commonplace thing devoid of heroism, and so you challenge yourself to the impossible: the revelation of it to the world. I can't touch your courage. I only wish I had some fragment of your cowardice.

I am nearly through 55 now. The person and the writing grow steadily in clarity and wisdom and beauty. It is a great saga of an individual, very possibly the greatest that exists. No important step is missing: the floundering, the searching, the backsliding, the bold and magnificent steps forward in consciousness and freedom.

This diary is the harvest of an angel-witch, nourished by all forms of light, candle, moon, sun, imagined lights, and reading it makes me feel like a warlock who has stumbled on a fortune in treasures that will last him all winter. I am glad you're not here as I'd be saying this and it would evaporate. I would have it in me but you would get nothing in return. I feel that I have to take the place of the entire world in my response to your work. All doors should be open to you, rose and cognac, adoration and gratitude for your courage and your record. I suppose they are being withheld in order to force you to continue it, in order to protect you from the spoilers. You have got all levels here, Anaïs, I never found this in other books, sensuality, intelligence, mysticism, and through no conscious organization of your own there is a fusion (you do not organize well, I must tell you that, and I must tell you why; it is not your job) that causes one level to comment on another, illuminate mutually.

Letter to Jim:

Your letter moved me deeply. It contained such a response and understanding. You have indeed given back to me whatever it is you feel the diaries give you. You have taken the place of the entire world, and what more can a writer want who has built a pyramid of writing, than that someone should be able to enter, feel at home, enjoy and inhabit this pyramid. It is as wonderful an experience as reciprocated love. In fact, it is the same. But as you well know, this is rare. I'm happy too that I can say I hear and understand and love every word in your diary. When one knows this is the secret self, then to be loved for that is the highest that can happen. You did say more than you realized, even if you believed you were feverish and drugged with reading. And the sharp awareness, too, when you say: you do not organize well and it is not your job. This is the problem I am trying to solve. I made one failed attempt in the novels. It has to be organized, not perhaps as I tried to, but like jazz. As you know from your own diary, the price you pay for improvisation is that it may sound like fragments. What holds jazz together? In the old jazz a trite theme, New Orleans folk tunes known to all. In the progressive, classical music, for they do borrow and embroider upon Bach, etc. A theme. Yes, it is my job, Jim, because no one else can do it for me. And I didn't do it in the novels.

The thread was the self, which stands condemned. Read Kronenberg's *Company Manners*. This is the mass age. To be a self is a great crime. For me the self was merely an oceanic container which could receive all experience. I never felt that this self effaced others but served to relate to them. You caught the meaning of *Les Mots Flottants*, the Floating Words, or Words Afloat. Your letter was wonderful to receive. In a sense Los Angeles is a desert. I have to start anew creating my own world. The friends I like live far away in Malibu. I see them rarely. You must imagine your letter arriving in a dull little town, in the tin drawer among others and how I take it to the coffee shop and sit there devouring it. I feel like the grounded aviator who receives his command to fly again. And immediately I obey. And now, like Scheherazade, I have to continue the diary to entertain you. About your own life, you will have the marvelous because it is within you, and inevitably it will take shape.

Waiting for Godot, one of the few antipodes of the mind mysteriously accepted by the people. Why? Because the dreamer and the
madman have smelly feet, the comic spirit is common, it is a rec-
ognizable hobo's fantasy of someone who will save him, of waiting
and boredom. They disregard the madness of Lucky—the inferno
of it. The language is not authentic (in the antipodes people speak
the language of dreams) but people have the illusion that they have
seen a profound spectacle. The intellectuals are tickled. As when
Tennessee Williams presented his private nightmare blown up in
Camino Real.

Waiting for Godot has quality, inventiveness, the courage of
"dépaysement." Some lines are moving, others stir laughter. It is
superior to most plays, and the aftertaste was good, an aftertaste of
quality. I don't know why it is not completely moving, no more
than Joyce. Is it because it is not born of the genuine antipodes but
an intellectual simulation again, the irrational reproduced, a reproduction, not a direct expression of it? It is carefully charted.
It comes altogether from the mind, and the dissociative process is
only a reflection of the true subconscious realm.

Jim and I tried to analyze why we were not carried away by the
play. Was it because the theme is personally distasteful? Passivity,
waiting, empty days, helplessness. Was it that blending of rough
humanity, sore feet, with Einstein complexities about time and
space? Whatever it is, we must be loyal to all the explorers of man's
dreams, even when the intellect meddles with both nightmare and
dream.

Story of a Possession continued:
Unknowingly I had continued to mourn my mother and to take
into myself some of her traits. It is a common form of mourning.
Failing to die with her of a heart ailment, I took in her irritability.
This ceased when I saw Dr. Bogner again. Failing to die, I suddenly
could not work on *Solar Barque.* I was not only arrested, the flow
was not only inhibited, but I felt total doubt of what I was doing. I

felt I could no longer write well. With this came anxiety and the need to see Dr. Bogner (I would go earlier to my appointment, wander around in her neighborhood).

Only yesterday, with Bogner, I remembered that my mother had condemned my writing: "How can you, who wrote so charmingly as a little girl, write now about that monster D. H. Lawrence?" I wept. Bogner, always tactful and gentle, became even more so. "I read *A Spy in the House of Love* just the other day. It is very poetic and very sensitive. I see nothing surrealistic or difficult to understand in it."

I wept on the way back. I ate dinner alone. Attending to those who write me letters, ordering books they cannot find. I read Pierre Molaine, another multidimensional writer. Before sleeping, another attack of anxiety. The heart beats irregularly. The body is cold. Finally slept. And this morning went on working on *Solar Barque*. Wrote about the party on the Mexican general's yacht. So I have been reliving the death of my mother and even obeying her in not being able to write. But I am coming out of this possession. *Solar Barque* is for the greater part invention, more invention than I have ever practiced. Very little taken from life. And now I realize it was difficult to write because I did not depend on diary events for it, it lay outside the periphery of the diary, and for the first time I felt truly thrust into the space of invention.

It was a student at Evanston who asked me a most important question: "If symbolism is the language of our dreams and our subconscious self, why can't the writer translate it for us so that we can receive the direct message?"

I could not answer at the time, but now I know that the reason the writer must not translate symbolic images is that we must *all learn the language of symbolism*. Otherwise we will never become familiar with it and we need to know it to interpret our daily acts, indirect acts of people around us, the meaning of dreams and certain expressions which escape us in humor or impulse. It is the language of our hidden self. Just as jazz created its own language, and translating it means conveying it to the intellect (and it was not intended for the intellect), symbolism was intended as another means of communication affecting us indirectly, reaching our own subconscious level. Using this imagery, becoming familiar with it, means communicating directly with our senses, our subconscious, and affecting it.

Letter to my nephew, Paul Chase:

I was very much amused by the wit of your TV play *Prometheus Rebound*. It is skillful and has a marvelous pace, and at the same time there is a deep underlying significance, all beautifully hidden. The bitter truth, the delusions and the tragedy are so wonderfully lightened. I was delighted with it. I wondered whether you would let me show it to someone who has an entry into TV? Not because I think it is on the mediocre level of most TV shows but that the humorous handling of it might make it pass where a seriously handled theme would not. Humor is a wonderful instrument. A passport to many closed places.

I am as busy as ever, between housework and typing, working on a new novel not yet finished, copying out diaries and preparing them for future publication, wishing I had my own Press again, and frequent trips to New York. It takes me a month to recover from the tensions of New York where too much happens, and to adapt to this place where nothing happens except fires, floods.

And by the way could you and Derith help me find the name and address of a man who was once a student at Chapel Hill who is said to have initiated the reading of my books at Chapel Hill, whose brother still teaches at Chapel Hill, who named one of his children Djuna? I meant to get his address when I was there, but I forgot.

Very interested in Derith's future child, and hope she will feel well all through and enjoy the experience. Even though I have no children I do consider it a beautiful experience, and I believe now that it is the only one which rids you of that troublesome child in yourself which haunts you all your life until you transmit it to the future, project it onto a human child who then makes you a grownup at last. This unborn child in ourselves is always looking in at the window.

And by the way, the most brilliant story I have read this year is *The Jet-Propelled Couch* by Lindner (an analyst). In paperback it is called *The Fifty-Minute Hour*. Read *The Jet-Propelled Couch* first as you may be discouraged by the others, although I personally think his is the best portrayal of a communist and a fascist from a psychological point of view. He has a wonderful understanding of rebellion and encourages it in a certain way, on certain levels. Died fairly young recently, in his forties. The title of *Rebel Without a Cause* was taken from his book.

———

Comment by Jim on what we call the Age of Mediocrity. "Kraft turned down *Gypsy at the Automat* because the young leading man is a writer. They say the public is not interested in writers. Naturally I refused to change it, and told the man that I thought his kind were responsible for the fact that the public is illiterate."

Huston understood *Moby Dick* and brought out its deeper meaning. It was an exceptional film. The captain's obsession was not a professional one, motivated by the need to earn his living whaling. He was not concerned with that or the well-being and safety of his crew, or his duty, but with the neurotic accounts to settle with Moby Dick, who had defeated and crippled him.

Every neurotic sacrifices other human beings and himself to such vindication or revenge for the past.

Copied volume 68, a total of 215 pages.
Cannot complete *Solar Barque*.
Enjoying the summer heat, the pool and the Campion children.

Phyllis, our neighbor on the left, daughter of a Swedish farmer, left her three children with me Sunday so that she could see the horse show with her husband. The baby is only a few months old, so I changed ten diapers and fed him two bottles. And everyone was laughing to see me in that role. Pam even telephoned her mother the news. Complete cycle of human experience!

I have now known community living. But I am still convinced that these people who are so proud of giving birth and raising three children are giving less to the world than Beethoven, or Paul Klee, or Proust. It is their conviction of their virtuousness which distresses me. I would like to see fewer children and more beauty around them, fewer children and better educated ones, fewer children and more food for all, more hope and less war. I was not proud at all of having helped three children with faces like puddings or oatmeal to live through a Sunday afternoon. I would have felt prouder if I had written a quartet to delight many generations.

These years in Sierra Madre, with relationships based entirely on human fraternity, proved to me that simple human life as laid out by uncreative human beings is impossible for creative people because it is narrow, monotonous and not deeply nourishing. Kindness, peace, routine, are not enough. I get desperately restless.

Louis and Bebe Barron worked on electronic sounds in New York and invented music for Ian Hugo's first film, *Bells of Atlantis*. It was very suitable for a film which depicted a dream. Hollywood thought it would be appropriate for a science-fiction film.

I thought it would be interesting to hear how they worked:

From the *Los Angeles Times* (by Philip K. Scheuer).

What the Musicians' Union will make of this I don't know—but a new Hollywood movie has a score "played" by no human agency.

This is MGM's *Forbidden Planet,* a startling science-fiction story conceived on a positively intellectual level. Where customary music credits would appear, the title card reads, "Electronic tonalities by Bebe and Louis Barron."

I've never heard any sounds quite like these, although at moments they bear a generic resemblance to the theremin. But the Barrons, who did their recording—four months of work—in their studios in New York, say the theremin had nothing to do with the case.

"The voice quality may sometimes be similar," Louis explained, "but the control is very different." No other musical instrument was used either; it was all done, he swore, by electronics.

The Barrons, who had been making experimental sounds—and films—in Manhattan, reached Doré Schary's ear by crashing an invitational art exhibit of Miriam Svet, who is Mrs. Schary. Fate and a trip to the Coast combined to bring them to MGM just when the producer and Music Czar Johnny Green were seeking a new kind of music to match the blend of fact and fantasy that is *Forbidden Planet.* The Barrons got the job.

They are a young, intense couple, he more intense than she. Both have studied music; but the sounds they produce are too inexact to be called that, Louis said. "We can't call it a score and we can't call ourselves musicians; although we are attached to the music department, we are, at the moment, artistic orphans."

Nevertheless, the Barrons have created musical themes distinctly conveying everything from the beauty and terror of the unknown to the alcoholic binge of Robby the Robot. Robby is an automaton designed by Walter Pidgeon, an earthling scientist stranded on Altair-4 in AD 2200, and a whimsical fellow he turns out to be, too. Robby, not Walter.

The Barrons make their music with electrons, which they activate to create electronic circuits. In fact, Louis' talk was full of circuits.

"The circuits are our actors," he said. "We set them up in a dramatic situation in relation to each other and then we stimulate them to behave in accordance with it; start with some sort of provocation to make them fight or make love or whatever."

"Electrons?" I repeated incredulously.

"Sound is produced by the behavior of the electrons in these circuits," Barron resumed patiently. "If left to their own behavior they will do what come natural to them. But they need prodding. We can torture these circuits without a guilty conscience—whereas if we did it musically, we might have to torture a musician."

An appalling prospect, I agreed.

Louis went right on: "We look on these circuits as genuinely suffering, but we don't feel compassion. Each circuit, as I say, has a tendency to do *something*, though it may rebel against instructions: When it does, we have to knock it around electronically."

I was still feeling sorry for that knocked-around circuit when Louis was off on a new tack.

"What we have is a new artistic tool: direct communication by pure emotion rather than by a symbol which must be retranslated in the mind. In studying the communication or information theory—how much information can be communicated from one mind to another, or one machine to another—"

"Oh, sure," I said. "Cybernetics." It was a wild guess.

"Precisely," Louis agreed, beaming. "Well, science has been borrowing from nature and the arts to prove *its* theories, so why shouldn't artists borrow the tools of science to express emotional ideas? What is evolving is a new art form, completely electronic."

I asked Barron if he could hear the sounds made by his circuits while they were being recorded.

He said he could. He doesn't use a "keyboard," he added, but uses various controls—and as the circuits are being knocked around, the resulting mayhem is taken down on tapes. It is then, as in the case of *Forbidden Planet,* transferred to the film track.

I remarked that the music really seemed to express varied emotions as the picture unfolds.

"Whether the circuits actually feel or not," Louis said, "they behave as if they do. They can be made to act, to sound unhappy, for example, and when we hear them we feel unhappy."

Well, that's the story of the Barrons and their "electronic tonalities." I don't pretend to do more than report it. But I can assure you a different listening experience at *Forbidden Planet.*

Because I was always confronted with reality when I expected pleasure from a person, a country, a way of life I had imagined as pleasurable, I felt that pleasure was unreachable. Pleasure is an attitude, not a person or place. Just as guilt was my greatest tormentor. Yesterday instead of getting restless in Sierra Madre I proceeded to find what I could enjoy: uninterrupted hours of work; Chris, Mollie and Kitty's visits.

I have a treasure trunk—old costumes, masquerade items, fake eyelashes, wigs, shawls, make-up, combs, castanets, my baby shoe, which is a wooden shoe from Holland.

Chris, Kitty and Mollie have looked into it with wonder. Yesterday I gave them my Spanish costumes to play with. They got dressed up in my dance costumes, and all afternoon I saw them trail them on the lawn while I worked on *Solar Barque*. I can see why people feel that in their children they begin life anew and are given a second chance.

[Summer, 1956]

To be closer to friends, I left Sierra Madre for Hollywood. A small, two-room apartment with a tiny patio which Tavi, now deaf and blind, looks upon as a jail. He was so used to roaming free in Sierra Madre, knew his way home from miles away, but here there is much traffic and I am afraid to let him out. He has wandered off and been picked up by the police and then I have to search for him in the dog pounds, which they call "animal shelters" here. Once I could not find him and I grew anxious. When I described him and his age, they took me to a special heated section for very old dogs and there he was.

Met a remarkable woman, Mildred Johnstone, called Millie by her friends. She had come to my reading at the YMHA and came to visit me with Annette Nancarrow. She has a beautiful face, with large blue eyes and very regular features, a warm smile and warm laughter. She was a dancer and found herself married to one of the directors of Bethlehem Steel and totally immersed in the world of Big Business. Her solution was the one I most admire: she proceeded to see how she could transform this world into one livable for her, how she could create something out of it.

This is what she did, in her own words:

Using industry as a theme for needlepoint seemed natural to our times —especially for those of us who live in Bethlehem. As neighbors we are drawn into the rhythm of its tensions and power—the percussive surge of production. Visually and emotionally we are related to steel. It is a powerful image in our daily lives.

Dust catchers, skip cars, sawtooth roofs or a blast furnace against a red sky . . . mechanical shapes lend themselves easily to a needlepoint medium. The visual excitement of turning hot metal into cold steel suggests infinite possibilities for working in thread—fluorescent red for the burning crackle of scrap iron or yellow angora for poured steel. Industry is alive with stitchable material. This sequence of needlepoint is what I found waiting inside the mill, with its magic mood of unknown happenings— men in masks pushing levers, switches and buttons. Colors and compositions were dictated by the dynamics of the industry, its dissonance, texture and drama, and by the symbolic forms of machinery in relation to men—poetry in a steel mill.

Each concept has come about by personal reactions to specific operations within the mill itself—the ritualistic sensations from the pounding beat of science refining raw material by modern alchemy.

Watching the world stretch forth with new sights and sounds, discovering parts and relationships—this makes needlepointing an endless adventure, experiments in the unexpected. I rip as much as I sew. Sewing on planes, trains and ships brings peace in a world of speed, moments away from time. Materials, tempo and mood organize themselves into a feminine logic, a personal commitment bound up with twentieth-century vibrations and the mystery behind a landscape of steel.

I went to see the tapestries, and they were rich in color. They had the beauty of primitive paintings, a primitive looking for the first time at machines and men at work. It was an extraordinary transposition, turning into decorative abstract motifs all the various aspects of steel-making.

I was touched, too, by the human motivation. As an artist, who had always been among artists, Millie entered a strange and foreign world. Instead of rejecting it, as I might have, she espoused it by translating it into terms she could love and take pleasure in. She exposed its potential inspiration as design.

I thought it was a metaphor, an indication of how the modern world, rather than destroy the artist, could be used by him to his own ends. That is what Millie did.

I read Simone de Beauvoir's *The Mandarins* with interest and admiration. Not because I believe in what she states but because she dramatizes the case so well, the tragic sacrifice of the individual to a political cause, and does it objectively, the whole drama of politics, conscience, abdication of the individual, sacrifice of the artist, and to no purpose. She does not say this, but the book proves it to me. Politics betray each one of the characters. It reveals that the personal element is never annihilated, that there is no objectivity or real self-sacrifice, but that people use political ideas to hurt and fight each other, that it is not a dedication to the hungry or the poor, but to an ideology which would make each man the enemy of the one who does not think as he does.

———

Titles I want to use sometime:

Archipelago of Guilt
The Burning Prisoner
On a Bed of Lime
Scream through the Eyes of a Statue
Astroblem
Star Wound
Pockmarks on the Moon
Hit by an Asteroid

Titles for the manuscript volumes of the diary:

Disintegration, The Woman Who Died. 1931.
Journal of a Possessed. 1932.
Apotheosis and Downfall. 1932.
La Folle Lucide Équilibre. 1932.
Uranus. 1933.
Audace. 1933.
Flagellation. 1933.
Incest. 1933.
Schizoid and Paranoiac; The Triumph of Magic, Black and White. 1933.
"And on the Seventh Day He Rested from His Work." Quoted Negligently from a Book I Never Read. 1933.
Definite Appearance of the Demon. 1934.
Flow. 1934.
The Real Play, The Birth of Humor. 1935.
Tubéreuse Aux Muqueuse Pleureuse. 1935.
Révolte. 1935.
Vive la Dynamite. 1936.
Drifting. 1936.
Fata Morgana—A God Who Laughs. 1937.
Fire. 1937.
Maya. 1937.
Isolation Circles: Consummation–Collective–Self-Abnegation–Le Monde. 1937.
Nearer the Moon. 1938.
Les Mots Flottants. 1938.
The Only Way to Conquer the World Is to Make It Transparent. Ne Touchant à la Terre que par le Sexe. 1939.

Death of the Mother. 1939.
Book of My Metamorphosis; Book of Maya. 1939.
House of Death and Escape. 1940.
Intermezzo: Book of Climacterics. 1941.
Birth of the Press. 1941.
À la Recherche des Jeux Perdus. 1942.
The Transparent Child. 1946.

Last night took a stroll with Jim through the Village. We sat at the Rienzi, on Macdougal Street. Italian coffee and pastry, as good an imitation of a Paris café as could be achieved in New York. We met Tambimuttu, the Hindu poet who ran *Poetry* magazine in London. But unlike most Hindu poets he likes Western drinks too much, and so his white costume is soiled, and his dark blue jacket stained. Negro musicians go about in bright red shirts and berets and beards looking like ancient Biblical Africans. Women in cloche hats pushed down over their faces, pale make-up and heavily made up eyes like the flappers of the twenties. New York climate, one day torrid jungle heat, the other North Pole iciness, must have an effect on one's nerves.

I met a child named after Djuna in my novels.

Read about the climbing of Everest, *Tiger of the Snows*, autobiography of Tensing of Everest. One evening everyone questioned the usefulness of such ventures. Just to satisfy one's ego? Not at all. It gives courage to others. You can choose to question the motivation or the application of it, but you cannot question the example of courage and endurance. I read it as a metaphor. It seemed to me that all of us are trying to climb Mount Everest. That we do risk wounds, falls, precipices, frozen feet and hands, snow burn, snow blindness.

Fell in love with Lippold's *Sun* at the Metropolitan. I go there and bathe in the golden radiance of its filaments. After all, our old sun only shows a flat round disk, and this has tentacles of such life that they seem to penetrate one, and fill one with light. When I am depressed it lifts my depression. I feel like a mystic who has received illumination. It is one of the most perfect symbols of what the artist can do with a concept already existing in nature. At times he can surpass nature in his interpretation. From the real sun we may receive warmth and life; from Lippold's we receive an inner illumination which reminds us of our hunger for light.

It is not well placed. The walls around it are hung with antique rugs. It should be in a dark room, to emphasize its powerful vibrations. The gold threads actually seem to tremble in the air. What the artist creates can shine on a war-torn world. The beauty in the sky of the artist can survive all the cruelty and horror of people killing each other.

On the same day a concert by Ravi Shankar. Such a beautiful, subtle, complex, incredible performance, all of it improvised, none of it ever written. An exhilarating challenge between drum and sitar as if trying to trip each other up but never able to do so, and they enjoy it as jazz musicians enjoy their own feats. The entire YMHA was filled with Hindus. I saw many old friends. Santha Rama Rau, the Indian writer, and her husband Faubion Bowers, who writes so exquisitely about the dance. After the concert we talked of new electronic machines which publishers are now using as critics. They are fed on statistics and decide whether a writer will or will not be a success. It may not be worse than the human prejudices and irrational opinions we have now. But machines have breakdowns, so we began to imagine a psychoanalyst machine to analyze neurotic machines. Imagine, I said, a machine lying down on a couch and saying to the electronic psychoanalyst: "Last night I had a nightmare. I imagined myself becoming human!"

The sitar player smelled so strongly of sandalwood that we all went away impregnated with his perfume, even though we had not shaken hands, as the Hindu way of salutation is to clasp hands like a Catholic at prayer and bow.

Anne Metzger, who translated *Ladders to Fire* out of love, showed the manuscript to the French publisher, Plon, and they offered to publish it if they could make cuts on the basis of not offending readers with the relationship between Lillian and Djuna.

It was so utterly ironic, because after twenty years of enduring the irrationality of American publishers, the puritanism and commercialism, I had formed an idealized image of French publishers who could publish the unequivocal Colette and Genêt. I imagined France liberal, tolerant, open-minded and still in love with good writing.

I wrote to Anne:

I give you the right to do anything with *Ladders to Fire* that you think wise. You can cut, eliminate, subtract and dilute, whatever Plon wants. They sound so much like American publishers, timorous and fearful of taboos, that it is no longer of any importance to me. My last illusions and hopes are gone. I do want to be published in France. If I am to be published by a narrow-minded publisher, it is my fatality. I would have preferred to appear first with the short stories in which there is nothing to censor, but my wishes in matters of publication are never to be fulfilled and I can see they won't in France either. The next thing I expect is French critics too will be saying my women should return to the kitchen and to bearing children, as they wrote in the *Saturday Review of Literature*, and I should not be writing about artists. I do hope, dear Anne, that after all the work and faith you expended on me, the contract will take care of you first, the translator. If they decide to leave out the Lillian and Djuna episode it might be too short and they might consider including *Winter of Artifice*. Do whatever you please. I surrender.

I met Betty at Sylvia Spencer's apartment. She had asked to meet me. She arrived from her job on a magazine, drank a cocktail, and fell asleep. She looked quite beautiful asleep, with her young face smooth and healthy, her gray hair and her catlike relaxation. When she opened her cat-gray eyes she explained that she had not slept for two nights.

On leaving she said to me casually: "I am leaving on vacation. Why don't you come with me?"

I thought of it as a light and free meeting. I gave her my books as a parting gift, and we corresponded.

When she came back she came to visit me. She was all in black, with silver jewelry tinkling. She looked sensuous, luxuriant, pale, alive, a startling incarnation of all my women characters.

She touched my arm so gently, and I thought, all the musicians, the artists of love know the power of the first light touch.

Before she left she whispered: "You're someone I want in my life for always. I love you."

All the women I had known and written about flowered in her, with an intensity and fever unknown to men.

I took her hand and answered very tenderly: "I never loved a woman sexually."

"But what about Sabina and Lillian?"

"My attraction to June was an unlived experience, so in imagination, in fiction, I completed it."

She continued to use all her power, her seductiveness. She would try to extract by vehemence words I would have to retract the next day.

One night she called me up rather late: "I'm so tired, and I'm getting a cold. I'm going to bed."

"No more nightmares," I said, referring to three she had told me.

"If I can imagine you beside me, I won't have nightmares. Will you let me imagine you beside me?"

I said yes as one would to a feverish child. But when she asked: "Is it absolutely impossible?" I answered: "Yes, absolutely."

Jim knew I felt bad at refusing to spend the evening with Betty; so, seeking a carefree time, we played games. For this kind of fun, I like to slip into black tights and a striped burnous, hair loose on my back. We started the evening with a parody of Betty's exigencies. I used the large clock for timing eggs and received Jim with it placed against my heart: "You are one minute late! When it rings exactly at zero you must say you love me."

He did.

Then I said: "Such a lovely spontaneous expression of love." But we gave up the game because it reminded us of the times when we ourselves had taken the clock too seriously. We went off walking lightly to the Rienzi. In this bohemian crowd I feel at ease. Years ago I had decided that if one must wear sports clothes they should be ski clothes, which had some charm, and now it is fashionable with the young. I do not know what they read but I share their love of jazz. I know they believe Beckett is profound, but I am not sure. He has deviated from the trite, but into a universe of death and ghosts; the antipodes of the mind must be explored, and Beckett's ramblings are more alive than some of the taxidermist novels we usually get.

Jim does not read him.

People think this exploration of self is self-centered and selfish, but I notice that whenever I clear up something for myself it quickly affects everyone around me, as if it were a psychic liberation which in turn affects others' conflicts. My change of mood affects shop-keepers, bus drivers, policemen, cleaners, messenger boys, besides those close to me. It is like the distribution of a positive current. It is more powerful than the self-sacrifice of the so-called selfless ones, for inevitably sacrifice brings some kind of inner depletion and all the gold vibrations are extinguished.

[Fall, 1956]

There is a difference in the aging of men and women which I hope one day we can eradicate. The aging of a man is accepted. He can age nobly like a prehistoric statue, he can age like a bronze statue, acquire a patina, can have character and quality. We do not forgive a woman aging. We demand that her beauty never change. The charming, beautiful women I have known, is it because their aging is frowned upon that they do not age nobly?

Italian women age nobly, Mexican women. The culture accepts it. They cease to wear dresses which clash with their bodies and faces. The charm of voice, laughter, the animation remain, but because we have associated femininity with silk, satin, lace, flower, veil, a woman is not allowed to acquire the beauty of a stone piece. Cornelia Runyon aged in that noble way. There was no defeat, no disintegration but a passing into stone and leather, as if to acquire a statue's quality. The slightest wilting is tragic in women because we make it so. A woman's skin has to rival the flower, her hair has to retain its buoyancy, aging does not constitute a new kind of beauty, hierarchic, gothic, classical. She can only seem incongruous, condemned, doomed among the silks and the flowers and the perfumes and the chiffon nightgowns, the white negligées. Why can she not efface her rivalries behind black gowns as the Greek women, as the Japanese women do? It is the rivalry among the elements we associate with women which prevents the transition to some other kind of beauty. Caresse Crosby gave me a shock when she appeared in a bright deep red dress, a buoyant dress, frou-frou, walking lightly on very high heels, but then her face appeared like a ruined mural, eroded with time. The powder and the lipstick did not adhere to its dryness but seemed about to crumble off. The sadness was that not all of Caresse aged simultaneously; her voice and laughter were younger, and her marvelous enthusiasm for "Citizens of the World."

The sadness was that the aging of woman is like crushed satin, wilted flowers, while that of man is more like that of architecture, as if the old belief that we love men for their character and women for the dewy, ephemeral quality we call beauty were still enforced.

Sold *Spy in the House of Love* to Avon paperbacks. Letter came from Thomas Payne, editor-in-chief. Advance sumptuous, it seems— 1250 dollars.

Jim remembers that in Black Mountain College I did not say this is good writing or this is bad writing, but go on, get deeper, go deeper, and it will become good. Find your level. This is not yet *you*.

A long time ago I wrote about the sympathy of Simenon for his characters, and now I am reading a study of him (*Simenon in Court* by John Raymond) in which the sympathy is stressed. "Nothing repels him. Physical sickness, crime, vices, perversions." He has sympathy for all of man and never judges.

This sympathy was once my main characteristic. As a child of seven I knew that the presents given to us by Mrs. Rodriguez were not sufficiently appreciated because of her wealth, and I made the following speech to her (which became a subject for jokes in the family): "You know, Alta Gracia, it isn't the luxuriousness of your presents to us children which I appreciate as much as your thoughtfulness in choosing them."

Was this sympathy partly corroded by neurosis? Neurosis is a kind of unhealable wound. A man with an unhealable wound does not have an ever-ready sympathy for others. People have always felt my sympathy in life but it does not come through in the work. This year I feel it was restored to me in its fullest vigor because I am not drained by my anxieties.

There is something beneficial in retracing steps. I pick up the errors and am forewarned of repetitions. Why did I consider my father's leaving as a defeat in love, a sexual defeat? Because somehow I became convinced that it was the sexual attractions which drew him out of the house and away from us (my mother and two brothers). Did I as a little girl compare myself with the women who came to the house and feel inadequate, puny and negligible in their perfumed, chic presence? Did I overhear my mother's scenes and was the sexual betrayal stressed? Is this where the concept originated that I preferred the mistress role to that of wife, that love and sensuality could only be reconciled if a woman remained primarily seductive?

Metaphor of change and rebirth. What I remember best of the beautiful film *Secrets of the Reef* are the births, the baby turtle pushing out of the egg shell, the baby octopus pushing out of an egg which seems made of plastic, the lobster painfully pushing out of his outworn shell.

Met William Goyen, whose writing I admire so much. He is a subtle poet, covering the unexplored ground of fantasy and reverie as they mix with life and color it. He is a master of atmosphere and suggestion.

Gray-haired, handsome. Another fatality in the world of publication. His books, though much admired and respected, did not sell enough so most of them are now out of print. Another wounded writer. But we made him feel successful. He read us one of his stories. Random House refused to publish his last book after sending it for approval to a *Time* magazine literary critic. They paid him 175 dollars for reading it, and as he said "No," Random House turned it down. A new kind of rigged game in publishing. Since *Time* has the power to make or break a writer, the publisher might as well know in advance. These critics make as much as 2000 dollars a week in this way. A friend of mine, a music critic, has retired at thirty-eight, having earned these extras from musicians and record companies. What a world we live in.

William Goyen is teaching at the New School. The students ask: "Where can I sell my story?" He answers: "I don't know. I can't sell my own!"

Note from Allan Ginsberg:

Ruth Witt Diamant said she would write you to substantiate this note of mine. I will be coming down to L.A. area for a visit to dig hollywood and some relatives I have in Riverside & be there in a week or so . . . coming down with a fellow poet, Gregory Corso. We have been giving interesting buddhist poetry readings (by buddhist I mean looney) in S.F. & I went with pack and sleeping bag to Northwest & Reed Coll hitchhiking with a young hipster monk, now in Japan on same purpose, & to travel. Anyway if you or anyone down there in hollywood or L.A. cares to pay us any attention we will be happy to sing some poetry at you. I had wanted a regular, formal reading maybe but there's no time to arrange; but I mean, we will be there for a week trying to make friends and see the town, and we have something to offer, free, for kicks, if anyone like yourself or anyone else wants to hear us, under any circumstances, time or place, provided everyone joins us in a little wine, which we'll foot the bill for, tho we are poor wanderers; yet we sing well. If you by chance know Huxley, we have all used Peyote &c. and have things to say on that, that he may be interested in. And if you know Marlon Brando, ask him to hear our poetry; but if not, and you know only strange beat citizens, we sing even more sweet for them. I don't know what you can do with us, but if you can figure anything you're welcome; and the occasion, whatever it is, will not, please understand, be just a big nowhere bore. I mean our poetry swings and is literate & O.K. We promise to be the only poesy in hollywood or anywhere for that matter, in eras, or seasons.

Isherwood and Jimmy Dean too. Also is there an old 1930's poet named Bernard Wolfe? Changed his name and wrote *Asphalt Jungle* under I dunno what name—wrote a great old powerful poem called *The City* in the 30's.

Lawrence Lipton arranged a reading to which I brought all my friends, not the ones he asked for. He wanted to sleep on the floor of my one-room place, but that I evaded, knowing I can neither drink all night nor talk all night.

The reading took place in a small wood frame house exactly like a million others in Hollywood. Ginsberg and Corso sat on opposite sides of a table with a gigantic bottle of red wine and read their poetry. One of Ginsberg's poems was called *Howl*. It was a great, long, desperate wail, a struggle to make poetry out of all the objects, surroundings and people he had known. At times, it reached a kind of American surrealism, a bitter irony; it had a savage power. At moments, it did seem like the howling of animals. It reminded me of Artaud's mad conference at the Sorbonne.

Then a man in the audience challenged Ginsberg in a stupid way. "Why must you write about the slums? Isn't it enough that we have them?"

Ginsberg was in a frenzy of anger. He proceeded to take off all his clothes, throwing each piece to the audience. My friend Ingrid received the soiled jockey shorts. He provoked and challenged the man to come and expose his feelings and his real self as nakedly

64

as he had. "Come and stand here, stand naked before the people. I dare you! The poet always stands naked before the world."

The man in the packed audience tried to leave. Ginsberg said: "Now let someone dare to insult a man who offers what he feels nakedly before everyone . . ." The way he did it was so violent and direct, it had so much meaning in terms of all our fears of unveiling ourselves. The man in the audience was booed and hissed until he left. People began to throw his clothes back at Ginsberg. But he sat at ease on the couch and showed no signs of dressing again. Lipton wanted the reading to go on, and said rather shyly: "There are women and children upstairs," which made us all laugh. The two poets went on reading for hours. I left, thinking it was like a new surrealism born of the Brooklyn gutter and supermarkets.

[Winter, 1956–1957]

I don't know why I can't give the diary the continuity and unity of a Proustian work.

I would have to leave out incomplete portraits, scenes, too sketchy at times.

I would have to fill in more details about character outside of the relationships. For example, Albert Mangones, I do not feel he is all there. I also lose sight of people. When Albert returned to Haiti, I no longer knew about his life. I very rarely resort to hearsay. I do not trust others' descriptions.

Sometimes I feel I concentrate too much on inner feelings and not enough on the outside.

I typed volume 66 all day, alternating with housework. Gonzalo, Jaeger, Frances Field, Thurema, Josephine Premice, Albert Mangones, etc. This made me grateful for the richness of my life.

Romain Gary wrote *Colors of the Day*. My French translator, Anne Metzger, suggested I read it. She had known him in the South of France. As soon as I began the book I found myself in the world of intelligence whose capital is Paris. I wrote him a letter. He was no longer at the United Nations but was the French Consul in Los Angeles.

Anne Metzger had given the manuscript of her translation of *Ladders to Fire* to Romain Gary so it would come to me by way of the *valise diplomatique*. When I arrived to call for it at the pseudo-Spanish house so dear to Californians, I was met by Lesley Blanch, his wife. I explained that Anne Metzger had sent my translation by *valise diplomatique*.

With English blue-eyed coldness she implied this was not legal. But after we talked, she softened, and later she invited me to their open house.

I was met at the door by Romain Gary. He looked startled and kissed my hand. After reading *Ladders to Fire* he did not expect me to look so feminine.

Slight of build, with large, beautiful sea-green eyes, a southern, warm-toned skin, and a mouth whose design was spoiled by a contraction, a sneer, a twist (from an old war wound), which marred the regularity of his features. But for his mouth, which gave him an underworld appearance, he would have been a handsome man. He offered us pink champagne and introduced me to Gregory Peck and his French wife. Gregory Peck is the very symbol of American physical beauty, without sparkle or expression. His French wife very beautiful and disquietingly alive, as alive as he was not. Mrs. Joseph Cotten shouted across the room: "If that is Anaïs Nin, I want to meet her!" Madame Gary took me over to a handsome blond woman, bold and powerful, who sat with me on the sofa and talked of how she gave *Ladders to Fire* to friends to read when they had difficulties in relationships, of her piano playing and of her house by the sea. She must have identified with Lillian. Joseph Cotten sat on a pillow by the fireplace, gentle and reserved. A genuine Russian played the accordion and sang French street songs. Old old Cole Porter, the composer, carried his shivering, autumn leaf fragile body by leaning on a cane, and the light shone on his denuded head. The pink champagne flowed. My talk with Mrs. Joseph Cotten was spoiled by a group surrounding her, and as she confessed that Joseph Cotten had given her a Rolls-Royce for her birthday, the talk turned to cars, jewels.

The French officers in their white uniforms, all gleaming buttons and gleaming smiles.

I had the sense of failure, which is the curse of my life. I had so wished for a writer friend. Gary, too, was talking of failure; he felt that one either fails in one's life or in one's work. And what depressed me most was his questioning why we write.

My answer, "to communicate with the world," did not convince him, and I myself began to doubt it recently because the world you create in a book you leave behind like a piece of architecture. When Betty came to make love to Sabina, Djuna, Lillian, Stella, she was not able to find me of course; I was already in another cycle. Why do we write? I was addressing the author of *Colors of the Day* and he was not anywhere in the book, he was not the romantic character but the cynic.

Gary went on a trip to South America and I was left with a sense of a failed friendship.

After reading his new book, *Les Racines du Ciel* (*Roots of Heaven*), I had a dream: I was in Paris. All the plumbing was out

67

of order (the greatest concern of my American friends visiting Paris) and the city was dirty. But I kept repeating, "In spite of this, it is the capital of intelligence."

Gary lived in a brilliant world inaccessible to me.

His book is a masterpiece. It is a bitter satire and proves the irrationality of the world. The elephants are a symbol, like the White Whale. What is dramatized is the erroneous interpretation everyone gives to facts and their personal distortion of events.

Then I read *The Wilder Shores of Love* by Lesley Blanch and became completely devoted to her writing. It is a book of great vitality, superb storytelling. She is herself Scheherazade telling about four remarkable women. I was fascinated by the charm and wit with which she tells biographical facts. The four women became my heroines. I read the book several times. My admiration for her was total, and I wondered why she received less attention than Romain Gary. His books were being filmed. *The Wilder Shores of Love* would have made colorful and entrancing films.

To the usual Christmas tree I added Japanese good-luck branches, so festive and tinkly, and a glass wind-chime at the top of the tree.

A few days at the beach were marred by the Malibu fire, which caused us anxiety for Cornelia and Renate. Later it reached up to Lloyd Wright's property but burnt only a small part of it. We watched the fire leaping across roads, with all the equipment, men, water and airplanes right there, impotent to stop it.

We did not enjoy our New Year's party. Renate with a new lover and Paul appearing at the same party did not add to our lightness.

The holiday neurosis. The one time of the year when your memory is forced by associations to return to the past. The superimposition of other Christmases, other New Years, the awful sense of time passing, all this causes sadness, regrets or revulsion. A forced gaiety is expected of me which I do not feel. The fire cast gloom over these holidays. Anxiety over friends. One professor of art lost the studio he built himself and all his lifework. Renate had a friend who, wrapped in wet blankets, sat on her roof and watered it all night because sparks from other fires fly about and cause new fires. So many tragedies. Many poor artists and others had shanty homes in the hills.

In neurotic relationships there are never just two persons. There is always a third. In almost every relationship there is another presence. It is not the simple figure of the other woman or the other man, the rivals. It is far more intricate. It appears in literature but oversimplified. It is not the rival, the younger man, but the guilt for having once been the younger man who rebelled or offended the father; so now he expects to be equally offended or harmed by the son, his son. It is not the rival, the other woman, but that the other woman represents the mother one has displaced, or rather the mother's avenger come to punish the daughter for her rebellion. Our real enemy is the guilt we all felt for wanting to interfere with the union of our father and mother, for having wanted to possess either the father's or the mother's love exclusively. We are the young rivals, fearful of defeat, crushed by the union of the other two, seeking to divide them and possess one. The third figure in all our marriages is the parent, who was never truly dispossessed, cast out or liquidated. In my case, the other women who took my father away (my first defeats) are the women who haunted my entire life once the pattern of defeat was set. So in every triangle there is one outsider. My way of rescuing myself was to identify with women. As an ally of women, I no longer feel like the defeated little girl who wanted to take her mother's place.

Another party at the Garys'. Madame Gary wore a caftan, beautifully embroidered, which, she said humorously, hid the bulges! She was maternal and protective towards her guests.

One of the secretaries was a beautiful young girl condemned to die soon of incurable cancer. I was told she was spending her last months making love as often as possible.

I sent them a Christmas card on Chinese paper, shocking pink with black lettering. Gary sent his staff hunting everywhere for the same paper. I bought him some and we met at the Café de Paris on the occasion of his winning the Prix Goncourt for *Les Racines du Ciel*. When we met I realized he was deeply moody, depressed. He explained that he had done everything for his mother. She wanted him to be a great soldier (he had campaigned with Malraux and was decorated), a great lover (there were many women to testify), and a great writer. She is dead and so the prize does not mean anything to him. It should have come when he was thirty. I read the review of his book later in the cold, empty consulate. I could not make contact with him. I do not know if it was his fault or mine. It may have been that I was connecting with the Romain Gary of *Colors of the Day* and he was no longer that Gary (as people often do with me)—or that I aimed too high in the jazz sense; I was high and he was low. Anyway the evening was dislocated and out of tune.

Another failed friendship. It was merely a friendship, but when I realized he was only interested in the pursuit of young girls I turned away and gave my love to Lesley Blanch.

The triangle is always the parents and me. Me seeking to displace one parent. As others come to displace me. So many of my women friends resembled my mother, and like my mother did not give me the total love I wanted.

Linked with all this I had the dream of *"La Fausse Petite Fille"*: I dreamed of three cold little girls. We were at the pool. The water was cold. I made them come out (as I did with the Campion children when I saw them shivering) and dried them. But the eldest died (Chris is the age I was when my father left me). She died of cold (no love?). Her bones were to be thrown off the high ledge of a mountain, to be scattered. When we reached the ledge I peered down and found it bottomless. I felt the bones would be scattered into infinity, irretrievable (after my father left I died, but I didn't want to be buried where I could not reconstruct myself). So I decided they should not be scattered there.

Thomas Payne, editor-in-chief at Avon, writes me that the advance sales on *Spy in the House of Love* are quite good.

Felix Pollak visited Djuna Barnes, writes me:

Found her a sick, sarcastically bitter old woman who made slighting remarks about a lot of writers, except Dylan Thomas, whose voice she admired. When I finally asked her in some exasperation: "What writers do you like?" she answered evenly: "I like nobody." I refrained from asking whether she liked herself, for she had given me the answer to that question already. Also poverty and bareness. Yet she rejected the offer she had received from a pocket book publisher to let *Nightwood* appear in paperback because they didn't offer enough money, she said. She just finished a verse play which will appear shortly. When I said upon leaving: "I hope you will feel better soon" (she has asthma and some back trouble), she replied: "Thanks. I probably won't." And closed the door.

Dream: We are invited to have dinner with Marlene Dietrich. I am fixing up my face. I take such a long time to make up my face that the dinner is over before I join them. I go off to some dangerous, gloomy place, full of wells, landslides, tunnels. I am in trouble.

I like to be in touch with human beings directly, not by way of television or newspapers. I find a moment of life more important than hours of information through news sources. Meeting the ex-governor of the Gold Coast and hearing about Africa from him, hearing about the Suez situation through Hilda Pole, Reginald's sister, who was working there as a social worker, means more to me than the canned news of the media. Ingrid's husband hesitates to come to our gathering at Curtis Harrington's home Sunday night because at nine o'clock Bernstein is going to talk about jazz on TV. When Hilda came from Jerusalem, traveling thousands of miles to see Reginald, and arrived at the house and sat down, Reginald was going to turn on the commentator at five o'clock as usual. Hilda had more to tell us than Mr. Edward R. Murrow. It is as if people prefer the indirect contact with events.

Most of the time TV news is an intrusion from a very ugly, petty world. It prevents reading and thinking. It is pedestrian, prosaic and on such a low level (I am referring to the news, not the commentators).

Renate and Paul separated. Renate is working as a hostess in Holiday House. She tells me about the eccentric people she meets there. When I first knew her she was a Viennese romantic, and now she is undergoing many changes. She is desecrating her own romanticism. She took as a lover a sweet, innocuous young man, the opposite of Paul, who sells advertisements and likes deep-sea diving.

She is inventing her own life. She turns it into a metaphor as she goes along. "My paintings have a life of their own. The woman and the cat aroused a scandal. The portrait of X burned in the fire, when nothing else did in his house."

In New York Jim was very light and gay because he sold his second play to Walter Starcke, to be directed by Van Druten.

Went to see *A Clearing in the Woods,* written by Arthur Laurents, author of *The Time of the Cuckoo.* Very moved, in fact entranced. First experiment with dramatizing the inside of a neurosis. An abstraction of relationships, a symbolical meeting of the woman with her past selves. The men rotate around her associations, called forth partially by her memory and certain incidents. The men (as Geismar described them, writing about *Spy in the House of Love*) are "shadowy figures." Strange the protest which arises when a woman is at the center of the drama and of the vision. It is the world seen through her. Wonderful lines. Through a dialogue with her past selves and her relationships, she confronts her true self as if by a process of peeling the false, as if by analysis. Daring truths. An amazing scene when she reaches her hand towards the audience to turn the knob of the door which opens on her daily job, and she cannot complete the gesture, she is paralyzed, cannot open the door. Not a work of art because the language and situation are trite, but a great step forward in the psychological dramatization of inner states.

I understand it is not a success and the actors had to sacrifice their salary to keep it going. In a few years it will be appreciated.

Jim did not want to see it because he had heard it was a somber play, no humor. Amazing that this play could be done at all, with all the forces pulling everyone to the surface, even Jim. The characters were ordinary, out of daily life, a secretary, a research worker, a drinking father. It should have been acceptable. Brooks Atkinson made the usual statements: Blanche Du Bois was so much better because you were outside. Here you are taken into a stifling inner world, inside one woman . . .

Fresh-air fiends! They have claustrophobia of the mind. They won't go inside of anything, but even less inside the feelings of a woman.

It was a subtle play produced and acted with imagination.

The characters in themselves were of no interest, the realistic pattern uninteresting. But the depiction and dramatization of a neurosis is wonderful, such as the scene of the woman saying in a dialogue with her father: You think I am a strong woman. So strong that when I went to work I stood in front of the door (she extended her hand as if to turn the knob) and I could not open it (her arm grows stiff, her fingers stiff). The relationships could have been more interesting.

The moment Jim described his liberation from fears, his moments of freedom, I felt a change of atmosphere I could not describe. I thought at first it was his liberation from me, a good thing, as he enlarged his world. But with success and his associations he entered a more superficial world. He not only gave up intimate talks, but intimacy with himself and with his diary. He wrote an objective comedy. He said he owed this freedom to me but it was not the kind my diary teaches. It was a shifting to an easier, shallower level. For the first time, as he read his play, *Crazy October,* I saw a Jim I do not know. It is based on a story I had not responded to. A fat, slobbery mother and an infantile son.

It must be this way with all one's spiritual children. At one moment they enter a world that is foreign to one.

When I went to call for twenty copies of *Spy in the House of Love* at Avon, I had a long lunch with Thomas Payne and we began a friendship. We talked about psychoanalysis. He drank too many martinis. He said he had thought of a way to present *Children of the Albatross* to Avon: "We will say on the jacket that children of the albatross is a name given to bastard children."

He has long-fingered, sensitive hands and long, dark hair, which he does not cut short in the crew-cut style adopted by most business-men. He has dark, intelligent eyes, a refined aquiline nose and a sensuous mouth with a smile which gathers first at the corners and then spreads. He wanted to be an architect but the war derailed him. His appearance is that of a writer.

I am looking at Stanley Haggart's photographs of Portuguese Fado singers. He tells me, "Anaïs, do not give parties. Everyone feels cheated. They all want, with you, a private, personal relationship.

At parties, even though you are gracious and a perfect hostess, you are not there yourself, because you do not really appear on that level."

The unattended party I describe in *Ladders to Fire* is my own. But I am here with Stanley and Tom. Tom's paintings are from the continent of Atlantis. We sit on the floor. When Betty arrives her first remark is, upon seeing my Japanese hair ornament: "Why didn't you tell me it was a party?"

"It wasn't at first. It grew."

When I was eleven, twelve, thirteen and my rich Cuban relatives would give me jewels, I always managed to give them away or lose them. They were a symbol of their world, in which the artist was disparaged ("All your tragedy came because your mother married a musician").

This has lasted all my life. I detest pearls, jewels and furs. All the symbols of bourgeois society. There is a difference between luxury and beauty. One can achieve beauty without luxury; I have done that all my life, in decoration, living quarters, in dress.

I was wrong about Jim. He entered a lighter world but did not surrender me, his diary or mine. When he finished *Crazy October* and celebrated its sale, he took up his own diary, our intimate talks, and his reading of volume 60. He telephoned me to read me passages from it, responding wildly and talking to me about the diaries giving him some kind of nourishment, a charge. "Every artist should be able to read it."

"I am aware, aware and frightened to see that those who started with me have already fallen by the wayside. People are wrong to say teen-age is the critical age. Not at all! In your teens your life is still being composed, you are studying, experimenting, but at thirty you have had your big encounters with life and you have to adopt a course . . ."

I had been afraid that he would adopt a course of "surface" living and writing. But last night he talked as before. It is not that I do not believe in external living, but that I think it is dangerous to stay on the surface without communication with the depths of the self, and the subconscious self.

Jim is my link with young America. The role I play is ironic, for

I am the one who encourages the jazz elements in his writing because jazz is the only American expression or manifestation of life rhythms, emotion, the senses and surrealism. Its equivalent in writing is to me the future of American writing, its rescue from puritanism and photographic reality. It has gone too far in its stultifying copy of life, and produced books as dead as postcards. Its only salvation is through jazz, improvisation, rhythm and color.

In *Solo*, the novel by Stanford Whitmore, there is life, a complexity of characters, a style which I feel has a pulse. Jazz or jazz writing expresses the lyrical, the tempo, the pulsation of heightened living. It is the equivalent of surrealism in France. It is no accident that the pianist Jones considers himself the last of the individualists, that what he rejects are the American idols, success, money, publicity. And he is destroyed by his resistance to being owned by the man in power.

These flights, these high moods unknown to middle-class writing, this pulsating life of jazz must find its equivalent in writing. I must find it, encourage it. Certainly the Academicians will not encourage it. The teen-agers can only hear it, not read it. I saw the jazz musicians reach and rouse these frozen and hardboiled teen-agers. I wish I could write it myself. But I was not born here. I do not speak the language of jazz. I have a sense of rhythm and pulse in writing but it is of a different order.

Dream of the Water Wheel: I am standing in front of a water wheel in full motion. There is someone else there; I do not know who it is. As I watch the wheel rotate I hear the cries for help of a little girl caught on the wheel. I feel helpless. I stand there, unable to move, frozen with terror. Then later, either it was a second dream or the second part of it. Same scene. Same wheel and same little girl crying, but this time I can act. I move forward and with great strength stop the wheel and pull the little girl out of danger.

Association with the wheel. Water. My obsession with *flow*, the flow of life currents and of images. Image of water frequent in my dreams. Either on a boat with difficulties, or facing engulfing tidal waves, or inundations, or flying above the sea, pulled by a helicopter. Thirst. I am never thirsty in reality. The new novel, *Solar Barque*, begins with a search for the sea or river which will enable the boat to flow, glide freely. Feelings on the houseboat the most wonderful

I ever had, being lulled, cradled by the river, being carried smoothly even when I lay asleep. Neurosis is really when everything is paralyzed, when nothing flows. Water makes the wheel turn but the child is caught, endangered. The childhood is stuck on the wheel. I have to rescue my childhood so that the wheel can turn harmlessly. Obviously the child in me.

Rambling talk with Dr. Bogner. Why does life in California seem unreal at times? Is it that I am not in my element, a fish out of water? Is it the attitude of the people, so uninterested in books, in life, in the rest of the world? Is it their concern with maintenance, as Renate says. Land, houses, problems of living on a material base?

Jim calls me up so excitedly about the page on my father's departure from Paris for Havana. Outwardly I had no feeling, I had frozen my emotions. I believed my love for him dead, but when I met him after he fainted at his last concert I felt acute and terrible pain. The page is a cry of despair. I love this man still and also hate all that he is. The emotion is so violent (recognition of feelings under controlled surface) that it made Jim jump up and call me. But I responded emotionally.

"Isn't it beautiful writing? Incredible writing?"

"I can't tell," I answered honestly. "I can't tell if I am feeling the experience or moved by the writing."

But talk with Dr. Bogner made me relive the incident.

Bogner: "When you do not want to experience great pain you withdraw. You withdraw from the great pain of separating from your father. He was leaving for Cuba and you might never see him again. Emptied of feeling then life becomes 'unreal.' Reality is achieved by feeling."

This unreality once frightened me. It seemed inhuman. There were certain things I did not want to feel. Millicent Fredericks, for instance, a great human being, does not behave this way in the face of experience. Her feelings are never turned off. When a relative of hers was taken to Bellevue the whole family suffered openly, they cried, they broke down.

The unreality of life in California because I cannot feel as others do. I am relieved to have discovered that this inhumanity is merely a freezing out of feeling and pain when it becomes intense. I have occasionally worried: How can I suddenly stop feeling for so-and-so and so-and-so? I remember the day I stopped feeling for my godmother because she made my mother unhappy. I once asked myself: Am I inhuman?

In certain areas I do seek escape from pain.

Jim: "What saved you from breaking under really hellish experiences, Anaïs, was your faculty for passing onto other levels."

Jim's writing in his diary is wonderful. It is the deepest Jim.

This constant search for depths and understanding is an experiment which, if many people had given themselves to it, might truly change the world far more effectively than a devotion to politics.

I would like to write the life of Millicent. But saints' lives are difficult to do, as for example the life of Schweitzer, which failed to move one, though it is a life of sainthood.

How can I give an inner illumination to my life in Los Angeles? It has yet to be created. I must remember to transform, transform.

Sunday at the Geismars'. Sunny enough to sit in the garden, with three children and four dogs, and all the talk about Henry James because Geismar is writing a study of him. I could never get interested in him. It seems to me that he writes as we say women write, too small, too fussy, too detailed, too mincing. I get tired of his indirectness, his close-ups and careful dialogue. What a surface world, where nothing is revealed, no earthquakes, no floods, no storms. Subdued and elegant, effeminate. What we once called feminine writing, except that many women do not do it.

Evening with Santha Rama Rau and Faubion Bowers. They made a long trip through India writing and photographing the dance. This time her sari was all red, black and gold, and I never tire of looking at her. Our dresses are so lacking in beauty and color. She says my writing is not writing but witchcraft.

Met Geoffrey Holder (not his wife, Carmen de Lavallade, because she is too near delivery of a child). Amazing beauty and grace. He is seven feet tall, dancing everywhere this year, at the Metropolitan Opera, in calypso programs, on TV. And I remembered my first sight of his group in Los Angeles, my great hopes for them. He is charming and intelligent and was telling us his way of handling stupid M.C.'s on television and radio. He says when they ask him a stupid question, he does not answer, he just waits, smiles, and then the audience realizes how foolish the question is. His timing and acting are so good, people suddenly begin to laugh at the M.C.

Read the life of Byron. He left a journal of his secret life, his darkest secrets. It was destroyed by friends and relatives and now people spend time trying to reconstruct his life. Did he or did he not sleep with his sister? Etc. Maurois is an excellent biographer. He gives just enough details, he fuses facts and interior states.

Surrealist film by Hans Richter, *8 × 8*. All the famous artists acting in it: Max Ernst, Cocteau, Caldwell, etc. Electronic sounds by the Barrons, lyrics by John Latouche. Paul Bowles appears in it with his young Arab friend. Scene opens in an empty swimming pool, with piano, bed, telephone. Paul Bowles plays the piano and the Arab boy his flute. It was too deliberate, calculated, and did not give the impression of a surrealist dream somehow. So much of the surrealist art gives the feeling that images did not come from free association or reverie but an intelligent imitation of the subconscious process. Possibly because when familiar with subconscious associations one knows there is a pattern and a link, it is not meaningless, no more meaningless than a dream.

In *The New York Times* Science Section:

BRAIN AS RECORDER. MEMORIES STORED THERE MAY GIVE DOUBLE CONSCIOUSNESS.

Observations revealing the existence of a tape recorder of one's past in the human brain were reported last week in the annual report of the Smithsonian Institution by Dr. Wilder Penfield, director of the Montreal Neurological Institute, one of the world's leading authorities on the brain's functioning.

Under certain circumstances, Dr. Penfield reports, a person may be possessed of two consciousnesses—one of the immediate surroundings and circumstances, and one of the surroundings and circumstances of something that has been subconsciously remembered. The phenomenon amounts to a "doubling of consciousness." One state of awareness is just as vivid as the other. The two are not likely to be confused.

This weird condition arises unpredictably, Dr. Penfield reports, when the cerebral cortex that covers one of the temporal lobes of the brain is stimulated with a gentle electric current, applied through a wireless needle during surgical operations.

Dr. Penfield advances a possible explanation of the phenomenon. Apparently every sensory experience—sight, sound, taste, smell, touch and the like—is carried by the appropriate nerves to a specific part of the cortex. There it is coordinated with other sensory impressions to make up a total pattern of experience. The temporal lobe observation indicates this pattern, or appropriate parts of it, is laid down or recorded in the cells of the cortex as though in a sound motion picture, or a tape recorder. It remains there forever, and although it may pass out of conscious memory, the path over the nerves remains permanently impressed in the cortex . . .

I did not describe William Goyen's visit one evening. A man in pain—gray-haired but with a youthfulness of gestures and face, a young man upon whose body age could only imprint a few lines and would never weigh down. A softness of voice, a gentleness of manner. He had gestures of disturbance, his hands made efforts to erase the lines of anxiety. What came to the surface was the injuries received, the disappointments, the injustices, the brutalities of the press. A wounded man. The ones who expected great love and are wounded at the beginning later cannot register the love they receive in the present, only the one denied them. The groove is made to receive only the insults and betrayals. Jim and his friend did not understand the vulnerability. They have not yet been wounded. They were expecting playfulness.

He read us a short story, and Jim read one. Goyen's books are out of print.

It was I who wrote to him about his books. He was ruthlessly handled by *Time* magazine.

He wrote me a note:

My play *House of Breath* (imagine!) opens at the Circle in the Square April 8. Please come. I need you there. And call the theatre at once to make reservations because to my astonishment there are only a few left. I must have you there. If you have any difficulty ask for me at the theatre. I am beside myself with anxiety and tension—it might be beautiful—if *only.* I'd love Jim to come too—all of you. But your face I need. More later. Where am I?

Over the telephone:
Anaïs: Hello, William Goyen?
Goyen: Hello, Anaïs.
Anaïs: I wasn't going to call you just before the opening of your play. I thought you might be harassed.
Goyen: What a good intuition you had to call. I'm sick in bed. I have been under such a great strain, the usual strain of putting on a play, besides my other anxieties.
Anaïs: Think only of your writing, of what you have to say, not of yourself as a human being, and you won't be afraid, for you are such a wonderful artist and can do no wrong. All you have written is beautiful.
Goyen: You always say what I need to hear.
Anaïs: Do you need anything? Any errands?
Goyen: No, only your errands high above where you are so effective.

Last night in the rain and slush we went to see William Goyen's *House of Breath* at the Circle in the Square. At last a bit of magic, poetry and subtle levels of feeling. What a contrast to Tennessee Williams, now dedicated to violence and melodrama. This was so emotional and full of poetry, like *The Glass Menagerie.* It seeks a free form for the theatre, an impressionism. Goyen calls it a ballad. A very moving theme. Seeking escape from home, parents, and never quite making it, even though in this case the home is death and stagnation.

It was a success. They dragged him onto the stage and he is so shy, he hung his head down and looked at the floor. It was beautifully cast; because of the young actors' respect for him, he obtained the best of them. The Village is full of vital theatre now. We all went to the coffee shop next door, full of young people, students from N.Y.U., actors, singers, jazz musicians. So much animation they do not go to the bars, do not drink. They sit over a coffee and plan the next show. Goyen had not seen this and he said: "The Village has a new aliveness." They were all genuine artists of one kind or another. It reminded me of the Paris cafés. At last.

[Spring, 1957]

The frightening experience I am traversing now is this: with Bogner I am acting out scenes which prove, in the end, the strength and vividness of my memories and fantasies superimposed over reality. It is such a subtle, elusive happening, that I cannot describe it. It is as if I see and hear you clearly for a while and then become drunk, confused, drugged. And all the time a part of me is aware of the distortions. It is frightening because it causes self-doubt, a doubt of what I have always believed in: my intuition.

For example: there are direct questions which I feel tempted to ask Bogner and have controlled for years because my intelligence tells me all too clearly that the function of analysis is not to answer such questions directly but to explore what lies behind them, what causes me to ask them. They always lie at the back of my mind— tabooed. Then once, such a question broke through the restraint, and as soon as I uttered it I censored it myself. I knew it was wrong to ask it. Why can't I choose one kind of life, one groove and totally give myself to it?

When Bogner realized I had withheld such questions she encouraged me to state them because nothing should be withheld from analysis. I allowed all of them to be expressed. They were the human questions everybody asks of me, which I seek to answer when people are not helped by analysis. (What shall I do? What shall I say? Why can't I make a choice, a decision, instead of living torn like this between two kinds of lives? In Sierra Madre I feel deprived of protection, of both Dr. Jacobson and Dr. Bogner.)

What was revealed by my questions and my shame at uttering them, was shame of dependency.

Asking questions is an expression of immaturity in my mind, it means you place before others an unsolved problem, and you are asking them to solve it. You are not working at solving it. This was what I construed from our last talk.

That is why Bogner does not answer the question but seeks to get into what lies behind it. To clear the ambivalence or the confusion.

Returning to Bogner and discussion of intuition. After her stressing the differentiation between intuition and fantasy and my reaction to this confusion with self-doubt, it became clear that this intuition, clairvoyance or insight I considered my one magic power against sorrows and difficulties. Deprived of my faith in its infallibility I felt poor and powerless. And as it is connected intimately with my writing, its source, I felt doubly weakened. Bogner had said repeatedly that she had no doubt I am particularly gifted in insight and understanding, intuition, but that in a few instances (fear of loss of love) I had let my imagination and fantasy take over (in the vivid imagining of catastrophe and loss). She pointed out that the idea of infallibility is unreal and inhuman. Dangerous too. I began to understand that there were times when I must question my intuition and separate it from my anxieties or fears. I must think, observe, question, seek facts and not trust blindly to my intuition. I have been so mistaken in judging people (Frances Keene, the Spewacks, Lawrence Maxwell).

Thomas Payne took me to lunch. One cocktail and he begins to talk:
"All the difficulties we had in arranging an evening with you, they were not natural, they came from my wife. The years she has spent away from New York, in a suburb, raising our children, she has lost her contact with the life of New York. When she was in college, at Bryn Mawr, she studied your work. She is afraid now, afraid of coming in, meeting you, disappointing you. When she has come in occasionally with me, she felt she could not understand what people were talking about. I love my New York life. And I love my life there in the suburbs. I must tell you . . . I come from a conservative background, Yale and all that. But I behaved so badly I was almost expelled from Yale. But I should go back further. My father died when I was three, and when I was seven my mother quite literally followed him. I was raised by aunts, only by women. I was afraid of what this would do to me. Then I went to war, and for a few years all went well, only when I returned I felt shellshocked. Just knowing it cured me, somehow. Then I made a choice and married an innocent girl of my own age and class, and we lived in the country, and I liked it, the wife, children, home. But among the executives I was the rebel, and when I was angry

I made it plain that I despised them and that I knew myself to be more intelligent. I would talk to a psychiatrist now, but I know what he will say. I know everything about myself. I am ready for any revelation. Nothing would surprise me, even to be told I am a homosexual. But the tension has grown. When I stay in New York overnight it affects my wife, and I have given up more and more. I do things alone. But I can't bring her into this life. If she had been a part of it I never would have married her. I married her because she was an angel and I'm a Calvinist. I feel like succumbing to the sensuous life, like sending everyone to hell, yet I can't do that."

It was all halting, vague, diffuse. He expressed a conventional attitude towards analysis: "It will make me conform."

I tried to remove his fear of it, and to explain it was not a battle of wits. "You do not engage in a battle of wits with your surgeon, do you?"

"I know everything about myself."

"But this knowledge is conscious and it masks a part of yourself you do not know. No matter how lucid, how intelligent you are, there is a self you cannot see. And analysis is not a duel of wits, it is an emotional drama, a primitive ritual in which the secret self is evoked and revealed."

I hope he did not regret his openness. People have hangovers after confidences.

Max Jacobson is illuminated, obsessed with his new discovery on cancer. People mistrust his experiments. He takes it for granted everyone wants to experiment, everyone is willing to gamble, everyone is willing to explore with him. I have always loved that trait in him. The safe and static doctors make mistakes too. I feel an identification with his research work.

It was born of all the work he did for the Jews from refugee camps. He set about repairing the damage done to their health. He involved all his patients in finding homes for them while they regained their health.

He sits quietly beside me now, but for the twenty years I have known him, I have never seen him sit down for more than a minute. He is filled with excitement. He tells me in his over-quick, skipping way something about finding more nourishment in kidneys than in liver. There is a word that sounds like "misty-poetic" but cannot be a medical term. His language is that of a specialist and unknown to me, but delight, certainty and faith animate the words. I ask him about his research. He says he has started enough trends to keep a big laboratory occupied, enough feelers, tests, checks. The magic potion which he has explained in technical language is bottled. He cured my anemia.

Last night dinner at Harold Feinstein's. A long loft room, all across one floor, floor uneven and with holes. Harold tall and round-faced, showing his work. His wife pale and blond, pregnant. In the front of the room all his photographic equipment. In the middle of the room, a double bed. In the back a stove, a table, an icebox. The dispossessed life of the bohemians I knew in Paris. The talk was rich. On the floor above him, live jazz musicians. That night crystallized my vision of jazz music linked to a way of life, another vision of life. It has passed into the bloodstream and separated people from material ambition. It is the only rebellion against conformity, automatism, commerce, middle-class values and death of the spirit. It all made a synthesis, *Really the Blues,* and *Solo,* and *The Man with the Golden Arm,* and *The Wild Party.* The only poetry in America, the only passion. I am not speaking of delinquency, or the lower depths of Nelson Algren, but a poetry, a heightened state, a search for ecstasy, the equivalent of surrealism. And the equivalent of jazz in writing.

We talked about this. I said: "I'm sorry I was not born here, or I could have written jazz in writing. But it is not native to me."

"I'm not sorry," said Feinstein. "If you had you would not have given us Bartók, that's what your writing is, what Bartók is to the jazz musicians. What happened to Miller when he returned to America?"

"He repudiated it, but how can we know if it was because it repudiated him? Every writer needs care, devotion, faith to blossom, and America denied him that which France gave him. He got that from France and from me. One of France's best writers, Blaise Cendrars, gave Miller a full accolade. How could Miller survive when critics like Maxwell Geismar say no writer unacquainted with Big Business can write the Big American Novel?"

What absurdity. There is not one novel of America. There are a thousand Americas. Big Business is only one of its inhuman, monstrous products. But jazz is the expression of America's romantic self, its sensual potency, its lyrical force. Big Business and Politics are twins, they are the monsters who kill everything, corrupt everything. Why not pay attention to the artists who humanize, keep the source of feeling alive, keep us alive?

In Los Angeles I feel cut off from all the sources of knowledge, experience, contact with interesting people, contact with foreign countries, contact with publishing and other activities.

In New York I am deprived of nature, peace, an inward personal life. The split is showing even in my handwriting. I am dividing my words.

At the same time I read about Proust. His unique insight into character (because he was willing to split the atom, psychologically speaking) was founded on the observation that a single face can wear a thousand masks, that personality is reducible to a discontinuous series of psychological states, not necessarily unified or consistent.

I must write my novels from my work in the Diary. I must find a way to make them flow together.

Note: The word I wanted and could not find at the time for the portrait of Caresse was "stance." How she had retained her stance, in spite of a bad heart, failing eyesight and outward withering.

The power of the diary to re-create the emotional intensity of the relationships I describe makes it so potent that while I am copying it I am reliving them and seeking to understand the mysteries, the mystifying quality of relationships altogether, when one sees the panorama, the opening (which often contains a warning one does not heed), the living core, the disintegration.

But when I meet these same people in reality, accidentally, I cannot understand or reconstruct the love, the friendship, the exchange and bonds between us. The encounters are deprived of the luminous incandescence I preserved in the diaries.

After such encounters I get very depressed and jittery, not at the actual meeting of a figure from the past, or because of any echo of the old feelings, but at the shocking disappearance of these feelings, their total death. It is the terrible experiences of death in life, which I have experienced more than most human beings because I have preserved them at their most heightened moments. It is very much as if love and friendship were a form of possession, a magic state of being, which can be killed by either party in a relationship, leaving no trace of its passage.

Is it the death of illusion, or a natural death of the ties between human beings?

When people say the novel is dead it is because the novelists won't write about the intimate, inner experiences, complex and unconscious, which are the living core of our experience: what we *feel,* not what we see, hear, tape record, photograph.

The novel did not give us what we most needed: The intimate knowledge of others. What is the greatest need of human beings? What is it they seek from me always? Intimacy. Being able to reveal themselves. The lack of this is so great in our time, the lack of a personal life, that all this had to be taken to the psychoanalyst. That is why no one is pleased when I give parties. That is why everyone wants to see me alone. It is my insistence on contacting the deep self. I listen with all my being, I am completely interested. I seek momentarily a full communion of eyes, feelings, thoughts. I have this expectancy so strongly that even taxi drivers tell me the entire story of their lives (and with taxi drivers I know that generally the opposite is true, it is people who talk to them, confide in them). The gift for creating intimacy, a personal world in which people feel they are entirely present, they exist, they have a clear and vivid identity.

The novel could give us this. The insistence on objectivity has destroyed this possibility.

Paul Mathiesen came and told me the story of Acapulco. When he went to Mexico he inquired where I was and was told I was staying in Acapulco. This was the year I had gone there alone. Paul drove down. He arrived during a party at the Mirador Hotel, a dinner dance. Annette and I were surrounded by young men and in a frivolous mood. Paul had come in a Gauguin mood, wanting a primitive life, and hoping that was what I had found in Acapulco, a thatched-roof native cabaña, a deserted beach, cocoanuts and bananas to eat, fish for fishing. Because I saw him as a dreamer, as a remote, legendary young man, a mystic, not as an earthy companion, he symbolized all that I was running away from. I made no effort to communicate with his inward self, inward journey. I was happy and joyous in a purely external world of swimming, dancing, music. His silence and remoteness I felt were endangering my pagan mood. I wanted pleasure and sensuality (he wanted pleasure and sensuality!). I always remember Paul in Acapulco. So blond, so Nordic, it set him apart from the dark-skinned Mexicans. His refusal to talk lightly and playfully seemed like a desire to take me from the world of sun and natural delights into the depths from which I had escaped.

He went to Revolcadero, a dangerous beach. The Mexican boys warned him of rip tides. But he was confident in his swimming, he swam out, and he was caught in one, which prevented him from returning to shore. He called for help. At that time they had no life savers, no boats, no floaters. Mexicans do not swim expertly enough. None dared to swim out. Paul was in the water several hours. He thought of his death. What he could not bear was the idea of darkness, of not seeing the sun any more. He could see the people on the beach, some unconcerned, drinking their tequila inside of cocoanuts, others just watching, and even at one moment a mariachi band playing. He was getting exhausted. He took off his bathing trunks because he felt that if he had to die he wanted to be naked, not wearing a foolish bathing suit marked "Catalina." Finally two Mexicans swam out and brought him back, unconscious. The water was pushed out of his lungs. He was ill for several days in his hotel room. And I never knew any of this. The beach boys did not tell me. When I heard this story I felt shocked. His muteness and his withdrawals baffled me. I felt even more lonely in his presence, out of contact, than with my dancing partners.

When we talked about this it seemed a shocking lack of communication, a sad misfire. Silence has always estranged me. I need demonstrativeness.

Later at the parties in Malibu, he seemed voluptuous and I thought: Renate has sensualized him. But it was not this. They suited each other.

In the sunny, small modern studio on North Occidental Boulevard, Paul and I talked. Kenneth Anger has invited him to Paris. Kenneth Anger's *Fireworks* attracted the attention of Cocteau and Cocteau has taken him under his wing.

Paul had just finished reading *Solar Barque* and found it beautiful. It was his reading which brought on our talk about Mexico.

His blue eyes close together give him a look more like that of a silver fox. His retreats into caverns of silence were invaded by Renate, who lives so actively, acts her fantasies, dreams, intuitions.

Paul said: "In all my love affairs I always had to be sure of an emergency exit!"

We both laughed at this.

Renate has a gift for romanticizing her experiences. Her affair with a twenty-four-year-old drug addict, an alcoholic, in the power of a gangster's "moll," who threatens Renate's life, even to this she can give a Viennese flavor. The older woman who keeps him in drugs is the dragon he cannot kill himself, but he wants Renate to deliver him from her tryanny. He is the sleeping beauty to be rescued.

Will there always be in emancipated women this daredevil challenge of destiny to prove their strength?

In rebellion against her romantic love, Paul, she wants to live sensationally free. "He is a combination of Jimmy Dean and Marlon Brando."

The danger in American life is that all distinctions are erased. I struggled all my life to maintain levels of quality. For some friends of mine there is no distinction between science fiction and my stories. Science fiction is America's expression of imagination and fantasy, in terms of science only. It will never be that of Giraudoux, Supervielle, Pierre Jean Jouve, Michaux, nor of mine. America's true romantics will be the jazz musicians and jazz writers, living by their lyrical emotions, their senses.

I can make the link with jazz, but not with science-fiction writing because it excludes all humanity. They leave out the human being; these are the dramas of technology and science. And just when we were about to discover the science of character, the mysteries of character, the mysteries of our unconscious selves.

Well, Anaïs, stick to your job.

At the Garys' party to celebrate his selling *Les Racines du Ciel* (*Roots of Heaven*) to the movies.

In the face of James Mason (whose roles I have interpreted for years, seeking to separate the man from the actor, who was at first the intense, the burning, severe piano teacher in *The Seventh Veil*, who became later the uninspired *Flying Dutchman*, whose beauty vanished) I found last night the consistent, essential sincerity of his own personal life which I had sensed beyond the roles, a man who has lost his fire. It may have been that it was his very role as the severe teacher which fixed my attention on him (didn't he bring down the lid of the piano on his niece's hands?) and that my curiosity about whether he was a man of feeling was because of that film. I saw in the Englishman who once had a beauty composed of dark, burning eyes, a pale skin, dark hair and an emotional mouth, the human story of a young man who came from a town in Yorkshire and who was poor, a hunger which helped him to portray intense reaching out for love and flights of emotion, but which now seemed unappeased and resigned. There is in his face the asymmetry of sadness.

He is quiet, slight of build, gray-haired. Talking of where we did and did not feel at home he told me: "When you reach middle age, you suddenly return to the small place you came from, which as a young man you hated and rebelled against, and you feel you belong, that you are at home with simple people, when all your life has taken you on such a long trajectory away from them. The fraternity of the artists, you say, but even in that I find they seem like displaced persons. In the South Sea Islands I experienced what you described feeling in Acapulco. I was making a film there. I didn't care either about the film, or the international crisis at Suez, or probable war. I cared about nothing at all except existing like a plant, or a sea shell."

We talked about the missing element in California. A place hung between art and nature. Nature not powerful enough to lull and entrance you, to drug you as the tropics do, and art absent from its life.

The sadness I had divined, the seriousness. He had such a gentle smile while talking of the delights of the South Sea Islands.

Baronne d'Erlanger, enormous, a mummy of ancient age, carrying trinkets, charms, pendants, tassels, textiles dug out of a grandmother's attic trunks, a dress made out of curtains like those we wore in charades, a long gold chain to hold a hearing aid, the sweet smile of a very tired queen.

Lesley Blanch, wearing a Chinese mandarin coat, with her blond hair piled up, the English beauty of watercolors, delicate features one fears may vanish like a chalk drawing on paper. I keep seeking to make contact with this extraordinary author of *The Wilder Shores of Love,* which should be at the bedside of every woman. The adventures of these women are deeper and more effective than *A Thousand and One Nights.* These four women shook off conventions and embarked on their own chosen journeys. It is difficult to contact a writer on the lyrical, romantic, dazzling effect of her work. Beneath the hostess, the wife, the Consul's assistant, is she one of those women she understood so well?

But there were many other women there who, unlike Lesley in her mandarin coat, did not hide their bulges, who in fact flaunted them in dresses that were too tight. Several bosoms were half out of their dresses. There was no need of imagination to visualize a bedroom scene.

Frank Sinatra made his boyish entrance with not one but three standard Hollywood beauties, as if made to order, so perfect in every detail, *"tirage en serie,"* that they seemed cut out of *Playboy* covers and advertisements, and I could not distinguish one from the other. His stance was one of pride in his triple conquest. Whereas Capucine, an exquisite French model, had a face I can remember in every detail, which appeared at first like the face of a *jeune fille* not yet opened to life, and then as she raised her eyes they contained all of a woman's knowledge of life, the finesse of a nose like Hepburn's, no symmetrical beauty but a surprise in the placing of the eyes, wide apart and slightly elongated.

Some women age with firmness. Age need not mean a loosening and flabbiness. I notice this kind of aging takes place in interesting women. Aging can be a concession to the inevitable withering, but each line can be a line of meaning, like a scroll, like the aging of wood or statues. It is a patina, printed on the outside by the inclemencies of time, but different from the aging of the weak, the empty, the self-indulgent, which is an external expression of the flabbiness of the soul. Emptiness gives flesh a lifelessness.

Mrs. Joseph Cotten is alive and vital.

Romain Gary, with his handsome Mediterranean eyes, long black hair brushed back à l'artiste, his mouth, which pulls up towards one side only, as if unable to smile fully, concealing his pleasure at his success, with irony.

Irving Lazar, the literary agent who sold Gary's two books; a French actress in a red dress, tanned, with laughing eyes and careless hair; another childish blonde, like a schoolgirl, a face that will never be born, never change.

Adventure into a difficult world. I find it hard to navigate on the surface, with games, roles, persiflage, flirtations, peripheral talk.

I understand Lesley Blanch better than Gary.

Paul wants to go to Paris to join Kenneth Anger. I gave him travel books and names of friends. He felt "wings growing out of his elbows." He said: "The artist is like a flute. He wants to throw this flute into the air to see what music it will make."

Up at seven A.M. Dishes and housework. Typing the diaries. My only walk is to the post office and errands. The geographical constriction of L.A. We all live far away from each other and I do not drive. Taxis are inordinately expensive. It takes an afternoon to get to Hollywood to buy paper and a typewriter ribbon.

Jim asks: "Why is it that with you everything becomes illuminated and exciting? That's the secret of your seduction. You create an intimacy, an atmosphere in which one has an intense feeling of *existing*."

We were talking about Renate's "spectacles." I said: "I'd like to be like Renate. She talks and behaves like my characters. She is propelled to act and say everything without controls. A marvelous spectacle."

"But," said Jim, "does she listen to others, does she always leave you with a feeling that there is much more to discover?"

"She has time for that too. But for a good performance it has to be a solo performance. All good performances are solos like Frank Lloyd Wright's. I'm too aware of the other. I am listening and waiting for the other, as you watch a dancing partner, and so much does stay inside of me."

"I prefer that," said Jim.

But I think of Renate's freedom to act and talk regardless of consequences. Her impulses carry one along.

Do I try to maintain the contact at whatever point it touches? Is it that I always respond? I always tune in when I am called. Before I act or speak I have to become aware of the other.

Tuning in.

Tuning in.

With Bogner we discovered that I cannot bear criticism (it was criticism that made me break with Dutton, with James Merrill, with Madame Chareau, with the Spewacks). I also cannot bear to criticize others so I direct it at other objects. When offended, criticized, I break away. But that is not all. I have to break when offended because I fear my anger. The real problem is what to do with the anger. I have stifled it so long that I have packed it like dynamite, I have stored it and now it threatens to come out in explosions I fear.

The day we discussed my anger I could only express bodily pain: a constricted throat, backache, headache, tension, tightness. I was using all my energy to repress it. And I left Bogner with this rising tide of anger controlled. It is my conviction that anger is corrosive. So I displace it, attach it to peripheral places or people.

After this I felt lighter. Just to have acknowledged the anger. But not the caricature of it I carried about (Anna Magnani!). Genuine anger can be useful and creative.

I gave Maxwell Geismar *Art and Artist* by Otto Rank. But I do not know what effect it had on him.

I love the Café Figaro on Bleecker Street. It has character. People sit and play chess and genuinely talk together. The waitresses are actresses out of work, or musicians out of work. They participate in the conversation. I went several times with Jim and his friends.

Haiti's best chess player was playing against an old Village Italian.

Annette comes with the same provocative walk, showing more of her luxuriant breasts, as fashion dictates. She asserts gallantly: "I am a dethroned Queen. But I enjoy being a dethroned Queen. My friends love me more than when I was the top billing star; they feel sorry for me. And there is much to enjoy backstage. I let the younger women worry about being at the top, quarrel and struggle. While young women take the center of the stage, there are still plenty of young men who prefer autumnal women. *Jeunes filles* are for the daytime, but autumnal women are for the night."

Her freedom to come and go, her gaiety and ability to live alone are admirable. She is back from a trip around the world, alone. She lives by her own caprices, changes, varieties. "Think of all the places in the world I have not yet seen and all that one can do with 150 dollars a month elsewhere, anywhere but New York." She gave up her apartment in New York. She is one of the adventurous women I admire.

When Thomas Payne writes me he is willing to show *Solar Barque* to Viking I get paralyzed and think: One more insulting letter to add to my file of Bitchy Comments. I cannot take it. The last letter from Viking was apropos of *Spy in the House of Love,* calling it an "erotic fantasy" and refusing to publish it. More damage. More anger. More feelings of my work being unwanted. I must learn to take the blows, the offenses. They are part of any work in the world. Dr. Bogner told me how often she is insulted in public in the name of psychoanalysis, by those who hate it. They make her the butt of jokes and criticism of the science. I don't want to put *Solar Barque* through that experience.

Dream after talk of offenses and insults: I am in a room. A tiger leaps into the room. I run out and close the door. I continue to run into other rooms and close doors, one upon another, more doors. No matter how many doors I close I know the tiger is there. I close the last door. I am given a knife. I will not use the knife.

Stormy session with Bogner. It is the conflict with aggression (the tiger) and I am unable to kill it. I had interpreted the tiger as those who criticized my work. I was holding back the anger.

I resisted the interpretation that the tiger was part of me. I was closing doors upon a part of myself.

Bogner: "You forget that resistance is necessary to survival. It is your character. Without it you would be a fluid nonentity. We have to include the tiger in ourselves. It is no crime to assert or defend what you consider your truth. I am only trying to show you that when you come to facing your aggressions, you go about closing doors upon it. It is natural for you to be angry at rejections of your work."

Professor Corey's humor at The Village Vanguard: "Marcel Marceau was a success only because he was French and he did his pantomime in French and since nobody knows French they thought it was good. I'm much better, but as I have a Brooklyn accent nobody really believes it."

Marcel Pagnol's latest quip has the same nonsense charm. He was asked about his imitators. He said: "I don't mind them at all. It must be a great pleasure to inspire your predecessors!"

Italian Fair on Bleecker Street to raise funds for the Catholic church. Jim and I walked through it enjoying the games, the gaiety, the food being cooked, roulette with a two dollar limit watched by a benevolent young priest. We won, and were about to go home with our evening's take of four dollars but felt guilty to have won at roulette from the profits of the church, so we returned and lost all we won. Our Catholic background was too strong to allow us such a profit!

I am not sure that the encounter of American realism with French surrealism gave birth to anything at this period, but who knows what will happen to Jim ten years from now?

Letter from Jim:

It has been a beautiful ten or twelve days. I have read voraciously from 1939 to 1943, about six volumes, and I have never in my life read with such involvement, pleasure, fascination. I *am* in this life that I'm reading as I have never been *in* anything else in literature. That is perhaps the most significant aspect of my response to the diary: I am gripped by it. And that is the art of literature. I'm amused by the references, even in the diary, to the artlessness of your work—because that is the most artful thing about it: your own faith in your voice. I'm certain that was the essential strength of Shakespeare and Dostoevski and D. H. Lawrence and Tennessee Williams—their fidelity to their own voice, no room for doubt, no time for it. You can't doubt a river when you are riding on it, when it is carrying you—you know that it will flow even if you drown in it, and that even then you will go on flowing with it. I have decided that the people who don't know how to read you are the ones doomed to sit on the banks all their lives loathing their own inability to navigate. You know, Anaïs, that I was unable to read anymore, that before the diaries I had lost my faith in the power of books to enchant me, hold me. These volumes restored that faith. Now I'm hungry for more, for the rest of it, and then for *Don Quixote* and Dostoevski and Proust in a way that I have not been for years—because they are writers and works that have held you.

Amazing that at the deepest moments of your neurosis you are still in contact with truth and beauty and love; they saved you. The analyst who wanted you to abandon the diary was sadly in error. This could have been a tragic mistake, advising a bird to abandon its wings while it is in flight. And it could have been tragic for everyone in your life, because your children, as you called them, were sustained by you, and you *were* the diary. I don't think there was anything split or schizoid or what-have-you about your contact with the diary: it was one of your organs, as vital to you as your heart. There are so many jokes about the mother-child metaphor of artists and their work; but it is not a joke, it is a *fact*. And it is more true of you probably because your work is more true; you don't make the separation of life and art, and so to an outsider (the analyst) the connection seems unwholesomely intimate. On the contrary: the further removed an artist is from his work (removed by artifice, invention, technique, etc.) the less wholesome his relation to the product.

Exciting this growth and its record, the privilege of witnessing an act of creation, not just reading about it. And the creation, of course, is you.

That is the quality of this diary that makes it unique in literature: it is alive. I have often described it to you as an organism. I see more and more how true that is, how accurate.

It may seem odd to you that I can see this so clearly when my own work seems to have taken a totally different turn. My own work is also becoming more and more *me*. I am beginning to find that there are in *me* a brood of mad children, simple, crazy, inexplicable people who are anxious to create me by speaking through me. I let them do as they please, and this is the closest to truth that I can reach, at least at the moment. I feel now very deeply and strongly that it is incumbent on me to love my children and let them breathe in their own simple and crazy tongues. The new play is another expression of this: it is a play that I would never in a million years have written if I had planned it in advance and decided to. It is so simple and light that at times I don't believe I'd have given it house room, if I'd known in advance how frivolous it would be. And at other moments it seems, along with its lightness and simplicity, just as dear and loving and profoundly alive as anything I've ever touched. All of which adds up to only one thing: we must not kill our progenies with judgments. We are creators, not judges. Let others do that. And I believe that if our children are properly loved, they'll survive even criticism.

For years you've been my one contact with a world that would otherwise have seemed by now illusory, nonexistent. You are, in other words, the only artist I have known through these many years who fulfills my child's dream of an artist: one who is true, devoted to beauty, and dedicated to transcending the world through it.

Watts Towers.

When Simon Rodia arrived from Italy he was twenty years old. His father had been a mason and had taught him his profession. He settled in a flat, sparsely built section of Los Angeles, next to a railroad track, because the gray wooden shack, built on an odd triangle of land, was inexpensive. He began to work.

He traveled in a dilapidated old Ford truck and returned each night to the lead-gray, wooden house. The patches on each side of the railroad track were neglected. Weeds, tin cans, broken bottles were the only flowers of these dismal gardens. A few discarded automobile tires attracted the neighborhood children to play. The only trees around were bare telephone poles. The landscape ran from burnt brown wild grass to the dirty brown of oil wells. The other houses were like his, wooden planks hastily nailed together, with toothless fences sheltering Negro and Mexican families. The doors whined on rusty hinges. Old newspapers fluttered like dying birds.

The Italian mason was now dressed in dark blue denim. His car was gray and dusty. But he was a skillful mason and had enough work. The radios were loud and harsh, and under the pretext of sharing news, told only of crimes, malice, gangsters, and never registered acts of devotion and sacrifice.

Only salesmen came to his door. One wanted to sell him a burial lot.

"No thanks," he said, "I want to be buried in Italy."

He worked hard. House after house, day after day. At the end of each day there was much to discard, broken tiles, broken mosaics, broken glass, which he brought back in his truck.

During his meals of red wine, sausage, spaghetti, he dreamed. It was almost always the same dream. It was in color. He remembered the tile floor in the kitchen of his childhood home, laid by his father. He remembered the intense midnight-blue of it. He remembered the fountains in the square of his village, decorated with mosaics. The ceiling of his church, and the scenes of heaven in gold and blue mosaics. He remembered the church steeple decorated with gold tiles which shone in the sun. Memories of color. Memories of arches, colonnades, steeples, stairways, patios, squares where the mosaics were delicately patterned.

What he had collected in his yard were fragments, as if all the beautiful things he had seen in Italy now lay wrecked. But the fragments, discards shone in the light even when broken. He began to see he could no longer live with such squalor around him. He cleared his own yard, erected a skeleton of iron, similar to the Eiffel Tower, and upon this he began to cement the broken pieces of tiles, glass, and even pottery he found in garbage dumps. It was not a reproduction of what he had seen in Italy. It was his dream of color, of light-catching fragments, diffused by time and memory. It was his very own creation, resembling none other, but capable of giving the same delight as the contemplation of the finished ceilings, towers, plazas of Italy. The fragments would be patterned, abstract floral designs, abstract mandalas, with the bottom of a bottle for a heart. There were turrets, archways, ogival passages, all richly encrusted with whatever had color and could catch the light. It was a Byzantine city seen in dreams, slightly blurred by time, as if the campaniles of Venice, the minarets of Rome, were all reflected in water, built of light, losing their sharp contours. Standing out from the flat masonry surfaces were strange lyric shapes: the swan neck of a broken teapot, the lyre-shaped handle of a cup. His Italian cities had left imprints of gold, green, red, silver, his churches the memory of colors seen through painted glass. Assembled lovingly in spiralling towers, they were more miraculous, built by one hand, in the midst of barrenness, rising among telephone poles and dead, brown devil grass.

The salesman came every year to sell him a burial lot.

The mason was forty years old. Two towers rose as high as oil rigs. Artists came from all over the world to see them.

One day when the salesman came to see him, the mason, now eighty years old, had gone. He had returned to Italy.

Ladies and Gentlemen, Pan American Flight 36 is now boarding for its tour around the world at Gate 9. Ladies and Gentlemen, passengers en route from Paris to Mexico, please enplane for Mexico, Flight 39 for Hawaii, Flight 40 for Japan.

The Hindu I wanted to speak to passed out of my life through Gate 9. An old man with beautiful, eloquent eyes, was I going to lose him too? I loved his long white hair and his restless hands. And the musician, every musician with an instrument entrances me. The woman he was talking to moved slowly to the right and revealed a black cello case. It didn't matter if he passed through Gate 9, I would not lose him. I would hear him play somewhere. He belonged in my world, the world of the artist. We were *"compadres."* The world of the artist is my only native country. Jazz is part of it. Jazz musicians have a language, a style, a way of life. They live lyrically and to the limit; they transcend poverty. They may die of it. But they are our troubadours and they keep us alive.

When I sorrow over love it is over the statement that all you have to do to be loved is to look beautiful. I exclude myself from this because I lost my first beauty contest. I would hear my father say about women: *"Elle est jolie, elle est belle."* That was the only requisite for his interest. But he had no interest in his little girl. It must have meant I was not *"jolie"* or *"belle."* The apple was never given to me. To lose one's first beauty contest means you lose them all. The final outcome was that beautiful women lured him away altogether, or so I thought. A child's notion of reality. As it happened his second wife was plain. But this was my first impression (the beautiful, perfumed, chic women who embraced me at concerts were all my rivals!). The first defeat, the first loss is the one which stamps itself upon the soul. From now on you obey the pattern. I did try to transcend it by making efforts to *become* the women he admired, not the maternal hausfrau, too busy to dress up. I not only wanted to grow inwardly, but also attain some beauty. I won. I was the prize model of the Artists and Models Club. But such triumphs do not erase the doubt. I won love, but I was never certain of it. And the loveliest irony was that I would be sad that the love was given to me for other reasons, other qualities than physical ones.

In the museum, in the store room, in the attic of the mind much dust and microbes are left. The past is preserved, intact, and the child in one is always staring out the windows. Whenever my love has a moment of inattention, not me, but this child, considers itself neglected. I have no memory of physical closeness to my father. He was incapable of tenderness. He was stiff and formal. His second wife complained of this. She said she did not mind the unfaithfulness so much as the absence of tenderness. I was physically close to my brothers and my mother. And so later I am at ease in the same constellations, the little brothers and the mother. Old forms of successful union.

Dr. Bogner, today I bring you only a curtain. I dreamt of a curtain. Just a curtain. Nothing else. There must be something behind this curtain. I remember Brussels, a big round library table with a green felt cover which hung to the floor and with a fringe at the edges. This was our playhouse. I was eight years old. One brother was six and the other two years old. I do not remember any sexual games, but it must have been warm and intimate and left a lingering yearning for tents, or canopied beds.

I began to remember moments of union with parents and brothers, moments of love, proofs of love. It was not as I had crystallized it, all pain and estrangement. I didn't believe in my father's love because he read a book during meals, and only appeared (in my memory) to spank us, or to watch whether I slept through my child's siesta (I refused to sleep so that he would come and watch me). Did he come and watch me and was I happy to have his attention?

"Fact or fantasy," said Bogner, "the guilt is the same."

I wanted to charm my father.

The diary was not originally a depository for secrets only. It was written at first for my father to read, to make him share our life, think of us, want to join us. My mother read it. I left it in the library with the other books. Anyone could read it. I never concealed it until I married.

It is only the neurotic who drags his past around and who decides that his life is like a novel which, once written, cannot be changed.

If today, as a mature woman, I have a propensity to break with those who hurt me, would it not be possible that from the first injury (desertion by my father) I developed hypersensitive apprehensions which make me leave first? Just as the criminal remembers only the wrongs society has done him, never the kindnesses he has received. So the child wanting *all* and obtaining but a relative fraction conceives an exaggerated grudge. The sulks so well portrayed by Simenon, whose characters sink into their grudges instead of dispelling them or laughing them away.

Children, like criminals, are absolute dictators, as we know.

But with the vision of psychoanalysis, a new aspect of relationships is uncovered, a new relationship to the parents born of the recognition of one's own role in the interpretation of their actions. Abandoning the exigencies of a child's loves, one begins to see the parents as fallible human beings. My mother's courage sometimes expressed in benefic tyranny, my father's Don Juanism necessary to his childish dependency on the mother.

The idea or concept of not being loved is a painful one, but the realization that one was loved in the only terms possible to the parents, in *the only way they knew* (my mother by physical care, my father by constantly photographing us) is even more painful, but at least curable. Breaks, separations, losses could be aggravated by one's own inflation of them, arising from the standard set by the child: a demand for a total, unshared, fanatical, exclusive and flawless love!

You can make extreme claims. You can make inflexible choices. But you cannot blame those who cannot respond to them!

The curtains, the doors are of your own making. I could say now that the world of dancing is closed to me. At this moment it is closed to me personally, but if I can no longer dance as deliriously as I did, I certainly can transfer this to others, and take pleasure in watching other dancers. Abdication is not the end of contact with a form of expression. One has to transfer the love and let others express the dance for you.

Life is not being at the center but being in contact with others. The center of attention is the child's prerogative.

At the center of the stage now is Bill Barker, a friend of Caresse Crosby, Zina his ex-wife, Diana his present mistress. I met him with Caresse in Los Angeles, in the guesthouse of Burton Holmes. Bill had barely spoken, once in English, and once in French, when I was able to re-create his entire atmosphere. Society, Paris, Rome, Cocteau, Prince Ruspoli, De Sica and the movies, Jean Genêt and ambisexuality. It was like oxygen. We could have talked then and there for twenty-four hours. A disturbing light in his eyes, irony, anger, passion.

He and Renate met, but there were no sparks. Bill is in an angry mood. He is hostile to his present environment, seeking return to his other world. He thinks of California as a tranquilizer, heroin mixed with bicarbonate. He looks for wilder forms of life.

We met again in New York and he brought Zina. Tall, the body of Venus and the head of a young Greek man. Her short blond curls are like a helmet, espousing ears, forehead, *casque d'or*. The ice-cold blue eyes are slanted, in a faunesque slyness. The nose is slightly flattened, the mouth just full enough but not sensuous. At times her expression is hard. She frowns. She peers into the café at others. She is like a man, inspecting. Then she laughs fully, throws her head back and she is a charming woman. One moment she talks so softly one cannot hear her; another moment she springs like a tigress and shouts. She wears her scarf not languidly or floatingly but severely stretched across her wide shoulders like a Greek costume on a statue. She may wear a dirty raincoat and shorts or a heavy dark wool dress. Her father was a Russian grand duke, her mother an American millionaire. She has acted in films, worked in nightclubs, married and divorced, married Bill Barker. At times she sits in the café completely abstracted, withdrawn. You never feel you are looking into the eyes of a human being. Bill said: "Zina is a myth."

You feel she would not bat an eyelash at the sight of someone suffering. She plays roles. She is an unfathomable abyss.

Jim and I begin to rebel against using the word "characters" to describe the people who either spring out of my novels (like attracting like) or will soon be inside of them, like Zina. "The word 'character' has been mutilated, corroded. Let's find a new one. What do you think of Flora and Fauna? Flora for the sweet ones, Fauna for the fascinating ones."

To our sorrow, both Flora and Fauna vanished to Europe.

Bill Barker's last words to me were: "Anaïs, you have a genius for life."

Their charm did affect me for a few days. A most mysterious thing happens when one writes books. They attract and magnetize only those who feel an affinity with the characters. The links between them bring more and more into the circle. They relate to the "characters" in the book, resemble them, extend them, and the world of fictionalized, half-invented, partly composite portraits multiplies, expands, becomes denser and richer. We all form a kind of family. Recognize each other. It is a startling and marvelous miracle, like the birth of a world from a small nucleus, like the multiplication of cells, like a certain nation being formed with certain loves, beliefs, loyalties, adhesions. Bill and Zina and Diana can go to Europe but the pull of the constellation is there.

Twenty years ago Lawrence Durrell appeared in Paris, small, blond, blue-eyed, soft-gestured, tanned, endless talker, poet, with a yoga suppleness of body and the power of words already manifested in *The Black Book*. *The Black Book* was banned from America, as well as *Black Spring* and *Winter of Artifice,* and remained known to a very few people. Then today Bill Barker brings me *Justine*. What a feast of images! What a banquet, an orgy of words and colors, a riot of the senses. Erratic, elusive, penetrating, a sensuous jungle. Durrell is a juggler, a master of prestidigitations. It is full of mysteries, suggestions, adventure and romance. At last, a book which brings life and color to a drab scene of naturalism. To my utter amazement, America responded. America who until now only loved the clipped, barren, puritanical language of the Hemingways, who hated efflorescence in writing, who hated "literature," who hated sensuality and exoticism! For the first time a writer's recognition, which was instantaneous, made me weep, not with a sense of jealousy or envy, which I have never had and could not have because of my love of the book, but at the injustice of America closing its door to my work, which I felt to be the feminine counterpart of Durrell.

There was a Durrell epidemic. As he announced there were more books to come, I felt he was going to write the book of our century, as Proust did for his. I was quickly consoled to think good writing had won. That civilized, developed, full-blown literature was at last recognized by America. That puritanism had lost its battle for the short, Anglo-Saxon words as against the Latinized roots. That wealth of vocabulary, wealth of images, all the excesses of a Byzantine court had become part of our daily reading.

By accident I read Kerouac's *On the Road* at the same time. I had put all my faith in jazz writing, in writing with a living tempo, beat, rhythm and life blood. Those seeking to live "high" were to restore lyric and sensuous writing to a parched America. But after *Justine,* the ecstasies of *On the Road* seemed primitive, and the myth of jazz writing ushering in a poetry of the senses exploded in my hands.

The image of Larry as a young man who came to visit me was so clear. He had a softly contoured face. He was not lean in spite of constantly sailing his boat and swimming in Greece. He had a rounded nose, humorous and earthy. I wrote to him. He passed certain judgments on Henry.

An absurd incident had cut the thread between us. It was he who paid for the publication of *Winter of Artifice* and *Black Spring* and *The Black Book.* During the war he found himself needing money. He wrote to Henry. It was at the time when I was drowning in debts, with the Press, Gonzalo and Helba and Henry himself. I could not help. Henry borrowed from friends. I felt so ashamed and guilt paralyzed me. We could have been writing to each other. I would have followed his life. He was the best writer of the three of us.

Letter from Eve Miller:

Larry [Durrell] just wrote on the back of a letter from the head of Dutton which was a marvel! from Publisher to Author. Of his (the editor's) discovery of *Justine* . . . his love for it, what plans he has for the entire bulk of Larry's work. On top of which he will be paid regularly . . . some contract arrangement wherein Larry can actually realize living and writing at the same time. He says it's the first time in fifteen years. Naturally Henry is delirious with joy. Chortles and laughs and feels so good it's acted like a springboard, and he's painting like crazy. That wonderful quality of his, where he identifies with someone or something he believes in . . . the "oneness" of everything is proven. Your success is my success . . . your joy my joy.

Henry is so completely free, he truly has reached that level of being wherein he "sees as a child." Pure. I admit, now and then he humanly aberrates and because of this quality someone he truly cares for is hurt. I consider you one of the very few women who were "right" in Henry's life. You did him nothing but right and goodness . . . lifted him morally and spiritually always. The tortures he's suffered from most of his women are far more lacerating to me than I can tell you. Because of his innocence and purity, he's never deserved the treatment. (And he's sure as hell no angel either!) But enough. I could go on and on. (I have the strange feeling that anything I could say you know already! Probably far better than I!) We are so sincerely happy that your life is so rich and beautiful and full that the ugly moments are forgotten. That's a great thing to be able to say. Yes, I would very much like to read *Wilder Shores of Love*. My reading taste would be akin to your own, I should think. I'm not abstracted . . . in any sense.

Letter to Durrell:

The advent of *Justine* was a phenomenon, after the miserly, sterile, frigid, plain, homely American novels. It was truly a fiesta, a banquet, an orgy. As soon as I began reading the world expanded. It was not only the great tactile richness, the colors, the smells, the flavors of the surface, the atmosphere, but the sudden depths of insight, the senses and the intelligence so keen. I was tempted to say this is not writing but witchcraft. Whatever it is, dear Larry, I must tell you I have an immense respect for what you have done. All these years, what you amassed in power and color. I went back immediately and reread *The Black Book*. The richness of writing was there, and the deftness of characterization, but more abstract, more mystifying, more distilled. Here the balance is perfect between realism and surrealism. Surface and depths. The interweaving and interplaying between various levels of consciousness, perfectly captured. The wavering boundaries between dreaming and feeling. The characters live vividly for the moment you grasp them, and then disappear again into the depths, and reappear into a flow of poetry. The poetry with which the city becomes the bodies, and the bodies a city. All the metamorphoses of mind and matter, senses and thought. I know this may sound extravagant but the writing is extravagantly beautiful. It resuscitated the young Larry of twenty-six or -eight who appeared in Paris and in the pages of the diary. From that day on, in the particular world I was going to traverse artistically, I was to be completely alone.

Nearby in Los Angeles live two old Belgian ladies, Irene Delanoeye and Agnes Dedecker. One of them gives massages. When my back troubles me after hours of typing I go there. We talk French. Their house could be my mother's, the same taste, same neatness and care for the silver objects, mended clothes, austerity, all the photographs and bric-à-brac from the past carefully hung up, framed, aligned on the mantelpiece. The orderly sewing basket. The lace making. *"Petite vie."* All ordered, tidy, regular. The massage is a sort of small family gathering which takes us back to Europe. We talk about life in Europe. How they came here. One of them is a practical nurse who married and left Belgium. The days of the First War with little food, and Irene going about on her bicycle to rich women's houses. Her hands froze. Their father had a little haberdashery. They know music, and have thoughtful, courteous manners. Though my father supplied the artistic romance of our life, my mother had these humble middle-class virtues. Strange to return to the atmosphere of one's childhood, which one rebelled against, and to return with human respect. How I once hated the Sèvres porcelain swan, the decorated Louis XV teacups, the silver set in its felt bags, the fussy flower vases, the numerous little tables.

The photograph of the living room of the apartment where I first lived was absolutely crammed with objects, lamps, shawls, photographs, bric-à-brac. Today I find their gentle courtesies a relief from harsh manners, their tidy, impeccable dressing touching.

The people I find irresistible are those in whom the child was not killed. The qualities of openness, trust, inquisitiveness, tenderness, eagerness, enthusiasm, others undefinable, come from the child in us and are the source of charm. The laughter and the smile that do not calculate, the spontaneity that is not arrested. I cannot remember "adult" charm or whether it even exists.

Henry had this child's charm to a supreme degree, but it is not as apparent in his books as in his watercolors.

Most of the artists I have known have that, Harry Partch, Janko Varda.

[Fall, 1957]

So much has happened this month. Lawrence Lipton introduced me to a new magazine, *Eve*.

I discussed your participation in *Eve* with Jane and we decided that, for the present, a kind of letter would be the best editorial form for your material. A kind of diary of your comings and goings, conversations with the people you meet and reports on things you do and places you go— whatever you think will be of interest to our imagined Eve, whom I am sure you know very well, for after all she is really you. I can think of no better description of the sort of thing we would like to have than your own reportage, to make women feel they have been there.

I tried to get in touch with Margaret Mead, Dr. Erich Fromm, sent photographs by Val Talberg, tried to reach Kay Boyle, Santha Rama Rau, suggested James Leo Herlihy, the Barrons on electronic music, and contacted everyone in New York Lawrence Lipton asked me to.

It is difficult to describe the feeling we all had about Peter, Renate's son. We never knew his father because Renate was divorced when we met her. Because he was such a sensitive child and so enormously talented, we all in a sense considered him our child. At five he was already drawing. At seven he made drawings which evoked, without imitating, the Mexican sculptures and murals. I chose them for *Solar Barque*. At the masquerades he always contributed his own happening. He wrote a story for the Arabian Nights party, read it. His drawings were an amazing combination of poetry, imagination and science. At times he drew futuristic airplanes and cars. At others, dreamlike figures. He was not an expansive child; he was shy and reserved. He had a visionary expression, the expression of a dreamer. He watched all our doings as if he were dreaming.

The drawings I selected for *Solar Barque* are strong. The book will be beautiful. It will be ready in February. *Eve* magazine promised to publish a fragment of it to launch it. Tom Payne promised to help with distribution.

I remember that when Dr. Janiger asked me if I knew a child who would be willing to try LSD I had suggested Peter because I felt he was familiar with dreaming and that it would not startle him.

But Renate has a horror of drugs and she refused.

Letter from Renate:

Your letter made me happy—an image came in with your letter—you are riding the crest of a wave, the reins are red threads—Ariadne's thread probably, the horses are foam and fish, the whole image is like the Persian miniatures you love so much. Yes on anything you have in mind about Peter's work. $100 is very generous and Peter was delighted. He was seven when he did the drawings. He has already done a few sketches for *Solar Barque*, cover in mind, in the same style as the others of course. A king holds a sun in one hand, a boat in the other. A sun medallion and a boat sailing through the sky, the boat in the shape of a dragon. He also designed a few boats in fish shapes. Have you inspired him!

Sometimes I feel you invented me (like a character in search of an author in Pirandello). But how the role fits. It's always the same thing with me. The dream, the role, the invention, seem more real to me than reality (what people call reality). I'm not surprised that India is publishing you.

Letter from Larry:

Well, I have been living very much *en poète* in a ravishing Turkish house in Cyprus until the situation catapulted me out of the island. I was sad at first, but things turned out magically different than I had feared. At the moment Languedoc is perfect—it's rather a bony, windswept department of France, untouristy and rugged. But the wine and food as elsewhere. I have abducted a young woman, French, from Alexandria, who writes light novels in English, is very pretty, cooks and makes love like the Arabian Nights. Claude by name. We ran away to France and worked our way slowly down here prospecting, with very little money. By luck we hit upon this rather lovely villa on a hillside, in a sea of vines, and took it for six months. Owing to the aforesaid resourceful and clever woman we got it for six months cheap and settled down to see if we could make even a bare living by writing; I didn't think we could, but it was heartening for the first time in my life to find a woman who was almost more anxious for me to write than I was myself—and who was determined to get a job to keep me if I couldn't keep myself. So I gave in and started knocking out a set of novels—*Justine* is the first of four, a rather complicated pattern. Then other miracles began to happen; Dutton suddenly woke up to me in USA and bought out all my books, and contracted for the ones to come. Then *Bitter Lemons* got a Book Society choice in England which meant several hundred unexpected pounds. In short we have secured the door against the wolf for a year ahead and are falling to work with a vengeance to stabilize the position if we possibly can.

Letter from Henry:

I hear from June now fairly often. She's improving rapidly thanks to our mutual friend in New York.

Three characters, Henry, June and I, found different ways of concealing the truth. Henry Miller by exaggerated realism.

Bogner: "When you are so intent on describing externals, so emphatic about externals, it is one way of concealing whatever thoughts, memories, or associations lie behind or beyond the facts, the other dimensions."

June, who not only lied about whether or not she had lovers, whether or not she was a Lesbian, whether or not she took drugs (neither Henry nor I ever found out), but about everything, things of no importance, such as the purchase of a trivial object.

Bogner: "When a person lies so desperately on all levels it is because the compulsive mechanism functions continuously, a symptom of great defensiveness, great fear of the truth leaking out."

I observed that Henry's realism did not capture June, but that as I could not reveal the truths contained in my diary, I had to find a way to tell the truth in a poetic, symbolic, surrealist fashion. The ambiguity and obliqueness of poetry suited me.

That Bogner should arrive, via psychological routes, at the same point at which I arrived artistically some time ago, was so exciting to me, like some discovery in science. It was a moment of illuminating truth.

Truth lay in the subtle interaction between all levels, and only after the obstacles were removed, the personal obstacles of defensiveness, neurosis.

A new concept, that psychoanalysis does not (as we have been taught) deal only with a personal mythology, but that by exploring and unraveling the personal mythology, it can reach an impersonal mythology.

Mr. Joseph Campbell, you are wrong to say mythology ended in 1400.

The only obstacle is that Americans cannot read either poetry or symbolism and so whatever I tried to tell through the novels was not understood.

Every act related to my writing was connected in me with an act of charm, seduction of my father. Every act was accompanied by guilt and retraction. Every act was doomed. I was doomed by the enormity of my sin (the wish to charm my father) to be punished, to fail.

Every act from selling a book, accepting a dollar, involving others, was charged with direct sexual associations: courting the world. In my dreams I did not publish *Under a Glass Bell* but I bought a vulgar parrot—green dress, a whorish dress. In my dreams at night I did not achieve a work of art and present the world with it, but I lay naked on a bed (with an invisible lover) and all the world could see me.

I worked for the magazine *Eve*, collected articles, made notes, saw Henrietta Weigel, whom I had not seen for ten years, as she is a friend of the editor. We spent hours recollecting when we were neighbors on Thirteenth Street, and admired each other's work.

Saw George Borchardt, literary agent. Saw Gunther Stuhlmann, literary editor.

Helped Peggy and Sylvia in their efforts to present Peggy's opera *Transposed Heads*.

Went to the Barrons' party, to Eric Hawkins' dance recital (maddeningly static), to Harlem with Stanley, Karon and Tom, Wilfredo Lam and his young wife. Narrated Persian poems for a film on Persian miniatures by Walter Lewisohn, three hours of work. Was paid 125 dollars. Saw Tambimuttu, who feels that because he published Durrell, Miller and me in England during the war he has rights over our works today.

I wrote my "Letter from New York" for *Eve:*

Eve in New York donned a leopard fur beret and a red dress to match the vivid mood of the city. Red dresses in the windows . . . the Rodeo marching down Fifth Avenue between the buses . . . the noble Black Watch in their kilts and leopard vests marching around Madison Square Garden calling forth wild shouts of excitement from a usually restrained New York audience. . . . church bells, holiday bells, Indian bells on bedroom slippers . . . talk of vast inter-cultural exchanges, so many books being translated which we could never read, so much of our music and so many of our books going to foreign countries . . . dirty blue jeans adopted by the women of Arabia as the symbol of independence, but our women of achievement displaying more and more femininity.

Intensely active on the contemporary scene, Peggy Glanville-Hicks preparing the production of her opera based on Thomas Mann's "Transposed Heads." This woman composer, considered the best, is frail, slight, with a lively charm, dressed with a simple elegance which says: do not look at me but at the musician. In her humorous moods she wears a Tyrolean hat with dash. She disserts on the most abstruse themes of modern music with a lightness, a smile, a waving of small delicate hands, and the strength of her music is impossible to guess from her charm and humor. Her femininity is expressed in her untiring protectiveness towards other composers. She has no sense of rivalry, but a keen sympathy with all composers; her flair for quality is unerring, her skillful articulateness rare in musicians, enabling her to situate, to evaluate, to illumine musical values, developments and trends simultaneously with creation. Thus she offers not only her rich musical productivity but also a far reaching, universal grasp of the tonal meaning of music. This quality of objective insight is not usually considered a feminine quality. Peggy and Eve discussed the delicate confusion between activity and aggressivity which disturbs modern woman. Women are themselves fearful of this new active role, having played so long a passive and indirect role. The sensitive ones are aware of the differences between activity and aggressivity. Activity is creative; aggressivity is a warrior's attack upon obstacles. According to the legend it was Lillian and not Eve who was born independent of man. Eve was made of the same substance, which made her indivisible. Her new activity and creativity were fraught with dangers. Peggy has remained the friend, the protector, the initiator, the organizer of other musicians. Her words about Olin Downes might be applied to her: "possessing a kind of radar for musicality."

Another type of musician is Bebe Barron, collaborating with her husband Louis, who composes with electronic sounds, a modern permutation of music born of physics. Bebe is a beautiful young woman with short dark hair, delicate features and large soft dark eyes, who threads her way gracefully through mazes of lights, wires, buttons, turntables, earphones and tubes. She speaks softly, moves about in feminine clothes, unobtrusively sharing in the development of this new intricate science.

One cold morning on Fourteenth Street Eve met the Becks (Julian Beck and Judith Malina), who for years gave bold and original freedom to productions of their "Living Theatre." They had just bought a building for their theatre, after moving from one loft to another. There are now thirty-eight off-Broadway theatres in New York. This one, the thirty-ninth, proves the strength of the effort made to create an artistic underground to counter the present commercial and conventional values. Many personal sacrifices nourished this now flourishing activity divorced from commerce. These small groups, long dedicated to basic research in the theatre, often in turn nourish a Broadway suffering from an anemia caused by the commonplace. The Becks say: "The theatre is love, dream, ritual, poetry, prose, reality. It is a place of intense experience . . . it is a place where the spectator must participate by feeling and comprehending. It is more than entertainment. It is life itself. . . ."

The most fascinating aspect of life in New York is this artistic underground. Lofts are rented to give exhibitions of paintings, concerts, films, readings, lectures and jazz sessions. They are advertised only by word of mouth. The crowd that attends these loft events is marked by a particular attentiveness, a deeper interest.

One of the loft sessions was a Symposium of Modern Music. Faced with the highly over-abstract music of John Cage and his European parallels, the crowd not only listened with absorption but demanded afterwards that the composers make clear their intent. A young Swede, newly arrived in the United States, heard this music on Second Avenue, weaving between hoboes and bar-leaners, and joined the group. Coming out with Eve and her friends, he commented: "This is an America we never heard about." This is what Eve has always called the Hidden Face of America, the one Europeans would love and understand.

From over-distilled sounds to the best jazz in town, the Five Spot on Cooper Square. The crowd does not wish to encounter the peepers and spectators who watch others in Village cafés. The waiters are mostly artists and musicians. Eve and her friends tried to divine their professions. In the group was Maxwell Geismar, the historian of American literature, now preparing a collection of his reviews. When asked if he were a painter the young waiter answered: "No, I am a writer, but I write something which wouldn't interest you. I'm an avant-garde writer."

At the bookshop two books were placed in Eve's hands: *Justine,* by Lawrence Durrell, and *My Father, My Son,* by Edward G. Robinson, Junior.

Justine is an exceptional adventure into intimate experience, a love affair with characters rarely encountered in modern fiction and with the sensuous, beautiful city of Alexandria. *Justine* has the deep, warm colors of a Chagall painting and an intoxicating use of language. The blending of humor, skillful analysis, poetic descriptions with realism and surrealism, gives it the smoky, mysterious, enticing quality of multiple dimensions . . .

a voyage to the antipodes of experience. The threads weave in and out as richly as oriental tapestries, as intricate as oriental cities, but with sudden, sharp moments of revelation in the development of relationships which brings them into the focus of our daily experiences among those concerned with moments of truth.

My Father, My Son is almost at the opposite pole. It is a document of the tragedy of people who cannot relate to each other, who fumble and stumble through all the distortions and errors of non-love and non-understanding. The story is an ancient tragedy of failed relationship between parent and child in the modern setting of Hollywood. The unfulfilled demand for total love creates revengefulness, the theme of modern delinquency. It is the environment of Hollywood that contributes to the disaster, through its publicity, which makes caricatures of relationships, destroying intimacy. The book arouses compassion for both parents and son. The ultimate tragedy is the boy's inability to find his own identity so that he can withstand defeats and emptiness. The obsession with retaliation and destruction takes the place of the creation of a world in which he could live.

In these two books the two worlds oppose each other—one rich, magic, full, the other empty and destructive. Robinson Junior has been able to create compassion for the displaced person who lacks a passport to an inner life.

Parties . . . at the Barrons', where through a soundproof window in their living room one looks upon the science-fiction room of electronic machines. . . . One sees first of all Geoffrey Holder, the dark dancer, who looks like a Giacometti statue, elongated into supreme grace, so tall that at times he walks into a room with his hands outstretched like those of a blind man, making way for himself as if delicately creating enough space so he will not collide with anyone. . . .

In one corner James Leo Herlihy sits Buddhist fashion. His play *Blue Denim,* written in collaboration with Bill Noble, is being rehearsed. Jim is a handsome young man who could act the hero of his own plays. . . . He has the tense, swift rhythm of New York, and of jazz. His many-faceted talk rushes out in dizzying improvisations with a casual elegance and facility which recalls one of the titles of his stories: "A Breeze from China," but which is of the purest American flavor and origin.

Joseph Campbell, author of *The Hero with a Thousand Faces,* the brilliant historian of mythology, is asserting that mythology expired in the fourteenth century, but all around him are people who, born in the reign of Freudian mythology, know there is a language of the myth we all share after having learned the translation of our dreams. . . . In this room, at this party, symbolism is a familiar guest, no esoteric one. The women assert it by their dressing. The symbolism of women's dressing has so lovingly been recorded by the novelists. Proust gave ten pages to the resemblance between Odette's negligées and the flowers she surrounded herself with through the Paris winters. D. H. Lawrence, without knowing anything of fashions, liked his heroines to wear magenta stockings on days of conflict. And a film star Eve knew owned a multitude of hats. The hats, properly perched on stands, as in all women's dreams of an actress's wardrobe, were never taken down. They required too much audacity. They demanded that a role be played to its maximum perfection. So each time she had reached into the joyous hat exhibit, looked at the treasured hats, she took again the little skullcap, the unobtrusive page and choirboy cap. . . . The moment when her small hand hesitated, lavishing only a caress over the arrogant feather, the challenging upward tilts, the regal velvets, the labyrinthian veils, the assertive gallant ribbons, the plumage and decorations of triumph, was it self-doubt which reached for the tiny skullcap of the priest, choirboy and scholar?

The distinction between colorless dressing and dressing to express character, a mood, the richness of a personality is the same one which separates a uniform from the art of dressing. The last originates from a knowledge of one's identity, an awareness of moods, a care for eloquence of body as well as of words. It is inseparable from the art of relationship or the art of living. A choice of scarf, a style of hair, the form of a shoe, a certain color, can play this lyrical note which reveals a woman's inner riches. The art of dress in living is not less valuable than the art of dress on the stage. The art of living is renewal, inventiveness, exploration, an openness to the unexpected, a love of surprises. Eve is not a spectator watching a fashion parade. She knows that even among textiles, she must choose with a feeling for the meaning of her life, the motifs and the patterns, the textures of her life and of those she loves, a harmonization of moods, temperaments and indications of the hidden selves which cannot appear badly dressed.

The way Jean Erdman, the modern dancer, stood in the middle of the Barrons' room distinguished her from all other women. There was a plumbline perfection to her standing which made other women seem to have collapsed inwardly, achieving what Martha Graham had once described as pelvic consciousness.

Two kinds of climate are clearly felt in the city of New York. One is the ozonated one which blows from the wide open East River and the United Nations Building. So many windows open upon the world, men of all races walking up and down the wide, windswept steps, all races meeting in the elevators. The visitors from other cities and other countries who are not sitting at the sessions wander in the basement into the shops, which carry objects from all over the world. An international bazaar, with flutes from Yugoslavia, basketry from Mexico, silverware from India, shawls from Persia, painted wood objects from Greece, dolls, spoons, toys. And near to it, a bookshop unlike any other. A network of written communication with the whole world: books in every language, on every subject, studies made by the United Nations of people's vital problems of living. America's gift to other countries here is in terms of technology, how to build bridges, how to develop agriculturally, how to organize communities, how to solve problems of food. A simple example of teaching people to mature economically was the task accomplished by the United Nations representative in Haiti. The Haitians were suffering great poverty, in spite of the fact that their sea contained abundant fish. They lacked fishing boats. They were too poor to construct them. They were helped to build these and to become, ultimately, independent and self-sustaining. It was also an American who discovered that they were painters of marvelous quality. Every year Haitian painters are exhibited in New York. It was he who had a story to tell of what happened during the last floods. American helicopters were picking off people who had been carried off to sea; flying them to Port-au-Prince, where they were given a full meal and a new set of clothes. Soon the fliers became aware that the more people they rescued the more appeared to be swimming in desperate clusters. And soon they realized that some poor Haitians were deliberately throwing themselves into the sea to be rescued, fed and clothed.

Together with this many-colored, many-flagged world, and the infinite sharing of one's privileges, there also blows upon New York the incandescent climate of jazz. Not only for our pleasure, not only as the truest art born of America, but as a revivifying influence upon American literature. Following the war there was in the novel a period which might kindly be described as "dead." The writing was pale, lifeless, without rhythm or vitality. No need to mention the writers. They were bored, listless, and dealing in clichés. But there was another trend. It first revealed itself in writers writing about jazzmen, such as in *Really the Blues,* or *Solo,* a remarkable novel of a jazz musician who clung to his individuality and whom the community destroyed. He carried about a visiting card which stated: "I am the last of the individuals." He was not the last. He was probably one of the jazzmen who was to influence our literature. A long prose poem was used in the film *The Wild Party.* It was not noticed then, but the stylized beauty of it is apparent today. In Kerouac's *On the Road,* the lyrical passages have a primitive beauty. All of them are alive. The basic research in American writing does not lie in surrealism, or in the flat dull realism of middle-class novels, but in this original language born of jazz, which has the tempo of American life, its rhythm, its vitality and colorfulness. The resistance to it, to its artistry, its uniqueness, only comes from a fear of freedom, the fear of individuality which has tried to make writing an anonymous, functional utility. New York is experiencing the influence of a climate which blows from the West Coast. . . .

[Winter, 1957–1958]

The liberation from guilt caused a rebirth, a freedom from fixation on the past. The past traumas caused crystals in the joints, spiritual arthritis. Suddenly I could relate to everyone, even those who had hurt me. I recaptured old friends like Wallace Fowlie. He hurt me once by leaving me out of his book on surrealism and including Henry Miller. The same people I knew before but could not connect with, I could work with now. I had forgotten to take change into account, a change in them and a change in me. Gunther is now a literary agent and is helping me. He is an intelligent man who loves literature, does translations, worked in films. I connected with Tom Payne. From the very first we talked openly.

One evening Tom brought Jack Kerouac. Kerouac greeted me in French and kissed me, saying: "You are beautiful." But he was already drunk and it was impossible to talk with him. He put a record of his own reading on the phonograph and listened raptly. It was as if he wanted the recording to speak for him because he was unable to. The telephone rang. Kerouac unhooked it and laid the arm of the telephone against the phonograph. Half an hour later the bell rang. Tom Payne felt it was a distressed friend and that he should leave by the kitchen door. He left. It was his friend at the door, who, hearing Kerouac's recording, felt Tom might be there. Her unhappiness touched me and I consoled her. After a while she left. Then I stayed with Kerouac, who was blubbering. I have an incurable prejudice against drunks. I suggested we go to the Cedar Bar where all our friends were. We sat at the bar. He had heard about my experience with LSD and so he began to pat his breast pocket vehemently and said: "If you have LSD, I have plenty of money to buy it." This offended me. I said: "I only took it once and it was given to me by a doctor." Then I said I had to telephone and I slipped out of the bar. A failed meeting because I am not a drinking partner.

I can see Tom is under a strain. He is articulate, adroit with words. He is emotional even though the intelligence dominates the feelings. But they are there. Once he spoke of himself as dead. "I am so dead." I suggested he buy the Chinese junk which Walter Trampler got from China. Tom had seen it from his car when he was driving uptown, and he almost drove off the freeway. "That would be a perfect way to live." Was I trying to suggest the way out of reality and restrictions? To make his life a separate poem as my life on the houseboat was for me?

I spent Sunday tracking down Walter Trampler, who wanted to sell the junk. I visited him with Peggy.

Excitement. The excitement of being once more in the world, able to act, to be spontaneous, to engage in activities when I had feared my life might end in isolation, the isolation and withdrawal of the wounded.

A pile of letters in the morning. Discoveries of analysis. Realism and surrealism. "Those are the things we should be discussing, and plans for publishing. Now it is all crises and conflicts."

"For the moment you need first aid. We will have time for all that later."

I entrusted Tom with the edited five hundred pages of the diary, to get his opinion of present reaction to it. He carried the box around. But after a few weeks, I quietly took the box back.

I met the Becks the day they bought their theatre on 14th Street. Judith keeps a diary and has written about Nina. I offered to compare our portraits, but she was reluctant. All these years I admired their audacity, their originality, their experimentation, their incredible courage. I first went to their productions in the Village, and I loaned my name, but the actual plays they put on I did not like: Rexroth and Stein, and others, so I told them how much I admired them and their acting, directing, but not the plays and withdrew my name. But we remained friends.

The recognition of how much neurosis interfered with my friendships, publications. My vulnerability and touchiness, and immediate withdrawal from the fray. Elation at freedom from this now. I kept telling Bogner of accomplishments. The Grove Press ignored my work and Don Allen was only interested in men writers. Ordinarily I would withdraw, refuse their parties, and erect a wall against them. I was able to drop in with Jim at a cocktail party, invulnerable and indifferent to their intrigues.

117

A moment of intolerable pain hearing that Gonzalo in Paris has cancer of the throat. Wilfredo describes the treatment by long radioactive needles through his throat. Hearing this I felt the pain in my own throat. Beautiful Gonzalo who used to say: "I won't be able to bear old age and physical decadence."

Then came a day of quiet acceptance, which comes from the knowledge of all our dooms, illnesses, and deaths. The intensely personal image of his death is finally dissolved by time and thrown back into some universal ocean where all our pains and deaths are one. We do not die individually but in each of these fragments of the death of those we love. There are days when I count the dead, like a ritual of black magic, as if calling up names and not being too certain mine is not among them.

The news of Gonzalo's illness came when I was preoccupied with completing my portrait of Henry because I had heard he was very ill.

I thought aging meant the loss of sensibilities, of vibrations, but I feel more intensely alive than ever. Music pours freely through me, the music by which I know the extent of my receptivity and response. I thought that while parting from the dead or the dying or the sick, one parts with fragments of one's own life. I thought so many deaths would create little cemeteries in me, but I am blessed with continuous aliveness, as if on the contrary, I am to be their preserver. Instead of dying in part with Gonzalo, and as in a great earthquake, seeing nine years of my life sink into death, I feel stronger than ever in my desire to assert Gonzalo's aliveness.

It is wonderful to lose the angers, the wounds. My scars are vanishing. I thank Dr. Bogner. When Tom told me about his differences with his psychiatrist, I had no qualms because Bogner has not once betrayed the precisions of truths even by a word misplaced, misused or carelessly defined. She is a semanticist. She has a genius for nuances and for expression. She seizes upon one's own confusions, such as mine between the words "activity" and "aggression."

When Tom first talked about analysis he approached it intellectually. He considered it like a chess game in which the cleverest one wins. But I insisted that was not what it was. You do not match your wits against your surgeon. He has a knowledge you do not have. You have to analyze his knowledge, yes, but not waste time fighting it.

My relationship with Jim made difficult because I do not like his plays. When I try to tell him how I feel, he is disturbed. He needs blind devotion at this moment.

Jim stopped writing in the diary and he surfaced into a more superficial life and circle of friends where I could not follow him. This weakened our connection because I felt the deepest Jim was in the diary.

When Antonin Artaud first became involved with films he was exhilarated because it would be such a perfect medium for the depiction of dreams. His wish was not fulfilled. But Ian Hugo has used film to depict exactly the atmosphere, the symbolism, the lure of dreams.

Melodic Inversion is a perfect example of a haunting dream. Inversion—the process of reality unmaking itself as it makes itself, as in an hourglass. This film is a visual melodic study of transposal in which brilliantly diffused colors with fluid movements are constantly revealing moods embedded in its theme. With imaginative boldness it stands alone. Images from dreams are often too diffuse to be captured, but Ian Hugo achieves this. The passage from one image to another is accomplished almost mysteriously, as it is in dreams. Haunting footage uncoils in a special world of shimmering lights and colors.

I have lost the sense of pain which had closed these portions of my life (opened only by the diary) and can relive them pure. A distillation has taken place which has dissolved the past, left the experience free of dregs. I can write freely to Henry and Eve, Eve having made the loving bridge. I can work with Lawrence Lipton as I could not work before. The first time I went to his cottage in Venice, California, and saw a little man whose glasses magnify his eyes and give him a fixed stare, whose teeth are blackened by cigar smoking, I was faced once more with what I call the antithesis of creation. The definition of creation for me was turning dross into gold. The definition of Lawrence Lipton and his friends is to give voice to the ugliness. His house was a motel without a single object I could admire, but filled with books, tapes, recordings. Prosaic, homely evening at which he played records of poetry readings instead of letting the poets who were there read. It was through him I met Ginsberg and Corso. But I did not go again. It was not my world. He called me up when the magazine *Eve* was born, and I responded because I had always a longing to be a roving editor, to rove as I usually do, garnering riches but at the same time earning my living. They will publish eight hundred words of *Solar Barque,* my "Letter from New York," and give me a salary.

The very evening I returned from New York I went to the poetry and jazz concert. Lawrence Lipton was backstage. I realized he had a large role in this new fusion of music and poetry. But the poetry was bad. Rexroth (as I knew long ago from the play presented by the Becks) is not a poet and his prose is lifeless. But in this attempt to fuse poetry and jazz there is more life, more freedom and possibilities of experiment than in the rest of American writing. The dead writing is left behind. Jazz has influenced the new writers. They are at least alive, they have rhythm.

My high standards have alienated me from error, trials, experiments. But here it was, an effort, an attempt to be encouraged.

Letter from Jim:

You have really got it made: you are the Sputnik of literature: your altitude continues and continues. Such fine excitement in your post cards. I'm very happy Lipton is taking my story. Is it *Pretty on the Bus at Nighttime?* I couldn't remember which you took. This makes the third story of mine placed by you.

The sun made by the artist far surpasses the ordinary sun so I chose it for the symbol of our new year of creation.

Lippold's *Sun* made of gold wire hung at the Metropolitan is the symbol I chose for my Christmas card. It seemed to me, watching the suffering of Hungary, the turmoil in Suez, the semi-wars, the monstrosities of the political world, work camps, slave labor in Russia, that the sun of the earth was an ugly sight, that human beings, while talking so much about collective life, communities and a United States of Europe, never loved each other less than now.

But Lippold the artist could make us forget the earth and a sun which does not always bring us joy.

Brooks Atkinson in *The New York Times:*

It's a story as old as the country. In America art lies outside the mainstream of national life. The American artist has less prestige and influence than he has in Europe and even in the Soviet Union where an artist is as respectable as an engineer.

But a culture in which art flourishes only within its own bailiwick is not complete. . . . Henry Myers asserts that there are two essential ways of looking at man in relation to the universe: "one from within, the other from without." Art, looking from within, brings illumination to the individual and releases him from his "lonely island in the sea of his isolation." Science, viewing him from outside, measures him by objective standards. "The poet and the scientist are not rivals," Professor Myers concludes, "but equal and trustworthy partners in the task of teaching man through insight, to see others as he sees himself, and through objectivity to see himself as others see him. . . . For society—the mass—is composed of individuals, and no society can be wholesome if the individuals are not individually fulfilled."

My connection with the world broke twice: the first time when my father left me. The second time when America slammed the door on my writing. What I have been busy reconstructing is my bridge to the world. I had to find an objective role for a comeback. I couldn't come back just as a writer—that would have been too difficult. But the magazine, *Eve*, helped me.

At first when I met Lipton, heard him speak and read his editorial, I felt ill at ease, distressed. I couldn't work in his atmosphere. But I persisted. I collected the best material I could in New York, Talberg's photographs, articles by Louis Barron, Peggy Glanville-Hicks, a story by James Leo Herlihy, etc. I wrote my "Letter from New York" sincerely, not playing down, on my own level, feeling I might be risking failure. I met the editor, Jane Morrison. I was direct, enthusiastic but I kept my integrity. Sunday she sent for me to see her alone at her home. She was distressed by Lipton's "On the Art of Love." She asked my opinion. I gave it. It was vulgar. He had given me my job yet I could not lie. I helped Jane not only to avoid a big error in publishing an article which was an offense to women's intelligence, but also to find a way to tell Lipton without hurting him. I suggested she lay stress on the feminine point of view. Jane told me that when she gave my "Letter from New York" to the switchboard operator the girl said: "She writes as if she felt I was an intelligent woman who could understand. It makes me feel like an individual."

I had worked thirty years to receive such praise. One of trust and leadership. This was the result of my efforts at integrity and maturity. I never aimed low. Jane said: "In your writing I feel you are being articulate for many women." All the subjects I had elaborated were meaningful here, the deeper meaning of dress, the deeper meaning of women's roles, the necessity to discard roles.

Underneath all this was my own drama evolving, from a child of a tyrannical father, which prevented me from assuming leadership in the realms I was capable of directing or clarifying, to a natural assertion of what I have learned. After helping Jane to discard Lipton's article was I going to feel as before a terrible guilt for surpassing a man, or anyone? I did not. I felt this is the truth. Lipton's article treated women patronizingly, as incapable of intellectual equality.

I also felt a joyous new strength. It seemed that at last I could manifest strength without castrating myself. I felt secure. I had achieved a victory not over Lipton but over my own vacillations and conflicts, and I was ready to help other women.

I was aware that I was articulate for other women. But that this could be used creatively gave me great joy.

All my work with Bogner bore fruit at this moment. I could talk to Jane, who is altogether different from me, different background, different experiences, different expressions.

When creativity is fulfilled there is less fatigue than in frustration. I have accomplished amazing work. I go from writing letters to editing volume 32 of the diary, to Xmas cards, to the articles for *Eve,* to notes, to housework, to telephones, but because all of it is living and creating I do not feel tired.

Editing diary 33. Writing fifteen letters. The bridge to the world is strengthening. I came too soon to America. I retrace my steps to understand what led me to solitude. My disappointment in my "children," who turned to science fiction for their flying carpets, to drugs, to alcoholism, who would not acknowledge their debt to

Proust, to Joyce, to surrealism, but pretended to have been born spontaneously, by chemical volition. They bow to jazz but jazz showed up the inadequacy of the writers. The other writers, the ones I protected and defended, Miller, Durrell, Djuna Barnes, were waiting backstage for the right time. I wish the jazzmen had the courage to shake off the poets, who are parasites. What alienated me was my disbelief in drugs, alcohol and the absence of art. You cannot influence by standing outside, only from within. When Gil came offering mescalin, at first I refused. I wrote *House of Incest* without drugs. But when I accepted LSD, I shared something in common with the present. At least I understand their need of it. They had nothing to help them dream. Dream was forbidden, and the artist who could teach it was in exile.

In New York I heard Harry Partch's music again. I saw Tawney's poetic weavings, filigree in wool. I saw her amazing studio on South Street near the Battery. It once belonged to a sail maker. There was an open well through which a chain brought up the sails to be repaired. The place was big enough for the sail to be spread out and repaired. The sign was still on the door.

I was distributing *Solar Barque*. My greatest pleasure was to receive wholehearted praise from Joaquin. I was filled with hope. I received a letter from William Kozlenko of MGM expressing interest in filming *Spy in the House of Love*. I had talked with him two evenings. He was intelligent, well read, and he gave me a copy of *Masterplots of 1954* in which *Spy in the House of Love* was described and analyzed favorably.

Kozlenko keeps me in suspense. He said my writing was spatial, not temporal. He said I was a great writer, that people would come to my writing. But he wanted me to write for TV.

As a violinist, he was a young prodigy. He drags a leg.

Letter from Lawrence Durrell:

Thank you so much for the good letter. We have just got back from London and I have just finished the third book of *Justine*—a straight novel in the naturalistic tradition; I want the four books to travel from subjective to objective and back—from being to seeming as it were. I want to give the poem *with* its rationale! Ach, we shall have to see! The last will be a continuum poem again. Dear I wanted to tell you the position with Dutton. They want literally all I do though they have not as yet signed for more than the Justine series and *Bitter Lemons*. Meanwhile I've found the text of *The Black Book* so full of errors that it would be quite impossible to photoprint from it. But Macrae will be in London in February to have a full dress conference about me and all the titles I have for sale. I've just had an offer for *Cefalu!* If he gets cold feet over *The Black Book* I'm sure we could photoprint from the London edition which I shall correct and which as I told you will have Eliot's blessing—a sort of Catholic cow-catcher! Tell me, when you plan your Brussels trip is there any way of planning the return via Marseilles? We could certainly meet you there. Paris may well be possible, but at present I am trying to escape English Income Tax and pay French instead; but initially I shall have to pay the French before reclaiming the British; and this period of double tax *paid* may make me terribly broke for just the period when I most need the dough to come and see you in Paris. I am just paying the French Tax now; but the English financial year begins in April and I doubt whether they will refund me before end of May. Do you see? If there were any way to organise your return via Marseilles we could certainly get across there for a few fond days whatever the state of the *fric*. It may not inconvenience you too much: think about it . . . will you?

I took your *Spy* with me and read it again; I think I must have expressed my admiration badly in saying you had grown more "deliberate" because I didn't mean it in the head-conscious manner at all. I meant that your sense of organic shape was new. Not in the conscious intellectual sense of a prefabricated design but in allowing the creature to take on the curvature and emplacement dictated by the germ which was unfolding in it—organic form just as rigid in a sense as an intellectual form but arrived at by greater surrender, greater identity with the book itself. An embryo isn't a thought-formation though it responds to laws almost as rigid as those of a mathematical calculus; what I felt in these books was a greater sense of relaxation, of play. It may be that you have reoriented your position vis a vis time in the diary sense; what I meant in the old days was precisely that. The pressure was so continuous, the material so uniformly excellent in the diaries that it was quite impossible to know how to cut them. One missed the feeling of flux and reflux, pressures applied and relaxed; the sustained top note produced its own anaesthesia—as pain does when it goes on too long. At that time too you were doing all your work *out of the diaries* and I could see that you shared my own perplexity about how to edit material so rich and dense, luxuriant as jungle. Now I notice in the books that you no longer waste your effects, but use all the richness of orchestration in patterns of emphasis which allow the reader to recover his balance before you knock him off the shelf again. A small passage of quite cold description. A list of things, clothes, gestures. The heat of the poetry is applied in *rhythms*. That is what I meant. A diary of course can have no form, being time-bound. I think the books have stepped beyond the time-binding, out of the diary into life. I am so delighted by your success—so well-merited. And it will be so wonderful to meet again after all this time. Just had a long letter from Joe. He has written a novel called *Love in the Ink Gutter!* Henry too is full of ginger and writes huge letters full of his children. Wants to tour the Orient with them if you please!

Justine has done quite well in the States and in April *Balthazar* comes out in England (2nd vol); I am just delivering *Mountolive* to Faber now (3rd). I've been working like a coal heaver. I only sent *Bitter Lemons* in lieu of a letter, to tell what I had been up to these last years. I wrote it in six weeks for money alas. It is a modish and somewhat irritating book, but it has had a strong political effect by its approach. But one problem was very much complicated by libel considerations and by the fact that there was a good deal of lead flying about in Cyprus at the time; an incautious word might have caused a Greek friend to be bumped off so I had to tread very cautiously indeed. Dutton is doing it in March I believe . . .

So far the grand plan seems to be shaping up okay and I don't need to get a job stone breaking this year. Claude has written a trio of light novels, comedies; she is still playing with forms in order to learn the job of book-making from the outside until she hears her own voice. Which is rather wise, to accumulate technique and experience while waiting for the geist to speak up. She's a good girl, hard working and gay and sensitive, *sans pretensions;* she just typed 140,000 words of *Mountolive* in a fortnight flat; speed typist, radio expert, cook . . . I'm rather lucky. We have just bought a tiny canoe for the river to amuse our children—they come out for the summer holidays to swim and sail here which is very strenuous but such fun. My eldest daughter Pinky is 17 now and a ballet dancer; she is coming in June for 3 weeks and the younger one Sapphy is 7 and coming in August.

No, Anaïs dear I've never kept a diary; always felt it would swallow me. The diaries in *Justine* represent symbolically the prismatic effect of personalities seen from different sides. Much is explained in *Balthazar* and *Mountolive*—new positions taken up. I think the *form* will intrigue you—multiple book-keeping. But it might repel! As soon as I have the others I'll send them to you to see. The French are excited about *Justine*—a very good press. Have you read our horoscope for this year? A great year—the best for ten years they say! Here's hoping it is! . . .

Did I thank you for the books? What a blessing, particularly the big Keyserling. What density and richness of spirit. I'm re-living it again. Bless you and 1000 thanks.

Only understood today why I was never drawn into the dramas of history and continue to give the science of relationships between human beings the primary place. In history the objective of the game is power. In human relationships love. Also history stems from the kind of human beings who gain the power and I feel we have to create a new kind of human being who won't misuse it. First of all man has to be able to relate to his fellow men.

Arrived in New York with typical Spanish flourish. One engine on fire, a reception committee of ambulances and fire equipment, in freezing weather, the center of interest of all Idlewild Airport and for a while I thought the end of my life. But all ended well, we didn't have to exit by way of a cord ladder like mountain climbers. We merely went out the first-class exit (they allow tourist class to use first-class exits in case of fire!).

The play *The Chairs* by Ionesco is one of the most remarkable I have ever seen. Impression of a dream, a profound symbolic event. What a marvelous use of imagination. Even Max Lerner wrote about it though it was symbolic; perhaps symbolism is beginning to be understood, and I am writing at length about it for *Eve*. Not a word from *Eve*. No check. No press card. No letters. I hate to work for deaf-mutes.

Meanwhile Ionesco had to defend himself against Mr. Tynan's saying that Ionesco is being deliberately, explicitly anti-realist, having declared that words have no meaning and that all language is incommunicable. Ionesco answers: "I simply hold that it is difficult to make oneself understood, not absolutely impossible, and my play *The Chairs* is a plea, pathetic perhaps, for mutual understanding." His whole defense is worth reading.

From *The New York Times,* January, 1958.

The Playwright's Role, by Eugene Ionesco

I was of course honoured by the article Mr. Tynan devoted to my two plays, *The Chairs* and *The Lesson,* in spite of the strictures it contained, which a critic has a perfect right to make. However, since some of his objections seem to me to be based on premises that are not only false but, strictly speaking, outside the domain of the theatre, I think I have the right to make certain comments.

In effect, Mr. Tynan says that it has been claimed, and that I myself have approved or supported this claim, that I was a sort of "messiah" of the theatre. This is doubly untrue because I do not like messiahs and I certainly do not consider the vocation of the artist or the playwright to lie in that direction. I have a distinct impression that it is Mr. Tynan who is in search of messiahs. But to deliver a message to the world, to wish to direct its course, to save it, is the business of the founders of religions, of the moralists or the politicians—who, incidentally, as we know only too well, make a pretty poor job of it. A playwright simply writes plays, in which he can offer only a testimony, not a didactic message—a personal, affective testimony of his anguish and the anguish of others or, which is rare, of his happiness—or he can express his feelings, comic or tragic, about life.

A work of art has nothing to do with doctrine. I have already written elsewhere that any work of art which was ideological and nothing else would be pointless, tautological, inferior to the doctrine it claimed to illustrate, which would already have been expressed in its proper language, that of discursive demonstration. An ideological play can be no more than the vulgarisation of an ideology. In my view, a work of art has its own unique system of expression, its own means of directly apprehending the real.

Mr. Tynan seems to accuse me of being deliberately, explicitly, anti-realist; of having declared that words have no meaning and that all language is incommunicable. That is only partly true, for the very fact of writing and presenting plays is surely incompatible with such a view. I simply hold that it is difficult to make oneself understood, not absolutely impossible, and my play *The Chairs* is a plea, pathetic perhaps, for mutual understanding. As for the idea of reality, Mr. Tynan seems (as he also made clear in an interview published in *Encounter*) to acknowledge only one plane of reality: what is called the "social" plane, which seems to me to be the most external, in other words the most superficial. That is why I think that writers like Sartre (Sartre the author of political melodramas), Osborne, Miller, Brecht, etc., are simply the new *auteurs du boulevard*, representatives of a left-wing conformism which is just as lamentable as the right-wing sort. These writers offer nothing that one does not know already, through books and political speeches.

But that is not all: it is not enough to be a social realist writer, one must also, apparently, be a militant believer in what is known as progress. The only worth-while authors, those who are on the "main road" of the theatre, would be those who thought in a certain clearly defined way, obeying certain pre-established principles or directives. This would be to make the "main road" a very narrow one; it would considerably restrict the planes of reality (which are innumerable) and limit the field open to the investigations of artistic research and creation.

I believe that what separates us all from one another is simply society itself, or, if you like, politics. This is what raises barriers between men, this is what creates misunderstanding.

If I may be allowed to express myself paradoxically, I should say that the true society, the authentic human community, is extra-social—a wider, deeper society, that which is revealed by our common anxieties, our desires, our secret nostalgias. The whole history of the world has been governed by these nostalgias and anxieties, which political action does no more than reflect and interpret, very imperfectly. No society has been able to abolish human sadness, no political system can deliver us from the pain of living, from our fear of death, our thirst for the absolute; it is the human condition that directs the social condition, not vice versa.

This "reality" seems to me much vaster and more complex than the one to which Mr. Tynan and many others want to limit themselves. The problem is to get to the source of our malady, to find the non-conventional language of this anguish, perhaps by breaking down this "social" language which is nothing but clichés, empty formulas, and slogans. The "robot" characters Mr. Tynan disapproves of seem to me to be precisely those who belong *solely* to this or that *milieu* or social "reality," who are prisoners of it, and who—being no more than social, seeking a solution to their problems only by so-called social means—have become impoverished, alienated, empty. It is precisely the conformist, the *petit-bourgeois*, the ideologist of *every* society who is lost and dehumanised. If anything needs demystifying it is our ideologies, which offer ready-made solutions (which history quickly overtakes and refutes) and a language that congeals *as soon as it is formulated*. It is these ideologies which must be continually re-examined in the light of our anxieties and dreams, and their congealed language must be relentlessly split apart in order to find the living sap beneath.

To discover the fundamental problem common to all mankind, I must ask myself what *my* fundamental problem is, what *my* most ineradicable fear is. I am certain, then, to find the problems and fears of literally everyone. That is the true road, into my own darkness, our darkness, which I try to bring to the light of day.

It would be amusing to try an experiment, which I have no room for here but which I hope to carry out some day. I could take almost any work of art, any play, and guarantee to give it in turn a Marxist, a Buddhist, a Christian, an Existentialist, a psycho-analytical interpretation and "prove" that the work subjected to each interpretation is a perfect and exclusive illustration of each creed, that it confirms this or that ideology beyond all doubt. For me this proves another thing: that every work of art (unless it is a pseudo-intellectualist work, a work already comprised in some ideology that it merely illustrates, as with Brecht) is outside ideology, is not reducible to ideology. Ideology circumscribes without penetrating it. The absence of ideology in a work does not mean an absence of ideas; on the contrary it fertilises them. In other words, it was not Sophocles who was inspired by Freud but, obviously, the other way round. Ideology is not the source of art. A work of art is the source and the raw material of ideologies to come.

What, then, should the critic do? Where should he look for his criteria? Inside the work itself, its universe and its mythology. He must look at it, listen to it, and simply say whether it is true to its own nature. The best judgment is a careful exposition of the work itself. For that, the work must be allowed to speak, uncoloured by preconception or prejudice.

Whether or not it is on the "main road"; whether or not it is what you would like it to be—to consider this is already to pass judgment, a judgment that is external, pointless and false. A work of art is the expression of an incommunicable reality that one tries to communicate—and which sometimes can be communicated. That is its paradox, and its truth.

New York. Snow on the trees, none on the ground. Jim busy with rehearsals. I work on material for *Eve*. Dodd Mead seriously considering ordering two or three thousand copies of *Solar Barque* and putting their own hard cover on it. Sent more articles to *Eve* by other people. Tracked down the history of the junk moored on the East River and was disillusioned. I wanted one so badly to moor in Los Angeles. The first man to get a junk bought it second hand in China; he paid only five hundred dollars, but had to dismantle it and pay five hundred more for shipping it. And then he had to put it together again. But now he is in business and he wants to make money out of it, selling new ones, more costly, made of teakwood, beautifully built all through. So to get one I can afford, I will have to go to China.

Strange cross-fertilization. In France they are interviewing Burroughs with Ginsberg and Corso. They tell the newspapers they are mystics, not literary figures. They explain the credo of the beat generation. The beat man, half-vagabond, half-criminal, who has rejected the American gods, business, television, publicity, for a life outside the pale but *lucid and pure.*

And the French writers are recognizing that jazz has expanded the sensibility of man limited by logic.

———

Stanley Haggart took a photograph of a gesture I had made during the session of LSD. I joined my hands as if in prayer in front of me. I am told it is a gesture made by the mystics and meaning that when they feel the energy is too strong they join the hands so it will flow in a circle and not dam up.

Eve was complimented on my "Letter from New York."

[Spring, 1958]

Receiving a letter from Dr. Betty Eisner reminded me of many things I never had the time to write down. In Louveciennes one day I had a visit from a young woman who had just received a fellowship to study in America. She was a violin prodigy and her name was Laura Archera. We had a long visit. She gave me her photograph. We met again in New York when I was doing controlled analysis under Otto Rank's guidance.

Now she is married to Aldous Huxley. Aldous Huxley is also a very old friend of Reginald Pole, so we were bound to meet. I respected his work but was never attracted to it, it was too intellectual and too scholarly. The contrast between him and D. H. Lawrence made it too clear on which side I developed.

When we went to lunch at his startlingly all-white house, which Laura felt helped him to see better, I was touched by his handsome and noble appearance, by his one clouded eye. He had invited Dr. Betty Eisner, who wanted to meet me. She brought a lively intelligence and naturalness to an otherwise rather formal Huxley. We discussed my LSD experience and Huxley asserted I had been given too strong a dose and explained that different temperaments should have different doses. He was rather indignant about that because, as he said, anyone could see I would react sensitively to a light dose.

I also ventured my opinion that if we had been properly trained to appreciate music, painting, poetry, meditation, dreams, we would not have needed drugs, for I had reached such "states" just listening to music, looking at certain paintings, reading certain books, or in nature at times.

But Huxley disagreed vehemently: "You happen to have direct communication with your unconscious, that is rare, but most people do not and for them drugs are necessary."

He also has a vehement attitude against Europe. He seems to be finished with it. I had no time to find out why he felt this. Dr. Eisner was describing her work with tremendous fervor and promised to send me some papers she had written, *Observations on Possible Order Within the Unconscious,* read before the First International Meeting of Neuro-psycho-pharmacology in Rome. Her dedication to me was: "To Anaïs Nin, who knows more about this than any of the scientists do."

Aldous Huxley and I disagree about the necessity of drugs for everyone. When I took LSD, I proved to myself that it only opened the same realms which one can have access to by way of dreams, poetry, writing. I wrote *House of Incest* without it.

Huxley and I do not communicate. He is too much the scientist and not a poet. I cannot imagine his friendship with Lawrence. They must have argued a lot. I find him too scientific, too literal, too precise. I still feel, as I always have, that the *effort* made to live, love and create without artificial stimulants is part of the enrichment. It strengthens the creative will, whereas those who are passive and fond of shortcuts will never be vigorous creators. There is also the matter of connecting the visions to life, using the visions to create one's life. Drug users do not take that second step. They see paradise, and decide they will return to the vision of it, and not bother with seeking to create it as Varda did. Michaux is an exception. He is still one of the great writers after ten years of using drugs, but that is because he was a powerful poet before he took drugs.

Hollywood is a mirage factory and so many things never come true. Curtis Harrington sold a story to the studios two years ago and it has not yet been filmed. Lesley Blanch sold one of the stories in *The Wilder Shores of Love,* and it was never filmed. So I went to dinner with Bill Kozlenko and a Mr. Pink without much faith.

Pink owns several movie houses, is an "independent" film producer, always raises the money and gets distribution through MGM. Kozlenko writes plays and TV and movie scripts. He understands *Spy in the House of Love* perfectly and said wonderful things: said the purity of my work would outlive all the fads and fashions, that it was deep, that Sabina was not a stock character. He plans to write the scenario. Having once been a musician, he might understand the musical quality of *Spy*. But for once in my life I cannot get excited, even though Kozlenko says people are tired of false psychology.

But I am happy in a quiet way because the venture is based on Kozlenko's genuine interest and understanding of the book.

Solar Barque does not stand alone. I describe the feelings of Lillian, who at one time tried to enter life by violence (*Ladders to Fire*) and failed, then by escaping from husband and children into the artist world of Paris (and failed), then by seeking nature. It is Lillian who is drugged by nature but finds she cannot have relationships (thus they are all sketched in) nor enter life deeply through nature because she has first to liquidate the past, the shadows, the subterranean life. The characters exist as she sees them (just as Sabina also saw her lovers partially). The vision from within is different from the objective one. Felix Pollak misses the objective, rounded description of character, but then you would not be inside of Lillian. I want people to see the world as Lillian sees it. It is quite different from other books. *House of Incest* was all dreams, not nature. *Winter of Artifice* an effort at awareness. Here in *Solar Barque,* nature is beautiful but Lillian cannot become entirely one with it. And now we are ready for the next development. The books are interdependent. Here Michael (in *Children of the Albatross,* painfully in love with the wrong person) has now withdrawn into exotic places. There is no passion because Lillian is not ready for it. It is a different atmosphere. Those who encounter *Solar Barque* for the first time will only find relationship to nature and to exile.

The simple attempt to take one into Djuna, into Sabina, into Lillian so that you see the world as they do was a dangerous experiment. For then everyone thinks I am the one who is seeing the world thus. Yes, the passive passion is an experience too, necessary to Lillian, who was far too aggressive. I give the key when I refer to drugs, Golconda as a drug. Lillian is learning passivity (remember her violence in *Ladders to Fire?*) or becoming feminine.

I wrote all this for Felix Pollak, who demanded conventional filling in. Outer reality. I should have made clear that the journey begins with *House of Incest,* proceeding from the dream outward (Jung). *House of Incest* was all dream, and all the characters moved in and out of it. Lillian enters the dream of voyage, of the tropics, and does come out *changed.* All my efforts in writing were to say what had not been said, and to do this I sometimes have to pursue a more oblique and circuitous route. For *Solar Barque* I bypassed the reviewers. I sent no copies to reviewers. I consider that they distorted my work and that without them people approach my work with far more natural intuition. This way I have arrived at a direct connection with those who read me.

Joaquin writes me:

Solar Barque was wonderful. Beautiful writing with amazing transpositions from one reality to another. You certainly have a genius for making the invisible real, for making sounds out of eloquent silence. Dialogue is not speech for you but something else, more remote, more deep seated and yet always more real. It would seem as if you were gifted with a tangible soul or an immaterial body. Take your pick.

Reading all of Anna Kavan.

Meanwhile meditating a continuation of *Solar Barque*. The gradual destruction of the fiction or persona by which characters have lived, and gradual evolution of deeper truths. Difficult to do, technically, with an invented or composite character.

All around me there is a keen interest in science fiction. Some of it appeals to me, but most of it contains a terrifying dehumanization. The human being is totally absent. There is an absence of human contact. Is that a prediction of the future, because of technology? I saw the biggest collection of science fiction in the world. Overflowing into the garage of Forest Ackerman. The monsters created for science-fiction films, a combination of the occult, black mass, Aleister Crowley, and *Popular Science*.

Yesterday a science-fiction day, with all Los Angeles poisoned by fumes from orchard heaters pushed back by the fog. Jim and I sat with a box of Kleenex in the center of the table. We should have had gas masks such as were distributed in the first days of the war in London.

Great admiration for Lili Saint Cyr. Women should learn from her. She does not express the narcissistic self-eroticism of stripteasers, she conveys the presence of the man, an expression of contact with the man. She uses her body with enormous grace and skill, to invite, to expose, to suggest, to respond, but it is always a gift, an offering. She is a great artist. She is never vulgar. The common men do not like her. I went all the way to Newark with the Barrons once to see her. Bebe wanted to know what I saw in her. I said: "Women should study with her. She is an artist in erotic lore." I saw her again in Hollywood. She stands apart. She does not make up or dress like other stripteasers. In one act she takes a bath. In another she tests her seduction before a painting of a Spanish matador. The man is always present, so it is charged with currents which flow out and around the audience.

Dream: I live in a kind of boardinghouse. I have a small room in which I do my writing. All the other rooms are occupied. A very ugly, pockmarked man invites me to his room as he walks up the stairs. I say I am too busy. Maria Schell occupies one room. A teen-age boy, red-haired, breaks off a conversation with me to join some girls of his age. I lose my key. A couple arrives who want to get in urgently. I say it does not matter about the key, I will get in through the window. I push the window open. There is an antique cabinet against the wall. I touch it and it begins to crumble. I have to hold it up. Somewhere in the house is my mother but I don't see her. I go up to the top floor but by mistake enter another room. The occupants are asleep and I notice the gas jet leaking. I stuff it up until it stops. There is an alarm whistle going on. I begin to knock on all the doors to get people out. Maria Schell answers angrily: "Leave me alone, I'm not coming out." The others leave the place. I have the usual problem about rescuing the diaries but this time (not as in other dreams) I walk out without them. The whistle resembles that for air raids. Down below, in the courtyard, I see many people. Greta Garbo is there, luxuriously dressed in silver-gray velvet with a large hat. I seem to be alone and unrelated to anyone else, all boarders. There are couples, and single persons. With another group I have a discussion on symbolism, how it was once overlooked and how it is coming into its own.

Atmosphere reminded me of our house on Seventy-fifth Street. That was what I remembered when I awakened. Memories of West Seventy-fifth Street. The brownstone house. Rooms rented out. We lived on the second floor back. I was fifteen; I was not in life. I did not like strangers in the house. It humiliated me. I had many duties. I was not intimate with any of the roomers. I sensed their lives, nevertheless. I remember them sharply now. Once in a while a friend. Enric Madriguera had a room on the very top floor, once a servant's room. I could hear his violin all day. He pulled my braids every time he passed. I thought a great deal about him at that time, but he was part of a joyous group led by his sister, Paquita Madriguera (who later married Segovia). Paquita's beauty, assurance, flirtatiousness dazzled and intimidated me. I wanted to be like her. But I was not. I was shy, withdrawn, and read obsessionally. I managed to keep a book open while making beds and washing dishes. I watched life and wanted to be a part of it but found it painfully difficult.

The ex-husband of Teresa Careño, the great South American pianist, lived in the basement room. Emilia Quintero, a well-known Spanish pianist, lived in our house too. She gave Joaquin piano lessons. She had been in love with Sarasate and showed me his white silk scarf, which she had stolen after a concert. She was incredibly homely, also incredibly loving and always praising us. Whenever we were at dinner in the dining room (which also served as a bedroom) she would peek in, pretend to be surprised, actually observing whether the dinner conformed to her plain diet. "Oh, boiled fish," she would say with such longing that my mother always ended by inviting her. When she went to Paris I wrote a letter to my father describing her with a child's unconscious honesty in terms which must have discouraged him, for he was obsessed with physical beauty. I insisted he invite her to dinner and serve the plain food permitted to her.

But I do not understand the dream, for I do not feel estranged any more; it is a past state. It would take too long to unravel. And I myself am wary of the trap of too long, too clear a dream. I do not know what set it off.

Is it being taken into the infernal core of Tom Payne's life without having any role to play but analyst? He is in hell, and suffering.

He had said that he wanted to be an artist: a musician first, then an architect, then a painter, then a writer. But that the psychiatrist could not help him because he knew nothing about art.

We talk about Kerouac. He knows him well. Yes, we know he is a compulsive treadmill seeking freedom which is not freedom. It is not a genuine freedom he acquired, but the external motions of freedom, that is, moving, breaking away, not being rooted, not taking on any human responsibilities. Nevertheless, he knows how to write about high moments.

Tom is diffuse and tormented. He takes me to the house he lives in. It is hidden by another house, in a courtyard. There had been a fire in another apartment and the burnt furniture is lying in the courtyard. The house is like a secret womb. It could be beautiful but he has not furnished it. He has not even set a match to the old papers in the fireplace. He has placed a table, a chair, in the radius of the lamp's light, which can be seen from the door. And that is all. It looks like the stage for *The Chairs* of Ionesco. He has no telephone hook up. This was supposed to be his secret home. But he gives his address to a friend who spreads it around and he does not feel safe any more. The apartment belonged to a friend who went away without paying the rent so Tom cannot acknowledge this friendship or put his real name on the door. A neighbor receives his mail.

When I laughed at the complexities, he laughed too and admitted he enjoyed the difficulties. They are a form of creation, misspent imagination. He is a master of the labyrinth. There is always a new corner I had not suspected.

I received a check for 310 dollars from *Eve* for a section of *Solar Barque* and my "Letter from New York." I feel very proud.

I went to Washington to interview Caresse [Crosby] for *Eve*.

Such an extraordinary woman. She designed a symbolic structure to express her concept of "Citizens of the World." It was erected in Delphi. She placed on it the flag of "Citizens of the World." The Greek government became alarmed. They considered it an "invasion" by subversive elements. They sent soldiers to arrest her and bring her to court. But the soldiers were the young peasants who knew her as Lady Bountiful and had helped to build the structure. They were devoted to her. They were in a painful quandary at the order to arrest her. They came carrying guns, as they were obliged to do when on duty. But they put a bunch of flowers at the tip of the guns. And thus with gallant escort she was led to court. A Greek bishop pleaded for her. Men of letters appeared to defend her. The trial was held. The outcome indefinite.

My article for *Eve:*

CITIZENS OF THE WORLD

The Greek shepherds were watching an American woman climbing the slope of Mount Parnassus. They knew her well. She has lively and gay blue eyes, a constant sparkling laughter, a short humorous nose, a warm manner which wins everyone and a gift for making friends. Her short, softly waved hair is white, but her stance, her responsiveness are young. She never commands, but whatever she asks is immediately accomplished.

She is Caresse Crosby, the head of the Citizens of the World, the owner of a promontory near Delphi which she has chosen as a fitting symbol for the place the citizens must have to be legally recognized.

Delphi is situated on the slopes of Mount Parnassus, overlooking Itea, on the Gulf of Corinth, once the most vital harbor of the ancient world.

On the Island of Salones, over 2,000 years ago, the Delphic Festivals were held.

Socrates had expressed the idea: "If you are asked from what city you come, do not reply I am an Athenian, or a Corinthian, but reply I am a Citizen of the World."

At that time there had been a democratic council—lawmakers, philosophers, teachers, poets—to draw up rules of life by which men might live in enlightenment and freedom.

Here was produced the First Document of Human Rights.

"In war no women or children were to be harmed.

No houses were to be burnt.

No wells were to be poisoned.

If a horse were wounded under a warrior during battle, this horse must be killed."

This document was one of the earliest expressions of humanism.

Caresse Crosby returned to Paris and on the Black Sun Press she printed the first World Citizen passport, reading:

"This passport has little meaning in itself. Its importance lies in the fact that you have sought and accepted it. It stands for something that cannot be printed on cards or imposed by leadership—your own willingness to respect your fellow man; your own readiness to try living at peace with him.

"You will note that you have made no pledge or promise. You are simply identified as one who will endeavor to recognize his responsibilities as a member of the single, total World Community. World citizenship is clearly inconsistent with prejudice, unreasoned fear, and impersonal hatred. It is not well served by war (which can be no more than a disorderly, local breach of peace among world citizens). It may call for resolute affirmation or positive acts of aid and comfort in some situations. But its applications in your life are left to you.

"This is trust—almost faith. The number on your passport is the number of human beings who have accepted this trust already. They count on you, and as their faith is justified in your own conscience, so may you count on them. The numbers grow. Our task, which you may share as fully as you will, is to keep it growing until so many of us stand together that the World Community emerges as a living actuality among us.

"All of us welcome you and honor the step you have taken. Now, as one of us, you are something which you were not yesterday. The difference is not slight, if you do not make it so."

Caresse Crosby and R. G. King

Caresse was dedicated to the idea of World Citizenship. This seemed to her the most valid and efficacious way to a true world community. Knowledge of people of quality had convinced her that it was between such individually developed people that communication was possible, and ultimately unification of nations.

The American Embassy in France was sympathetic. Caresse Crosby printed more passports. She wrote an article on "Women Against War" in the *Herald Tribune:*

"Women against war is an unofficial alliance of women from every land seeking the abandonment of war as an instrument of national policy. Our number is millions.

"We, the women, according to the last world census, are a majority in every land and in many lands we hold the vote. Women, wives and mothers, are more terrified of power politics and war potentials than men are.

"Why is it then, in matters that concern us so deeply, we are so docily silent?"

Caresse Crosby suggested that we educate our children as Citizens of the World.

A book has been published—*Rufus King's Manifesto for Individual Accession into World Community*. This book was read by a young man, Gary Davis. With a youthful idealistic impetus and regardless of consequences, he made a symbolic gesture of giving up his American passport to join the Citizens of the World. This was not intended as an offense to his native country, but as an adoption of the whole world, a transcending of boundaries, as a consideration of the whole world as one community, an attempt to dissolve the causes of war.

Gary Davis had served in the war. He had experienced the horrors of it, the increasing hostilities created by frontiers, and he believed that the dissolving of frontiers was a solution to a humanist existence.

This incident had a powerful impact upon the young, and created many disciples. It was reported in the papers in London, Washington, New York. Gary Davis was now a follower of Caresse Crosby. Many young people wanted to join the movement.

Rufus King gave Gary Davis all the legal help he could, for he was now a young man without a country and subject to extradition. Gary Davis sat on the steps of the United Nations in Paris in a gesture of protest. He was not allowed inside of the United Nations. The only courtesy extended him was the use of the lavatory, but not that of the cafeteria. So Monsieur Lescaret, the printer of the Black Sun Press, hero printer for the Resistance all through the war, would come every day to bring Gary Davis cheese and wine.

The whole world was waiting for the United States to support a daring idea far ahead of its time, one which the world was not ready for. So much could have been gained in one stroke of leadership. The true meaning of leadership should be guidance into the future.

But instead Gary Davis was arrested. The press, true to its negative function, caricatured and discredited him. He had unfortunately brought damaging publicity to the Citizens of the World and delayed its progress. Even today, when Citizens of the World is mentioned, there are people who exclaim: "Oh, this was a movement started by that crackpot Davis." But Caresse Crosby was still seeking to re-establish the truth. She went to Rome and talked with the Mayor and with the head of the police. She asked that Davis should be given the keys of the city so he could address the youth at the Piazza del Popolo. They consented. She went back to Paris and planned to re-enter Italy with Davis. He drove her car. But Davis panicked, and stopped at a monastery in the south of France. Six months later it was too late. After ten days of meditation he had returned to Paris and called a press conference. He was young, inarticulate, inexperienced and found nothing to say. From then on, his desire to act on his own rendered him ineffectual.

Caresse Crosby returned that year to Greece and consulted with Prime Minister Venizelos, with poets, writers, religious men, about making Delphi a symbol for Citizens of the World.

According to folklore of the shepherds in that region, it was on the promontory that the Councils had held their meeting. Pausanias described the promontory, which is just west of Delphi, overlooking the sacred grove of Apollo on the lowest slope of Mount Parnassus. On one side is a sheer drop of 300 feet to the town of Krissa, and from there the road runs level through the grove for about two miles, to Itea, which was used in the era of Pericles. The treasuries of Corinth, of Athens, of Sparta, were built to express the idea of union among different Hellenic tribes and settlements. When they were built over 2000 years ago, they were pre-fabricated. There was no marble in Delphi. Great sculptors such as Phidias and his disciples had the marble blocks cut in different islands. They were carved, and marked as we mark building materials today, brought in sailing boats, or triremes, from the islands to Itea, and carried on the backs of mules or pulled by mules up the path to Delphi. At that time there were no roads to the Delphic Temples.

Caresse Crosby decided that this was the place she must acquire for the Citizens of the World.

The family who owned it were goat herders. The oldest member spent most of his time far up in the mountains with his goats. He was difficult to find, but two young relatives offered to search for him, Yani and Paracles. The rest of the family lived in Delphi.

The two young men hiked for days and returned with the old patriarch. He was told that Caresse Crosby wanted to buy the promontory. His comment was: "Land no good, not even for goats."

Then as Caresse Crosby insisted, he made a typical Greek gesture and said he would give it away. After further *pourparlers* he agreed to sell Caresse two acres for $250. In order to sign the deed the entire family had to be collected. It had been acquired by the family in the year 900. They were finally assembled, and one night by the light of a candle, with the presence of the Mayor, a lawyer, and the gendarmes, with the assistance of Greek resin wine, eighteen members of the shepherd family signed the document which made the Citizens of the World landowners of one of the most beautiful and most symbolic spots in the world.

In order to dedicate this land Caresse Crosby sent invitations to World Citizens everywhere, to diplomatic corps, to the Athenian government.

The American Ambassador was skeptical, but cooperative. The Greek Premier answered he could not be present but would send his right-hand man, Mr. Sifneos. An invitation had been printed in both English and Greek, which read:

Dedication at Delphi:

The Minister to the Prime Minister, Mr. P. Sifneos—for Freedom from Fear.

The Archbishop of Amfissa—for Freedom of Worship.

The Mayor of Delphi—for Freedom from Want.

Caresse Crosby, Citizen of the World, will dedicate the land.

Hugh Schonfield, founder of the Commonwealth, will make the acceptance address.

As the Greek Government had objected that Caresse Crosby had no official organization and that such a dedication and inauguration could not be done without the stamp of an official status, she had merged with the Commonwealth in England, created by Hugh Schonfield, which had elaborated a constitution and a legal status. The Schonfields had agreed to come to the inauguration, which then seemed to make the ritual legal. Caresse went up to Delphi two days ahead of the date set. While she was in Delphi, the press (always at its favorite pastime of caricaturing man's endeavors) reported that World Citizens, organized in England, intended to occupy property in Delphi and fly a World Flag and let the planes fly over it.

The symbolic project had ceased to be a myth to inspire men. It was now considered a realistic encroachment upon Greek sovereignty.

On Sunday agents from Reuters asked Caresse Crosby: "Are you going ahead with the ceremony?"

"Yes."

"We are sending people to cover the story."

She received a notification from Athens: "Stop the ceremony." It was delivered by the police. The message added: "We are sending out militia."

She tried to reach the Minister of Defense. He was travelling. The American Ambassador was out hunting. The King and Queen of Greece were on their yacht.

Caresse Crosby's humanistic plan had turned into a minor war! While struggling to rescue her project, her sense of humor and irony registered the absurdities, the comic opera aspects of the situation. The home guard, who knew her well and were fond of her, had started the day carrying bouquets of flowers to present to her. They had not dropped them to fulfill the new orders. They carried them in the left hand, and their guns in the right hand. They looked embarrassed, and puzzled, not knowing which they were going to use.

Reporters arrived on motorcycles. Caresse was carrying her useless flag. The military began firing across the road that led to the promontory. The reporter from the *New York Times* said: "This is your territory, Mrs. Crosby. We are Americans. We will go up anyway." Caresse Crosby said: "I have a right to read the dedication."

A man started to take a newsreel. He was arrested and taken to jail. The buses with the people had been stopped at Delphi.

They were treated like an invading army. Caresse Crosby had not foreseen that the Greeks would interpret this ceremony as an invasion and a founding of a new nation.

She was brought back to her home in Delphi under arrest. She stepped out on the terrace. A delicate moon was rising over the enchanted country. She could also see the heads of the Carabineros all around her. A few steps away was her Art Gallery of Delphi, exposing Mirós, Calders, Picassos, Tanguys, etc. Her friends (and they were many) were in distress over her plight. They had interviews with the Minister of Defense, who maintained that a large organization had set up headquarters (or tried to) in Delphi, and Delphi was a National Monument.

Christian du Bois Larson

Anaïs Nin at work in Los Angeles, 1963

Stanley Mills Haggart

James Leo Herlihy at
the time of publication
of *Midnight Cowboy*, 196

Millie Johnstone,
a tea ceremony

A tapestry by Millie Johnstone

Caresse Crosby at her castle,
Roccasinibalda

Aldous Huxley, a drawing
from life by Don Bachardy,
August 2, 1962

Variation within a Sphere,
No. 10: The Sun,
by Richard Lippold

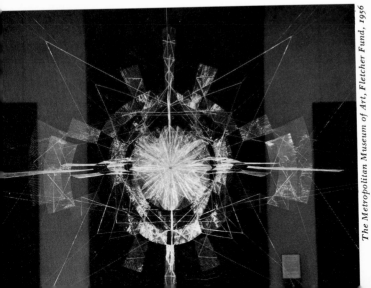

The Metropolitan Museum of Art, Fletcher Fund, 1956

Rupert Pole

Watts Towers,
Los Angeles

Louis and Bebe Barron

Lawrence Durrell, 1958

Anaïs Nin during her visit with Durrell
as photographed for the French press

Anaïs Nin with Lawrence Durrell
and his family in the South of France, 1958

UNE AMERICAINE A SOMMIERES

Dr. Inge Bogner, 1963

Peter Gowland

Anaïs Nin at home in Los Angeles

Caresse Crosby maintained: "I have a right to a peaceful assembly, and freedom of expression."

"You have a right to appeal for a hearing," she was told.

Greece had been the first nation to include the United Nations Bill of Rights in the Greek constitution.

Caresse Crosby now started action against the government.

On December 1953 the Council of State dismissed the appeal of World Citizen Crosby. In 1955 Mr. Rollis, Minister of Defense, accorded Caresse Crosby "permission to hold exhibitions, receive visitors, build on her property, bring together meetings of her friends, and to express freely as an individual her artistic, cultured, and humanist ideology at Delphi."

Professor Pikionis, the most highly considered of the restorers of ancient buildings in Greece, has drawn up plans for a World Treasury (in the old sense of the word, the Treasury in Greece was a building in which were conserved tablets, engraved principles of government, such as the humanist philosophy of Plato. The Treasury at that time was not for gold, but a *spiritual bank* for works of art, rare statues, documents). Caresse Crosby has received donations for such a treasury. The foundations are laid. It will be a circular building of white pantellic marble like the marble on the Parthenon. On it will be carved in both English and Greek, "Citizens of the World." The outer rim will be carved in five points, Truth, Beauty, Love, Justice, Choice. We now have Choice, said Caresse. Under the round piece will be a *coffers* with scrolls of the great documents of our day, such as the Constitution of the United States, and all other democratic pronouncements. Caresse Crosby will invite every government to send what they consider the greatest utterance of their unity and democracy.

This is for the myth which man needs as he needs a blueprint for his constructions.

Now for the practical manifestations. In 1957 Caresse Crosby drew up a proposal for the Independence of Cyprus. She was on her way to present this at the United Nations when she fell ill. But nothing will deter this smiling, charming woman from her conviction that there is a solution to the impasses and barriers which occur between governments. She remains, whether in action or in temporary inactivity, the woman who worked all her life to unify various ethnic groups through her personal genius for intimate relationships. A feminine way of dealing with aggressions. With her native humor she added: "Women can solve it. Remember the legend of Lysistrata? The women of Greece threatened to deny themselves to their husbands if they went to war. Nowadays, in a less romantic period, such a threat might not be as effective. But women own 85 per cent of the national wealth, and in this more practical civilization it might be very possible for women to take a stand against war by threatening to withdraw their investments from war manufacturers. *The next war will be woman's war, voted and financed by women.*"

So spoke this *chargée d'affaires* of the heart of the world.

I asked Tom why *Justine* had been treated with more fairness than my novels when there is an affinity between them.

Tom answered: "There are several factors. One, your work is purer than his. He mixes the poetry and the unconscious with long stretches of almost conventional novel writing. People can follow that. Another factor is that of time. Your work came too soon. The timing was wrong. You were on the front line and received all the aggressions. The third factor is that you are a woman and all the critics are men."

He examined the copy of *Eve*. He has an enormous knowledge of publishing. He advised me on my story of "Citizens of the World."

Letter to Bill Goyen:

We are all hurt that loving you so much you have deserted us and no word from you to any of us. I am now the publisher of beautiful, paperbound editions of special books. In a fit of frustration I started reprinting *Under a Glass Bell* (offset), a lovely book for $1. It was always in demand. I sold 500 copies on my own, without help. It impressed Tom Payne, who guaranteed me distribution for any book I do. I can print 1000 copies and give the writer all the profits after printing is paid for. It is very simple. Say your book will cost $.50 to reprint. Either you get the cost of printing back from distributor when he sells 500, or 500 can be sold directly, as I did mine, for $1 and you make $250 dollars, and if we print more (in your case 2000) you can make $500 or more. But I know it is not the making of money which concerns you, but having the books available to those who want to read them. It is the only solution. I have a selected mailing list. Frances Steloff told me *House of Breath* was out of print but constantly in demand. She promises to take many copies if we do it. One book can feed another, it is a beginning, but if we can help each other we can be free of publishers. Think of it, we can design our own book covers. Each one of us has a loyal following. I will do whatever you wish. If your play is put on again, it would be so good to have *House of Breath* available. Or the manuscript you mentioned which was not published. Edward Brothers in Ann Arbor is a very reasonable printer. This may free us of the pain of working with publishers who do not love writing. I am sick to death of commercialism. Let's go underground in an aesthetic, pure and uncorrupted way.

Letter to Jane Morrison:

What I could not explain to you over the telephone was this: of course I believe in your integrity, that is your basic quality. But I also know you have a job to do for a most difficult person. Now just as I believe that when the owner chose you as editor, she should give you complete trust and let you perform to your fullest gifts and capabilities (I think she should abide by her choice of you and' your gifts as editor), I also think that the editor should give his writer the same trust if he has chosen him because he is competent. I felt that at a certain point I was not writing for you but for the owner. The editor who chooses a piece of writing and then wants to change it all around is the one who is basically using the writer to write what *he* would want to write, not choosing a piece for its quality, or rejecting it for genuine incompetence. For example, changing the end of John Hinshaw's story, or changing *Solar Barque* (I know you did not but the owner wanted to). This, dear Jane, I believe is the reason why magazines are so boring to read, they sound like assembly-line work, factory-made, lifeless. If we inject into the writer our own personal needs or ideas of how a thing should be written, it is an act of the ego and will always sound ersatz. I think the failure of many films and many magazines is due to this, a medley of too many opinions, too many points of view in an effort to seek a mass approval, and the lack of respect for the individual work. I respect you as an editor but I have held out all my life against writing to order. I sincerely think it is what has obstructed the development and growth of America. A basic, unique, individual point of view is necessary to produce an original, integrated work or person. For this principle I have sacrificed a great deal. When I first wrote my short stories every one of them could have appeared in a magazine if I had changed this or that. They all said my stories had no ending. Instead of doing that I bought a printing press and printed them. Today they are used in six colleges as textbooks. I feel that the owner has a conventional and literal turn of mind. But I do believe a story should be either accepted or rejected, not changed. To have rewritten it implies the writer is incompetent. Just recently a publisher in New York presented with one of Giraudoux's gemlike novels said he would take it if Giraudoux would make a few changes! (Giraudoux now dead and one of the purest classics of French literature.) I believe this comes from the fact that no matter how good a writer is, he will not write the things the editor has in his own mind. I do know that *Time* magazine makes its writers rewrite a thing until it sounds like *Time* magazine (James Agee told me he sometimes had to rewrite a thing over seventy times). But why should the execrable tone of *Time* magazine be superior to the beautiful writing of James Agee? No wonder it sounds as if written by the same person. Somehow I feel this is what the owner is going to do. *Eve* will sound and talk and think like her. And who is she? Neither a writer nor a creative personality in any sense of the word, just a woman endowed with money. I am devoted to you, and I understand both your human and editor's problem. I believe in you. I would not know what to do in your place. And I know you have been wonderfully understanding of me, and of my writing. And I know too you are going to do some very good writing. I know that you will understand that having given up so much for the core and truth of every word I write, I cannot now do the very thing which has made me a symbol, for others, of integrity and consistency of attitude. A point of view permeates everything. You have that in everything you write. Maintain it. It is the most precious source of strength and effectiveness. The other, the ersatz, crumbles away.

The backer, after issuing one number of *Eve*, lost interest. I received a charming letter from Jane:

You are unquestioningly the most giving and loving person I have ever known and I am sure that because of your integrity and what it has cost you to gain and maintain it, my own integrity and my passionate rebellion against those seeking to change me is strengthened. This must be the chain reaction that Caresse spoke of. I'm referring to the effect people can have on other people by what they do and what they refrain from doing. Your wonderful letter came tonight after I had spent the whole afternoon listening to —— tell me how I needed to learn to dissemble, to cheat, to overlook lack of principles and values in others, etc. I will compose a letter of resignation after I've written to you and Caresse. Her autobiography has had a profound effect on me, as has her achievement *Citizens of the World*. Dear Anaïs, this whole *Eve* business has been worth it to me just to have been in touch with you.

I fell asleep the night before, remembering a "character" in the diary and adding to the portrait, and I realized it was the first time I had looked upon the personages in the diary as "characters," and that it revealed I was tending towards the work of art and transcending the personal diary, for I also began to see it as peopled, in fact, crowded as any so-called social novel might be. Oh, yes, the minor characters were lovingly depicted, but not the ordinary standard ones. The ones so beloved by America. The cellist with the red shirt and the pipe who does not talk, the scientist who talks about science intelligently but only reads *Reader's Digest*, the horse-loving violinist who looks like the horsey women of English novels, the brilliant mathematician who makes corny jokes, the wives who knit or read *Look* magazine; no, it is true I have not included them, because they have not included themselves. They have chosen anonymity even in their own eyes. They have lived according to a wholesale pattern not to be recorded by their own eyes. I have often listened patiently for them to demonstrate signs of individual life. They wear an unbroken mask of trivialities. At times I feel great pity and think: they are imprisoned. They are imprisoned in a limited vocabulary, in jokes dating from college days. I look at the books in their bookcases and they reveal mediocrity and under-nourishment. I cannot distinguish one house from another. I seek landmarks so I may remember. I finally can tell them apart. But if I am not careful they melt into one undistinguishable, diffused mass. I seek in vain for signs of separate identities. It is a depersonalization that is willed. And so when I do not describe them and they rarely enter into the diary it is their wish, not mine. We make a distinct or an indistinct effect upon each other according to what we choose to give of ourselves, not what we retain. It is not I who lack interest, for I have endless curiosity and attentiveness. But I like the extraordinary because it is an indication of generosity. It is generosity which increases our eloquence, our means of expression, the abundance of our sharing, the effervescence of our growth and overflow. I like richness of being as I like the efflorescence of the tropics. Those who seek to conceal themselves, to remain anonymous, those cannot enter the diary as characters. There must be some reward for those who made a greater effort at *being* and *becoming.*

The character I was trying to remember. Did he appear in a dream? It concerns me. Was it the faceless one, the voiceless one, the unborn? Have I not been attentive enough? Failed to see or hear someone?

Tonight I tried to explain to Reginald Pole what might prevent him from destroying his friends' affection and devotion, trying to tell him that the actor in him is playing a role, the role of the deathbed agony, as a plea for love, but that this was in actual fact a destruction of love because people felt it like an undertow from the world of the dead, sweeping them into the shadows too. But he did not understand.

I cannot find my character.

Nor my dreams.

Letter from Eve Miller:

Forgive the typewriter again. Your own letters are so richly "you" and I know the handwriting plays a large part in the music. I should be able to splash my own with colors, too! Funny, about your inability to write in answer to that last letter of mine. I knew it. Somehow, even as I wrote it, I sensed the echo, in fact I felt strongly as if I was writing to myself. I'm quite sure there are few answers to certain problems, especially emotional ones, nor do I look for them. The relief, or help I think must come from identifying with another long enough to gain some further perspective. The one thing that came like a revelation to me in your answer is the thought you mention that the love of one's children is almost self-love. I'd never considered it. And so simply true! Yes, I have often felt that Henry gives, emotionally, only to his children. It's before me constantly. I'm not jealous of that. Perplexed is closer to it. He is able to give to them, of himself, but not to the woman he loves. It's a strange thing, to me. Loving him, it crushes me that something in me cannot open the sluices and allow him this gift of being able to give yourself fully, wholly. What got blocked off, when and where? (Even though I feel I know.) I met his mother on her deathbed. At 86, dying. She frightened the hell out of me. A real tyrant, cold as ice, and she died without "recognizing" Henry. This hurt him deeply. I think he's clung to the hope that one day, if only in a glance, the hatred, the rejection would drop away. The mother-image would settle itself. Well, it didn't. In any case, do know Anaïs that I know Henry loves me. I can most certainly live with his kind of love. It's been some struggle to come to this sort of strength within myself. One day, I will so love to talk with you. Arthur Knight was at Emil's one day, and spoke of meeting you. Of how remarkably beautiful and young you are. You would not let him photograph you. I loathe the fellow personally, one of those chemical "hates." His brand of brashness rubs me like sandpaper. The people Henry tolerates often make me gnash my teeth.

Hans Wolfert writes in *An Act of Love:*

A new conception of what is human reality is rising. A new conception of what is reality at all is rising. Dr. Freud and Dr. Einstein have opened no new world to the artist. But they have presented him, if he is a novelist, with the challenge of a new dimension. This new dimension is enlarging the consciousness of readers of fiction. Unless novelists learn how to deal with it, the novel will perish.

While copying the diaries, I am filled with thoughts, excitements, memories, a rich world in my head. The excitement generated during the day is dissolved not in the great themes of our history but in the petty details of the family squabbles of nations, the corruption of politicians, the competitive spirit of science, which proves only arrogance, rivalry, self-love, not the love of science. Of course I respond to essential, vital events but not this muddy stream of low-level information given by newspapers and radios. The contrast in level between the atmosphere in which I live within my work, and the level on which we are asked to live, is violent. My paradises and my infernos are of another kind. I do not want the company of the men who rule our lives, for they are not much better than the men they jail. Thousands and thousands of luminous cells, like the accumulated light of fireflies, slowly die at contact with the world. Whatever we destroy in human beings, elations, flights, and scintillations of the psyche, causes a strange phenomenon and then society is amazed when it creates monsters without feelings. By its emphasis and focus on the lowest level of existence, it causes stratification. By contagion, people learn to kill, to destroy. Nothing in the papers about creation or humanism. Vanity, competition, airplane accidents, robberies, crimes, marriages of movie stars, shootings in Jerusalem, all the ugliness of human beings and none of their accomplishments. No sooner do we hear about the vaccine for polio than we hear about squabbles between those who are to provide it, or even of deaths due to neglect or greed. We only hear about the degradation of France's political men, but not about the three thousand modern churches built by French artists. We have headlines on the death of Mike Todd but none whatever on the death of Dr. Otto Rank and so little on the death of Einstein.

There is a selection permitted on the information we receive. I reject almost all of it. Its intent is to debase us. *"La vie descendente."* The toxics only.

Why does this generation live destructively, saying it is because any day we may be blown to pieces? What a poor excuse. Men have lived magnificently, have created, discovered, loved in spite of the ultimate certitude of death. And even today, while the beat generation lives destructively, others are creating, discovering, exploring and giving life.

One of the most fascinating new fields is this exploration of man's unconscious by way of drugs. For certain closed, hermetically sealed people, it could not be done otherwise. Dr. Janiger calls it exploring Inner Space.

An evening with Aldous and Laura Huxley, Dr. Janiger and his beautiful wife and Lesley Blanch. Huxley's learning is overwhelming, immense. He is not a poet, but he has a curious, scientific, exploratory mind. Dr. Janiger read us Alan Watts' description of his LSD experience. Watts is a teacher of Eastern religions. He described his experience, covered all the philosophic implications and ended by comparing LSD with two mystical experiences he had. He asserted that the mystical experiences were superior in that they were organized, whereas the LSD was not. He compared LSD to a complex dream that lacked cohesion and would need to be interpreted and organized later to be understood. He did not describe the mystical experiences, implying that they were not describable. Why, I asked myself, should they not be describable if they were more organized, more harmonious than the LSD one?

Dr. Janiger wants to publish all these descriptions but says he lacks a priest, a child and an uneducated ordinary person. One of his most interesting stories was of a wife who felt she had an artistic temperament but never knew what medium she could use until she took LSD and asked for clay and became, from that moment on, a sculptress. Another experience was rather frightening: a woman who kept repeating the experience of giving birth to a child, re-enacting it over and over again, with all the pain, and could not emerge into any other cycle.

I behaved very badly toward Jim, like a parent who expected his child to bear a strong resemblance. His writing turned out to be so different than I expected. I rejoice over his success, because it will make his life easier; I am sad that I cannot respond to it. He is out of the nest for good. No family resemblance. In fact, he seems like an adopted son, and after all, he was! *Blue Denim* is well received, reviewed favorably.

After the failure of *Eve*, I was still determined to carry out my romantic fantasy of becoming a roving editor. I made arrangements with magazines to do articles on the Brussels World's Fair (1958) and perhaps on Paris, Venice, Florence, etc. (Some of the articles later appeared unsigned and unrecognizable.) Then I began to make plans to get to Europe.

I was invited to Brussels by the American Cultural Center. My cousin Gilbert Chase, musicologist, was then Cultural Attaché, and they felt a lecture from me would be appropriate during the Brussels Fair. Also, I had been invited to stay with Baroness Hansi de Lambert for a week of the Fair's opening, and I felt this would give me material for several free-lance articles. In addition to that, whenever my life was not rich or colorful enough my remedy was always to plunge into an orgy of novel reading. I was seeking direction.

I reread all the novels of Pierre Jean Jouve. There was a trilogy entirely devoted to an actress called Catherine Crachat. Why he gave her such a repulsive name ("*crachat*" means spit in French), I never knew. But Catherine suffered a cruel and broken love affair and accepted the invitation of one of her devoted admirers, an Austrian Baroness. I always remember Catherine's arrival at the castle, the giant bouquet of flowers, the Baroness's magnificent welcome, and in the heart of this magnificence, a woman suffering and in need of another woman's friendship. I made an association between the Austrian Baroness and Baronne Hansi de Lambert, who is also Austrian and married to a Rothschild.

Who ever said literature does not help one to live? I was prepared for the atmosphere of my new adventure.

Landing in Brussels I was met by the chauffeur of the Baroness Lambert, who said to me: "Madame La Baronne is waiting in the car." And took care of my baggage.

The Baroness in Pierre Jean Jouve's novel was sensual and possessive. Baroness Lambert was subdued, with smiling dark eyes, a warm smile. She was dressed with neutral elegance but her talk touched instantly upon the heart of events with a sense of their meaning, the important and the unimportant events taking place at the Fair.

As always, upon entering a European city, I was touched by the human scale, the small station, the small people, the small streets, the small cars, small buses, small trolleys. After the giant proportions of America, they almost seemed childlike, diminutive, tender.

Every gesture was dictated by manners, good manners not born of formality but of humanism, a respect for each other's dignity, an effort to save face. Human scale, human behavior, intimate and personal. It was even demonstrated in the direct simplicity of the Baroness's dealing with servants. No arrogance, only clarity in her orders, kindness. The chauffeur's response was respect, self-dignity, pride in his job. Madame la Baronne was not only giving orders but they were reasonable ones. Would he be able to stop at such-and-such a place at this time? To his duties he added an intelligent protectiveness which was more than an impersonal assignment. His own identity was precise and stable in relation to the well-being of the household. The problems of so many guests arriving at different hours was his to solve. He took pride in his responsibilities.

As we entered the hall filled with hundreds of bouquets from the guests, Nicolas the butler received us, distributed the baggage magically and led me to my room.

The guest room was hung with yellow velvet. This gave to all sounds a muted tone. While the maids unpacked my bag, I studied a telephone next to my bed which showed fifteen buttons: one to call the cleaner, one for the laundry, one for the shoes, one for the seamstress, the cook, the room service, the butler, the chauffeur, the errand boy, etc.

The bed was downy and warm. The valises had been emptied, the clothes hung up. The bath was filled with perfumed oil. The bathtowels were being heated on warm pipes. The edge of the bathtub was of wood. No hard surfaces, no new paint, no gloss. Everything was soft, unobtrusive. The only painting on the wall was a Paul Klee. The desk, to my delight, had all one needed to write letters. Writing paper with a small crown on it, stamps in a silver box, the white blotter with crowns on the corner. Crowns were embroidered on the sheets and pillowcases.

I walked down the curving stairway to the salon, where a fire was burning in the fireplace, and the Baroness had gathered her guests for lunch. In the bookcases I could see the most exquisite selection of books. On the walls, hung with red brocade, the best of Paul Klee and some moderns I did not know.

By American standards the house was modest, on a quiet square, but it was filled with an unostentatious luxury (one discovered gradually) quite different from the garish American luxury intent on dazzling you all at once with gloss, shine, newness. All the textures were soft, and the only polish came from silver, silver candelabra, silver cigarette boxes, silver lighters. It was a curious quality I had not seen since 1939, a luxury which was soft, unobtrusive, mellow, neither cold nor formal nor stiff.

It was all concentrated on quality, the exquisite quality of the food, of the conversation, of the paintings on the walls, of the books in the bookcase.

I entered suddenly into a world in which all the themes, interests and talk were familiar: literature, painting, music, theatre. Even Musil, who was being read in the United States so seriously, was dismissed lightly as "yes, a *Roman fleuve* but a river of boredom." An art dealer was talking ardently about a certain modern painting of Buffet when Baroness Lambert asked him: "You must show it to me when I come to your gallery." He answered: "I do not own it. It is owned by another gallery, but I am in love with this painting and you must see it." At my right sat a young professor who had just written a book on Pierre Jean Jouve! In front of me sat a couple from Zurich who discussed psychoanalysis, LSD.

A week began which I will not believe even after I have written it down. I met all the talent, beauty and wit of Europe. Names which glitter in history, in politics, in the arts. We visited the Brussels Fair in various groups. It was overwhelming. But to extract a single impression: Europe was *alive,* alive in every cell, every nerve, every part of its being, creative, inventive, dynamic. At first I thought it was because Hansi selected the best, but afterwards I noticed that it was unselected: art gallery dealers, newspaper men, politicians, all the filmmakers whose films were being selected for prizes, Abel Gance, who invented the Cinerama concept, Edgar Varèse, the German Cultural Attaché, the Swedish Cultural Attaché, Claudel's son, Chagall's son.

Hansi is a marvelous woman, interested in everything, open, receptive, full of insight and humanity.

Ten or twelve people to dinner every night. Le Corbusier, Varèse. Conversations in many languages. *"Oui, c'est ravissant. Ist Liebe nicht schön? Cara mia."* I have enjoyed the stream of people as much as the Fair. The Dukes, the Barons, the Counts, all straight out of Proust's novels. C. L. Sulzberger, with fresh news, Zurich journalists. The beautiful names of the guests (my father would have been in heaven!):

Comte Jacques de Grugge

Comte de Lesloy

Duc d'Ursell

Madame Duroy de Blitney

Comtesse de Greffult, descendant of the one who inspired the Duchesse de Guermantes in Proust.

Next to my bed not a Bible but a book of poetry.

One evening, after dinner, we walked up the stairs to the large living room. At each curve of the stairs there was a butler in a red uniform, holding a silver tray with a candle, a box of cigars and a cigar cutter. It was like court life in the eighteenth century.

A friend of Hansi said: "Hansi is not a happy woman. She feeds on this variety and flow, which distracts her." I was reminded of the Baroness in Pierre Jean Jouve, and I felt if I stayed, I could help her. But there was no time for intimate talk.

Breakfast in bed, which was the only luxury I envied the wealthy. A fire in the fireplace. Outside the window I could see Brussels, where I lived as a child of eight because my father wanted to be near the violinist Isaye so they could rehearse together for their travels as a trio, with Casals as the cellist. We moved to a suburb called Uccles, where my father sent us to a German school because music was good in Germany and someday we would go there. I learned to read and write German. It was in Uccles that I nearly died of peritonitis. The local doctor had made the wrong diagnosis and when he left our house that evening he met a neighbor who had a daughter my age. He told him: "Nin's daughter won't live through the night." I still remember the neighbor's name because I was told I owed him my life. Mr. Hostele called my father. My father called a famous surgeon from Brussels. I was rushed to the hospital and operated on just in time. It took me three months to recover. It was the adhesions from this operation that strangled my child, causing the stillbirth. But the past did not haunt me. At ten o'clock we would all meet downstairs and separate into different groups to visit the Fair. Baroness Lambert always wanted me with her. Her chauffeur had invented tying a bunch of fresh red roses to the car's antenna so she would be able to find it among the thousands of cars parked near the Fair.

The American pavilion was designed by Edward Stone, who produced a combination of birdcage and birthday cake. In a glass case, like a jewel, lay a giant Idaho potato. There was a wall covered with automobile plates. A tasteless fashion show was going on. But fortunately three things attracted the Europeans: early American painters, a reproduction of the beautiful glass chapel designed for the Swedenborg Church in Los Angeles (which mistakenly bore the name of Frank Lloyd Wright and which I obliged them to change to Lloyd Wright) and the film show, at which half the entries were American, and in which America's qualities of humor and rhythm predominated. Abel Gance, now ninety years old, was receiving a prize for his invention of Cinerama, which in 1926 he was not able to develop financially and exploit. He was presenting a film in "polivision" to demonstrate the humor of juxtapositions, comical parallelisms, contrasting images. His first use of Cinerama was to depict the battle of Waterloo, and I still remember the effect of the two extra screens suddenly unveiled to portray the two armies marching against each other. It seemed like a belated homage, which the commercial exploiters of Cinerama had never thought of doing. In the American pavilion another popular spectacle was the IBM machine. You wrote down a question and received an answer almost immediately. I asked what happened the year I was born and was told: "The first airplane was launched and Picasso painted his first blue painting."

The Swiss pavilion was dull, solemn, and of course showed a magnified reproduction of the inside of a watch. A big banner read: "The art of Switzerland is measuring time."

The Russian pavilion was solemn. The portraits of leaders exceeded all human proportions. There was a heavy emphasis on propaganda and self-glorification.

The German pavilion was a fascinating demonstration of science creating its own aesthetics. For example, an entire factory built of glass was like a glance at future transparency. Machine models made of black and white plastic, with accents of red and orange, and the statistical charts as beautiful as a Mondrian or a Kandinsky.

The Phillips building was designed by Le Corbusier. It was like a sail in motion, or a white whale turning over in the sea, or a white foaming wave curving and rolling, the essence of motion captured in a silver surface enmeshed in a silver net. It was a setting for Edgar Varèse's *Electronic Poem*. The sound came from all directions, engulfed and drowned one.

Electronic Poem could be considered as the overall title of this World's Fair.

A humorous touch (though I'm not sure it was meant that way) was supplied by the English pavilion. You enter what might be described as a small, dark chapel. Voices turn to whispers. A hymn is being played. On the altar, a painting of Queen Elizabeth surrounded by candlelight and flowers. The swords, medals, headgear, crowns are exhibited like saintly objects or relics. It was an altar to royalty. In contrast to the exaggerated solemnity, the museum next door was a delight: the first raincoat invented by the English, the first mailbox, the first electronic fog detector, twenty-five Nobel prizewinners.

I loved the Austrian pavilion. It featured manuscripts by all the famous composers, modern pianos. But entering, I was amazed to see people lying in old-fashioned grandfather's armchairs, apparently drugged. When I sat in one of them I found that by laying my head against the cushioned headrest of the armchair I could hear taped music, and I sat like everyone else, eyes closed, in a state of beatitude.

The Japanese pavilion made me sad. A beautiful house, with the usual silky natural wood, the exquisite design, a few art objects, screens, but in the garden a giant tractor to show progress!

The whole world was watching America and Russia, comparing them as the two powers affecting the destiny of other countries. The American exhibit won hearts by its gaiety, but the Russian pavilion was too solemn and pompous. But at the same time people would have liked to see how the middle class lived in America, as was tastefully shown by the photographic reportage of the Israeli pavilion. By means of murals painted by Jean David and M. Bezem, the whole history of the Jews was dramatized. The murals cover the entire wall of a long hall, and by subject, color and lighting give the full tragedy of the first half of its history. But the passageway leads into a well-organized, cheerfully lighted photographic representation of life in Israel today. By means of enlarged photographs one is made aware of the history of the people.

Almost all of the exhibits being made of glass, aluminum, plastic, it was a sensuous pleasure to come upon Finland's building of beautiful wood, shaped like a modern version of a child's woodblock castle, with only a few windows. Inside was a wealth of wood products, wood carvings, wooden dishes, furniture, skis. Fishing rods hung from the ceilings.

The dramatic core of the Fair is the Atomium, built by the Metal Industries of Belgium. A huge edifice demonstrating the new potentialities of metal, expressing the hope that nuclear energy might be used to benefit mankind instead of destroying it. The Atomium has the form of a metal cell magnified 150 million times. It is created out of nine spherical shapes linked by tubular spans. The entire surface is covered by an aluminum composition. At night the spheres shine like actively winking stars. To travel up the elevator through its passageways is like a voyage into science-fiction worlds. It contains demonstrations of all the steps and developments of nuclear energy. For the uninitiated, it is a new world. One can even listen over the telephone to the sounds emitted by the atoms. The emphasis is upon the creative uses of atomic energy. There are plastic models of nuclear reactors, constantly projected films on the application of radioactivity in medicine, biology, agriculture. The United States, Germany, Italy and Belgium collaborated in this exhibit.

The most beautiful of all the buildings was designed by architect M. J. Van Doosselaere as a symbol of Belgium's civic genius. It has the form of a bird with an extraordinary wing span of cement in an abstract form, long familiar through Brancusi's sculptures. It expresses hope and flight into space, new aspirations, new dimensions for Europe. Under the huge wings, there is a relief map of all the Belgian industries.

The Vatican exhibited a modern church designed by M. P. Rome, with glass windows designed by modern artists as abstract as any paintings shown at the Fair. Even religion has accepted abstract art as a new expression of ancient beliefs.

Back at dinner I met two professors of Russian who were just back from a visit to Russia. Because of their profession and their knowledge of Russian, they were allowed to go about unaccompanied. They told all they had observed. People are still living in crowded houses, several couples in one apartment. They have no luxuries. Almost everyone is dressed in the simplest clothes. They are a solemn and dedicated people, believe that America wants to make war on them, that they are now living in a socialist state but will soon reach the communist ideal and be rewarded for their unremitting toil. They do feel they are working for themselves, for their own development. They know nothing about other countries, they are not allowed foreign books or foreign magazines. Libraries in universities are restricted and carefully oriented. The only admirable innovation the professors had noticed was the transformation of all the old palaces into "Palaces for Pioneers." These are centers of education for the young and the old. Anyone can go there after school or after work and study any subject in which they are interested: painting, the dance, filmmaking, crafts. They can engage in sports, in producing plays, and it is all free. The Russian people stopped them in the streets, saying: "Please tell everyone at home we do not want war."

We were to have a farewell dinner, all of us, about twenty-five guests. We all dressed for it. How beautiful everyone looked in candlelight, reflected in gold-framed mirrors, against the rich blood-red velvet walls. How quiet the butlers, how jewel-like the wines, how delicate the flower smells. Suddenly we became aware that Baroness Lambert was not there. A friend explained: "Her mother was taken ill during the night. Hansi did not want to spoil our last evening together and so she left early in the morning without telling anyone." One last act of exquisite thoughtfulness, so like her. But at the same time I felt that the rules of courtesy, of social life, left a human being alone with sorrows and troubles, inaccessible to sympathy.

After Brussels, I left for Paris. I had longed for its beauty but I had forgotten the loveliness of its muted tones, like the muted tone of Hansi's luxury, the exact features of its face, the scales of grays and charcoal, the engraved and etched buildings in harmony with opaline skies. Arrived early in the morning, driving through the poorest streets, unpainted houses, the dark entrances of medieval houses, a glimpse of puny plants in patios, leprous façades, all seemed beautiful because gentle and silent. No screaming billboards in raw colors, no empty whiskey bottles on the sidewalk, no unnatural gigantism of buildings. A human city at last, human scale, and human textures. Not the enameled bathtub glint but the soft grays of cement eroded by time and climate. Dust allowed to settle. An ugliness that is not as ugly as the brassy, shining, new, ever-new movie sets of American houses. The impossible gloss, hard on the eyes, the plastic brittleness. What a relief, the gray palette, the texture of etching, the depth of ink and coal and pearls, and a sky of Indian saris. All of Paris is caressable, *La ville caresse, la ville caressante,* with its outer life all grace and wit, at heart a mystic lover, a philosopher, a man of taste.

In its ancient decor, it is always youthful because its source of life is inner, and always renewed. The past is so vivid that it fills the streets. It is full. Later, walking along the Seine, a cool spring day, I lost another fear. That I would suffer from the absence of those I loved in the past. But when a life is lived for its meaning, for the creation of a poetic or philosophic essence, then the residue of the past is poetry, not anguish, death or loss. Nothing left of the past but its great illuminations like the soft illumination of Paris at night, focusing on its churches, monuments, palaces, spires, a selection by light only of the moments of beauty. So it is not Gonzalo who is acting with madness and violence, on the Quai, but a serene river Seine flowing, different houseboats, lovers, new waters, new boats, new loves.

Having taken my first walk along the Seine and discovered that it was not a walk into the past, I began to feel joy. The magic of its unity and harmony of colors and textures and styles. When there were contrasts, they were contrasts between medieval somberness and modern gaiety. At the Beaux Arts, against a background as somber as a bone structure, in the courtyard the students had set up tents for a rummage sale for their school. They had painted the tents in mock Miró, mock Picasso, mock Mondrian, with much humor and playfulness. And on the uneven cobblestones, they had set up a mock jazz band and were dancing.

The dead were not absent. They were a part of the present life. My father's music was being played, and Joaquin's concerto contained all the feeling and the color my father had prefigured but not completed. Artaud's work, long unavailable, was being reprinted in two volumes. Allendy's works are in use and well displayed at the bookstore for psychological works. Otto Rank's works are being read. Friends of Moricand had just reprinted a manuscript he left.

No ghosts awaited me at street corners, though once by the river, I did hear the voice of Artaud saying vehemently: *"Entre nous, il pourrait être question d'un meurtre."* This melodramatic threat prompted me to write a long letter to say I was not in love.

And again, the humanity of Paris touched me. I felt tender and vulnerable. A worn Paris, like an old, very much loved parent, but alive, oh, so alive. Personal and intimate. No barriers between human beings. No persona. Marvelous intimate connections, not ashamed to share their lives, loves, ideas.

Fabulous talks with taxi drivers, on existentialism, modern theatre, personalities.

At the hotel, so near to where I had my houseboat, I lie on the bed and have an LSD ecstasy just staring at the chandelier. The bedspread of gold brocade is worn. I do not like lace headpieces on faded tapestry chairs. Yet what is this air one breathes, what are these life currents and vibrations one receives? Everything is transformed into gold. A mysterious essence born of legends, the figures from history, from biographies, from novels. Other loves, other beauties, full loves and deeper beauties. The setting is crowded with them. The uncomfortable wardrobe, clumsy and not holding enough dresses, the bathroom with all its pipes showing, but it is the Paris of Colette, of Proust, of Flaubert, of Carco, of Simenon, of Erik Satie and Suzanne Valadon, of Gide and Ninon de Lenclos, of George Sand and Chopin. There is a glow, it does not come alone from my love of it, it is an essence from the past, it is a compound of grace, intelligence, love of pleasure, and sensuality. All the city has it. A compound of humanity, learning, and a constant flow of essential values. The elevator man does not say: "It is raining today." He invents his own greeting. We are twenty thousand miles away from clichés and platitudes.

I went out for a walk. It was cool and damp. I walked along the Seine and the beauty of the city overwhelmed me. The trees always present, the fountains, the river always present, the small cafés, the small restaurants, the small theatres. No feeling of a gigantic mass of people around you as in New York, Gulliver's country.

Intelligence in the newspapers, in the faces, in everyone's talk. Genuine talk, no ready-made phrases. Identity. Character. Everyone knows who he is, what he is, the meaning of his life. We are twenty thousand miles away from chaos, confusion and robots who think and say predictable things.

Is it that America discarded its past, and lost its flavor? These are the descendants of Erik Satie, of George Sand, of Proust. If in the hotel room everything turned to gold, in the streets every building was an engraving, a charcoal drawing against an opaline sky.

I made some ill-fated pilgrimages which turned out to be visits to the cemetery. I went to the grimy, soot-covered Grand Guignol Theatre which once gave us all chills of horror, petrified us with terror. On its stage were enacted all our nightmares of sadism, of perversion. It was the last performance. The theatre was empty. As a friend explained: "With the war, concentration camps, occupation horrors, what the theatre presented seemed mild and childish." Only the words had passed into the dictionary, as an expression of sadism and torture. Only a phrase was left of scenes which took place in a chapel, to increase the feeling of desecration and evil.

In my ventures into the past I ran into another funeral, that of the *Cirque Medrano,* so famous among the artists and painters. There also I was attending one of its last performances, and the clown never seemed as wistful as in this empty circus. The public consisted of about ten persons. The trappings were worn. The performers had lost heart. I was watching a once-glowing and dazzling, intimate, small circus expiring.

I had feared ghosts from the past, regrets, but there was only the heady perfume of it, not the pain. I lived the pain so deeply that it consumed itself and left nothing but a perfume. In fact when I stepped on the cobblestones of the Villa Seurat, I felt lighter than I did in my twenties when I was prey to all the anxieties of those starting to live and love.

I could walk along the Seine and not long for *La Belle Aurore.* Remembering only the moments of passion. I could eat in the Arabian Restaurant, with all its *Thousand and One Nights* settings, dim copper lamps, velvet cushions, partitions, copper trays, where Gonzalo enacted the wildest of all scenes of jealousy, worthy of Othello.

I could visit the apartment in Passy, overlooking the Seine, where Lawrence Durrell and I sat on pillows in the balcony watching the spectacle of the *"Exposition Universelle."* I went to visit the apartment on the Rue Cassini, next to the house where Balzac wrote *Séraphita.*

I did not seek out the past. It sprang up accidentally. A publisher invited me to his house in the suburbs, and so I had to take the same train at Gare Saint-Lazare that I used to take for Louveciennes. His house was similar to my house in Louveciennes. But it was a beautiful summer day. I wore a gay cotton dress of East

Indian colors. I felt beautiful and free. The same day a filmmaker invited me to see his films, and he lived in the Villa Seurat, across the way from Henry's old studio. After twenty years, I should have walked along the uneven cobblestones of the Villa Seurat haltingly, heavily, but here I was lighter than ever on high heels, jumping as children do from one cobblestone to the next and wondering how I felt then and remembering I was neither as free nor as happy nor as light. I had escaped from many tragic traps set for me. The egoism of some, the self-destruction of others, the dark world of Gonzalo and Helba.

My cotton dress was swelling in the breeze. I had escaped the rough cobblestones, the caved-in ones, the over-polished ones, the treacherous ones hidden under moss.

Place de la Concorde seemed more softly beautiful than ever, the fountains so graceful, the lights diffused, the soft-grained stones of the buildings smoky like old etchings.

I visited Pierre Jean Jouve, one of my favorite writers. His apartment was somber, he seemed very old, bald, and like a Protestant professor, but my visit made him happy. He has had a heart attack. He told me no one had come to visit him for fifteen years, which I could not believe. He told me poets had been forgotten during the war, and after the war only the realists like Sartre were read. But I also realized that the French writers, like the Japanese, surround themselves with formalities (you cannot visit them without the proper introduction) which protect them and also isolate them. He said he envied the American informality. He was amazed that I could have printed and sold my own books without losing face. People do not write to writers, invade their privacy, call them up as they do in America. His only regret was that I loved his novels more than I loved his poetry, but I explained this by telling him I was primarily a novelist and it was from his novels I had learned to fuse poetics with prose.

I had promised to visit the Durrells in the South of France. I took a sleeper to Nîmes, and Larry was at the station early that morning. We recognized each other instantly, showing how little eighteen years had changed us. Larry said: "How gallant of you, my dear." Claude was waiting at the hotel. Claude younger than Larry and looking more Irish than French, very lively, laughing already at seven A.M. We started a two-day nonstop talk. The house, a farmhouse on a hillside looking down on the most beautiful Provence landscape, a Roman castle, and a river with a Roman bridge spanning it. The house had the wonderful solidity of old peasant stone houses.

Larry's paintings, very joyous and colorful, were pinned all over the walls, his reviews, photographs. Monastic and primitive. A garden with vineyards Larry kept trimming. Much red wine. Food partly from the garden itself. Claude talks excitedly, more than Larry. Larry seems to me like a wounded person. His body quiet while Claude does all the moving about, cooking, serving, taking care of everyone. I had received *Balthazar* just before leaving for Brussels so we could talk about it.

Claude was lively and bright. But Durrell gave me a strange feeling of absence of contact. I did not remember him so impersonal. I missed the warmth and understanding of my other friends. It was as if he gave nothing of himself but a persona.

We went to a cave to visit the Black Virgin who has been seen to weep. We had a picnic at the beach. The best moment I remember was at dinner when Durrell was describing his life in Brazil or Argentina, I forget which, where everything grew so fast and so gigantic. As he said this he stood up in his chair as if the plants were literally sprouting beneath him.

What distressed me was that Claude had expected a lady with a pearl necklace and a brooch, which indicated how falsely Durrell had pictured me from the Paris days. He did not remember the special way I had of dressing, unconventional, with blouses cut out of Spanish shawls, jackets of textiles from Morocco, sandals, seeking a touch of character. imagination or folklore, everything in opposition to the fashions.

Larry is still poor. They have so many children. And I think he takes care of his ex-wife. We talked endlessly about the next books, about *Mountolive,* about America, about Henry and Eve (Larry played the record of interview with Miller), about Paris. Until his work is finished he is, in a way, hiding, and does not welcome excitement. He said he had had enough traveling and people.

In the evening we drank a bottle of champagne I had brought, plus several bottles of red wine, and became hysterically gay until we fell asleep and slept around the clock. The next day early in the afternoon we went to Nîmes to do errands, to have dinner in town before I took the train back. We met Temple, the writer who printed a small booklet given to him by a friend who inherited Moricand's papers (a booklet on astrology and professions) and who translated a book Henry Miller likes on the discovery of America.

We covered centuries in space. Wondered why Henry Miller had not stayed in France, where he was better loved. Larry loves France and dreams of living between Provence and Paris. Larry has that curious quality of being immersed in experience, yet maintaining a constant control over its meaning. Claude is devoted and loyal, not as fond of intricacies but has a gift of humor to save him from the depths. The beauty and warmth of the southern countryside surrounded us.

Larry does want me to print *Asylum in the Snow* and *Zero,* two pieces dedicated to Miller and to me, because George Leite left out the dedications.

Larry so deep and Claude so gay. The Arlesienne countryside, the Nîmes region, the river, the houses, the Roman town, the bridges and the castles so beautiful. The Durrells have a lovely, lush garden. They grow all their vegetables. No hot water, no bathroom, no W.C. It is like Mexico. Larry cools the wine bottles by lowering them down the well. They have two sets of children, which the other parents take over half the time. Both married before. Claude is Irish, French, brought up in Alexandria, in New Zealand, in France. A saucy young woman. They took me to a "royale," an arena where bulls wear tassels on their horns and the men have to remove them for a prize. They try, and then run for their lives and jump the barriers to escape the angered bull and some of the bulls jump too and the whole thing is very gay as there is no death. The men do get hurt now and then but not as seriously as at bullfights. They drink red wine all day, which keeps everyone in beatitude but never really supine.

Durrell has known so much poverty that he is obsessed with succeeding. The French admire him deeply. Durrell hates cities, loves the sea. They sail a canoe and swim in the river.

Political situation disturbed. Sad for me to know that the French are in a mess *because* they are so wonderful spiritually, because they have lived only for spiritual values, because they are impractical and unrealistic, they are all artists at heart, and helpless in the reality of the modern world. They care more about reading a new book or buying a new painting. It is as if the artists we know tried to run the world, Varda, Lloyd Wright. The whole French race, peasant or factory worker, are artists and like the Mexicans so in love with life in the present they cannot plan for the future. They are not indifferent to the plight of the workman, they are indifferent to their own personal fate in the practical world, if not indifferent, then incapable. I remembered a story Durrell told me: He went over to the butcher in the little town where he lives and the butcher said: "Monsieur Durrell, I saw an advertisement of your book *Justine* in our butcher's magazine yesterday. They say it is a beautiful book, and so well written. I may not have time to read it, but nevertheless I am very proud to serve you the best I have so you may go on writing beautiful books."

The Peking Opera, a mixture of opera, ballet, acrobatics, mime, an incredible defiance of gravity. The very opposite of Kabuki. All dynamism. The women fight sword duels. The finale is a dragon of illumined paper, which fills the whole stage, which seems to fly and undulate in space, its fiery mouth pursuing a lantern. Modern painting, films, acrobats, all combined. The dazzling colors of costumes, and the strange music.

Joaquin tells me another story similar to Durrell's. A taxi driver in Madrid who drove him to his concert and would not charge him because he was a music aficionado and said he was proud to have driven a composer. The last musician he drove to his concert was Casals. Then he parked his taxi and went to the concert.

And another taxi driver again talking about politics in Paris. Shaking his head: "Poor France, she is like a woman without a husband, she has no leader, and she is lost!"

Dinner at the house of a man who makes ovens for steel works. Among the best collections of paintings. His mistress is the daughter of the archeologist who gave Proust all his information on church architecture. As Proust was ill, and the archeologist too old to climb stairs, they met at the concierge's lodge and held their discussions. The old archeologist could not stand the smell of Proust's asthma cigarettes.

Every street has trees, there are so many parks and gardens that Paris smells like a garden.

The fountains and the wit. Where else would they say of a woman: "She has witty legs"?

The old friends like old wine grown richer, and the new so lively. The sensuality and openness of the plays, the atmosphere of both excitement and repose, gardens and tranquil rivers and feverish conversations. A city only gives herself to her lover. Paris opened her secret charms because of the love I bear her. The joy I felt to be in love again. I took my shoes off to feel the cobblestones. I met a banker who rises at five A.M. every day to write a History of France before going to work.

So many sequels to *Under a Glass Bell*.

The drab period of Sartre is over, I hope. He suited the after-the-war guilts and depressions, but it is a lifeless and colorless philosophy, creating nothing but despair. He certainly does not teach how to transcend events but how to allow yourself to be suffocated by them.

Came back with *L'Homme sans Qualité* of Musil, translated from the German. How could anyone compare him with Proust? It is heavy, opaque, boring, and without psychological insight. Now I know why someone spoke at Hansi's of the *"roman fleuve,"* and someone else said: "Better say a river of boredom."

Brought back *Lolita,* which should be wildly loved in America, where so many men are afraid of maturity and love adolescence.

Never realized the extent of taboos we live with in America. The French theatre actually shocked me by its openness.

I saw marionettes done with gloved hands (four pairs), giving illusion of undersea life to the tune of *Gymnopédies,* acting out the lovemaking of a couple at the beach. The nightclub *L'Écluse,* small and intimate, so full of imagination and humor.

The restaurant where the woman who cooks for everyone also entertains, sings songs, tells stories and engages diners in repartee. Someone turned the radio on. It was immediately turned off angrily by young students there who said: "We can entertain ourselves." And they did. Anecdotes, stories, confessions, descriptions. The contrast with America where no one *talks,* deeply, personally, was violent. Here about twenty persons engaged in a spontaneous humorous happening, some engaging in imitations, take-offs. They re-enacted Ionesco's *La Leçon* with more sharpness and even more erotic implications, more outrageous and more irrational. I laughed until the muscles ached.

At another place, a private house, I saw paintings by Braque, Utrillo, Buffet, da Silva, Picasso. And in the bookcase all the books I could dream of reading. They showed me manuscripts of Proust, and one wall was covered with drawings and engravings made by writers. But they were not ornamental. The owner picked up Genêt and read a quotation for me to admire the style. He read de Tocqueville's prophecies on America written one hundred years ago. I met the actress who once acted in *Les Enfants Terribles* of Cocteau.

The men here are in business, but business does not occupy all their attention. In fact, it does not appear in their conversation or their social lives at all. The place of business is where it should be, with the furnace, food storage, the other functional necessities of life; but it is not a cult.

Jean Carteret was changed into a prematurely old man. It was a shock to find him in the same apartment, surrounded by the same objects I had described in *Under a Glass Bell,* but with added layers of dust. But the poetry of his talk was unchanged, and I could see in his ravaged face his delight at his own verbal fireworks. A few times he tried to draw me into his sickness, to expatiate on his symptoms and on his triumphs over the psychoanalysts who had tried to cure him, but I did not want to enter the labyrinth of his schizophrenia. We quarreled over the fact that he had always found it difficult to write, and easy to talk, and now he felt the right time had come, writing would disappear, and everything would be on tape. As a writer I naturally protested. But he carried other things in his gypsy bag besides pills. Notes on astrology, rare books, photographs of driftwood statues, horoscopes. Looking at Fance Frank, an artist, across the café table he said: *"La course au trésor."* And one minute earlier, Fance had been talking to me in a very low voice, for my ears only, about her pursuit of the myth.

One evening I walked near Montparnasse looking for the studio of Rachel Rosenthal's friends. I came upon a dark feudal Impasse du Mont Tonnerre, with its charcoal silhouettes of uneven rooftops against a shell-pink sky. The feeling in the air was that whoever would lean out of any of those windows had made love to the limit, and would proclaim its full-bodied existence, a happiness born of the intense aliveness of every cell. Next to Impasse Tonnerre and its silent shuttered windows and the infinite probabilities that any character out of Proust or Balzac or Zola might lean out of the window, lay the Rue de l'Astrolabe. The humidity of caves, of deep medieval castles, of ancient history. Madame de Pompadour leaping over the cobblestones in high-heeled satin shoes (or carried in a chaise, hidden by curtains) but leaving forever in the streets the scent of her petticoats and the intelligence of her interest in architecture, in gardening, in the embellishment of Paris.

Paris is peopled. We are far from science fiction, the dream and fantasy of America to explore empty planets. The human being has vanished from the world of science. It does not bother them. They love to imagine planets where earlier versions of man were annihilated. They consider the annihilation of man (already half achieved in the U.S.A.) an inevitability. If science fiction is a prophecy of the future, I prefer my planet Paris with its boiling, steaming human life. Paris is peopled by those who did not think it necessary to throw the past overboard, who use it to enrich and illumine the present. The spire of the Sainte-Chapelle, even if we no longer pray in it, is still more beautiful than a satellite and it travels further into the inhabited planets of the psyche.

Paris lies in the palm of your hand. You can walk all of its surface area.

No billboards, no shop signs. No gas stations showing. When the taxi wanted to refill its tank, the driver veered into an inner patio behind a wall, and a quiet sign said: *"Essence,"* which made it seem like a perfume. No prices screaming at you, in large and crass colors.

ESSENCE

A taxi driver who advises me to read Claudel, and who utters the word *"hybride"* in his conversation. The word *"cachet"* acquires a profound meaning. *"Cachet"* is used for things which have a subtle elegance or style. *"Cachet"* also means hidden. Perfume and quality not visible. *"Savoir faire"* becomes an essential quality. *"Savoir vivre."*

Americans care about human beings in general, but the French care for intimacy with human beings. Americans are dying of loneliness with all their collective and group activities.

In Paris I went to visit more Tinguely machines. There was one which broke bottles instead of corking them, another which swallowed the paper on which writing appeared, another which filled bottles with colored liquid that then exploded, another which produced an unexpected fountain, another smoke, another which printed big blobs of ink, tore the paper and handed it to you like a work of art.

It seems that when he proceeded from his studio to the gallery with his machines, rolling them along the streets, one tied to the other, he was arrested, suspected of having manufactured secret engines of destruction.

Before I left Los Angeles I was reading all the science-fiction books recommended by Gil Henderson. He said I must read them, that they were not mere science fiction but a prophecy of the future.

"If they are a prophecy of the future we are in deep trouble, and there is no hope for human beings, because the human being is totally absent from this science fiction."

But certainly not absent from Parisian life. Vividly present, engaged, involved, alert, keen, passionate. Such an interest people have in each other. Time to sit in cafés and talk. Time to sit after dinner in a restaurant and meditate, dream over a cup of coffee. If you are sitting in a café and a new person comes in, everyone is alert to see him, observe him. In the theatre they actually turn their backs on the stage and examine the public. Their palate for life, their taste for it, is as keen as it can be.

Los Angeles:
I wrote this for Jim Herlihy's *The Sleep of Baby Filbertson,* to be published by Dutton.
"These stories, written in a quick jazz tempo, contain the compressed vitality of a compassionate writer, alive in every cell of his awareness."

Letter to Larry and Claude:

At six oclock while you are still asleep I like to take a glass of red wine while I cook dinner to be transported to your little house and remember the talks we had. Larry, was it the red wine or did you really say: "While we are looking at Justine, while we think we are discovering Justine, it is Larry you will see and know." While we ate the lovely garden salad (Americans love very young girls because their vegetables are so overgrown and tough, suffering from gigantism) did we listen to Henry's opinion of Tolstoy? Are you in your new house? Send me photographs. Eve's response to my letter about our visit together was beautiful. It seems I made them feel they were there.

Had lunch with the Huxleys and a woman doctor, Betty Eisner, who believes LSD will cure the neurosis of the world. They feel it not only opens up the unconscious but that you understand and are aware at the same time. I only took it once to prove to myself and others that it is the unconscious and the world of the artist, not a *new* world. Huxley is a scientist, not a poet. He is an intellectual and admits to having no visual sense at all. For him the experience of LSD is a new world.

I feel less lonely since I went to France. I was beginning to think I was an eccentric and no one else thought as I did. But as soon as I stepped on the soil of France I realized I had a whole continent behind me. As Giraudoux expressed it: *"L'Amérique, c'est tout simplement le contraire de la France."*

In Paris a new perfume appeared: "Rock and Roll" by Marquay. Advertised as "the most dionysiac perfume in the world."

In America there are only two choices of life. The square, which is too rigid, too limited, too narrow, and the beat, which is self-destructive, like the romantics, like the bohemians (see life of

Utrillo, Erik Satie, etc.). The life in Europe escapes both these categories. It is human, intimate and intensely alive.

Letter from Dr. Betty Eisner:

. . . Next I was struck by your observation that your analysis was your method by which negative aspects were prevented from taking over in an individual always close to the unconscious. This is extremely meaningful to me. There is another aspect by which the negative can become understood and used creatively instead of being limiting and destructive: this has become clearer to me with continuing experience with LSD. I think this occurs when the individual makes contact with the deep Innerness—call it what you will—which lies within us all and which probably has some common ground. Certainly it is a unifying and creative force. LSD when properly used enables the individual to make contact with this and to experience it so that life can become very different. Also there is that certain category of individual who experiences this and yet is unable to change his or her life in accordance with his perception of this change. Why does this happen and how? It seems to be some early shriveling of the possibilities; some warping of the character; perhaps some constitutional inadequacy for strain and stress. I am also finding out that for certain levels of the unconscious, drugs are not necessary. I know this has been self-evident for you all your life, but for those of us who never had an image, a vision, or a fantasy in color until LSD it is a revelation that such an infinity of worlds exists within us, accessible to us at almost any time under proper conditions. These conditions we must find, and how they can be used, and how deeply one can go without biochemical help. And what are the types of people to whom this is most possible? The artist certainly; the mystic, without doubt. But what are we saying? Possibly some redundancy because those are certainly individuals who have more access to their unconscious than others.

Letter from Jim:

You do not discover new Golcondas—you *are* Golconda. How I love your search for beauty and finding it. Rare! So few have that secret. I can't tell you how happy I am with your letters from Europe and the success of your summer. I know what odds were against it, but you ignore the odds and proceed.

Crazy October is going into rehearsal but I am also going to direct it. So far we have signed Talullah Bankhead, Joan Blondel . . . and Estelle Winwood. Starcke is behaving like a magnificent producer. I saw the Key West house, but only for a few days. I love it. It is a self-contained world, distilled beauty, usefulness. Remember my old dream of winter sun Anaïs? My old journals were filled with it. Now I have it. I have everything. Strange and miraculous.

All reference to my own Press now means contacting an offset printer and offsetting the books as they go out of print. I offset *House of Incest* with new photomontages by Val Talberg. Bypassing the reviewers, I have found the most wonderful direct contact with my readers. They write me, they order books from me, they send books to friends.

I sell the books at cost.

I have created too rich a life and now I cannot write at the time things happen. I have fallen way behind.

But reprinting the books has been wonderfully wise, for I no longer feel I am writing in a vacuum. How I wish every writer could do this. Perhaps my Press will grow and I can do others' works one day.

Dinner with Frances and Michael Field. His cooking is magnificent, with *brio* and style. Frances and I have a strange friendship. There can be long periods when we do not see each other, but we always pick up as if no break had occurred, because there is an affinity of vision. Her painting is very poetic and delicate. During her last bout with tuberculosis she painted lying on her back, on a contraption over her head.

I sold *Children of the Albatross* and *Four-Chambered Heart* to England. I am distributing *Solar Barque* on my own.

Reading Blaise Cendrars, an incredible writer, an acrobat of language, an adventurer whom the Americans should have liked, seeking gold, loving cars, wanting to be the first man on the moon, wanting to make films in Hollywood, penetrating impenetrable jungles, familiar with gypsies, with international exotic women. He admired Henry Miller. Henry admired him. I never met him but read each word with delectation. He should be translated.

I asked Lawrence Durrell to write a preface for the English edition of *Children of the Albatross*. He wrote one so off the mark that we could only use half of it. He does not understand me or my work. He called me a child of palace hotels! So ironic in view of the fact that when I was born in Neuilly my father earned the modest salary of a music professor at the Schola Cantorum, and that, everyone knows, is minimal. If it were not for the help of my mother's father we would have fared badly. Why does he have to imagine me privileged by wealth?

Time magazine made a ruthless parody of *Four-Chambered Heart* and treats James Leo Herlihy with respect.

Letter to Lesley Blanch:

What you have done [*The Sabers of Paradise*] is marvelous. It is an adventure, history, biography and more, because it is infused with so much life, color and vigor. Quite truthfully, I did not expect to be as excited as I was by this violent life, but once more you took such a weight of facts and animated them with your own curious mixture of dynamism and insight. Every personage comes to life, both in history and as a unique individual. The chapters you gave me dealt less with your central figure, yet in just these three I was captivated by the completeness of atmosphere, background, the gift you have for reality, for bringing to life by a mixture of a real storyteller's colorfulness and a wisdom of interpretation. I am not a great reader of history, but the animation was so successful that I felt, my God, this woman fills any place, any century, any character with such intensity of life and makes it all fascinating. I awoke at five A.M. to read the last chapter. I liked the study of character which is so steadfast under all the color and vividness. The warmth of it, in only three chapters. I thought part of the seduction was in the way of telling but also in your theme, but now I see more clearly that it is all you, with a unique gift for giving life to any history you touch. It is a quality sadly lacking in biographies. And the humor and the irony. And amazing, too, for a woman to depict violence, pride, courage, so powerfully. Salut!

Letter to . . .

I understand loneliness better than anyone in the world, that is why I do answer letters and when you speak of your poverty of people I remember the times and places which were not life-giving. Must you stay there? One should make a courageous effort to leave empty or lonely places. Life is much too precious. Looking back I can see how we create our own destiny, the negative aspects by our passivity. We should never accept poverty of life. I know it's difficult to face the unknown, to create another job, or another way of life. But if it is up to you, do not accept the void.

Henry publicized my birth date and caused me anxiety. Eve [Miller] writes me such human, lovable letters:

Do not allow your affection for Henry to be destroyed. He is too great a man and you are too great a woman. He is thoughtless, unable to give of himself emotionally, is stubborn, egocentric, but he is Henry Miller. Everyone who comes in contact with him receives great rewards, as well as blows. One cannot question this, but accept the whole. Who knows why he does this or that . . . what price he has paid for the genius he has expressed so well? What price all the rest of us have paid, or are paying . . . is part of our individual destinies.

This return to France fills my whole soul. Once I am deeply certain over what I must do in life, nothing can alter the direction of whatever force I have. Henry must "see." If we are to remain together, that is. Here . . . I am literally starving to death . . . and it cannot go on any longer. The life we live here in the Sur is built on quicksands. It has been since the first. One cannot build a life together on the wreckage of another woman's fiasco. "Children" are no excuse, in all honesty, for trying the impossible. One gets beaten from all sides, emotionally, in every way, and finally you are nothing but an aching pulp. Provided you really want to start *living* . . . there's always a way out!

I wonder if the same expectation of a marvelous life attracted poor Lepska [Henry's ex-wife], who was even younger than Eve, and never imagined the solitude, the isolation of Big Sur, the constricted life.

Larry introduced me to Jean Fanchette. He had just won a poetry prize, he was a medical student, and was planning a bilingual magazine to be called *Two Cities*. He already has written a critique of my work, and has contributions promised from Larry, Miller, George Sykes, Richard Aldington, F. Temple.

He is a handsome, dark young man from Mauritius. He met Larry when he wrote about him in the medical students' magazine. He seems to be a good critic as well as a good poet.

Letter to Marguerite Rebois in Paris:

I was quite willing to suggest you for the translation of *Spy in the House of Love* but did not succeed in interesting the two publishers suggested by Miller and Durrell, so Jean Fanchette wants to try his own publisher, but in that case, if he succeeds, he will be the translator. I do feel if *Spy* is done it will open the way for the other books and then I will be able to suggest you as translator. Jean feels something will happen after *Two Cities* appears because he is writing an article on l'Art d'Anaïs Nin. This is to me a symbolic link with France. As you know, the reason I have been so obsessed with getting published in France is that I was afraid my failure in America would influence all of Europe, and it has. I have been made to feel I belong *there*, not *here*, and want to return there gradually.

Henry Miller is going to France in April with his wife Eve, who is thirty-five, whom I have never met but with whom I correspond affectionately.

I am working nine to eleven hours a day.

I am so grateful to you for sending Desoille's *Le Rêve Éveillé*. A prodigious book, inspiring, powerful. It increases one's dream capacity.

I have such sympathy for Eve's desire for a richer life. One never expects a writer to hibernate, to retreat, to seek seclusion. Not a writer like Henry but even in Paris he was already showing signs of withdrawing from too active a life in order to write.

Explaining the Beats to my French friends:

To understand any of the trends in America it is necessary first of all to strip them of their caricatural aspect, for America relishes farces and caricatures more than insight. Gross exaggeration often destroys insight altogether. Inevitably what grows in such a climate requires toughness. Bunions of the heart and callouses of the psyche are common proliferating native plants.

The fanfare and distortion surrounding the Beats (translated by me as bohemians, or as referring to the beat in jazz or the beat of the heart, and by them linked with beatitude or mystic states) has obscured their affinities with the bohemians of Europe, the artists who lived in poverty rather than become slaves to some work they hated, and sustained each other by a mysterious fraternity. But the American Beat, to escape the American disdain for the artist, for the poet, acknowledges no such affiliation and is more often seen in company of François Villon characters. They are creating a new atmosphere, but secretly they feed on Michaux, Rimbaud, Artaud, and create a defensive way of dressing, talking, behaving which merely attests to the revolt against commercialism, bourgeois standards, robotizing forms of life, no different than the Dadaists. But the deforming lens of publicity did not make the accurate distinction between revolt and mutiny made by Dr. Lindner (in *The Fifty-Minute Hour*). Revolt is inseparable from evolution and growth. In the puritan mind all revolt against the bourgeois life is criminal.

Part of the distortion is due to the fact that the Beats themselves affiliate with drug addicts, thieves, etc., rather than painters or poets or musicians. They are closer to Villon than to Michaux.

They selected Zen Buddhism as a religion because it is the opposite of American pragmatism. They had to find a counter-poison against the powerful American practicality. The Beats had a greater problem than the bohemians. All the bohemians had to do was to make a vow of poverty and do their work. The bourgeois did not relish all their antics, but they loved and respected their work. It is only in France that a writer like Genêt is treated primarily as a great writer and not as a criminal. But the Beats have a more complex problem in a society which is actively hostile to their work. Hence the necessity of a pose of callousness, indifference, toughness. Hence secrecy about the intimate side of their life. If the Beats made a symbol of Jimmy Dean because he died young in a racing car, it was because in dying he repudiated the American obsession with possessions. True, Jimmy Dean is no cultural symbol, such as the consumptive Keats was to his generation.

The Beats try to create a life severed from commercial values. They have found no other way than to refuse all jobs, because they know what enormous pressure will be placed on them (a pressure whose tonnage is unknown in Europe) to adopt completely the cult of work, ambition, greed, success in material terms. So the job is repudiated as a trap which will involve them in more abdications.

Their one concession to the powerful mores is to disclaim all affinities with cultural values. They make extraordinary efforts to discover the writers who are not known, the composers who are not played, because they sense that they have been cheated of true values by salesmanship. This is also part of the process of discovering their own gifts. This is a delicate matter, not for public eyes. What they will create will be different.

Léon-Paul Fargue, the most imaginative, the most aristocratic of all bohemians, was an inspired storyteller. The young Beats have adopted a pose of inarticulateness. But it may be that they are discovering their own language. Symptoms of this originality are showing in their writings. The writing is influenced by jazz and the American lingo.

They receive little help and are treated as freaks. I sense in them a new kind of poet.

Letter from Eve Miller:

The great news! Henry has at last agreed to a trip to France! He thinks of it as such. For me I pray it turns out to be more than that. A "return" if you wish. I've done nothing but dream of this for the past six years. Nor is it entirely a selfish need, on my part. Henry *needs* France. This hunk of veritable Paradise in which he's put down taproots is insidious for him, and he refuses to recognize it. I watch this vital man dissolving. He is another person in Europe. How long can an artist feed on himself? The stimulus he needs is there, not here. In any case . . . I've reached profound decisions in these past months of desperation. I'll move mountains if necessary, in order to help him to "see." My own personal needs . . . I'm fully aware of. I'll never realize my potential in this country. I've got to breathe, at this point. Start living. The inertia that breeds like a fungus here! How do you tolerate it, Anaïs?

Voilà. Henry wants you to know he is most certainly doing that piece for your friend in Paris. (Fanchette).

But back to our plans. I'm so excited I can hardly believe in the reality . . . but it is true, it is happening. I won't breathe freely until I step off the jet liner in Paris!

We will take the two children with us. Their mother has given permission that they have this opportunity (this has always been the "excuse" for not being able to go back). We want six weeks in Paris, I insist. After which we'll go to the South of France and spend the summer. Probably where Durrell is. He'll have a houseful of assorted children through the summer months, and with Val and Tony along . . . It's essential that they have other children, if they're to taste "living" in France. It is planned that they should return the middle of August, but I'm hoping that M. Dieu is on my side, this time, and plans are altered. *La vie est très compliqué!* Henry is unaware of all these hidden dreams and hopes, of course. I doubt he has ever asked me once, in these entire seven years together, what my hopes and dreams might include!

Kinsey Collection bought a batch of my erotica, which I wrote for a dollar a page in the 1940s and which was maliciously presented as my diary, and sold to them under false pretenses. Unfortunately I cannot defend myself in this case if the Kinsey librarians do not know the difference between a genuine diary and pages written to order with tongue in cheek.

Letter to Anna Kavan in London:

Many years ago I wrote to your American publisher to get your address and intending to write you a long letter. Doubleday returned my letter. At that time I was so moved by *Asylum Pieces*. It seemed to me that this was the first time anyone entered the world of madness with such clarity and compassion. For the first time all the feelings were made clear and very humanly understandable. I gave the book to many people to read. I was amazed at how few knew you. Then I read your other books. I loved them. I felt a great affinity with them. Then Peter Owen came to see me (he has become my publisher) and for the first time I knew something about you. But I hesitated to write you before rereading the books. I had carried a letter in my head so long that I felt as if I had written it. You did so beautifully, so perfectly what I feel is the task of the writer of our generation. You entered the realm which it was inevitable and necessary to explore: the irrational. All of us so aware of the age of neurosis and the need to understand the irrational, and yet the novelist has disregarded this, particularly in America. I move in and out of conscious and subconscious and was reviled and ignored for years. But a new generation is becoming aware, a generation who has faced the unconscious. Not all of them are running away to the moon. And I hope they will read you and rediscover you as they are rediscovering me. I am sending you my *House of Incest* which has parallels to your *House of Sleep*. You have such a beautiful style, and such clarity in dealing with mysterious, confusing realms.

I would like to invite you to contribute to a magazine I am affiliated with, *Two Cities*, in French and English. The editor is Jean Fanchette, a poet, novelist, critic of twenty-three. They cannot pay yet but I believe it will become important. I met Jean Fanchette through Lawrence Durrell, who admires you. If you have something to send us I would be grateful.

As nobody would publish me in America, I printed my books myself. I had hopes that my Press would grow to include other writers. When *Asylum Pieces* came out, America was not ready for it, but the climate is changing and it should be reprinted. Peter Owen sent me your last two books. I felt like quoting De Gaulle: You are going to the moon? That is not very far away. We have so much further to go within ourselves.

The greatest pleasure I had this month was an article by Jean Fanchette on my work. It was so nearly perfect, so near the target in insight, that I dreamed I swallowed it. Yes, exact praise is nourishment, which one should not be ashamed of eating, any more than eating for the body! Plenty of people have fed on my praise and understanding.

Comments by Jean Fanchette on *House of Incest:* "Anaïs Nin projects an almost dazzling light upon what generations of writers have only dared to express in paraphrases.

"The gift of Anaïs Nin is to name and define the alchemy of body and soul, to explore the roots of obscure instincts, define them. A constant dialogue between the dream and lucidity."

Mount Sinai Hospital. New York City, March 9, 1959.

I named this volume *The Fallen Jet.* The strongest impression I received when I returned to New York was a story I read about a jet plane which was flying between Paris and New York. Suddenly it began to fall. The pilot was out of the cabin talking to passengers. The pressure paralyzed them. The pilot struggled against the weight and painfully, step by step, superhumanly, reached the controls and righted the jet a few thousand feet from the ground. The automatic electronic controls had failed.

The accident stayed in my mind so vividly that I realized it was an image of what was happening to me inwardly. I was seeking to right my flight and it took a great effort against the downward pull, the negative pressures. All year I had tried to control my career, my relationships, my unconscious, and the downward pull. The weights and pressures, the obstacles.

Then came the double pneumonia. It started with a cold. I had a deep cough. I was going to bed when Tana called me: "I must see you. I have just divorced my husband and closed my apartment."

"I'm ill," I said, feebly. But Tana came. I listened to her, but felt strange and detached, as if for the first time unable to feel another's sorrow. At four A.M. I wakened with violent chills. A hot bath, the electric radiator, two blankets, nothing could warm me. I started to call doctors. Most of them had answering services. Others would not come to the house. I had a fever of 104 degrees and was vomiting. At dawn Jacobson came. "I believe you have pneumonia." Millicent took me to the hospital in a taxi. With a raging fever, they put me through a questionnaire I could not answer and asked for a cash payment.

Double pneumonia, said the X-rays.

Today is the eighth day. It is snowing. The room is full of flowers, and friends came, Jim from Key West, Stanley Haggart, Woody Parrish-Martin, Sylvia Spencer, Peggy Glanville-Hicks, Bebe Barron, Dr. Bogner.

I write letters.

I wear my red burnous to the X-ray room and amuse everyone. The nurses seem grateful because I am made up and do not look as if I were expiring.

Letter to Louise Varèse:

I'm so excited to discover someone who shares my absolute devotion to Henri Michaux, and for that book in particular. I have much to tell you about this. I would love to publish the book. The situation is this: all my books were out of print and no publisher would do them, so this year I started to reprint them and it will take some time before I finish. But as I do have a following, the reprinting is working out, with no reviews, no publicity, with only the help of friends. So I do hope to include other writers. I would love to do Michaux and Durrell's *Black Book*. Please tell me what I would have to pay for the translation. This is a nonprofit organization, I planned to give the writers all returns after expenses of printing are paid.

Yes, America is baffling. They prefer the analytical approach of Aldous Huxley to the poetics of Michaux. They do not want to be carried into experience. They want to examine it. They won't trust the artist to give them ecstasy, but they will rush to take the drugs themselves instead of experiencing them through the far more subtle and receptive instrument of Michaux's tentacles.

I am sending you Jean Fanchette's article. If it appeals to you then I will accept your translating it into English. I am sending you some announcements too, if you would be so kind as to mail them to people interested in *Two Cities* and in my work. This is the only solution, the only remedy against an overpowering commercialism.

Jean Fanchette is translating *Spy* into French. For twenty years I have been vilified, and excluded, and for the first time this summer felt appreciated.

I have a feeling that Varèse is experiencing the same justice—so many years when his imitators were given what he alone deserved.

Letter to Karl Shapiro:

I had read your poems and critiques some time ago but reread them recently with more insight. Was struck by the same curious blend of deep humanity and a keen clairvoyance.

I was wondering if you would have something to contribute to our magazine *Two Cities*. I am the American editor (Oh, irony, since I was ostracized from every American literary activity). There is no money involved but good company and there is some hope of being backed by one of the French publishers. I would be proud to have something from you. Please help me get my Press known. This is the only way I have found to keep my work from being buried alive. Not a single American publisher will publish me. I know there are other writers in the same situation. I long to publish them too. Some out of print, some forgotten, some dropped, and some new ones nobody wants. Durrell, Miller and I started out together before the war, and the old constellation is being re-formed after twenty years of isolation and underground devotion.

I am in the hospital now with double pneumonia, but when I get home I will write you in detail about your books. I lack the energy now.

Letter to Claude and Larry:

I'm in the hospital recovering from double pneumonia (Spanish extravagance!) and catching up with my correspondence. This month I gave my energy to *Two Cities,* which will be good for all of us. I want to thank you for introducing me to Jean Fanchette. His friendship is a delight. Larry, so strange that you spoke of sproutings and many healings due to Claude and France. My summation of all my impressions of you, Larry, when I left in the train, was: he is a wounded man. But I didn't know how deeply.

Irony is that I didn't know the extent of the damage done by life in America. Jean seems to be healing that completely. Until I get the magazine itself I won't be able to get as many subscriptions as we need. Few American writers will write without pay. It will be good for Henry and Eve to be with you.

In your preface to *Children of the Albatross* I had to cut out "child of palace hotel life," as the truth was when I was born my father at twenty-three was the youngest professor of music at the Schola Cantorum, and you know how musicians are paid in France. We lived with help from my mother's father, who gave them a piano for a wedding gift and a small income. You will see pictures of the small apartment in Rue Henrion Berthier in Neuilly where I was born. When my father left us, and grandfather died, my mother's small income ceased. Her rich sisters felt she had received enough and should not partake of inheritance. So in America we were most unromantically poor, with my mother working and renting rooms. When I protected Henry it was out of denials, not out of abundance. I finally gave up Louveciennes, and the car and the Spanish maid (ten dollars a month). I was not raised in a jewel casket. In New York I did all the housework. I think you confused my life with my father's life later when he married an heiress, and had a private house in Passy and lived in luxury. I realized your fantasy about me when you spoke of the diaries delivered by a chauffeur. We only had a car when we lived in Louveciennes, but never had a chauffeur. But if this fantasy gives you pleasure, it is the right of a great fiction writer!

Letter from Elizabeth Moore:

In *House of Incest,* as in *Children of the Albatross* and in *Under a Glass Bell,* I found again that curious sense of someone working behind a thin skin—a drum skin, perhaps, from which certain melodies, frail and yet as strong as wire, are struck with increasing or decreasing rapidity. A spin of a silver coin on marble, a flicked crystal goblet. Your writing is to me everything strong, yet tender, muted yet triumphant. Sometimes a trumpet, sometimes a violin. Perhaps more than any writer this strong rhythmic and musical association is almost interchangeable; it has always made me marvel how you have plaited, as it were, music and prose together (which of course equates poetry). This is why, perhaps, one receives so strongly that extra-dimensional perception. You know how mysterious the tapping of a bird's beak can be—before dawn, outside the window. The sound penetrates your sleep, penetrates your awareness *before you are aware;* an impression is slipped in, together with night's tangling images, half-thoughts, wheeling worlds, before the slow coming of the day-self. Virginia Woolf has done this, Elizabeth Bowen, to a lesser degree Anna Kavan. But each of these writers seemed touched with neurosis. They show their wounds. Oddly enough, it occurs to me that you do not. You *flow* with life—whereas many writers (particularly of the sensitive school) have opted out and show it by a certain sterility.

Varda is in New York, and gives a party to celebrate his divorce from his Greek wife, Chryssa. He took one of the plainest, drabbest, homeliest of all lofts, painted it all white with sky-blue ceilings, filled it with hanging plants, hung his collages on the wall, and there was a beautiful, spacious place where you expected birds to start singing, and fountains to dance. Chryssa has another studio above, filled with her enormous drawings and paintings, heavy and coarse. Varda has never abandoned the fairytale.

I recovered in time to do my reading at Harvard. Harvard was wonderful and it did me good. Two editors of *The Advocate* met me at the plane, and one was French. We had lunch in a French restaurant, then we went to visit the Grolier Book Shop, who have been loyal to me from the beginning and always carry my books, but Gordon Cairnie was ill at home. It was bitter cold, and the famous ivy looked quite tubercular. The reading was in a big hall, overflowing, hushed attention, much clapping and demand for more. I read for an hour in all. Then somewhere else for a big reception where hundreds of students talked to me, all saying more or less the same thing: we are tired of realism, tired of flat writing, we want poetry and imagination. It was not the English Department who invited me, but the students, who pooled their resources to pay my plane fare and dinner and drinks. They were articulate, well read, sophisticated, in touch with the whole world.

More amusing my meeting an old man from the State Department at a party, who told me I had caused him a lot of trouble once during the Marshall Plan, when books were being sent to the army, to Europe. Among them somebody sent *House of Incest,* and the Ambassador from Brussels *cabled* a protest; he had to go down to the Library of Congress and sit down and read the book through to see what could corrupt the American army; he could not find anything but a surrealist dream!

After my pleasant visit to Harvard, Vincent Capanzano in *The Harvard Advocate* wrote a long story of my publishing my own books, which amounted to this deduction: If big publishers did not publish me, it meant I was not an important writer!

Daisy Aldan and I exchange letters on our mutual interest in publishing. She came to see me some time ago when she intended to write a thesis on American surrealist writers. I gave her all my books. I took an interest in *Folder* and in her poetry, and we have promised to meet.

When the books were out of print, I would receive letters asking me where they could be found. The letters are sincere, and I don't know what to answer.

Another thing which concerns me is that people are reading the novels out of order. I had intended them to follow one another, and the design of the characters became clearer from volume to volume. But the publishers did not want to say it was a continuous novel.

They said the American public would not want to think they had to read several volumes to reach completion. That they never read the second volume of anything. So nothing was said about the novels being interrelated. They were read as separate novels. I began to think that if I offset them all in the right order, their development would become clear. I found an offset place in Ann Arbor. I put all the novels together, with a few engravings by Ian Hugo, and had them offset under the overall title of *Cities of the Interior*. Woody laughed at the title, said it would be taken literally, as a geographic study, but the symbolism appealed to me and I kept it.

There was one handicap. The numbers of the pages in the original novels were masked. But I could not afford a new numbering, and so the edition came out unnumbered, and each volume in different print, which puzzled people and annoyed those studying the novels because they could not be indexed. But all this was less important than having the novels in print for those who wanted them. The correspondence was the nourishing affirmative response which kept me going. That and the expression in people's faces at bookshop parties. They never approached me with mere words of politeness. Their faces were full of emotion, the eyes full of messages, the words often inchoate because of the feeling overwhelming them. It was such a deep, such an emotional exchange always. The work could not be useless.

Letter from Alyse Gregory:

Your writing has on me the effect of poetry, so many undertones and overtones, so conjured a use of words to express so intangible an underflow of emotions and sensations. I think your gift is unique and it is not strange that you have not received the full recognition that your originality should be able to command. In the words of Cocteau: *"Ce que le public te reproche, cultive-le, c'est toi."* The coupling of your name with Virginia Woolf is somewhat misleading. I think you begin where she leaves off. You write on quite a different level. One is carried down into the life stream itself in your writing and the final feeling I carry away with me is that of a quite new illumination being turned on the beautiful, perjured, mysterious, subtle and dolorous enchantment that compels lovers into one another's arms only to find in the end that the gulf has been widened between them. To have treated this infinitely complicated yet so stark and overworked subject with so much poetical insight, so free of all contemporaneous vulgarity, so delicate and inspired a candor, amounts to an art in itself, one that should preserve your books long beyond the ephemeral pinpricks of your critics, if there are such.

Isn't it strange how much more wonderful letters are than reviews, how generous and warm and lucid people are when they are not writing formal criticism. How much more they see, respond to, when not intent on evaluating for the public.

Such letters are my best reward.

D. H. Lawrence book very rare. Gotham Book Mart has a copy now and then at a very high price. *Ladders to Fire* is out of print but will be included in *Cities of the Interior*. It will also include *This Hunger*. *Winter of Artifice* will be reprinted in paperback with three other novelettes in May or June. *Realism and Reality* is out of print but a section of it has appeared in *Two Cities*.

Note to Maude Hutchins inviting her to collaborate with *Two Cities:* "I have always admired your *Diary of Love*. The wit, the sensuousness and the intelligence of it."

Writers I sought out: William Goyen
Anna Kavan
Wallace Fowlie
Daisy Aldan
Karl Shapiro
Nabokov.

Karl Shapiro answers:

It makes me ashamed of literature that someone with your beautiful gifts must try to print their own books. The writers pay you the highest compliments and that doesn't seem to help. It is the same with Miller. People are afraid of your books and Miller's, but they are my kind of books and I am discovering what it is to be lonely in one's love of certain authors. I find myself reading your novels in secret and crying. You really are a poet and what you say and the beauty of your language go right through me. In a way I want to keep you a secret.

With such letters I must go on. The danger of oblivion has passed. All the books will be in print. But I often wonder how many writers we have lost. How many did not continue to write.

Two of my books exist in Swedish.
Miss Lonelyhearts sold only eight hundred copies!
If ever I make money I will start publishing the writers I like.

The business of *Two Cities* has taken much of my time. The rest is typing out the diaries so I can put away the originals.
Correspondence all about *Two Cities* and work of distributing books I reprinted. The Phoenix Bookshop will handle them.

I do feel Anna Kavan, with all her brilliance, has gone too far into the exploration of the labyrinth without renewing her oxygen supply through life. She seems to have stopped living, and is moving into an impasse. I admire her and only fear sterility for her later.

Can't believe I copied seventy-one volumes of the diary. On to my next twenty volumes now. But still weak from pneumonia.

Today I remembered Dr. Allendy's house. Not sure I described it before. It was in a quiet, residential quarter. There was a small, well-tended garden in the front. A dark hallway led to a dark salon, and this salon opened on a greenhouse. There was a small pool with goldfish, and a pebble path. The light came through a greenish glass. Several cats lurked in the shadows. The armchairs were deep, velvety. At all hours of the day the light was the same, diffused interior. And it seemed appropriate for this entry into submerged worlds.

Dr. Allendy's office was soundproofed by a heavy black Chinese curtain, black with a few gold-embroidered papyrus branches. It made his office seem less that of a doctor than a magician. When he was ready he would slide the door open, then slide the curtain. He was tall, but he seemed even taller in the small rooms. His enormous Celtic blue eyes were the most vivid, alive part of his body. He had the eyes of a seer. He was heavy, and his bearded face and large nose gave him the air of a moujik. He could have been a fanatic. It was unexpected to find an analyst who sat quietly behind his armchair, rustling notepaper, talking softly. He had beautiful teeth, but he rarely laughed, and never heartily.

The room he worked in was lined with books. It contained only a desk and two chairs. The light there was also soft, and early in the afternoon the lamp on his desk had to be lighted.

After his appearance behind the black Chinese curtain, he effaced himself. And only when leaving did I see him again. He would see me to the door. When he opened the heavy curtain he looked like a magician, a magician who would persist in prying open your secrets. At the door, saying goodbye in the light of the street, he seemed like a kindly doctor.

It was strange always to enter into the sunken garden mood of the house, to pass through a painful adventure, and out into the world again, the sunny bourgeois street.

[Spring, 1959]

What I have done for my own work, rescue it from oblivion, I wish I could do for other writers, but I can't both write and publish and I was overworked last year with masses of details. It costs so little to offset already printed books which have been dropped by commercial publishers, such as William Goyen's, Isabel Bolton's, Anna Kavan's, and one can always find two or three thousand readers for such books, enough to keep them in print.

I read all of Artaud, Michaux, and Kafka, and could not sleep for several nights. Such tormented human beings! It is incredible, the tortures caused by the psyche, their intensity.

Rejoicing over the success of Harry Partch in New York. *The Bewitched.* Everyone writes me how beautiful it was, how he made beauty out of American folklore, how fluid and marvelous the music was.

In New York, when Varda was separating from Chryssa, and was going through difficulties, I bought one of his collages. They are enchanting, a magic antidote to the barren abstractions, doodlings, and empty spaces called modern art. No matter how sad he may be, in his work he only expresses joyousness, airiness, the floating gardens of the spirit, making the invisible visible as even the dictionary admits to be the function of symbolism.

Jim Macy tells me: "We have overdeveloped minds. It is the mind which makes us live in the past, or in the future, and wrecks the present. It is the mind which seeks a knowledge of reality which is always false. The present is all we have, the present moment. Zen encourages this consciousness."

"But if the mind is ill, and lives in the past or in the future, will Zen cure it?"

"No."

Would it not be better, since we have developed this instrument, to learn to think our way out of our predicament? We can use this mind to direct our lives, to explore the unconscious mind. It is a valuable instrument. It can help you to become what you are, reach what you want, whereas instinct and feeling alone can destroy us.

The kind of Zen living in the present which Henry and Gonzalo did I understand, but I cannot understand what it can do for us now. It is the opposite of analysis, which ultimately takes us back to the unconscious, and therefore enables us to rejoin the present, having liquidated the past and ceased to live in the future.

When Larry Durrell wrote to me in Paris to look up Jean Fanchette, and I did, I did not know that he was giving me a link with France.

I sat waiting at the Deux Magots, and there came a young and beautiful Negro, slim, not tall, delicate features like those of the Haitians, small, straight nose, soft, warm eyes and a sensuous mouth. He was a student of medicine. He published a small newspaper for medical students. He had just received a prize for his poetry.

He was full of charm, with a balance between earth and poetry. He had written a critique of Durrell, and Durrell spent much time with him in Paris.

Later I felt his friendship with Durrell suffered from the same disappointment that mine did: he refused Fanchette a preface. He did not refuse me one but he wrote one so shallow I was never proud of it.

I helped the magazine. I was grateful for Fanchette's understanding. I count him my best friend in France. The magic link. It was strange that at the time I felt bad to be returning to the same old constellation, Miller-Durrell. It seemed like regression. But then I realized it was not a return to Miller and Durrell, but to France and to Fanchette. The present asserted itself.

Jacques Senelier. He wrote me that during the war he had found in Algeria a copy of a torn magazine with a fragment of *Je Suis le Plus Malade des Surréalistes*. Found my name and address in *Two Cities*. He writes like an heir of Artaud.

I want to add another section to *Solar Barque*. But I have not been able to. I do believe that the constant flux of analysis keeps my vision rotating so rapidly that I have no time to transcribe reality before a new aspect of it emerges. I start with a character or a story and it changes every moment. Today I saw Henry's obsession with June's lying as a projection of his constant invention, only the world calls his lies creation and imagination, and poor June's mythomania.

Dinner with Renate and John. He is very tall, exceptionally beautiful, tousled wavy gold hair, clear, keen, sharp blue eyes, dazzling teeth, heavy eyebrows, a clear small-nosed profile, a full mouth curved like a woman's, radiantly young and clear-skinned. They are happy together. They went to Mexico. He describes how in the middle of a brutal game, with a hobnailed shoe hovering over his face, about to mutilate him, he asked himself: "What am I doing here, I am a poet."

Renate said: "You can't imagine the perfection of his body. He is a Greek god, flawless."

He wants to buy a boat and sail around the world.

Anaïs, begin a book.
Write.
Begin anywhere.
Begin with Lillian, after she returned from Golconda, having refused to talk to the doctor. Then the experience of his death shocked her out of her evasions and she began to talk, to see, to understand.
She went through the labyrinth.
She did not select the lie detector as a guardian, policeman, traffic director, chief of inner confusions, but as a sifter, a clarifier.
Lillian talked, talked through turns, twists, light and dark alleyways.
And Sabina appeared at last on a real stage and became famous. Not on Broadway but on off-Broadway stages. Her name was on the marquee of the same streets she had wandered through, a drug addict of love and erotica. She was not acting out her own nightmares, but those of Tennessee Williams. She acted them well.

I am imprisoned in the diary. Wherever I begin it leads me back to characters already painted.

I am submerged by the enormity of my material.

I have been spontaneous, capricious, for so long that I cannot construct.

Now will I construct a chaos of meaningless experiences as Kerouac does?

Where am I?

Am I seeking a rational construction like the continuity of Proust?

Kerouac lives in the present, but in fragments. But I see a connecting link between all these fragments.

I am reading Lawrence Lipton's book, *The Holy Barbarians.*

[Summer, 1959]

What should have been one of the most beautiful parties I ever attended turned out to be the greatest failure of all.

It was a beach party to which we were invited by Gil Henderson. Gil had designed a tent for a group of his friends. Each group had to build his own tent, and bring pennants. When we arrived, the pennants were flying gaily, all shapes and colors, some medieval, some modern. There were campfires, and inside the tents candles, in glass jars. There was music. The moon was high. The sound of the waves was gentle. It was a summer night.

At first we could not find Gil's tent, so we walked about asking for him. Young and beautiful people were lying about. But the astonishing, the shocking, the appalling thing to me was that they were all silent, without gaiety or interest in each other. No smiles, no laughter, no exuberance, none of that hungry curiosity about each other I was used to. They barely answered us, sullen and detached. It was as if they had drunk a potion of indifference. When we reached Gil's tent it was the same. No sparkle, no ignition, no life.

Gil grunted a welcome and then we became invisible. Olympia gave a pale smile.

I remembered Haitian parties, Tahitian parties, bohemian parties in Paris, Spanish parties, Italian parties, Cuban parties, Mexican parties; I remembered exuberance, the sensuous delight, the embracing, the spiritedness, the physical vibrations. Here there was plenty of music, plenty of wine, such a dreamlike setting, and no life. It never came to life.

I remembered my own description of the party no one attended. The disillusion was so great that I left early.

I was sent to Venice to cover fashions for magazines. When the train approaches Venice, it seems to be running on water because there is water on each side of the rails. The dream begins even in the train, as one leaves the earth to enter a new planet. Venice at night. In the train, across from me sat an Italian with gray hair, such a warm-toned skin and glowing eyes and resplendent teeth. We could not talk very much because I do not speak Italian, but with a few words in Spanish, and his few words in English we managed at least to create friendliness. I thought he was being kind to a weary woman. I understood his Italian. He was simple but all he said was alive. In tone, texture, physical presence. It was getting dark. It was he who opened the window so I could see the first lights of Venice.

The first layer of still water and the floating lights.

When we reached Venice he helped me get on the motorboat, carried my bag. And instead of saying goodbye he leaped on at the last minute and sat beside me, to see me safely to my hotel. And so I entered Venice properly welcomed with words of courtship. "I wish I could steal a million kisses!" I smiled behind my veil and wished instead I could concentrate on my first sight of Venice. Venice at night. Fluid, golden, all lights, and multiple reflections of lights, ghostly houses, a beauty one cannot seize at first because it is so subtle and intricate and has the evanescent quality of a dream. The laciness of the buildings, the sculptured modeling, the carvings, the statues, the trellises of shadows and white colonnades and such a fusion of a city and reflections of a city that half of it seems sunk into water. The music of the water, the slapping sound of the wavelets as the boats pass, against walls, bridges, and stairways. The long gliding black gondolas, the rhythm, the voices mingling, laughter, everything softened, flowing, muted by the presence of the water.

All this passed marvelously, delicate, accompanied by the Italian's courtship. The temperature of his feelings rose until I said someone is waiting for me; then he immediately vanished into the night after depositing me and my bag on the hotel landing.

The city which rose out of the sea has the wistful beauty of a dream about to vanish.

The ritual which is celebrated each year struck me with a poignant fear. A wedding ring is thrown into the sea to celebrate the wedding of Venice with the sea. But it seemed to me a wedding which might at any time submerge the bride and take her into the deeps forever. I had a fear of the city vanishing. Because it cradles emotion and the senses, stirs and lulls them, enchants and hypnotizes, one feels dissolved and melted into it. It is like Acapulco, not a city but a drug. The entire palette of chalky colors, all patined with gold, rocked by a constant rhythm and eddies around buildings, around the boats. As you sit in the gondola you are carried, swept along, lulled into passivity and contemplation.

Steps are worn by the licking waves, houses lean towards each other, spanned by lines of laundry. Children stare from balconies. Some deserted houses with nailed-down shutters, disintegrating. Then a window filled with flowers, another with a red brocade hanging to be sunned, another window revealing an inside room, candelabra and tapestries, or gaping into medieval darkness, with iron grilles. Some doorways are suppurating with age; others give their last rays of declining colors, the fading golds, the indescribable patina of time. Damp russets and mildews become rich brocades in the setting sun. Like a great courtesan, Venice changes its aspects, its costumes to please many lovers, but all of them, sad or gay, festive or somber, tragic or frivolous, have the sensuous texture of fruit, skin, flowers, of cotton or sand. The ornate façades are like the magnificent dresses of the Medicis, encrusted with jewels. On the black stones the rain creates snowy rivulets or capricious designs of its own making. Some roofs undulate, others shine softly, the balconies give animation, there is always a face peering, a child intensely curious or an old man or woman seeking a little sun. Both humble working Venice and elegant Venice expose their lives. The workmen carry meat on the barges, furniture, wine casks, fruit. Weddings appear suddenly on gondolas, or funerals, or two mythological aristocrats from the past decked in their finery going to the opera. The past and the present are superimposed, happen simultaneously. The destructive motorboats bring the ruthless present, destroy the dreamlike rhythm.

Descendents of pigeons once fed by Keats, Byron, George Sand, Chopin and many other famous lovers are still being fed, and the sudden sound when they all rise together, frightened away, is like the sound of giant sails flapping. Rituals and fiestas bring out the old costumes. The wooden poles to which they tie the gondolas are painted like striped candy bars. As the gondolas bob up and down when the *vaporetto* passes, they move like dancers in unison.

The waters from which the houses rise give them an ephemeral beauty as if they were ships which might pass on and vanish in the horizon. The variations of ornamentation make it difficult to recognize them, and when you seek to see the same house again you may have a sense of loss.

And the gondolas, though of similar design, are yet endlessly varied in tone and quality. They are black with silver tips shaped like profiles of warriors or fish or birds. Half-winged, they seem like birds skimming the water, barely touching the surface. There are the shining polished ones bearing aristocrats to fiestas. The silver tips are carved like an effigy, knife-sharp to cut a passageway. A red brocade is thrown over the seat; the aristocrats sit accepting one's stare but not looking back, legendary and symbolic. One gondola, draped in black and silver, carries the dead to the cemetery. One gondola carries the tourists, and they are raping the beauty with cameras. A gondola passes carrying garbage out to sea. A barge carries cement, bricks, fishing nets. A hospital gondola carries a woman in a coma, another gondola carries a policeman.

Hungry, lean dogs prowl the quays.

Some of the houses are workshops. They are printing newspapers in somber, high-ceilinged rooms, they are manufacturing glass, they are selling antiques. An ancient doll in a Medici dress leans out of the window. In one courtyard carpenters saw wood, in another they repair gondolas. Some of the canals are the canals of poverty; they are stagnant and narrow and the laundry hanging above receives no sun. Some are canals for tourists, and some are so beautiful, so secretive, so hidden in flowering bushes that they evoke instantly all the stories of passion one has read. The house of Byron, the house of Verdi, of Wagner, of Marco Polo, of Nietzsche, of Chopin and George Sand. The painters, the glass makers, the lace makers, the sculptors created a city which the sea plunges into the dream.

In charcoal-black doorways there are heavily grilled windows which suggest echoes of murders and cruelties that fill the history of Venice. But it is all outweighed by the beauty, and beauty always suggests life and passion. There is a way of molding a clay or cement or marble cornice which is like the caress of a lover. The sensuous accumulation of silk, gold, fuses with the dank vapors of past history. But in Venice one cannot experience the past as ashes because it is too powerful and it catches you by the throat. Rich lives exhale a perfume and it is not that of death. An accumulation of fervors can never suggest death. There are canals which shiver with mysteries but even if Venice should be swallowed by the sea, its disappearance hastened by the infamous motorboats, its past will remain as glittering as its lights.

At night the palaces are illumined and one can gaze into them through the many windows open to the canals. Vast rooms, walls covered with paintings, tapestries and murals, gold brocade curtains seeking to fly out of the windows, the last flutter of coquetry from a vanishing lady. The gondolas are ornamented with candlelight or Christmas lights on garlands of artificial flowers. Once I am sure they were banked with fresh flowers. But the gondolas which bore reclining figures on pillows, making love in the shelter of a rounded canopy with tiny side windows to spot a jealous husband, are not there. I discover the canopies stored away in a deserted courtyard. Are they to be brought out in the winter only, or has the art of lovemaking in a gondola vanished?

At night the gondolas grow mysterious, lit only by small lights. The silence as they glide is only broken by the cries of the gondoliers, announcing their arrival at a sharp turn of the canal or emergence from under a bridge.

Walking through the narrow streets one contacts the entire population. The shops are full of surprises. The restaurants smell of fresh fruit and wines. Harry's Bar shelters the international set dressed either in extravagant fashions or in jeans.

I entered a bookshop in the fashionable section to admire *Under a Glass Bell* in Italian, the title sounding so much lovelier, *La Campana di Vetro*. And outside, looking in longingly, was my Italian friend from the train journey. He mistook a casual friend for my lover and promptly disappeared. But while my friend was paying for a book, my Italian waited for me outside and with a swiftness and precision inherited from centuries of intrigue, he slipped me a little note which said: "Write to me!" and vanished into the crowd. Pure Italian romance.

One evening I sat at one of the red velvet upholstered cafés along the Piazza San Marco, all woodwork and bright red sofas. It looked like the backdrop for seduction found in eighteenth-century ribald stories.

Just as Venice offers the most gold-threaded, succulent brocades in all its Oriental wealth of gaiety, it offers too these prisons, alleys of medieval horrors. Dilapidated houses like ransacked tombs, water-sodden cellars, half-torn shutters, walls spattered by storms which seemed like the marks of bullets, leaning towers sinking into the mud, cobblestones dismantled by the tides. There were *"oubliettes"* where prisoners were forgotten and left to rot, some had traps in the middle through which the prisoner might be pushed into the canal.

I read Venice's history. It had horrors comparable to Hitler's crimes. The streets were made narrow on purpose to prevent invasion by armies. But this city of the past gave love stories as well as horrors, and today we are not even given the elements which can console one and help one to dream.

Met Sam Kramer, the filmmaker, who is here painting. He is married to a beautiful Danish girl. There is a law that the façades of old houses cannot be renovated but this very beautiful one was made livable by redesigning the inside. It is in the Academia quarter, the bohemian village of Venice. It is big, with all modern comforts, an enormous room overlooking a junction of two canals, for 67 dollars a month, furnished. For a moment I dreamed of living here. There is a bedroom for their child, one for them, a studio for him, a salon and dining room, and the incredible view! It is ten o'clock. Until now I have not heard any singing in Venice. But now the Serenade tour comes by, ten gondolas gliding very slowly, following the one on which their best singer stands at the prow. What singing! Cascading, with more power than the tender Mexican voices, operatic really, flamboyant voices, sending ripples of echoes down other canals. As I stand there I have that overflowing intensity, ecstatic dissolution I experience only at extremes of beauty or love, as in my first sight of Portofino from the boat, as during the soft nights in Acapulco, and I weep on the dark balcony, weep with joy. The Kramers have this every evening. He is studying guitar and they are both doing mosaics. The life of a modern artist in Venice.

Saw Peggy Guggenheim pass by in her private gondola with two private gondoliers dressed in white and crimson.

I pick up a wounded pigeon who is floating and save it from drowning. I am told there was a clinic for pigeons. I visit a hospital; once it had been a monastery. In the Middle Ages the nuns did all the nursing alone. Now it has a new wing and good modern doctors.

This city striving to rise out of the water each day has the magic which only the sea can create for it, has the same pulse as that of our heart and blood; it cradles emotions and the senses, it lulls them, enchants them, hypnotizes them. It is not a city but a drug.

In the sunlight the chalky colors are patined with gold, rocked by the rhythm of the tides which sway the houses and bridges. These are the canals of the womb. The sleep of the womb. The gondolas are so silky and quiet that you feel you are swimming through the water. You are carried on a current of passivity and contemplation.

In the sun it is an orgy for the eyes, a fiesta, a shimmering and tinkling of lights. Between the ochres and sepias, gray engraving smoke filters, faded corals and silky turquoise. Then suddenly a dark alleyway, mildewed, coal-dusted, pockmarked, a death alley, haunted by rats, scarred by past crimes. Deserted houses, crumbling, swallowed by the sea. A constant friction, an eternal wearing caress binds city and sea, the sea struggling to submerge Venice.

Some roofs are peaked, and some are flat, with crumbling edges. All of them house statues with missing noses, arms or legs. Some are those of the men who sang of Venice, painted it, wrote it, ruled it, and others demons and gargoyles, angels and saints. Some windows are boarded, some wide open. The balconies give them all expressions, a frown, an invitation or a secret.

The wooden poles painted like banderillas are planted in the canal to chain the gondolas at rest, but they still dance up and down, evenly, like a well-trained ballet.

The houses rising from the water have an ephemeral quality, as they seem to lack moorings, they seem as restless, as heaving as the gondolas.

The intricacy of an ornament has to be learned like a scroll and the differences between ornaments are elusive. The gondolas are black, like black swans flying over the surface of the water with their heads and necks thrust out, proudly. Other gondolas are covered with flowers and carry coffins to the cemetery. Others carry meat, bottles of wine, furniture, coal, garbage, statues. One of them carries a red velvet couch just freshly upholstered. Some, decorated like wedding cars, with artificial flowers and small lights, carry tourists about. Another gondola carries a wedding couple, half submerged in white flowers. Another carries extra chairs for the church, a woman who has fainted, cardinals. The heads of the gondolas carved like a warrior's helmet, sharp-profiled, cut a passageway through reflections, or at times through black canals like black mirrors.

What the sea carries away, the painters, the glass makers, the lace makers rebuild anonymously at night.

One still sees the medieval cruelty of Venice but this is outweighed by the lovers. The sensuous accumulations of silk, gold, lights, lovers, and water leave no ashes. Cities which have so rich a life exhale a perfume that is ever new.

Venice. The meaning of Venice. Even Proust, the hunter of meaning, did not uncover the meaning of Venice. It is not, as Chopin said, a city haunted by the past. It is a drama between city and sea, a struggle for a city to resist submersion; it contains both past and a vivid present, and for me the meaning lay in the ritual performed each year. Each year when a golden wedding ring is thrown into the canal, to signify the wedding of Venice to the sea, it is not a wedding, it is a fusion which threatens the existence of Venice, and some day Venice will lie at the bottom of the sea.

[Fall, 1959]

A long article about my work by Hugo Raes, a Belgian writer, in October issue of the *Vlaamse Gids*. Books translated into Dutch, *Ladders to Fire* and *Under a Glass Bell*.

Jean Fanchette is planning *Two Cities* number 3. Introduced Harry Partch to Peggy Glanville-Hicks and she responded as I did to his strange music. She said he was ahead of his time, and she will help him. She directs Composers' Forum and will also get Joaquin back for a concert. The meeting took place in that fabulous place I love, the sailmaker's loft down by the Battery. We saw a film made of Harry's work, his instruments, and how he wraps up and mails his own recordings as I did my own books. It seems that when he saw *The Pleasure Dome* he withdrew his music. It was the first time I heard it. It affected me like Balinese music. He lives on the sale of his recordings.

With the Barrons I visited Billy Kluver, a scientist, and his wife Hill. She came to see us today in a state of shock and threatening suicide again. "I have lost Billy. He really loves that woman in Paris. I don't want to live." Looking down, childlike, doll-like, with a small turned-up nose. So this morning I had to take her to a psychiatrist. The last time she only survived because Billy came back for something he had forgotten and he was able to take her to the hospital and have her stomach pumped. I tried to tell her it was wrong to give Billy a sense of guilt for the rest of his life for something he could not help, falling in love with another woman. He loves her so much he is willing to fly all night to spend a day with her and fly back in time for work.

I asked John to write the story of how a football hero suddenly became a poet. He writes these touching words: "The story led me by its kind hand, so I followed, but a little frightened because of some of the dark shadows, for I am seeing as a child and still afraid of the dark. And he talked to me like a stranger from the paper but I enjoyed the conversation. I hope he visits me again soon."

The five novels are out in one volume, *Cities of the Interior*. I read at the Becks' Living Theatre. I read the Party Scene at the end of *Ladders to Fire*. There was an opening at the Guggenheim Museum the same night, which put my friends in a terrible spot, but they all came, faithfully, warmed up the hall, no defections! One person came with a two-month-old baby, who cried until I began to read. There was a parrot in the entrance hallway which had to be covered. They serve coffee and sell books. Good atmosphere. The Becks' last play, *The Connection,* got the worst reviews any play ever had. It was gruesome but exceedingly well done. Between the acts, the actors went about pretending to be drug addicts and begging for a fix. But they got one good review from the *New Yorker,* so all uptown people are now coming to see it, and for the first time the poor things are making money. I remember the days when they collected bottles of milk from all the floors of their apartment house to feed the actors while they rehearsed.

Caresse came, the day before entering the hospital for a cataract operation, telling the story of the castle she bought for fifteen thousand dollars, a historic monument between Rome and Spoleto. She is having the roof repaired to make it livable. Three hundred and sixty rooms! She just had the imagination to get it, to persuade the Italian government to repair the roof (once the roof goes, the whole castle falls into ruins; I saw that so often in France; the castle walls of stone endured, but once the roof caved in, the rain would erode from within and soon the whole castle would tumble). Her relatives and friends will share the cost of making certain parts habitable. We are all sending books for her library. It is to be the home of "Citizens of the World" and "Women for Peace." She invites us all to stay there, in the summer when it is habitable. She offers wine and spaghetti. She is no longer wealthy but she has a genius for living (as Varda has with even less money). What a spirit she has, half blind and unable to climb steps because of her bad heart.

All seats were sold. I gave a good reading. The Becks said I had the power to create magic without acting.

Lecture Monday at City College. And what do you think they invented to draw a crowd? "Anaïs Nin will talk about Kerouac." I was very angry.

I discuss with Bogner the unfortunate habit I have of cutting off friendships as soon as someone hurts me or betrays me. If they damage, disappoint me, I pack off and leave, and that is no solution. Even my novels are full of "cuts." "Cut!" says director Nin, as if it were a film being made, and one could cut out people's cruelties or thoughtlessness.

"You want so deeply to relate to others," says Dr. Bogner, "but your vulnerability and your fears of damage make you withdraw, separate, break off. Everybody sooner or later commits what you call treachery. In the case of Jean Fanchette asking for more and more financial help, why don't you explain that you cannot give it, that you have worked very hard for the magazine and all you can give is your time and energy. Instead you feel hurt and begin to withdraw. Durrell probably told him you were well off. You told me he has always spread that story of your wealth. Fanchette may have believed him."

By cutting off friendships you create your own solitude. After this talk I dreamed I was beset by bees and had to defend myself. Relationships which fed on me, stung me?

Every letter is a request, a demand, every telephone call is a call for help, every activity becomes an unbearable burden. The work for *Two Cities* took all my time, stopped my writing.

In the mail, a letter from Fanchette asking me to advance him 100 dollars, which the Phoenix Book Shop has not paid him. Sara Berenson: "Please read my story which *Evergreen* turned down, I need your encouragement." Gil asks me: "Show the slides of my paintings to the New York galleries."

I dream of carrying a bomb.

Living Theatre in debt so of course I will not be paid for my reading, which filled the theatre.

I write to Fanchette truthfully, but I do not break.

Evidently I am trying to change a pattern and it is complicated. The new one is not yet born. It was I who said: "I identify with the taker. I prefer to be the one who gives."

Daisy Aldan and Serge Gavronsky will be co-editors of *Two Cities*.

One more evening of Japanese films. The magic quality and the poetry. External beauty, conflict between exquisite form and violence. There is a constant element of surprise, of the incredible. The hero is always engaged in a single-handed sword battle against fifty enemies but he always wins. The scenes in the theatre become scenes in the life dramas. The actor turns out to be a Prince who has run away. They announce a spectacle. At six oclock the Princess will arrive. It is a real Princess who arrives trying to escape her pursuers. The Prince-actor is the best swordsman. But all of them can leap in the air to the roof and escape. All of them are masters of disguise, men into women, or into actors. Magicians are numerous. Ambushes, intrigues, counterplots, a jail (made of wood) burning, lovers in a boat which looks like a paper boat, lighted with candles, cellar jails, new forms of fighting, throwing chains and darts. A world of constant metamorphosis almost entirely based on fairytales. Intrigues so intricate, I never know what they are, but happy endings are certain. There is always a surprise, a fiesta, a marionette show, a scene from a play, a temple with people praying. The costumes are endlessly beautiful and varied. The women are never undressed. The comics, like Shakespeare, are always from the people and always picture fear, cowardice or greed. The greatest charm in men and women until faced with battle. Then an amazing ferocity appears. Last night a woman samurai. In periods of violence the houses are slashed to pieces, panels fall, screens of great beauty are pierced with swords. In between, gentleness, music, poetry. Codes of honor. They easily give up life when they lose face or are defeated.

One day in autumn, I remember walking with Daisy Aldan at our second meeting, after corresponding. I remember it was a wistful walk, because we were both overwhelmed with the actual work of self-publishing.

Her poems are of the finest quality, published in small magazines, and she did much for other poets and artists through *Folder Editions*. Yet she has to do her own publishing, and neither one of us can find a distributor who will take over the chores of disseminating books, dealing with bookshops. What we discovered is that bookshops are afraid to leave bills from big publishers unpaid, as their book supplies will be cut off, but are not afraid to ignore bills from small magazines and self-publishers. They know we have no power. The labor is overwhelming.

On that first walk Daisy and I shared our disappointments and our difficulties. We established empathy. But actually Daisy is a very spirited and cheerful young woman, who has been an actress, who studied with Anna Balakian and might have been the first woman to do a study of American surrealist writers. She teaches creative writing at the New York High School of Art and Design, where the students are exceptional and are prepared to enter the art fields. She is teaching my stories from *Under a Glass Bell*. She now shares the editing of *Two Cities*.

I wrote to Fanchette that I could no longer carry the editorship of *Two Cities*. I promised that when I came across good writing I would send it to him. What happened with Fanchette was that he never returned material sent to him, or answered my friends, and I was losing friendships because I would encourage them to mail stories, photographs, poems, and nothing would either come back or be published.

I begged him to send me the material he did not want to use. I explained I was losing friends and creating enemies for *Two Cities*. No answer.

I sent important things: stories by Maude Hutchins, a translation by Louise Varèse of Michaux's *Miserable Miracle,* and Daisy sent articles and poems. We are trying to divide the labor of reading into three parts.

Fanchette writes me: "If you give up *Two Cities* it is the end of our friendship."

I recommend Anna Kavan to my very active Belgian critic, Hugo Raes: Anna Kavan, William Goyen, Isabel Bolton, Maude Hutchins, Djuna Barnes. He writes to Anna Kavan, and she answers *Asylum Pieces* is out of print. He can't find any of the books except Djuna Barnes' *Nightwood*.

Daisy is selling *Under a Glass Bell* to her students at cost.

Jim is finishing a novel, *All Fall Down*. He feels that my novels gained in being printed together. "The pattern you were creating seems to define itself by the association of its parts. Each part is stronger in this context than when it stands alone."

I had read a fragment from a novel *Miss MacIntosh, My Darling,* by Marguerite Young in *New World Writing*. It was extraordinarily imaginative and poetic. The writing flowed like mercury, and the atmosphere was elusive and seductive. I decided to look her up. We had met once, before she left for Italy. She had accepted a fragment from *Children of the Albatross* for *The Tiger's Eye* when she was one of the editors.

Her smile and her talk are enchanting. They are a continuation of her writing, an accompaniment to it. There is an extraordinary force of imagination and language there.

On her father's side she is a relative of Brigham Young, the Mormon. She talks lovingly about her grandmother. Her grandmother raised her. She is dedicating her book to her. She has been at work on this book for years. She lives in a decor which is reminiscent of childhood, antiques, love seats, sofas, chairs, little tables, artificial flowers, dolls, stars, bonbonnières, boxes, lamps, statuettes. Partly a child's playroom, with a collection of dolls, dolls' houses and doll's furniture, a horse from a merry-go-round, tin soldiers, old photographs. It is crowded and nestlike.

Her hair hangs absolutely straight on each side of her face. She monologues, without pauses. Her talk is like her writing: it proliferates, each cell leading to another cell, one character growing out of the other by a chain of associations.

She has studied philosophy and history. She abandoned lyric poetry because her love of human beings and interest in history could not be contained in poems. She considers the novel the modern epic poem.

Everyone in her eyes is beautiful. She endows all her friends with beauty; but her own charm lies in the kaleidoscopic variations of her imagination, her power of storytelling, her human warmth. She uses the word both symbolically and physically. She is related to Melville and to Boswell, Lord Byron, Jane Welsh Carlisle and Knox. She makes one think of Beethoven, and in her crowded room, she seems a giant who has strayed into a child's room. She has beautiful hands, slender, well shaped, aristocratic.

When I arrived in this curiosity shop, treading carefully so as not to upset vases, flowers, pennants, paintings and books which overflowed from the bookcase, she was annoyed because she had been revising the six-hundredth page of her book and had found repetitions.

"The subconscious repeats itself," I said, "so does poetry."

Of my writing she said: "Controlled wildness." And she praised its stylization; "I'm tired of slovenly writers like Kerouac," she said.

We agreed that the unconscious is not slovenly. That improvisation and spontaneity did not need to be slovenly. I like the pulsing rhythm of Kerouac.

She was ambivalent about the attitude of her students and friends who kept asking: "You haven't finished your book yet?" It irritated her, and yet she admitted that she lived inside of her book and was happy while writing, and was in no hurry to finish it, still writing every day from nine to five.

A friend of hers, a Viennese psychoanalyst, said later that she would never finish it, that it had become a way of life, that she was satisfied while she was working, which was true, but that psychologically she would never let go of it. He felt I might be useful to Marguerite if I urged her to finish this book she has been writing for so many years. Marguerite said today: "Anaïs, you are wise. You know that the true experience is in the writing, and there should be no haste to publish the incomplete, the half-realized, the wholly adventitious. The love you gave me through all my life is to me the most precious gift. Like my Scottish ancestors you keep your eye on the golf ball like a good golf player and your ego is totally lost in the worship of art itself, regardless of the infinity of the green course, the turf which meets the surf as at St. Andrews."

I do not know yet why I have retained from childhood the fear of imagining and inventing, which I did plentifully at the time even though I was scolded for this. Did I feel it would carry me away from human life? In New York, in the brownstone house, when a room was unrented, I would slip into it, and indulge, alone, in deep states of reverie I would today call the waking dream. I felt then a kind of drunkenness.

One day I awakened to my mother's need of me. Reveries lessened. I gave myself to my task, first of being a second mother to my two brothers, then to earning a living.

I clung to the diary as reality. It was my way to make contact with my daily earthly life. I somehow began to equate the imaginative work of man with a separation from human life. Man the creator was not human, not as human as my unimaginative mother.

In any case, I devoted myself to the diary and did not attempt fiction until Henry prodded me into it. Or else until I felt tired of my secret life.

When I met Marguerite Young the old anxiety returned. She is, in my mind, a genius. Again the gift for invention, for imaginative treatment of history, for flights of fantasy seemed daring to me and connected with her distance and separation from ordinary human daily happenings. She was interested in politics, passionately so. She was loving and affectionate with students and friends. But she lived in a world of her own and her descriptions of people did not seem to fit them. They are not faithful. They are fiction.

She described herself as Raggedy Ann.

The work of imagination might be said to be one long dream, as in the case of James Joyce, but even though he allowed himself automatic play on words to lead him into unusual images, he gave the outpourings a form taken from the structure of the myth.

Marguerite Young does not use old myths to hang her reveries on. She uses folklore, her knowledge of American life and characters drawn from the very earthy Middle West, from Indiana where she was born.

The folkloric stock characters of *Miss MacIntosh, My Darling* are revealed not to be stock characters at all because she goes deep inside of them, and if you go deep inside, nobody is ordinary or simple. There lies the uniqueness of her work. The suffragette, the bone breaker, the bible salesman, the country doctor, the old maid, the nurse. All of them in her hands become extraordinary.

She will be what Cervantes was for Spain, and Joyce for Ireland.

Whenever I come to New York now, Marguerite Young reads to me from her book over the telephone. The main theme seems to be Illusion and Reality. But there are no boundaries. I am becoming acquainted with a multitude of characters, allegorical, symbolic, comical, extravagant. Her eloquence animates all of them. At last, an eloquent writer, not a stutterer, not a clipped, denuded one. No telegraphic tap-taps. But fullness and expansion. She catches them at first on the surface of a prosaic life, then plunges them into the waters of the unconscious, and astonishing personages appear. There is a recurrent theme of drowning, drowning in the oceanic unconscious. Characters like the old country doctor who took care of everybody, but who while traveling through a storm at night in his battered Ford drowned; but one is not certain he drowned into reality or just into hallucinations. The drowning and the dreaming exist in every character. When the doctor disappears in the flood waters he goes on answering calls from people who never called him.

Perhaps all things are illusion, this crying, this crumbling, this falling away, this vanishing, this revelation of that which is no more, and there is nothing given but this dream. Perhaps this dream is not given but earned.

I like to watch women at work, I like to write about one of the most extraordinary women of our times, a woman who will be one day as much studied, analyzed, interpreted, commented upon as James Joyce. And not because of scholarship, linguistic acrobatics, play on semantics, intellectual prestidigitations, but because she creates a complete, entire and immense world of her own, a world of dreamers. In this world she has installed herself as comfortably as any Middlewesterner installs himself in the harsh daily realities. She is at ease; she can take off her shoes in the heart of the dream as in the center of the most ordinary events. The entire book is one long dream, in which even the animals partake of this ability. Through the entire journey, illusion and reality are dramatically questioned. Readers are so lazy today; but more than lazy, they are afraid to enter worlds vaster and more complex than their own. And a world entirely composed of dreams which never end and from which no one awakens is beyond their courage. A small fragment of a dream, a minor one, an interrupted one is reassuring. But a dream which is unbroken seems dangerous.

The dreamer was untouchable, taboo, weak, escapist, to be discarded. In Marguerite Young's book he reappears in all his splendor.

The typical characters are cracked open and reveal a metaphysical universe, proving the startling magnitude of the unconscious content of the most ordinary human being. New lands. New archeology of the soul, a new vision. Someone wrote lately that the sign of the creative mind was its ability to make new connections, new relations not made before. That is Marguerite Young. Because of the depth, because all the characters are plunged into the ocean of the unconscious, the journey gives me a sense of timelessness and space such as is given to us in the outer world by the scientists. Marguerite can start with a man going through his old check stubs, proceed to the other side of the mirror and into a metaphysical journey.

She has been able to cut the umbilical cord which ties woman to human reality, she has given full rein to the imagination, but as she says: "No matter how far imagination carries us, this wave of living fable, it must always return to shore." Shore is humanity. The shore is Marguerite walking the streets of the Village in New York to eat her breakfast at the Bloom brothers' drugstore. It is Marguerite walking along Bleecker Street looking into the windows of antique shops for more dolls to add to her collection.

Her apartment is a paradise for a dreamer or a child. The predominant color red gives it a Christmas mood. The merry-go-round horse has a fine long silver mane. Mobiles, chimes; there is so much to see that one can only remember a few objects at a time. By some touching, unconscious modesty, the table on which she does her heavy voluminous work is a shaky old card table always about to fold up and give up.

Who has ever encountered an old maid, a suffragette like Cousin Hannah, who had "wished to overthrow man," and yet left, when she died, a trunk filled with forty wedding dresses? The story, like all others in *Miss MacIntosh,* is based on reality.

Who has ever made a journey through the mother's ear?

Who has ever met a Mr. Spitzer, the surviving member of identical twins, who is never sure which one died and which one lived? Mr. Spitzer is a lawyer, a respected citizen yet an oddity in his own right. His brother was a gambler, a member of the underworld. But the gambler continues to intrude in the identity of the lawyer until it seems to the lawyer that his brother the gambler is alive and that he himself is dead. He is his own brother. Each one of us contains his opposite. They had built a twin house. Mr. Spitzer was always trying to separate his own knowledge of musical composition from his gambler brother's knowledge of natural sounds, such as his imitation of a moose call, which he swore was answered several times by a real moose in the streets of Boston.

Marguerite tells me: "Our predominant art is poetry. Fantasy to the point of madness. Europe has stability, tradition, art forms, architecture, rituals, social classes, patterns, structures. America has nothing, only freeways, supermarkets. So an American can be anything. He is more fantastic. He only has the WORD."

Another time she said: "I want to dramatize obsession. When I get hold of a character I have to play it to the very end until I trap the obsession."

Where else would you meet in literature a hangman who took up his profession out of humanitarianism? Because he knew he could tie the knot and kill without causing pain. No one he ever hanged came back to complain about his technique. When his first wife hanged herself, he shook his head and commented: "It was a most unskillful job."

Today when I picked up the telephone to call Marguerite I heard a full description of the death of the last passenger pigeon, a prophecy of what might happen to all the pigeons of New York City.

I am reminded of Lewis Carroll, other times of Charlie Chaplin. Marguerite, wearing comfortable shoes, reading the newspapers, listening to Long John at night when sleepless, eating in drugstores with a Middlewesterner's ease in homely worlds, while continuing to dream as Don Quixote did, as Thurber did.

We often discuss expansion, because she expands to the very limit and I condense. She said once in defense of her proliferation: "I just try to put down every pebble on the road so that no one can get lost."

Her feeling is that if one is to follow the full expansion of a flight of imagination it is necessary to complete the cycle. Joyce is not her model. America is her ideal. Its vast spaces, its gigantic expansion. A book must match its size and vastness.

The first twelve years of her life were given to poetry. As a child even, she wrote so much that the papers would be spread all over the floor of the living room, and her grandmother would tell callers they had to enter by the back door because "my granddaughter is writing." She could have papered the walls with them.

Very American too, her concern with history and politics. Her first prose poem was a study of the first socialist town of Harmony, Indiana, on the banks of the Wabash—the scene of two utopias, that of Father George Rapp, mystic of Württemberg, and that of Robert Owen, father of the British labor movement. She knew this town intimately.

I would always begin her portrait with her very delicate and fine hands and matching feet, when she kicked off her shoes as she reached home. Then with her voice, which has a chanting quality, like James Joyce's, revealing that her writing has a musical tone, which is a kind of canto.

"Mr. Spitzer," she announces over the telephone, "dead for the last time." It was a mournful day, when Mr. Spitzer finally died.

The same day I was walking along Houston Street looking for a famous "Fix It" place. There are several tomb designers on that street. In one of the windows was a marble tombstone engraved: SPITZER.

A beehive of images, a work with a disappearing shoreline, like Calderón's *La Vida Es Sueño*. America, her great love—its comic spirit, its playfulness. She revealed to me an America I could love.

"The sea is not harmful if you sleep under it, not over it, best place for keeping pearls."

That is where I feel Marguerite sleeps.

Someone asked her: "Do you love children?"

"Of course I love them. My children are all the letters of the alphabet."

She talks about the visitors she might have had. I can well imagine Henry James fascinated with her erudite conversation.

"I never have anything but artificial flowers in case Proust should visit me. He was allergic to fresh flowers." In honor of Poe, she dusts an old stuffed raven. Irene Rice Pereira gave her, in celebration of *Miss MacIntosh,* her painting of doves. She loves Dreiser because he too was a Hoosier. "He is part of our tradition. The Middle West has a peculiar history. Indiana had a strange conglomeration of pioneers, disillusioned French idealists, lovers of Rousseau, sophisticated Europeans, Utopians, individualists." She also loves St. Augustine, Berkeley, Bishop Hume, Laurence Sterne, Blake, Melville and Henry and William James. One day after talking I said: "I'm going back to my submarine world."

Marguerite said: "Your periscope is showing."

There is nothing more wonderful than a writer who creates a complete, well-rounded world, who demonstrates the power of man's imagination to create a new planet. Marguerite is a new planet. The scientists are not alert enough to planets created by the imagination, on which human life can thrive.

Marguerite reveals to me an America I once knew as a teen-ager, when I fed on Emerson, Poe, Melville, Whitman and the concept of transcendentalism. When I returned from Europe, I found an

America that seemed to have gone in the opposite direction in literature. Anti-poetic, anti-spirit, anti-metaphysical.

My discovery of Marguerite is not only that of an individual but of America, the comic spirit of America, the poetic imagination of America.

Marguerite believes in doing things thoroughly. When she contemplated suicide at an early age, Werther's age (for she had been a child orphaned by her parents' divorce when she was three), she studiously worked out a method which could not fail, a three-way project. A teen-ager then, she was going to prepare a noose, but before letting herself fall and strangle she was going to take poison and slash her wrists. The noose was also hung from a tree branch over a river, so that she would be sure to drown. To prepare herself, however, for the departure, she sat down to write a poem, a suicide note for the world, and by the time the long poem was written she had experienced the suicide emotionally and it did not need to be carried out.

For those who are so vociferous in their war against poetry, let them contemplate for a moment a dreamless world such as the one depicted by the newspapers. For those who consider the dream a peculiarity, an eccentricity, given to the few as a form of madness, let them contemplate a poet who proves the existence of the dreamer in the most ordinary man, the power of the most ordinary man to exist on several levels, tragedy and comedy, absurdity and depth. It is betrayed by night dreams, by reveries, by obsessions.

To the question we all have asked in the midst of tragedy or comedy: What is reality? Marguerite answers: "Man's dreams. Without them he is lost." "If only a frog had died, if no one else had ever died, if all had been perfection, changeless and unchanging, he probably would still have been the universal mourner," she writes of the pseudo-musician Mr. Spitzer.

"Do you have doubts, Marguerite?"

"Oh, yes, everyone has at moments. Only the mediocre never have doubts."

"The doubts you may have, Marguerite, are because you live so deeply inside the subconscious stream that you do not know how it sounds to others. And then what people are most frightened of is what you constantly describe: metamorphosis; everything is in the process of becoming something else."

Sometime before the death of Mr. Spitzer I said to her: "You'll soon be at the end of Mr. Spitzer."

"I don't want to," said Marguerite. And I understood then how vividly she lived with her characters, they were living organisms, incorporated into her life, a part of it, as difficult to part with as a relative, a friend.

"He comes back at the end of the book."

A refusal of ultimate death. Death and separation equal. What power the poet has to repudiate a physical world and assert a metaphysical one.

When Mr. Spitzer finally died Marguerite said: "Mr. Spitzer is the only composer I know and he is dead."

I answered: "Nobody is definitely dead. I'm not one for conclusions, I love basking in uncertainty. You said he would return at the end of the book."

"Elizabeth Hardwick is anti-poetic," I said once, referring to her literalness.

"I don't think she has even that amount of conviction."

Marguerite gave a party, although she said she did not enjoy her own parties. "A party is a gift to my friends."

She said she could not keep a diary because she was "devoid of personal life. I am never introspective about myself. I delve into others. I think it is sad that I should not explore myself in an autobiographical sense. I am not aware of how it happened. I'm totally diffused into the writing, that is where I exist as a human being."

"You built a world."

"I either had to do that or disappear."

When she writes about Esther Longtree she "is known for her everlasting pregnancy and her loving heart which knew no lover." The everlasting pregnancy is Marguerite's vast work, interminable, timeless. It is of Mr. Spitzer that she writes: "Perhaps his sympathies always would be with those who had missed their loves . . . with musicians who had lost their harps, bridge menders who had lost their bridges, great warriors who had won every battle but the last one, great lawyers who had lost their clients for whom they had drawn up testaments and wills leaving their properties which were never theirs to leave. Mr. Spitzer having come upon some remarkable instances of the non-existent leaving their non-existent properties to the non-existent whom he had traced for years before he had found out that they were not real."

Marguerite was amazed that I had made up my face when I thought I would die in stillbirth. This aesthetic discipline which carries over into nonexistence. Painted eyelashes, painted lips. This kind of trait would be understandable only to the Japanese, for whom aesthetics is a form of religion.

At times the American indifference to aesthetics and the European obsession with it clash. She does not care where she eats, does not mind clatter and homeliness.

"Being deprived by nature of normal motherhood I took up giving birth to characters."

Suddenly I understood why she would not part with her book or finish it. She enjoyed the state of pregnancy.

Marguerite thinks it is strange that instead of wailing, sobbing at the stillbirth experience, I find a moment of ecstasy, even in that.

"Because I always had a sense of the mythological nature of experience. I always leaped just in time from under the crushing weight of human sorrows into mythology, our mythological journey."

Marguerite said: "A search for God?"

"Oh, no, for oneness with others, and with nature. God to me has become the figure of a most unsatisfactory father. I learned to live without him."

We compare her playing upon characters endlessly and my letting go of them. She says the pursuit of psychological icons and motives and the search for the ultimate flowering are necessary to describe obsession. She feels we are all obsessed. "Obsession does not let go of us."

Her roots are so native, yet I feel she is unique.

"Every real writer is unique," said Marguerite. "Where he comes from is not as important as racial memories, which reach into antiquity or prefigure the future."

Marguerite reminds me of Calderón's *Life Is a Dream*.

Long ago Otto Rank, who had written so much about the artist, stated that woman had not created imaginative works such as *Don Quixote* or *Ulysses* because she feared to cut the umbilical cord, to separate from the human and the personal. I had this fear. Out of it was born the diary.

Marguerite solved this by developing a cellular structure, an unbroken cellular development, a vast mesh which would capture everything rather than separate, divide. She *englobed*. The female need to nourish, to encompass, to hold, commune with, was fulfilled in the spider-like web. Thus was life contained, no intellectual invention like Joyce's, every beginning taken from life and then magnified, expanded, but rooted in some natural seed: a newspaper clipping, people she had known or had read about, anecdotes, history, biography. Her research in her reading is extensive. Every character and event in the book is interconnected, interrelated by associative thinking. So she had no need to cut the umbilical cord and seek abstraction.

The occasional chill I feel in the corridors of her ghostly voyages is that the unfamiliar invisible spirit life touches us with such concrete fingers that we grow fearful of its power.

Language used to hypnotize. Her work is a symphony. She is the acrobat of space, flying from image to image, word to word in an unbroken rhythm.

She includes the crippled, the blind, the deaf, the mute, the failures, the eccentrics. She writes lovingly of defects, about weddings that never took place, mirages, confusion of identities, hallucinations, nightmares.

Saw a film of Tennessee Williams', *Orpheus Descending* [*The Fugitive Kind*]. The cameraman, Kaufman, is a poet. The young man who wrote the script is Meade Roberts. There is a wonderful scene in the cemetery when the girl says: "Do you hear the dead talk?"

"The dead don't talk," answers the young man.

"Oh, yes they do, they say LIVE LIVE LIVE LIVE." In the end it turns into Grand Guignol, but the early part is good, and Magnani and Joanne Woodward are excellent. Even Marlon Brando takes it to heart and does not ham it up.

Ottone Riccio, the poet, writes: "The poem's blade cuts deep." I write him that I do not believe in too much revision. The material begins to wither in your hand. It is best to go on, and try anew so that it keeps its freshness for you. It is when you get tired of it that it withers. As long as you are vitally interested, it will remain alive.

———

Maude Hutchins lives in a world of total silence around her work and I am trying to awaken waves and vibrations around her.

Though Daisy is now the official editor of *Two Cities*, we continue to collaborate in every way possible.

I write to a woman editor that it would be such a relief to publish some women's writings, Maude Hutchins, Anna Kavan, Isabel Bolton, Marguerite Young. Such a relief from the violence, war, rape, castration, cannibalism that we are getting.

Answer to letter from poet in prison:

It is true I do not have much time for letters and that after writing all day I would rather hear music, talk to friends, or see Japanese films (Los Angeles has such a large Japanese population that I can see four films a week, beautiful ones, and so complex in plot that it becomes a challenge to unravel them). But as I know you are deprived of all this I like to bring you news. How do you keep so well informed on books, magazines, theatre, films?

The prejudice you speak of, against ex-cons, is there, but the world is full of prejudice of all kinds and one learns to live in spite of them. There is a way of reversing the negative aspects of violence. It can become the active will of the artist, the assertion of creative power. We have so much crime because commercialism, technology, has destroyed man's creative abilities. If you can't create, you destroy. I have been reading many biographies of the French artists: Modigliani, Dégas, Toulouse-Lautrec, Picasso, Utrillo. There is a vast difference between them and the Beats. They produced, created and lived so fully that there was no destructiveness in them except that created by hunger and poverty. So much of their drinking was caused by the necessity to keep warm in heatless studios.

Just read the life of Suzanne Valadon, the mother of Utrillo, model, painter, mistress. When you come out think of the legend of the Eskimos, who believe that no matter what they have done in the past they need only climb to the top of a mountain, discard their old name, adopt a new one and when they walk down the other side they leave their former self behind.

The prison does not allow him to send out his poetry or I might get it into *Two Cities*. He has been jailed for eight years for violence.

[Winter, 1959–1960]

Jim finishes his polished version of *All Fall Down*. Daisy Aldan, now American editor of *Two Cities,* sends Fanchette poems and photographs of quality.

The students of the New York High School of Art and Design ask me to come and talk to them. "We like you, Anaïs Nin, you're new, refreshing, unconventional. We'd like to be too. Help us."

Letter to Jim:

This is a difficult letter to write and I hope you will bear with me. Because I love you so deeply I cannot lie to you. Take into account the world I have lived in, and the one you cover in *All Fall Down*. It is so alien to me I cannot feel for it. I am limited and tone deaf, and my remarks about the novel will be of no value. So when I say I cannot feel it, do not be distressed. From the beginning, you remember, we had a discussion about your putting yourself inside of little people. This is what you have done now in this novel, and even though I know the theme of the brother's love is deeply felt by you, I still could only regret that it should be imbedded in such limited, shrunken, inarticulate, almost subnormal people. Why, why, I wondered, must we put such emotional experiences of complex feelings in such characters? I do not overlook the humor, and I am fully aware that it is precisely the lives of such people which interest you, fascinate you, and that thousands will love you for it, will recognize themselves, perhaps, or their neighbors, so that my responding or not, in the end, is of no importance. I wanted to say something because I love you, I believe in your writing, I believe in you, in your intelligence, perception, and intuitions. I cannot question why these people interest you. It seems like deliberately putting one's bigger self inside of dwarfs, mental dwarfs. But this is something one has no right to quarrel with. I am only mentioning it to justify my incapacity to respond to the novel, to become involved in the feelings. The characters seem stunted and half-alive. But so were Sherwood Anderson's people. You have a perfect right to choose them, to devote care and skill to their stories. They may appear worthy of it to many people. They seem quite incredible to me.

Letter from Jim:

Your letter is beautiful and courageous, and it means more to me than any other I have received from you in the last two or three years, or perhaps even longer. It has a vitality of the sort our correspondence has lacked recently—partly, perhaps, because our lives have taken us to different corners of the earth—but more likely the deeper reason is that our world, as artists, seems to have developed in disparate ways; and perhaps we feel that this might be a threat to our friendship, our human relationship which is deeper and more important than our artistic connection. But I feel that you have broken this fear for us, and have proven that our concern for one another on that level was unnecessary. You wrote me with love and respect—and in those terms, in that framework, there is nothing I could not accept from you, even your quite severe criticism. Because I know that you would offer it with love, I felt quite safe in inviting it and as I expected it has been meaningful to me in an extraordinary way; it has forced me to a reaffirmation of my own values, my own vision. Nothing could be more vital to any artist. You have done all this for me, and I feel I must do the same for you: answer you with equal honesty, love, courage.

I must begin by telling you that I understand your inability to respond to my novel [*All Fall Down*]: an alien world of alien manners, language. Your own life was formed in the artist's world. In your childhood and throughout your life you have been forced to reject the ordinary, the subordinary, the "oatmeal" people as you call them. One of the miracles of our relationship has always been that these two backgrounds had found such a vital connection in us; we have often remarked on the twinship of spirit that has survived these contrasts. Through you, I have learned much about the workings of the artist, the artist in others and in myself, the processes of the artist, his spirit and psychology, his endless discontent and the creation it fosters. This is the province of your work and the scope of your influence; it is your specialty, as they say, and you are magnificently qualified for it; no one else touches this material with even comparable incisiveness, power, beauty. I am talking about the material of your work, which is the artist himself, not his product. Your greatest body of work, your major achievement, is the journal itself, in which you have made palpable the very spirit of the artist; and as far as I know, no one in history has produced the equal of it. You say in your letter that this work, or this life (they are interchangeable in the journal) has given you a kind of blindness, tone deafness, to certain other worlds. You even say that there are kinds of human beings, "limited, inarticulate, shrunken, dwarfed," who are not worth writing about. Can you mean it? Is there such a thing on earth as a human being of so little value that he is outside of a writer's focus? Did I misunderstand you?

Letter to Jim:

I did not mean that, Jim. I often wrote about what we call the under-dogs with sympathy and love: the mouse in the houseboat, the ragpickers, the madman, etc. In daily life, I am in tune with non-artists, with Milli-cent's life in Harlem, with the life of taxi drivers, doormen, handymen, carpenters. But there are times when a world is alien to one, and one fails to empathize. I could not feel for Main Street, for the puritans, for the repressed characters of some Middlewestern novels. It is true your char-acters did not touch me. It is my loss. Everything which happens to you touches me. I should extend that to the characters who occupied your life or your interest. Don't worry too much about it. We all have our blind spots, or areas of unresponsiveness. I was trying to explain even to myself, why I respond so much to your diary, and less to the novels and plays. I could only explain it in terms of "foreign worlds." Just as my artist world is foreign to so many Americans. The reason must be that you are an artist, struggling for expression and to be re-created into an articulate, fer-tile writer. But losing me as reader of your novels is a small loss, when you have gained my personal love, and respect for your diary writing, which, after all, is more you than the novels.

I do not overlook the humor, and the fact that thousands of people will recognize themselves in your characters and love you for it. I believe in you, your writing. I should not question why these people interest you.

Letter to Jim:

You were right in doubting I could mean: There are kinds of human beings, limited, inarticulate, shrunken, dwarfed, who are unworthy of the serious attention of literary creation. No, I did not mean that. My first letter was emotional, and you know why; I feared that these differences would threaten our relationship, and I overstated the case. I mean some-thing else. (You remember I criticized people who objected that Proust wrote about society people or homosexuals, or those who objected to my writing about artists.) I feel that in choosing people of such limitation, you deliberately shut off an enormous part of your richness, of your potentiali-ties. Take, for example, your personal eloquence, your flights and improvi-sations, or the relationships around you, so subtle and intricate, which you described so well in your diary. I feel that you chose too limited a char-acter and that all the skill, color, power of expression was not given a chance to manifest itself. I did not mean that you should pour your talent on the world of the artist, your own, but that it is best when the characters are a challenge to your own expanding vision. If you were playing a role on the stage, would you not prefer a role which involved all your richness?

It is the best image I can think of, a role into which you could throw all your range of abilities.

In your choice of character there is inevitably a constriction, like a painter who chooses to paint in only two colors. I hope this makes more sense than my first letter. Possibly I'm influenced here by my feeling that the writer can expand the world. The world we are thrust into is narrow. You know the world I was thrust into (the family) was narrow in a different way than yours.

Anyway, let us not give all this too much importance. I'm comparing the people you write about to you, and that is not fair. But some day, promise me, you will write out of yourself, and not get inside of others' skins, with your own eloquence and color and rhythm. The gifts you have, reach for them, give the characters some of your luminescence, fantasy and freedom. We do have a different concept of writing. I know. Yours is objective. But good things come of certain collisions. Strange how our first talk in Hollywood had to do with the choice of characters, remember? I may not be your best reader, as you have been mine, and I regret that, but perhaps I am your best reader in listening and watching for the fullest flowering of a not yet explored or discovered Herlihy. Your best reader of James Leo Herlihy in person, the creator and not the characters created. Will this help you to forgive me?

Letter from Jim:

Today I received your letter on the lovely Domjan paper, which evoked you as sharply as the words you wrote. I also received your first letter in which you clarified our discussion of the novel, character selection, etc. Your point of view is much clearer now; and there is so much to be said about it that I don't know if it is possible even to begin. I understand and accept your point of view. I even like it. But it is no longer mine. Does that seem to be contradictory? Perhaps it is, on the surface; but on a deeper level I'm certain it is not. My work has become a part of the total of my life in a way that it had not been previously: my subjects and characters select me as much as I select them. They are like friendships or love affairs to me. If I find myself fascinated, delighted, preoccupied more and more with a group of people, or a character, or a situation, or a combination of them, I come to the typewriter and let them have their lives. (It is a far less objective process than you know; and the novel, for instance, was deeply personal, in that the dilemma and the characters are in my own family.) Since I found myself working in that way, my life has found a new integration and form; it is at once more natural to me, and happier—and I feel it has made me freer in profound ways, particularly in the freedom to love. By contrast with these powers, writing, in itself, is of no importance to me—only in that it contributes and forms an essential part of the whole, which is my life. I am not really tempted to concern myself with whether this makes me a more or less significant writer, though I confess I am tempted to believe that, in my case, my work is better for it. I agree with you that the writer must accept every challenge to his vision, so that it can expand. Any kind of freedom in which there is stasis, a lack of growth, expansion, is false. You must trust me to know that my expansion has been tremendous; if in your own view of my work, this does not seem to be true, it is purely a matter of vantage point, the difference between yours and mine. Yours is of great value to me when I am in shadows and in darkness; your insights have cast much light on those moods and conditions in me, and you have contributed to my freedom. Now that my work has taken a face that is strange and unexpected, from the point of view of your own tastes, preferences, I can understand why you would be tempted to place upon it this interpretation, that I am not using my full powers. I can only say, again, that I deeply appreciate your devotion, which is what made you speak out at all; and most important, I hope you will trust me that I have not turned away from the challenging in favor of the easy. Oddly enough, I demand more of myself than ever before.

The young poet in jail writes me:

I've tried to have my writing sent out but it's just impossible . . . However, I have some small consolation. Nathan Leopold and Roger Touhy also had to wait until they were released before they could get their things published. Perhaps it's just as well. Everything I've written recently is permeated with the exudations of my soul—bitterness and self-pity. I need fresh perspective. It's good I'll be out soon. Soon—well, eighteen months does seem soon after eight and a half years.

Then he writes about literature, Zen, Japanese films, D'Annunzio, Kabuki theatre.

I was trying to get some of his writing for *Two Cities*. But I don't have much hope for him. He wrote: "Perhaps crime can be creative."

Letter from poet in prison:

No, I'm still suffering the effects of my rebellion without knowing the cause. Perhaps in a sense I do know, but can't quite reach it. It could be a denial of the "I." That would be appropriate. It's hard to explain when I read your letter. I wanted to see you—talk to you. What you have accomplished is what I have been trying to do for the past 4 or 5 years.

I have Rank's *Art and Artist*. I've also read Colby's *Energy Structure in Psychoanalysis*, Mowrer's *Psychotherapy: Theory and Research*. French and Alexander's *Psychoanalytic Therapy*. I've read Berg on *Deep Analysis*, even Sartre's *Psychoanalysis*, but . . . nothing. Artists are neurotics who cure themselves with their art—granted. I know my writing will remain a dead, inert thing until I can detach this whole creative process, and this is impossible until I find why I am unable to "get beyond this destructive preliminary work," this anger, rebellion. Not being able to find this cause is why I suggest a more violent, more intense return to the old forms and patterns. The purpose would be self-destruction, yes, but a quick total destruction. In the other direction lies creative repression, which is a form of self-destruction itself, a slower, gnawing type of destruction. This must sound like the confession of an unresolved neurotic. Sorry.

Letter to poet in prison:

I am sorry you cannot receive books. Are you allowed to order books from a bookstore? The Phoenix Book Shop will accept your orders and charge it against sales of my own books. You must not be uneasy at what I may do for you. I cannot imagine a more painful thing than the loss of freedom and as you are deprived of physical freedom I want to compensate a little with the other freedom of imagination and creation. I still cannot understand why they do not give you psychological help, considering your gifts and insight and efforts to solve your own conflicts. It is so hard to do it alone. Not even Freud succeeded in his self-analysis. I can understand the loss of freedom by empathy. I always thought that was the one experience I could not survive. I have had plenty of symbolic imprisonment but it is not the same, and it was voluntary, for the sake of another person's happiness.

Letter from poet in prison:

. . . In *Ladders to Fire* you wrote: "The man who was once starved may revenge himself upon the world not by stealing just once, or by stealing only what he needs, but by taking from the world an endless toll in payment for something irreplaceable which is the lost faith." And again: "In the underworld of nature debts must be paid in the same species: no false money accepted. Hunger with hunger, pain with pain, destruction with destruction." Wonder how I will react after ten years without freedom. Glad you mentioned those two books by Lindner, *Fifty-minute Hour* and *Rebel Without a Cause*. I have read so many on the criminal, so many that didn't have anything to say, that I disregarded these. Rank's dualistic conflict is, in some respects, much like the inner conflict I'm experiencing.

Henry Miller started a correspondence with a man in Missouri State Penitentiary, Roger Bloom. He is serving a life sentence for holding up a bank with a toy gun when he was seventeen. He never engaged in violence. He had once thought to become a writer, and tried his hand at plays. Henry gave him my address when he was convinced of Roger Bloom's passion for reading, and I received his first letter: "Obtaining good reading would have been nil without the help of Henry Miller, bless him. I would love to read more *Two Cities,* and most specially one or all of yours for you are something special."

Letter to Roger Bloom:

I do not blame you for confusing me with Djuna Barnes. Her book *Nightwood* did have enormous influence on me, the level on which she writes, between conscious and unconscious, poetry and prose. As I see the rules are that you can only get books from publishers, not private persons, I will ask the Phoenix Book Shop to send you mine. Your statement that you are a man of feeling, which is revealed in your letter, made me feel friendship, as I value that quality more than any other.

I have been working at copying and editing the diaries Henry wrote about and I am only at volume 70. But for human reasons (hurting others) I cannot publish it yet. This is a secret which is becoming harder and harder to keep as it is my major work.

I write you without asking what might have sent you to jail but you must know that when one has looked deeply into the truth about one's character, one knows one is capable of all acts, and that only a small thread separates us from those who act out their violent emotions. I suppose we feel that under certain circumstances we might have acted out our anger. The one who takes such action, in a Dostoevskian sense, does it for us! And we feel—at least I do—that I should share in the consequences, we the dreamers who only get angry and kill in our nightmares. It must be harder for you because you are a man of feeling.

Letter from Roger Bloom:

Please know that I love your books—truly they are beautiful and while one of them is held in my hands I am completely out of this life of sordidness and despair. Please God arrangements can be made so that I shall be permitted to learn more of you and your life through your books or any books you choose for me.

You will, in time, come to learn that I am a very emotional person—

that I am forever giving way to my emotions—to those I love specially—and when I opened your letter I had to glance to the bottom of the page at first to make certain it really was from you. Too, I cannot allow the most important of your kindnesses to go unthanked—that you left other letters to one side to write to me—how can one determine the magnitude of friendship—regardless of my present stature, no matter the cause of what might have sent me to a place of this kind, without a single word of reproach, you simply share your life with me.

The only word which can describe the general flowing of life here or in any prison is abnormal. From the moment one enters an institution of this kind, or perhaps any institution where one's life is suppressed, harried, brought to a state of regimentation, one begins to feel as tho' he had entered an eerie world. There are rules, regulations, whistles at 15 minute intervals from each tower surrounding the prison—bells which tell you when to extinguish the cell-light—to arise in the morning—to stand for count—to begin eating—to leave the dining room, and every waking moment you are conscious of the fact that each act or movement can be misconstrued as one of rebellion against the RULES and REGULATIONS or the whim of a keeper or guard and can mean further punishment of various kinds.

[Spring, 1960]

I was invited to Sweden to read and lecture because two of my novels had been published there. Several Swedish friends had planned the trip.

The light of Sweden, the midnight sun and the perpetual light of *Miss Julie*. The light which literature sheds upon our lives. The poor starved human beings who do not read. Ibsen is here, and his plays. And all the Swedish novelists I read, *Hunger* by Knut Hamsun, Stig Dagerman, who committed suicide at thirty-one when he felt he could no longer write, all the light of books, the madness of Strindberg. The light of folklore, booklore, and its reality now, when I cannot sleep because it is not dark, and the body is confused, the eyes stay open. It is not daylight. It is not dawn. It is a light of glaciers, of planets unknown to us. It has a strange quality of suspense. It is neither warm nor cold. It is disquieting. It gives nostalgia, you do not sleep and you are not awake. There is a flutter from the heart that says you must not sleep for the earth is awake. Expectancy. Somehow the cycle of light and dark is interrupted by this no-daylight, no-nightlight existence. Neither the moon nor the sun is present. Is this limbo? Has the earth forgotten to turn? Are we flung out of the orbit, in the light from an unknown planet? I feel anxiety.

Suddenly I was flooded with journalists, cameras, interviews. It was my first taste of celebrity. It was fun as a novelty and a great trial to my secret, hidden shyness. They compared me with Marlene Dietrich, who was here last week, spoke of my chic and glamor. Next morning three big newspaper front-page articles. Telephone calls and flowers. Afternoon interview with Isak Dinesen's nephew. Reading at the Museum of Modern Art. Such a big crowd we had to change from a small hall to the main hall. The beautiful actress Ingrid Thulin was there. Her husband was one of the first to review my books. Two parties were to be given tonight, and they finally agreed to make it all one party at the house of Hulten, the museum director. I have met all the writers, poets and other actors from the Bergman films. But Bergman himself was ill and my Swedish publisher broke a leg at Cannes. But I saw my agent, whose son is in charge of paperbacks for Bonnier and may do *Spy in the House of Love*. Today at one thirty I go through a long interview with Artur Lundkvist, Sweden's finest poet and critic. When I walk into a restaurant I am asked for my autograph. After America's indifference, it is very elating.

The secret is not as I thought, an affinity between Sweden and my work, but the attraction of opposites. They are earthy, almost like peasants, their literature is plain and folkloric, their lives plain, stodgy. Bars close at midnight. So much dignity and order.

Tomorrow is a holiday so I will have a peaceful day at the country house of Gelber with Hill and Billy Kluver.

Yesterday a short, to-the-point interview with Artur Lundkvist on the radio. He told me about the earthquake at Agadir. He and his wife were staying in one of the hotels. They had almost agreed to separate, the marriage was about to dissolve. Then the earthquake came, ripped the whole façade of the hotel down, and left them standing on the fourth floor, shaken, so frightened at the near death they had experienced that they were reconciled.

The party at Hulten's. Four big bare studio rooms filled with his mobiles and Tinguely's. A real artist's home. Orange-crate bookcases painted orange. Very little furniture. For refreshment, red wine, a huge round homemade loaf of bread, hors d'oeuvres of smoked reindeer, yoghurt with ginger flavor. I met fascinating people, Ingrid Thulin and her husband Harry Schein, another beautiful woman ceramist, Gunilla Palmstjerna, married to Peter Weiss, a writer. Jazz on the phonograph. Dancing. Lundkvist and his Danish wife, who wears her hair *à la* Veronica Lake. Ingrid has such an emotional face, dark intense eyes in a blond face, and a lovely dusky voice. It was she who wanted to persuade Bergman to do *Spy in the House of Love*. But he likes to write his own scripts.

Yesterday was a holiday, so Nils and Arnita, Billy and Hill packed a picnic lunch and drove me to the country. First they showed me a suburban development project which looked as monotonous, as dull as our own, uniform, seeming more like jails than apartments. But then Nils drove to his family property, twenty-five acres overlooking a lake, so much like Bergman's settings for *Illicit Interlude*. A cold lake, gulls, but spring vegetation, wild flowers of all kinds, birch trees, deer and snakes. His childhood home, like a big Southern home, all of wood, ruined by vandals because unoccupied and finally even partly burnt by teen-agers who prowled about. While we were there a man came up with his fishing rod, and Nils argued with him because it was Nils' property and the man should not be fishing there. They almost had a fist fight. Billy went to fetch the police. They pay no attention to private property. Socialism has taken care of all the problems except the cussedness of human nature. Country full of restrictions, on drinking, kissing, etc. All the wives do social work. It is paid like any other job.

As they talked about their childhood, about the short summers, it seemed wistful. Too short a summer to enjoy nature, the lakes, the boating, the fishing and swimming.

The long winters at home make them read so much.

Every newspaper has an article on me, what I do, wear, say.

Yesterday, after the day in the country, we visited Gunilla, the wife of Peter Weiss. Top-floor apartment in old quarter, blond pine-wood floors as smooth as those in the Japanese house I saw in the Museum of Modern Art, low ceilings with beautiful old beams, big white plaster fireplace. Beautiful ceramics.

I forgot to mention my first impression from the airplane. Lakes, islands covered with pines, small red houses like the German candy houses in pastry shops, forests dark green. Stockholm itself would seem dull but for the rivers, canals, boats. Billy is all ears, which he leaves out of his skiing cap. Hill is all freckles. Small cars, gray buildings. Staying at a small hotel in the center of town, facing a bookshop which has all my books in the window. All the luxury is concentrated on heavy embroidered linen, but the bath-room is down the hall. Bathtub big enough for four persons. I almost drowned in it. It is all familiar to me because of Bergman's films, which I know by heart. I saw the kind of boat the ballet dancer took in *Illicit Interlude* when she went in quest of memories. The palace is earth color. I am not seeing my Sweden but Bergman's. Winter cold still. A northern Venice. Buildings such strange colors, brown, vichyssoise, dark red. Ponderous restaurant rooms, bars. A melancholic cast of colors. As against that, the bright, modern de-signs of textiles, pottery, kitchenware, furniture. The needed bright-ness. I took a walk through the city. They do not allow cars through the small narrow streets, so one can enjoy walking, window-shopping.

Dinner at Gelber's, with his two little girls waiting at the door to say two words in English. English is compulsory in school. In a once-rough quarter, eighteenth century, now invaded by the artists because there is a shortage of apartments. Up a hill, dung-colored houses relieved by peaked red roofs. A view of the river, and most interesting the effect of the midnight sun. It is like a long twilight. The sun seems about to go down and does not. At twelve when I left it looked like early dawn. Strange feeling of *dépaysement*.

The last evening was the most interesting one of all, in the old quarter. Medieval houses. Because they have no caretaker or automatic door opener, we all stood in the narrow cobblestone street shouting: "Here we are!" The painter leaned out of his attic window and threw the key inside of a glove. We climbed crooked worn steps to the fifth floor. Jazz recordings played. The painter had baked a giant round loaf of bread, beautiful peasant bread, and this with wine was all that was served. I loved the simplicity of it. His paintings quite amazing, a world of design, on paper which was one continuous roll around the room. A major painter.

I loved them all. We almost wept at parting. My room full of flowers but not florist flowers, flowers they pick on country drives, wild lilies of the valley, wild blue bells, wild violets, wild lilac.

They are passionate people frozen in old forms and conventions, in puritanism. The cult of nakedness is part of athletic love of physical fitness, not sensuality.

Return from Sweden via my beloved Paris.

I saw the life of Paris as one of openness, no compromises, natural, impulsive, instinctive, giving free rein to eroticism, imagination and creation. Even the evil is more honest. More maturity in insight. Max Frisch's *Biedermann et les Incendières* treats of the militant revolutionary, full of verbal fireworks, until the revolution starts and then he cannot take the violence, and becomes abjectly terrorized by bombs and fire. How honest the world of the prostitutes. Out of my window I saw wisps of fog trailing over the city and I wished to change substance, not to be trapped by the many duties and obligations of life. I envied the wisps of fog.

Simenon has described a hundred times a man awakening to his total disconnection from the life he is living, the persons he is living with. How he awakened a stranger, all links broken. This caused such fear in me that I fell asleep and dreamed, as usual, that the sea overcame me and drowned me.

The taxi driver quotes Socrates and Balzac. I love the small, intimate restaurants, the personal and intimate feeling between people.

I visited Henri Michaux. I had a letter of introduction from Louise Varèse, who had translated *Misérable Miracle,* which I had spent much time and energy trying to get published until I finally placed it with City Lights.

He is about seventy, ill, and withdrawn from public life. Louise had shown me a poem which he later withdrew from publication, which explained the tragic element in his life. His young and beautiful South American wife was wearing one of the new nylon nightgowns; it caught fire from the fireplace and she was burned to death. After a while he withdrew the poem. I wonder why. Was it too primitive a cry of pain?

He lives in one of those magnificent vast, shabby houses on the Left Bank, left over from the *Belle Époque,* high ceilings, grandiose entrances, royal staircase, no heat but marble floors, frescoes on the walls, sumptuous chandeliers. We sat in a book-lined room and he talked sparklingly about his discovery not of poetry but of the infinite. He talks exactly as he writes. He explained that he does not take drugs often, perhaps once a year, and then spends the rest of the time struggling to find the most perfect expression of the experience. He works at this with enormous care, meticulousness. I told him about my LSD experience.

He expected America to show greater interest in his books. I explained first of all that very few Americans read French and very few of his works were translated, but also that Americans were not interested in the subtle poetry born of drugs, that they preferred experiences to be reported plainly, factually, clinically, like case histories. They had more faith in the scientific intellectual commentaries of Huxley. The young had been misled into thinking the drug experience, like the mystical experience, could not be described. I always protested this. I said the poets could do it. Michaux could do it.

It is true that very few people read him in America.

The same day I was invited to dinner by a French collector who placed beside me a pile of books by Michaux as tall as myself, most of them out of print, and most of them unknown in America.

Michaux seems to be suffering from what Artaud described as a *"fatigue de fin du monde."* What I felt in his presence was such a lack of warmth that he also seemed like a man come down from the Ice Age.

Sylvia Beach was preparing to take her collection of letters and photographs to London. She remembered my very early visit to her to try and interest her in Henry Miller. She commented: "Of course, women were always steppingstones for men artists."

I met Kenneth Anger at the Deux Magots. He told me he was filming the life of Marquis de Sade in the actual castle of Sologne for Prince Ruspoli.

Strange how some meetings release no sparks of life, create no echoes, no reverberations. This mystery always baffled me. What blocks, what prevents any connection taking place between one human being and another, one life and another? At other times, this spark flares instantly. Kenneth lived entirely in a world of his own. Who entered into it, who inhabited it, whom did he love or trust or confide in? It seemed to me I had *always* been preoccupied with what made human beings strangers to each other. Was it that my father was so utterly disconnected, that no one knew him intimately, that he only gave his persona, that I never met anyone who could say: I knew your father intimately? Was it the great distance he maintained between himself and his wife, between himself and his children which first implanted in me the desire, the need, the search for intimacy?

I could see human beings floating in space like the planets. And so many meetings were like that, with Michaux, with Pierre Jean Jouve, with Kenneth Anger, with Lawrence Durrell and very often, in spite of my devotion to her, with Marguerite Young.

A quiet Sunday lunch at the restaurant Paul on the Île de la Cité. Jean-Louis Barrault and his wife eating at the next table. Outside in the little park, hobos cooking sausages over a small grill, with the inevitable bottle of red wine. Hobos at night, sleeping in the middle of the sidewalk. A woman hobo asleep in front of the police station, over a baker's grill, surrounded with smoke, as if she were being cooked.

The young girls all trying to look like Brigitte Bardot. A concert of *musique concrète*. A nightmare of distorted sounds, including a tape of a woman's voice which sounded like birth screams. A film made by Pierre Shaeffer to explain his theories.

In Paris I saw an exhibit called *"Noir."* It was black indeed. Sculptures of burnt wood, black iron, black figures, circles, black carvings, with a *musique concrète* background. The walls were hung with black, the lights hooded with black. It all looked as the world might after an atomic bomb or an earthquake and fire, all burnt and lava-covered. Is this prophetic art?

Dinner with Peter Weiss and Gunilla in a Chinese restaurant, walked through the Left Bank, sat at a café on the Place de la Contrescarpe. Weiss is a somber, bitter man. Has made films and written plays.

Paris is tense, full of police, there is shooting by Algerians. Bombs thrown a few nights ago in the café we are sitting at.

Last night our taxi was stopped by the police searching for bombs. Out of it came two old, distinguished figures, decorated, both of them, with the Legion of Honor: Roger Vieillard and Stuart Gilbert, translator of Malraux's *Psychologie d'Art.*

The police apologized.

The walk between Place Clichy and Place Blanche is a walk into multiple worlds. It is the tough Paris, cafés full of pimps, pushers. Side streets dark, lit up only by a few hotel signs and standing by the door real prostitutes, interesting, like the ones in Mexico. So vivid, painted, challenging. Many movie houses, pocket books from America sold on the sidewalk, crowds sauntering, jazz musicians playing in open cafés, nightclubs, barkers, dirty postcard sellers, penny movies all pornographic, as animated as the streets of Spain. Pinball games as on Broadway, a Japanese review at the Moulin Rouge, so alive and sensuous. All of it in unreal colors, like neon, too bright, varnished. Waking the night life in all of us.

The day before, I saw a Greek painter whose paintings had been turned down at all the exhibits. So he hung them on the walls under the bridge, the dark, sooty arched walls. Plenty of room for his big paintings, illuminated by the floodlights under the Pont Neuf. And the French, being people with a sense of humor, actually gave him a policeman to watch over his work, which all Paris came to see. As I was looking over the parapet later, a group of folk singers sang American songs. They passed big Western hats. I asked them: "Where are you from?" "From England," they answered, "We're fakes. Do you want your money back?"

Visited Stuart Gilbert. He is very old now, but his wit as sharp as ever. He tells wonderful stories about the twenty years he spent in Burma as a judge. How he tried to understand their sense of justice. When they retired him he came to Paris and Caresse blithely suggested he translate Saint-Exupéry and, equally blithely, James Joyce. Which he did. He is highly considered as a translator. He has lived for all these years, before the war and now, in an apartment overlooking the Seine, on one of those beautiful and still medieval islands. Unchanged. I could swear the same books are still lying on the small tables in the salon and that he has sat for hundreds of years in the same brown velvet armchair. It was here I met James Joyce, who refused to talk, but sang for us. We indulged in much literary gossip. During the war he went to Wales. Meanwhile his concierge drank all the wine in his cellar. He told me Gertrude Stein made you choose between herself and Joyce, you could not see them both.

Everyone talking about the world crumbling, but I don't see the crumbling. I see only artists everywhere, working, producing beautiful things, living austerely like priests, without possessions. The lovely, serene Paris where the café is not just a place to drink and talk but to sit in contemplation of a tree, of passers-by, the sweetness of life when we step out of history and politics. A city with a feeling for nature. So many trees, fountains. The fountains at the Rond Point incredibly delicate, spurting from amber glass, becoming under your eyes lace and smoke. Everywhere people happy over little things, strolling. Nowhere is simple human life so highly valued. Work is easily forgotten. People take their lunch in a basket and sit by the Seine. Time to dream! A sleepy dreamy city on Sundays. Opaline skies, old trees.

An exhibit of Polish painters remarkable, but melancholic. All in blacks and grays, with a few rare spots of color, abstractions which look like the inside of a body cut open.

A concert of *musique concrète* in the same Salle Gaveau where my father gave a thousand concerts. Science-fiction sounds not to be

233

taken seriously. Distortion of voices, sounds as from satellites, or wind in the Grand Canyon, much of it like the noise of jet planes taking off, electric motors, icebox motors, our dog's nails scratching on glass doors, his metal tag hitting his dinner plate. Conductor stands by a board of colored push buttons. Sounds come from all directions out of giant plastic forms like Mexican pottery. People go to sleep, it is so monotonous. Whistles, factory machinery, choked voices. A female voice is suddenly cut off as a Frenchman says aloud: "She has a tough life." The international composers come on stage for a bow. Poor little old Salle Gaveau, where I believe Chopin once played.

Invited to "Radiodiffusion," outside of Paris to see a film on *musique concrète* made by the leader, Pierre Shaeffer. The intellectual explanation sounds more interesting than the effects. As in science, he says, we have to split the atom to release new energies. We can no longer use or work with violin, piano, cello, which are always the same. We must break them down to obtain new sounds (Varèse, Cage), new combinations. As in painting, a distortion of a commonplace image creates a new image. So we distort a violin note, a bell note, with tape and scissors, like cutting a film, and we create new effects more like our own life.

Only effect I responded to was the echo, which gave a feeling of immense space, of it all happening on other planets.

Met with Roger Blin, a mysterious actor with an Asiatic face. I brought a message from The Living Theatre, who want to produce *The Blacks*. He was the first producer-actor of *Waiting for Godot*. Like many actors, he earned his living from television. But all those who signed plea for Algeria, cessation of hostilities, are out of work and in trouble. Actors suffered most, as television is government-owned.

I felt bad to be encouraging him to come to America when I knew The Living Theatre could not earn its own living and I finally told him the truth. To be without work in France was bad enough, but to be stranded in New York far worse.

A pop art exhibit. A mockery of art in every way. A big piece of plywood, size of a wall, covered with sponges sprayed with cobalt blue, representing the surface of the moon.

Spill a pot of ink on a large piece of paper, fold, open, exhibit. We did that as children too.

On one wall there was an exact drawing of a saw, repeated five or six times. At the end, a real saw on a hook.

Why?

Plastic bombs planted in apartments of government officials. Everybody nervous. Had dinner with Roger Vieillard and Anita de Caro, famous and interesting artists. A bomb had exploded in their hallway, intended for a government official. The maid was so nervous serving dinner that her hands were trembling. We took a taxi to go to the theatre, and on the way called for Stuart Gilbert.

Coming out of the theatre, we saw the hobos asleep on the sidewalks. They prefer their freedom to a hospital or a home for the aged. They choose to sleep over the gratings of restaurant kitchens for warmth. The heat from the bakeries or subways rises and turns to steam so they seem to be sleeping in a bed of smoke.

To see the moon over the dented silhouettes of medieval roofs makes it seem like a different moon from that of the new world. A wiser and sadder moon.

My stay in Paris ended in sorrow. Heard of the death of Gonzalo from cancer of the throat; and the death of Baroness Lambert on the operating table.

In Paris I was invited to visit an Italian businessman and his wife at their home in Florence. How can anyone say that literature does not prepare you for life? I found myself quite suddenly in a totally unfamiliar atmosphere. The home was in a monastery, on top of a hill. The beautiful square building, so simple, of stone the color of earth. In the center of it a serene patio, with flowers and a fountain.

But the unfamiliarity had begun at the airport. Rena, small and intensely alive, with a polish to her wit and a glaze over her gestures which seemed like a surface that would never reveal the inner woman. The persona was too well constructed, without fissures, well defended by humor and social grace. It was the behavior of the chauffeur which gave me the key. I knew then I was inside a novel by Pierre Jean Jouve, when the actress who has just suffered a failed love affair leaves Paris to visit an Austrian Countess. In the splendor of the background, in the formality and aesthetic perfection of the castle, the two women seek an unattainable intimacy. The Countess's only acknowledgment of the actress's suffering is to send flowers every day with her breakfast.

The chauffeur had this unbelievable blend of formal respect for his patrons and arrogance towards porters which only identification with the status of the household gives to European servants. He proclaimed, more loudly than anything, the prestige of the family.

As we entered the flagstone courtyard I felt thrown immediately into medieval Florence. The household activity was similar to the chauffeur. I was shown to my room, and to my first sight through three open windows of the landscape of Florence. The whole landscape of soft hills, of vineyards, of earth-colored low houses, of cypress trees and dirt roads, gave a picture in diffuse colors, the opposite of flamboyant, as if equally patined by centuries of unchanged life. It gave off, what so few landscapes will do, an aura of eternity. It had the tones of timelessness.

At dinner at the long refectory nun's table covered with a red tablecloth, Rena looked like a pixie in a beaded evening dress. One chair was devoted to a lifesize Pinocchio, a rag doll, which she spoke to now and then. He bore the burden of her reproaches to her husband, who was away "on business." Pinocchio had to listen to all her ironic complaints.

The red tablecloth was embroidered with flowers. The dishes were black. Each guest had one candle, and one perfect rose in a long-stemmed glass. There were rose petals in the finger bowls.

At the end of the evening, which was like a series of *tableaux vivants,* with no one saying anything to disturb the atmosphere of the finest liqueurs and the finest cigars, I went back to my room. Only in novels and eighteenth-century prints had I seen canopied beds, but they had always enticed me. The feeling of secrecy in those heavy brocade curtains, which could be drawn around the bed. The more extraordinary feeling of being plunged into the past. I felt outside of the body of Anaïs and inside all the bodies I had so carefully read about in books of history. This was intensified when I opened the night table to see what books were available to read myself to sleep, and a wave of sandalwood perfume came out of the shelves. Not only was the wood sandalwood, but the shelves were lined with brocade.

The rest of the furniture lay in darkness in the room, but by its stature and imposing weight seemed to be more present than modern furniture, and I felt if I opened the wardrobe the Borgia family would appear, and if I leaned out of the windows I would see one of the Florentine burial processions at which everyone wore a hood, because at one time the poisoner, the murderer, might be among the mourners.

My room was invaded by figures I was familiar with. The Austrian Countess and the ailing actress, who maintained a formal distance while barely suggesting the tragedies in their lives and why the Countess loved the actress.

Then my door opened, and Rena entered, wearing a long dark red robe. She sat at the foot of my bed and talked. She was suddenly a very young and very vulnerable girl, lonely in a brilliant worldly setting. She was suffering from her marriage. It was a suffocating marriage, in which she herself could not move, expand, breathe. She was cast in the role of a waiting wife, waiting for a husband who was always elsewhere, pursuing fortune and fame.

Without Pierre Jean Jouve's help, his masterful description of overwhelming settings, and the effort of two women of the world to reach intimacy, I might have been deceived by Rena's apparent control of her luxuriant and polished world, but when she entered my room at midnight I was not at all unprepared. This was the beautiful moment behind all the trappings, and no amount of aesthetic, aristocratic or historic background could cover the pain of a young wife betrayed by a husband's ambition.

I let her talk. She had written a novel, and I sought my usual remedy, to shift the emphasis onto storytelling, the story aspect of one's tragedies. For a writer this is a possible remedy. Soon we were talking about the comedy of his "absence" as if it would make a good drama. Rena had read Pierre Jean Jouve. We were shifting from pain to creation. Dawn came. Inside of her large, long dark red robe, she looked less fragile and less vulnerable. She left quietly. Pierre Jean Jouve's novel had a different ending. The actress steals the Countess's lover. With Rena, I gave her back a novelist to sustain a lonely wife.

Letter from Roger Bloom:

I grew up during the twenties, in a small town in Pennsylvania. My father labored for his wages when there was work to be had. He was honest
and good. Poverty seemed to be everywhere and in our home as well, at
times. And so I stole to provide food for our table. But always told my
people that I had earned the money . . . whether or not they always believed me will remain a mystery . . . finally my father lost our home to
the bank . . . foreclosure . . . and my folks had to leave town and accept
help from relatives until my father could recover. There was a lot of bitterness in my heart towards institutions which could take away from anyone
. . . anyway, I came to Chicago . . . with a laxity of morals any normal
boy should have. I became a lone wolf, so to speak . . . highjacking, boot-
legging, and even a few robberies. There were "hot car" rings . . . where
one could dispose of stolen cars for profit . . . and with this way of life
there was a complete loss of consideration for what is or was good. I might
say tho, that my lawlessness did not extend to hurting normal people . . .
or friends . . . or women . . . It was simply don't take from the have-
nots . . . take from the haves. In between there was the being caught and
convicted . . . the rebellion against the police and the guards and the
keepers who held sway over us. Certainly they should have been tough
. . . today I can understand why they treated all criminals with contempt
. . . but back through the years when I didn't understand, all such treatment made me even more determined to get even. And so, I graduated to
the higher form of getting what I could . . . with but one thought in
mind . . . go where the loot is. And so I began to get even . . . or so I
thought. To my deep sorrow, dear Anaïs, I came to know a great many
good honest people. My association with them had to be as theirs . . .
honest and as law-abiding as one could be. It was like living two lives. And
yet, even with the enjoyment I received through knowing these fine people
I still had to have this abnormal thinking. And I am now paying the price
of that thinking . . . but with a deeper sense of punishment . . . the loss
of association with those I had come to love and respect. . . . Henry Miller has helped me so much to become more firmly convinced that there is
so much to be had through honorable living. And then you came into my
life and your presence has added oh, so much more to my life. The United
Artists Studios representatives are due here today to film several scenes
for their picture *The Hoodlum Priest,* a story of Father Dismas Clark of

St. Louis. He and I are old friends (circa 1954 ABR, After Bank Robbery). I may see them again . . .

Letter to Roger Bloom:

I was very moved by the story of your life. I was sure it was something like that, understandable, human, quite possible for any one of us, and an offense you should have been forgiven long ago. The most natural impulse in the world, when there is so much injustice in the distribution of money. When will they come to believe that a man of seventeen is not the same man today? How far we are from understanding man's changes, evolutions.

And how wonderful, Roger Bloom writes me from jail: "I will mention books and authors many times in my letters to you, but only because of some reason I find that they might have, some influence on my life or my attitude towards life . . ."

Letter from Roger Bloom:

You and Miller both having an article in the same issue reminds me of my introduction to you and Miller's work. It was either in 1946 or 1947, when I was in my second year or third year in high school, that I read a book entitled *Spearhead*. It was published by New Directions in 1942 I think. The book included contributions by you, Paul Goodman, Kenneth Patchen and an excerpt from Henry Miller's *Tropic of Capricorn*. My father saw me reading it, and about a month later gifted me with under-the-counter copies of *Tropic of Cancer* and *Tropic of Capricorn*. He told me he was thankful my literary taste had matured, and words to that effect that it was time I got off the Thomas Wolfe kick. So I had to keep my newly purchased copy of *Time and the River* under the mattress so he would not be disappointed. I've been experimenting with what I thought to be a new form of poetry. After reading *New World Writing 14* I see that Octavio Paz does it much better. It's an exciting form to work with. I feel guilty about writing this. I know how busy you are and I don't want you to feel compelled to answer this. There is a lot of discrimination towards ex-cons because of the rising crime rate, and I don't know how to react to it or what adjustment I'll make. Whatever literary talents I may have may be discarded in favor of the old forms and patterns you spoke of. I don't think this likely but that possibility still remains. I don't want to lead a negative existence.

A friend lost his faith in astrology because he thinks the Sputnik will alter star radiations and our horoscopes will be thrown out of kilter.

Letter from poet in prison:

Received Rank's *Birth of the Hero* and other writings last week. He was young to see so deeply—just twenty-five when he wrote the *Birth of the Hero*. It's tragic that he didn't live to finish *Beyond Psychology*. I have his *Art and Artist*. Wonder if it would have changed things had I read *Art and Artist* ten years ago. I would have understood so much more and, possibly, have averted some of this—possibly not, also.

Recently read some books on semantics; Walpole's *Semantics,* Hayakawa['s] *Language in Truth and Action,* and (this one threw me) *Meaning and Necessity* by Rudolph Carnap. If confusion is necessary to profundity then this is a very profound book. I staggered through Carnap's symbols, L concepts, variables, etc. until it left my brain crinkling like tinfoil over a hot fire. Things went easy for a while, then I hit this: ". . . let us now consider the pragmatical investigation of the language of a robot rather than that of a human being." I left Mr. Carnap and his robot to their own devices and hope they live happily together. Hereafter, I'll confine my semantical pursuits to Kenneth Burke and I. A. Richards.

I'm glad you liked *Night Image.* Lately I've been experimenting with new forms—but mostly getting notes together for some longer things I'll write when I'm free. Too difficult now. Have some plays and novels in outline. Lived with the characters so long and know them so well they seem real. One play (*The Reincarnation of Casey Dudek*) will be in a seriocomic vein. Odd that I didn't think of writing for the theatre when I had my brief fling at acting. For I was writing then, but mostly mood pieces and some poetry. I'll always write—a necessity! If I can only contain the anger, etc., in my writing as you suggested and as Miller and others have done. Yes, October 1961 isn't too far off. Forgive me if I sound a little sad. Had the earphones on, listening to a jazz program, and they played one of my favorites. It was John Coltrain on sax blowing *While My Lady Sleeps* (too many memories). Coltrain is at his best on slow, moody, smooth-flowing bits like this. So much soul. When the piece is over the mood lingers like the slowly dissolving smoke of a freshly put-out cigarette. At times I wish I weren't so sensitive—too sensitive. Lack of sophistication. Nineteen when I came to prison and in many ways I'm probably not much older. Hope it doesn't show too much.

The concert of *musique concrète.* It's wonderful that you went. I've been following this type of thing for a long time. The new sounds, etc. Especially the things of Anton Webern, Varèse, John Cage, Stockhausen, Křenek, etc. So many exciting things happening. . . . I read and reread your letter until I nearly wore the paper thin. Felt guilty that you should devote so much time writing me, but was glad you did. . . . Criminals are supposed to be hard, cunning, and unscrupulous. I'm none of these, probably too much the opposite, and, well, I don't know how to phrase it but your letters have already done much for me. The news you bring to me and confidence in myself they have given me.

I did not know the prison rules about typewriters. I sent my own. The rules are they must be new, and mailed from the shop. So mine was returned, as it might have been tampered with? Roger's disappointment concerned me. I wrote to him:

Whatever the reason for the rule, I think it is very unwise and contrary to humanistic rules to frustrate a human being who is seeking to develop his gifts and re-enter society as a writer. They should help a man re-create his new self instead of thwarting his efforts, his creativity, they should encourage the one who wants to expand and grow. All they do is to create more resentment. So few of the men put in charge of prisons seem to care about helping the prisoners worth helping. He knew from our correspondence that I was sending one of my typewriters so it could not be new. As you say, one cannot expect laws to be human, but big men always know when they can be made flexible. When I return to New York I will send you a new typewriter from a typewriter shop. It may be your Warden does not think Henry Miller and I are good influences, being artists. But the artist is the very one who has made creative use of his faculties and tries to create a world of beauty and freedom. I'll be in New York in October.

Renate and John bought a sailboat in Holland and named it *Solar Barque*. But the voyage through European canals was short. It seems that John did not study navigation seriously, and that Renate was expected to assist in maneuvers which were described in a book in a language unknown to her. John felt the boat would guide itself. In the middle of one river he lost control and *Solar Barque* began to circle like a dervish while other boats bore down on them. Another time he guided the boat under a historic bridge, too low for the mast, and damaged an ancient treasure, to the great anger of the population. Navigating according to a book written in navigation terms was disastrous. To reach Villefranche they finally put *Solar Barque* on a train. It was exposed to sun and dry air for days. When it reached Villefranche and was set afloat, it sank immediately. And Renate's latest postcard came from Vienna, saying *Solar Barque* was in dry dock.

Though Roger Bloom is serving a life sentence, they evidently consider him a special person. He writes:

There is so little about a prison worth writing of or about. The everyday existence contains so little change from day to day. I am serving my sixth year here and thanks to Henry Miller, George Dibbern and now you, Anaïs, I have managed to retain a normal life. Last December I was selected by the Warden along with other inmates to go to St. Louis to represent the inmate body in distributing gifts purchased by all of us to the children of two orphanages there in the city. We wore "outside clothing" and were accompanied by two of the Warden's children. There were no guns, fetters, handcuffs or words about "being on our honor." We were just five people bent on a mission of goodwill. During the trip we were interviewed by the Press and on two occasions I was mistaken for the Warden. My gray and white hair had a lot to do with it. Too, we were on TV and altogether we had a wonderful trip. My reason for telling you this is that it became all the more important to me because of the fact that I am serving a life sentence.

[Fall, 1960]

Letter to Marguerite:

I plunged into your book reading at night and all day, everywhere, absorbed, moved, delighted, touched, bemused, hypnotized, lost, opiumized, amused, enchanted, saddened, frightened. It is a world on another planet, yet very intimate, personal, and familiar to me. An extraordinary sweep, depth, dimension, the constant shift between realism and reality, life and death, putting everything in question, extraordinary flights of fantasy, imagery, a gentle kind of humanity which dreamers usually cannot maintain. The love of details for their meaning, glasses, objects worn by Miss MacIntosh, the black umbrella, etc. It is so vast a world one cannot write about it all, and especially at first reading one must allow one's self to be swept into it as into a vast ocean. It is cosmic, musical, and immense. Its dimensions engulf smaller voyages, annihilate daily existence, cities, people, noises. It is made for solitude and meditation, for the night. One should read it every night and then go off on your large wingspan, to explore space, the infinite, time, life and death. There is a greatness in it, an absolutism. It took courage to write, to let the imagination run away as the surrealists wanted to do and never did. You yielded to all the waves, the wavelength of the soul, encompassed the wider meshes of the spirit in every shade and tone. Yes, quarter tones like those of Eastern music. Your way will not be easy. I do not predict a nonchalant reading from the lazy ones, the one-dimensional ones. But those who feel as I do will consider this the Bible of poetry, an oceanic world. The key seems to me to be Calderón's *La Vida Es Sueño*, all is a dream, in the end, boundaries do not exist.

Resistance to writing is a frequent experience with many writers. Henry Miller in Paris much preferred to write forty-page letters, Durrell writes of preferring to build a wall, and I at times enjoyed printing, bathing the dog, stacking wood for the fireplace, etc., more than writing. But when I am typing a diary (now volume 79) the entire life is re-created and it is such an intense pleasure to re-create a moment of life and love that it is worth the struggle. Often I did not know what I had done, or that I had done it. It was when I seemed most careless and casual that I would miraculously give the sensation I had experienced *sur le vif*. Writing is a curse only when there are no readers. Almost every other occupation gives more pleasure: cooking, sewing, gardening, swimming, but *none of them give you back the life which is flowing away from us every moment.*

Daisy [Aldan] is a loyal friend. We have shared many projects together. We read together at the Maison Française, Mallarmé's *Un Coup de Dés.* She read her translation and I read the original French. It was taped and played on the radio. We shared the vicissitudes of *Two Cities,* the helping of friends. Daisy is a magnificent poet, of the highest quality, yet she has to publish her poetry herself. Her teacher's salary goes into that. For my sake, she has also endangered her teacher's job. She has unusually gifted students who cannot go to college and will go from this school into their professional work. She made them study *Under a Glass Bell* stories. They wrote remarkable papers, more understanding than the critics. But one mother came in to object to the "Birth" story, saying she did not want her daughter to read such a tragic story and get the wrong idea about birth. Daisy defended the story well. She showed the mother the five-cent magazines children can buy around the corner from the school with vulgar, sensational stories. She insisted that anything which was written with grace and a sense of meaning and sincerity was better for an adolescent than what they were given to read on the newspaper stands. She won her point, not with the mother, but with the school.

Letter to Jim:

Still on that volume 79 and the lines which turned out to be prophetic, "I have a feeling Jim is going to succeed, and his success in the world will fully compensate me for my failure. When he is accepted, I feel it as if he were a mystical son, and I regain my faith in the world. It does not matter if life condemned me to an isolation cell as a writer, at least he will be in it, part of it, at the heart of it."

This prophecy came true. And it must not concern you as I have fully accepted this and I have given up novel writing. I have decided to enjoy what I have, typing out the diaries for the far-off future, stacking wood, enjoying sunsets and martinis, and forget I am a writer. When I was nine years old I had decided to live for others, and I should have stuck to my decision. But do tell me all the good things that your success has brought you, your pleasures, because as I say, they balance in the books of the mystics.

When Renate went away to sail on *Solar Barque* with John, Peter was left in care of an American family. Renate thought that he would be happy because Peter was always asking Renate to give him more of a family existence. He did not realize that with a stable family you have to play your part. He was asked to get up on time for breakfast, to help carry groceries from the market. Meals were at stable hours, the day was planned ahead. Peter lost all his freedom, his spontaneity. He had protested Renate's casual, un-planned life. Now he found himself in an organized life. He fell into a depression.

Meanwhile John, writes Renate, took guitar lessons from a wispy, lisping Catalonian "music professor." Not only did she have to be present to translate but the professor's large family sat around the room making shoes. When a musical problem came up, they all stopped to interfere in the lesson with Spanish passion and bravado. "We discovered too late that the 'professor' cannot read music, nor does he have an absolute ear for music, and with the exception of flamenco numbers and *paso doble* he plays everything off key in cacophony. John does not have the heart to quit because he loves the little Catalonian and his shoemaking family and fifty cents a lesson is a small fee. And so he is learning to play a *paso doble* and one flamenco piece."

Renate is in Barcelona, which holds so many memories for me, happy memories: Carmen, the Spanish maid who sang all day. Granados, the kindly paternal figure who let my mother teach sing-ing at the Conservatory. A modest but cheerful apartment, with a balcony overlooking the sea. The warmth of the nuns who taught us. The faith in the Virgin who would bring my father back. The view from the balcony. Everything white and sky-blue. Children dancing in the street. Music always.

Roger Bloom is fighting for parole. I showed his letters to a psychiatrist and obtained an opinion of his character and state of mind, all favorable. He did appear before the Board on his forty-eighth birthday. He was given thirty-five minutes to state his case.

For twenty-eight of those forty-eight years, he was involved with the law. Now he feels a changed man.

I wrote letters:

Letter To Whom it May Concern:

I am a writer who studied psychoanalysis and practiced it for two years as assistant to Dr. Otto Rank. I have corresponded with Roger Bloom over a period of years and have had the opportunity to be taken into his confidence both about his past, his family, his background, and his present state of mind and character. I believe he has undergone a great change; a gain in wisdom, understanding, and objectivity about himself. By the cultivation of friendships, reading, and psychological studies, he has gained much insight. I believe he has a fund of natural goodness, humanity, and a desire to help others; he is capable of sympathy, of generosity, and is far from being what is usually described as a natural criminal. He has no cruelty, no selfishness, and no love of violence. He did make a false start, based on youthful rebellion, and understands what motivated him. I have found him thoughtful of others, sensitive to others' feelings, emotionally responsive to kindness and understanding. I trust him.

What I consider the principal motivation for crime is absent here; he is not revengeful; he is not angry, or bitter. He does not blame society or shift responsibility. He has honestly studied and examined his own character.

Letters written over such a long period are very revealing. He has written in many moods, also under many kinds of circumstances. I detect no desire to injure others or even to excuse himself and blame others for his past.

Letter to Miss Bacon:

I have heard that you are seeking to help Roger Bloom, and I am writing this letter on his behalf. Being a novelist and writing for twenty years, I feel that I am a fairly good judge of character. I have corresponded with Roger Bloom over a period of years. I feel that he has undergone a great change, that he is no longer the person who first entered the jail. I feel he can be very useful to society outside, that he is basically a generous and emotional man. I never detect in any of his letters the kind of attitude he demonstrated as a youth of seventeen. He has grown spiritually, has matured, has maintained a very human relation to people both inside and outside of the jail. All these small details which inevitably betray themselves in a man writing letters are absent in his. He has an understanding of his life, he has been reading a great deal, he has even undergone a kind of self-analysis to understand what motivated his youthful acts. I would trust him.

May I add that I studied and practiced psychoanalysis under Dr. Otto Rank and that I feel this helped me to distinguish the person who will repeat offenses from the one who has uttery re-created himself into a man with a conscience, awareness, and a control of his life and thinking.

The remarkable fact about Daisy Aldan is that all her education came from hard-won grants and fellowships, that as soon as she won her degrees she began teaching and being self-supporting, that she always printed her own books and *Folder,* which was an anthology of the best American poets and painters. Her translation of Mallarmé's *Un Coup de Dés* (*A Throw of the Dice*) was authorized by Gallimard and the heirs of Mallarmé. It was said to be the most untranslatable of poems in any language.

She visited Varèse, and writes me: "It hurts me to think that this great imagination had to wait so long for recognition, and that even now there is no place in America where his work can be played properly. I sense within him a great restlessness and fear that there is not too much time left. He told me that his life had been like that of a prisoner who sees the sky and the freedom without but remains within his cell."

It is that she is not only a high-quality poet, one of the greatest integrity, but that she is always devoted to other poets.

Lawrence Durrell's preface to *Justine* is similar to one of Proust's letters: "There is a plane geometry, and a geometry of space. And so for me the novel is not only plane psychology but psychology in space and time, I try to isolate. . . . Such characters will later reveal themselves as different from what they were in the present, different from what one believes them to be, a circumstance which indeed occurs frequently enough in life."

Letter to poet in prison:

At Xmas I talked about you to a writer your age, and he became so interested he said he would write you—Robert Baldock—I hope he has. Phoenix promised to send you a Reich book—did he? No, I don't feel you indulge in self-pity at all. The situation is tragic, for you are gifted, and you analyzed so well what takes place when creation fails. But you have all the elements to win as an artist. When you come out, I want you to meet the Living Theatre group, James Herlihy, all the artists of your age who have worked through difficulties, obstructions. Bitterness is the thing to watch—toxic. I watch it in myself; when I see it forming like an abscess, I operate fast. Da Vinci's life, *filled* with frustrations, humiliations, a million projects defeated by others—but each time one failed, he picked up another. If he could not get a mural order he wanted, he took up the study of anatomy; when his airplane failed, he took up the study of birds; when his patrons poisoned his life, he designed a church, or took up astronomy. We all have plenty of causes for anger, but if we let it grow it becomes war and leads to death of all life. Did you know Genêt no longer needs to steal now that he is fulfilled as a writer? What a writer! You're a fine writer—I can tell from your letters. I take my correspondence wherever I go, and this time could not finish my letter to you. Now I am back with Tennessee Williams' *One Arm* stories, rereading them. Limited edition. I like his stories and novels better than his last plays which I felt were distorted to the point of vulgarization, what I call the Grand Guignol school, which I saw again when I was in Paris. It belongs to the 1800's. It takes place in a theatre built like a Catholic chapel, all wood and confessionals, and cloistered boxes, etc. Red carpets and old gaslight lamps. It is the old horror story, carried to exaggeration, grotesque and so far beyond belief that it creates laughter. It created a form of writing but one which was never taken seriously. It is always dangerous to go back to these places. One never knows at which point it will die. Well, Grand Guignol has not died yet. In Williams I think it came from his taking symbolism and extending it into action, into literal action (the boys eating the young man, etc.). The curse of American writing is action. The same with our rebellions. And Lindner made this point wonderfully. In Europe our rebellions were against the bourgeois world, or whatever, but they were made to affirm what the individual stood for. Romantic rebels, overthrowing what existed to affirm itself. Here, the rebel goes in a pack, set on destroying but not for any reason at all. Just anger. Surrealism was such a rebellion, preceded by Dadaism. And what did the Beats accomplish? Action in this way becomes meaningless. The cult of action . . . To return to Williams; he practically killed symbolism. He had genius for the theatre. But when he sets on the theatre cannibalism, castration, etc., he is profoundly and deeply betraying the symbol. For horror takes the place of feeling. Action takes the place of feeling. It is as empty in the end as the cries, wailings and murders of Medea, killing her children. No, creation begins somewhere else. Where we understand the symbol (the symbolism of the bullfight even, of eating a wafer in place of the Christ, etc.). Not in action certainly. I realize this in Williams with *Camino Real*. He was burlesquing the dream. Destroying it. For laughs and for chills. At that moment I lost my respect for him. It may have been in reaction against violent action that so many of the modern artists took an interest in Zen. I notice you did too. But I feel that is only a step, a step of suspense, while the meaning of our acts takes shape within ourselves so they might not become suicides. Williams tried to drag us into his suicidal nightmares, castration, etc. His own. There is a difference here with Genêt, who uses violent material but understands it. And in *The Balcony* reverses the process. Symbolic action to be transposed into living.

When you are free, what did you think of doing? Prepare all your writing for me to see what we can do with it. Do you need paper, carbons, etc.? Also do what I did as a child, in the diary: analyze in one column what makes you angry, and in another what makes you love and admire. They balance each other. I would do that whenever I was depressed. Even today. I set side by side on my desk a letter from a child of fourteen about my stories, and a letter of rejection from a publisher. And I'm satisfied. Your letter about my work was beautiful. It counts heavily in the balance!

Letter to Roger Bloom:

I know you fear freedom itself, that you may repeat the errors of the past, but what I hope for you is this: that the infinite value and beauty of freedom, its preciousness, will be so strong that it will resolve the conflict just as a great love can resolve a conflict by being so much stronger than the obstacle. Your enjoyment of freedom will become stronger than feelings of bitterness, rebellion, doubts of yourself. What I hope will happen is that life will seem so precious, so enhanced that it will erase resentments. You will be so hungry for everything. There is a choice to be made. We do choose people, situations, to prove whatever we seek to prove. At one time you wanted revenge upon society for the bank which took your home away from you. But you have done that. It is behind you. Now you can live out the other side of yourself, the side which inspired love in a little boy, friendships. . . . It all begins with a feeling. If we awake angry we tune in and find the events or people who will make us angry. This death you have known, do not let it deprive you of your life. A new life begins. Having been an actor, having written plays, can you imagine yourself beginning completely anew, a new self?

We have just heard of an experience with LSD which is enough to frighten anyone. A doctor friend of ours took too heavy a dose as an experiment. He was staying with friends up in Lake Arrowhead. He purposely stayed with them because they were very close and loving friends. But once under the influence of LSD he felt they wanted to kill him. He was so convinced he ran away. He ran down the road. He signaled to a car passing. They stopped. It was filled with people going to a masquerade, but for the doctor it was an intensification of his nightmare. Their grinning faces, their laughter, their joking, became another persecution. His friends came to the rescue. They gave him a sedative. He still talks about it, as if he still believed the nightmare was a reality.

Letter from Roger Bloom:

George Dibbern wrote recently and as I had told him that nothing had been done concerning an adjustment of time for some of us here he told me that if I wished he would make an effort to have me paroled to New Zealand. I immediately answered and told him that if the Authorities would accept me on the terms of my being an "habitual criminal" I would be most happy to join him. I spoke to the secretary of the Board and asked that my March "review" be set back until May, of this year. By so doing I can have some idea of what might be done by George "down under." I have wanted to speak of this to the Warden but I feel that it is best to wait until something definite has been made—then I will do it. The biggest problem will be to convince the Board that they would be doing a good thing by permitting me to go there. I am sure the Federal Courts will approve, so I am made to believe, and if they concur I am sure that this Board here will go along. Too, am still awaiting some action from Milwaukee and the Federal Court regarding a return to that Court.

I fully believe that since I have come to know you I have made a complete turn to reality—not that there wasn't a spark of it all the while—but through the many kindnesses you have bestowed I have found the verve to seek—to regain some measure of happiness—but mostly to prove my worthiness for this friendship. I will stop. This is not what I intended to write. May I do so again come Sunday??????

Letter to Roger:

I do admire George Dibbern. I will do all I can to help him, as he is trying to get you paroled to New Zealand.

But about Mailer, I feel differently. I think it is too bad that because he is so vociferous, so loud a writer, his work is not considered as it should be, a case of mental unbalance. It is unsound and dangerous. . . . In *The White Negro* he wrote that it takes courage to kill an old lady. He influences young people. A young poet who writes me from jail admires Mailer and thinks an act of violence would liberate his creativity. On the contrary, violence is a symptom of impotence.

Letter to George Dibbern:

I have come to know you through Roger Bloom's references to you in his letters and of course the piece in *Two Cities*. I regret to say I do not know Roger Bloom personally, but from the first letter I received from him I judged him to be a sincere man and a man of feeling who had gone through a great change and responded to kindness. It so happened I was receiving at the same time letters from a young writer in jail and the contrast between them brought out A FINE quality in Roger (the young writer after 10 years in jail is still angry and violent and will surely repeat his rebellion, whereas Roger responded to the books I sent, to my writing to him to be sure and understand *Why* he had acted thus in the past so as to avoid repetition, etc.). His willingness not to blame society or any others, to examine his past, to respond to kindness, his freedom from bitterness or revengefulness—all point to a changed man. And as you know neither books nor psychiatric help are given to men in jail. He also seems to have an influence on the others around him. He is generous and he does not try to embellish his acts; he could have blamed his environment. In short I would trust him. I have corresponded with him for over a year and as you and I both know writing reveals character as well as a friendship.

My only supporting reference is that for two years I was a psychoanalyst under control of Dr. Rank—that I believe I am a good judge of character objectively—Dr. Rank used to say to me: "A man who has a sense of guilt, of right and wrong is never dangerous to society." I hope this is enough.

Letter to Daisy Aldan:

Thinking today about poetry I wanted to be sure you did not feel I did not appreciate yours. I really do. When I speak of not being interested in poetry in general it is because I am more interested in poetry in the novel, in prose writers such as Virginia Woolf or Djuna Barnes, or Marguerite Young. But this is purely personal. I feel the novel needed the poets. I felt that Genêt went further than Rimbaud, Giraudoux further than Claudel, Djuna Barnes further than Dylan Thomas. I am always trying to convert poets to the novel because it is dying. What a novel you would write! But you are an exceptional poet and poetry is right for you. It is just that my devotion went to the novel. But you also have a sound critical faculty and are rendering poetry an enormous service. You are teaching it, inspiring it, encouraging it in others. You not only have written superlative poetry but you have fought for quality and discrimination.

I wish someone would make a record of our reading of *Un Coup de Dés* in French and in English.

[Spring, 1961]

Back in New York, I found myself faced with the sordid aspects of publication and distribution. Four thousand copies of *Cities of the Interior* were offset. Many requests from bookshops, but because I was not one of the big publishers, they never paid me. I had to package and mail books in answer to individual requests. It was time-consuming, and, in the case of the bookshops, shabby.

After many months of this, in desperation I wrote to Alan Swallow in Denver. I had been told that he started as a poet himself, printing other poets by hand in his garage, that he was a one-man, idealistic publisher, doing only the books he loved and content with small profits. Reginald Pole had introduced me to him when I was passing through Denver.

I explained my situation in a letter to Alan Swallow:

It is many years since we visited you, when I was on my first visit West. I was reminded of it when I saw your name on the books of Glenn Clairmonte and talked about you with Maude Hutchins, whose *Victorine* you published.

As you probably know, for years I continued with my own Press doing my own books, but I am having difficulties with distributors who do not pay, and so I am two books behind and seeking a new solution. I have one new unpublished manuscript, and one which has long been out of print and which I get orders for: *Winter of Artifice* (which I meant to put together with *The Voice,* and *Stella,* as three novelettes). I wonder if there is anything we can work out together? Would you care to do the new manuscript, *Seduction of the Minotaur,* or the reprint? I could guarantee that I myself would sell one thousand copies. Do you have any organization so that you might consider distributing my books? They have sold well and continuously without advertisement, without reviews, without any outside help, at the rate of 2 or 3 thousand a year. The paper edition of *Spy in the House of Love* sold in Avon books 170 thousand copies. (But the editor who worked with Avon is no longer with them and now with Hearst ownership the titles and qualities of the books have changed.) Have you any suggestions? I know you only print hard-cover books. Would you like to do an omnibus of *Cities of the Interior* which I did in a limited edition and put a hard cover on it and your imprint? Do think this over and write me. There is one added factor, that I have always said whatever publisher puts out my novels I will give an option on the diaries (for the future).

For the distribution of the books I would give sixty per cent on condition that they are paid for in cash. Do you have copies of my books? Shall I send you some?

Letter from Alan Swallow:

I have now read the materials you sent me, including the manuscript of the new novel which came from Mr. Gunther Stuhlmann. (I am sending a copy of this letter to Mr. Stuhlmann as your agent.)

I think it makes just about perfect sense that I become your U.S. publisher. The sales of your works have apparently demonstrated that they are not suitable or of interest to the large commercial publishers. Yet, there is a kind of victimization involved for an author to be handled by too many smallish "avant garde" publishers—who seem to be fly-by-night much of the time, who appeal to a certain clientele (an avid one but a limited and changeable one); or for you to be attempting self publication of the works. I fall in between. I don't manage the very large, large sales; but I am a determined and persistent devil, and I manage a very respectable sale for the materials in which I am interested. (Indeed, for many books, I feel that my methods will get more sales over a period of time than can be achieved by others—for I have seemed to develop them for the kind of work in which I am interested, which I find will not support themselves well upon a publishing situation of high overhead, etc., but are quite satisfying to me and, in the end, to the author.) As I say, for the kind of sale which seems to me your destiny in this country, I feel that I am in a better situation than anyone else. I am loyal to my titles; I keep them in print if humanly possible (for example, such a book as Winters' *In Defense of Reason,* which bigwigs in NY publishing told me I could not sell in 2,000 quantity, is now in its third edition, has sold more than 5,000 copies and still sells as fast as it ever did; and eight years ago I did his *Collected Poems,* stuck with them, sold them out, then in 1960 reissued a new, slightly augmented edition, placed it both in cloth and in Swallow Paperbooks, and it won the big Bollingen Prize for 1960 and was one of thirteen finalists for the National Book Award in poetry). This is the sort of thing I can do better, I feel, than other publishers and is the particular role I can play in the over-all field of publishing.

Furthermore, I publish only what I admire, and everybody knows this; and I admire your work. So it should be a fairly good "wedding" of work and publisher, I think. I shall hope so, anyway!

Now as I see it, the over-all problem is to "rationalize," to make sense of your works in a publishing "package" way. If I have all the work of consequence now, I seem to see it shaping up this way. One cannot achieve it just overnight, but it should be achieved as rapidly as possible.

1. The novels. You wish ultimately that all of these (five in present volume and the new *Seduction of the Minotaur*) be in one volume . . .

2. The novelettes. These should be the three—*Winter of Artifice, The Voice,* and *Stella*—in one volume, which should be available ultimately in both paper and cloth editions . . .

3. *The House of Incest.* You have this in paperback. I do not have it clear in mind if you have this in present stock. If so, I should take over this stock and add it to the list, then plan to reprint; or if you do not have it any longer in stock, I should agree to publish it as rapidly as possible . . .

4. The short stories. Now in your letters you have not mentioned this, but when the present volume *Under a Glass Bell* sells out and then the two novelettes in it (*Winter of Artifice* and *The Voice*) are pulled out to make up the new volume of three novelettes, then the short stories in that volume would be left out of print. In the over-all plan, I should think that one would want to do a volume of these stories alone—that these stories and *The House of Incest,* as quite small volumes, should be kept in paper editions (Swallow Paperbooks editions) alone.

Now I hope I have seen clearly the problem and your wishes. If I have failed to see something or have misinterpreted, please set me straight . . .

All right, in summary: I am willing to embark on the long-range project for your work as it seems best. First steps would be preparation of a contract for *Seduction of the Minotaur;* your indication of exact stock you have in the material in print, and your cost figure for that stock, and its exact condition—cloth, paper, unbound sheets, etc.; signature of contracts covering rights and royalties upon such stock; signature of contracts for books "intended" as above. I am indicating my willingness, even my eagerness to do this. I would sign any contracts, of course, after seeing your willingness in the over-all plan and the particular contracts, etc., that is, that they be such that I can approve. I don't think we would have any problems there. The big problem now is the ultimate intent and then the development of the plans.

A genuine association started. I review and help his writers. He distributes the books as well as he can. Big newspapers never review small press books. That is the greatest handicap. I soon found out that to be distributed by Alan Swallow was almost as frustrating as to be my own distributor. He could not get reviews except in college magazines.

I helped him with my appearances on the Pacifica Foundation

F.M. stations in Los Angeles, San Francisco, and in New York. They were playing my reading of the "Party" from *Ladders to Fire* which I had given at The Living Theatre.

Letter to Alan Swallow:

We both want to make things as easy as possible. I consider our association as a partnership among non-commercials. I don't want you to lose money; we must pool our efforts so we can enjoy the success of a sincere effort.

Story of Alan Swallow: Born February 11, 1915, in Powell, Wyoming, according to *Current Biography*. His father was a farmer. He graduated from the University of Wyoming. Began to write poetry and prose in his teens. Founded his own literary magazine. He published and edited *Modern Verse*. "Has long been connected with literary quarterlies and little magazines. In 1949 he published *Index to Little Magazines*. Little magazines, in his opinion, perform an important corrective and supplementary function, since they serve as a forum for poetry, and new and experimental writing is seldom published in mass magazines. The function of the little publisher, according to Swallow, is analogous to that of the little magazine. He has been a little publisher for over 20 years; firm has become the best known of its kind. From 1940 to 1954 he published on a part-time basis, and in 1954, the first year in which his business yielded enough profit, he left teaching and engaged in publishing on a full-time basis.

" 'So now I feel I'm one of the world's luckiest guys, to be concentrating so single-mindedly, working so many hours, on something I want so much to see done and have a modest living out of it!' "

Swallow is a man of quality, a modest man, with courage and integrity. He knows that by protecting the minority writers he is enriching the majority just as research scientists enrich science itself. By his absence of greed, he shows the same vision of future needs as the foresters who are concerned with replanting lost trees. He is the last of the idealists. His concept should not be allowed to die out. He should not die without progeny.

His own writing is wise, human and warm, and his poems crystal clear.

———

Karl Shapiro went off to Europe without giving me a comment which would have helped the books, after writing me such emotional letters. In one he said my books had to be read in secret, in a locked room, and that he had wept. This is like Maxwell Geismar repeating over the telephone: *"Spy in the House of Love* is so *alive,* so *alive,"* and then writing a perfunctory review. Private and public statements are so different.

Alan Swallow published Maude Hutchins, a writer I admire, the equivalent of Colette, meticulous and lyrical studies of family relationships, and a fine suggestive touch in erotic subjects.

Cities of the Interior was never sent to reviewers, and was considered a reprint, though it contained a new section, *Solar Barque*.

Gore Vidal is now a critic, which means he is cremating people.

New York.

Women look like flowerpots, hats of lilies, poppies, cherries. Windows full of orange and shocking-pink dresses. An explosion of color. Dogs running away from their masters in the park. Central Park much better for Piccolo [my poodle]. The Village is full of Bowery bums, beggars, staring tourists.

Lila in conference with a millionaire from Phoenix about magazine she wants to start.

Albee is a fascinating writer. Went early to see *Zoo Story* and *The American Dream* as I had no tickets. Expected to eat a sandwich while waiting. Bought one and was told I was not allowed to eat it in the shop. Woman cast me out in the rain. Next door to the old theatre a house was being wrecked. A pile of stones, twisted iron, wood glistening with oily stains, a ragpicker's atmosphere. Sat there and ate my sandwich in the rain. Perfect preparation for the plays. A torn, faded, rusty, toothless house, a rundown theatre, but a young crowd. *Zoo Story* tense and dramatic; *American Dream* wild surrealism, satire, wit, interesting every moment.

Fantasy of roving editor, which I pursued all these years because it meant freedom of movement and an income, which made me write articles under pseudonyms, or articles other people signed, which seemed about to become true with magazines *Two Cities* and then *Eve,* and then ended with their failure, was revived by Lila Rosenblum. My friendship with Lila lasted through the years although I saw little of her when I began to stay away from New York. But she was close to Jim Herlihy, to Stanley Haggart, to other friends of mine. She was in ill health but always courageous and spirited. She came to see me in Sierra Madre in a car which had tremors and always made me think of her fragility. Her illness, lupus, was a mystery to me. It was considered fatal. When I first visited her she was bedridden, but her intelligence was lively and her understanding of people accurate.

Now she was planning a magazine, the kind we all dreamed about. Her enthusiasm, her concepts were so contagious that her friends gave up their jobs in dull places to work on her magazine. Stanley Haggart was to be staff photographer, I the roving editor. Lila had found a designer for the dummy and for our writing paper. She was busy raising the capital. Her father had promised to raise half of it. She was in telephone communication with a young millionaire from Phoenix. Lila herself wrote a profile of Millie Johnstone. Millie's story interested us because she had been a dancer and an artist who had married into Bethlehem Steel. And at first she hated the steel mill as a monster who devoured her husband. She is only there as a nurse to a man shattered by gigantic responsibilities, gigantic ambitions, gigantic projects. We admired how she made her peace with the steel mill. She began to take an interest in it as an artist. She depicted the dramatic scenes of labor in her tapestries. Man in a death struggle with an element which had to be tamed. Then she took an interest in the workmen and initiated reforms. She tried to humanize the absolutely nonhuman offices and hallways. She introduced paintings and sculptures.

Lila understood the drama behind the luxury and the drama of woman.

I wrote a profile of the Barrons, as they are composing electronic sounds for Gore Vidal's play, *Visit to a Small Planet. Time* magazine wrote about them but I wanted to show one can write a lively profile without carbolic acid.

The magazine will be called *Fair Sex,* but an intelligent Fair Sex. At last!

We spent the evening at the apartment of Lila's co-editor, Don Combs. His friend of many years is dying of cancer at twenty-eight. He only has a few weeks to live. We all spontaneously created the illusion that he was essential to the first number, that he had to design the office (he designs stage sets), help select material. He was handsome, and the shock of conceding that this young body would die made our task difficult.

Lila wrote to me that she had her first meeting with the young millionaire, that he was about twenty-five, that he looked like Gary Cooper, that he had made his first million in copper mines when he was twenty. He would give her enough money for two years, more later if she needed it. He also gave her carte blanche as editor. He left town and would be back in five weeks with his lawyers to sign all the papers. Lila has designed the dummy of the first number. It would have to be a Christmas number now. By pooling all our friends we found we had a distinguished list of contributors: Daisy Aldan, Lesley Blanch, James Leo Herlihy.

I suggested I would like to do profiles of interesting and creative women. We had one of Millie Johnstone. I could write about Lesley. We are all so hopeful, dreaming of magnificent achievements.

We waited for the young millionaire from Phoenix to arrive at Lila's apartment with his lawyer to sign the papers. We had bought champagne on "the expense account." I had bought the first transparent plastic umbrella which lit up like a Christmas tree when opened. Tiny bulbs were hidden in bunches of lilac. We were delirious with happiness. I was going to Paris for the *Fair Sex*. We each had cards printed with our names.

James Leo Herlihy had promised a story. I was going to write about my favorite women, Kim Stanley, Cornelia Runyon, Jeanne Moreau. Stanley had beautiful photographs of a Fado singer in Portugal.

The young millionaire from Phoenix never appeared.

We found out later that he was the gardener for millionaires in Phoenix, that while clipping hedges he heard all these fabulous projects discussed, that this inspired him to play the role for a few weeks, "investing" here and there, over the telephone, and no wonder to all our projects and suggestions he assented with enthusiasm, it was all his dream and ours conjugated, interlocked.

All those magazines we were going to surpass, outshine, to demonstrate the talents, the intelligence of the *Fair Sex*. All the dull jobs we abandoned, the treasures we were to discover, neglected books of immense value, so much talent in all of us!

Letter from Roger Bloom:

Twenty-nine years ago I first entered prison. I had just passed my twentieth birthday. I had been hitchhiking from Pennsylvania to Los Angeles. A man picked me up in St. Louis and was driving to Oklahoma. We were stopped in a small town south of St. Louis and the driver disappeared. The police arrested me and sent me here for two years because there was something about the car and its contents which loomed darkly. It took six days from the day of arrest until I was a full-fledged inmate of this prison, and retained a bitter attitude for many years. Born March 3, 1912.

Letter from poet in prison:

Yes, in six months the abominable walls enclosing the tensions of a gray existence will dissolve and the fade-in will be on brighter forms. . . . It's kind of you wanting to put me in touch with your friends in case you are not in New York now that freedom is nearer. Having seen so much, experienced so much, how can you be so genuinely sincere, still possess feelings of altruism and compassion when you know what a vile, base, depraved thing man's inherent nature is? When I discovered the cruelty of an ugly world I reacted by becoming more cruel and violent than they—showing them the rebellion of a man though chronologically a boy. Your way "to create a world of your own, peopled with your own people." Yes, you have succeeded . . .

Letter to poet in prison:

. . . My only concern is your unhealed anger, and your pessimism, what I call, when I'm guilty of it, hemophilia of the soul, unhealing wounds caused by others' cruelties. But such pains are part of life and your capacity for writing and creating will have to be opposed (as they are in many of us) to self-destruction. For you are too intelligent not to admit destruction is ultimately self-destruction.

Varda was here yesterday. He has plenty to be bitter about. His joyous and really beautiful collages are never exhibited in San Francisco, where he lives, no museums have any of his collages. But he said yesterday the moment an artist becomes bitter he has ceased to possess his own world, he has gone over to the enemy camp, the enemies of his work, who had intended to embitter him, knowing it kills creativity. Why the present love for big, empty, sterile abstractions, for deserts? When you discovered the cruelty of the world, why did you not join forces with those who strive for beauty and humanity? As a girl I started to give myself to whatever neutralized the ugliness. There is another aspect to man which is not destructive. Destruction is going on all around us, but so is creation. We can choose sides. When you are free return not as you say to the gutter, but to your acting, writing.

I write to you in a desperate effort to eradicate the feelings of revengefulness for past hurts. I don't feel that you are healed. All of us have been at some time or other humiliated, betrayed, but our real life depends on how we react to such experiences. The tide of violence is too great. I fight it individually as much as I can.

Interview with Antonin Artaud, a few days before his death, by Claude Nerguy in *Pléiades* magazine, no. 49 (my translation):

Ivry . . . An iron grille gate, a park. We are at the rest home. I had heard about Artaud, his madness, and had read *The Theatre and Its Double*. He granted me an interview for this Saturday between ten A.M. and one o'clock. A young guard conducted us towards a small square building. We walked around it before knocking at a small, low door.

"Yes? Come in! Who is there?"

The anxious, deep voice surprised us. There was no time lapse between the questions. We entered and the guard introduced us. I was never so startled: a large square room, the floor stained, the bed with holes, one sofa and two armchairs. The closed shutters gave to the room an impression of frightening neglect.

Artaud is sitting by the fireplace where a wood fire is burning. Dark gray pants, a dirty shirt, open in front, revealing a red scarf around his neck, his hair falling over his eyes, he seems to us to be frightfully emaciated.

Artaud placed his two index fingers behind his ears searching for a spot for a long time and began to talk. He had memorized my letter! Then he talked: "I have just published three books: *Artaud le Morro, Ci-Gît* and *La Culture Indienne*. Those you do not have. You could not have them, they are too expensive for you. I asked the publisher to issue the books in a cheaper edition following the de luxe one. I don't know if he has done it. The other one, the third, *Van Gogh* is not expensive. Buy it." He turned towards us, his hands in front of him, his hair hanging on each side of his fantastic face, pale and suffering, a face incarnating suffering. His blue-green eyes enlarged and staring at the infinite. "My real public are young men of your age, students. They are not speculators. Those I hate." He sat once more by the fire. "You have not read anything else of mine? I came out a few months ago from my asylums, from my insane asylums. I have a hole in my back. The doctors struck me with hammers and bars of iron." I looked at him. It was an extraordinary face in our time, the face of someone having hallucinations, of a passionate nature, a man who might be at the same time a demon. He rose and seized a hammer. My friend and I became anxious but fortunately the cleaning woman reassured us with a smile. Artaud came nearer to us, his eyes dilated, the pupils small and black. "You see, this is the way I test the meter of my poems. It gives them greater force, breath." And he began to strike at a block of wood, his hair growing wild, his lips moist, screaming a poem of which I could only catch the first word: "Cain." It was unbelievable, terrible. This suffering being striking the rhythm with a hammer, these almost inarticulate cries which seemed like the war cry of the Indians, this sort of shout of victory and death in an almost empty room, bare walls facing only one drawing which seemed to be staring at us.

When the poem was finished, he stopped, exhausted, the hammer, now useless, hung in his hand, and small pieces of wood splattered the floor.

He went to the table, which served as a desk, covered with papers in disorder, searching through his papers for a copy of *La Culture Indienne* which he might give us. He did not find it, but he came back with a small sketchbook with a blue cover in which he wrote down his poems. "I draw too. The drawings add strength to the poems. See, there are drawings here and there over all the poems." He leaves the sketchbook with us and takes up the hammer blows again, then he came back to me and said gently and solemnly: "You are looking at the drawings upside down." I feared an explosion and retreated a little. His voice was so strange, with its inflexions of *grand seigneur*. He took back the sketchbook. "That was a man, and the chains which are killing him came from the infinite. This is a flying machine which has traversed the interplanetary spaces. It is stopped, broken, destroyed." Then he stood facing me and placed one finger on my chest, his left hand holding a drawing, and looked at me. I had the feeling that magnetic waves went through me. He returned the drawing to his table and walked around the room humming. He seemed like an animal in a cage, searching for an exit, and I was reminded of an early poem of his:

Ah, give us skulls.

I held out my book for him to sign and taking up his fountain pen he wrote: "To Claude Nerguy, on condition that he be alone because I am an enemy of sexuality, Antonin Artaud."

He took a package of cigarettes and offered one to each of us, and then took a card out of a package of white cards, wrote a few words on it, handed it to me: "Come Monday evening at the reading of my *Pour en Finir avec le Jugement de Dieu*. This card is strictly personal, as I wrote on it, there will only be three more seats. You, Mademoiselle, can go eight days later, it will be read again."

We parted and he said: "We'll see you Monday."

His eyes still shone with a strange sparkle, indescribable, eyes of a seer.

"Perhaps he died rhyming a death poem on his wood block," said my friend. "I do not dare think of it."

And she added: "He did not have eyes but a beam of light."

With Artaud it was the revenge of time. Time gave him his due. But as I do not believe in afterlife, I realize the gift artists make to the world is a selfless one ultimately, and that the knowledge that it may survive the self must be due to a belief in immortality. Or can one really work for those one will never see? Do I ever think of those who will read me after my death? The "self" disappears, as we know from LSD, from anesthesia. The core and center vanish. So if our words or music continue to enter others' bloodstreams they are no longer identifiable. I love Proust and his writing. All I have of him is an essence. It is not Proust or Artaud who will know who loves them.

Sometimes I think of what the dead would have hated to see if they were still alive, and I am grateful for their death. For my mother's sake, I am glad she did not see the Cuban revolution.

One night Jack Hirschman invited several people interested in Artaud. But they only love his madness and his use of drugs. They knew nothing of the seven volumes of collected works. Artaud would have repudiated them.

He was influenced by Edgar Allan Poe. He was haunted by the cruelty inherent in life itself. Do people die at the right time? Would Artaud have admired the drugged generation? If in his lifetime he was misunderstood, I do not think he would have preferred what is said and written about him now.

Ian Hugo's film, *Venice, Étude Number One,* is a poem of Venice which captures for the first time both Venice and the dreams it arouses. His use of superimpositions expresses the many layers of our impressions: color, textures, dreams, legends and memory. Scenes pass before our eyes in a free, apparently unrelated flow but which resembles the way our imagination and our emotions respond. We accumulate impressions rather as a series of musical moods. Our emotional view of Venice is fluid, symphonic. At times we are aware only of light upon water, of a gliding black gondola, of a square of blue, of laundry fluttering like pennants, of statues coming to life, of red brocade, candlelight and silver-necked gondolas. The film opens with the shadow of a gondolier reflected upon the red flanks of an enormous ship. The gondolas, tied to candy-striped poles, dance, as in a ballet, to the waves created by the ferry boats. A woman's lacy wedding gown in the foreground veils the passing of a funeral gondola. Reflections are a constant theme, gondolas reflected in windows, buildings reflected in the water, people reflected in mirrors, a church spire seen through a heart-shaped, sculptured frieze. The images are in rich tones, with the quality of painting, and are so vivid and sensuous that one can hear the sound of church bells, glass, metal, wood, the sudden windstorm of pigeons flying off, the lapping waters of the canal, the cries of the gondoliers as they warn of their approaching a turn, the barking of dogs, the laughter of children.

The climax dramatizes the conflict of a city always about to be swallowed by the sea. The cathedrals are reflected in the flood waters and seem to be lying at the bottom of the sea. Blue predominates.

[Summer, 1961]

Letter to Roger Bloom:

They should spend less time on rules and regulations, holding back books and records, typewriters, etc., and more on helping a man find his unused, unknown creative energy, his real self.

He received and read Lindner's books, Rimbaud's *Illuminations,* and from someone else, *Cast the First Stone,* a book about the oldest profession by Judge John Murtagh, Chief Magistrate of N.Y.C.

I correspond with that wonderful George Dibbern, author of *Quest,* who is trying to get Roger Bloom paroled to New Zealand. We are collecting reference letters.

I sent Roger Bloom two recordings of my readings and they were not given to him; they were returned to me. I was disappointed that the Warden did not relent. I do see the sense of some laws but I do not see any sense or usefulness in depriving Roger of something sent by a friend when all I sent inspired him to write and to read. I should think that when they see a man making efforts at expanding, enriching his understanding, they would help. The psychological effect of unjust deprivations is something they should consider.

Met Tracey Roberts at Kozlenko's one evening. She has vivid red hair, enormous blue eyes, she is both intelligent and emotional. She is slender, and her voice is rich in tones. She illuminated the room, she glowed. I felt she was the essence of all my women characters. When she talks to me over the telephone I never know which of them is going to appear, clear-minded Djuna, vehement Lillian, confused, fragmented Sabina.

I feel she is Sabina, but not sure yet. She has what I call a Russian beauty, that is, the ice-blue of the eyes, the heavy hair, the translucent skin still convey as much intensity as the dark-eyed, dark-haired Mediterranean.

She always begins the conversation: "I don't want to be negative . . ." but proceeds to manifest just that. She is an exquisite actress, accomplished, seductive, yet she has not reached the status these accomplishments should have produced. Again I am faced with the mystery of self-undoing. I feel it is there but cannot pin it down. Is it when she refuses countless roles offered to her for one reason or another?

Her voice is moving, she is elusive and mobile, she could act Sabina.

When she arrived in a sweater dress and string of pearls I was reminded that she was not one of Dostoevski's beauties, but a Hollywood actress. I wanted to wash the make-up off, pull out the false eyelashes. So much life in her, and fear, and a magnetic force pulling her back.

Very little exchange would take place when we met, but over the telephone she wept, confided, described chaos, dualities, complexities, ending always by convincing me that she was a victim of accidents, circumstances, of others. I confided in her. Then when we came face to face, it was as if we knew too much. Soon I was trapped in my usual empathy for those who suffer. True to my habit, I began determinedly to change the downward course of her life, trying to spot the errors, the destructive decisions.

Letter from Roger Bloom:

Have just reread several of my recent letters to you and one or two of yours—this I received today is in answer to that which I wrote on the tenth—and, as I mentioned in the first of these two, I shall forget Rosset and await a letter from Henry—he may have something in mind, since he has asked Rosset to take an interest. [About Dibbern and his mss. and Quest.]

Because I spend so much of each day in the shop—and when I am not serving a customer I spend most of the remaining time in reading—there are many disturbances during the course of each day—but, comes the nighttime I can be found here in my small cubicle with a book. After a while, after the newness of the place becomes commonplace one makes some effort to make adjustments in a manner which can provide a measure of living with others who are cursed with having lost their freedom—once within a place of this kind every trend of thought makes itself evident—at one time or another. The possible and the impossible, wish and fact, poetry and thought, belief and knowledge and, at times, all mixed up. One wonders—why think, brood, ponder or make plans? we don't want to fight against life—just let it bring some small measure of happiness and hope. We learn to accept whatever is considered a privilege—regimentation and all which it entails has an irksome itch with us—we don't like it but it must be accepted, else there is trouble.

Something I read just recently has prompted me to speak of this routine —it concerned an article in the prison paper about letters. I have sent you a copy of it and you can read it much easier than I might quote here—too, you spoke of the blues in your last letter and did not feel you should write when you were in such a mood.

There is so much pleasure in this sharing of your life—your belonging so completely to the beguiling world that is just beyond my reach—this, I assure you, has much to do with any man's existence in a prison. Would you know that with some of your letters, one can, if one wishes, breathe the perfumes, taste the wines, eat wonderful and strange foods, admire beautiful paintings, "feel" the murmur of muted voices in a salon—all this —and more, in the world within your letters. And, especially, when you write of your visits to foreign places—browsing in Le Mistral Book Shop— truly, they give one a more vivid meaning—an intense reality—and, you might ask, how can this help—how can this void the harshness of imprisonment behind bars and walls—it is so easy to answer—and who is in a better position to give an answer than I—since May 1st—1960, I have hardly known I have been imprisoned. At least I have spent less time thinking of the fact that I *am* in prison than I have in the years prior to Anaïs Nin. To be sure, Henry provided so much over the past six years— occasional letters, and books, of course—but for some reason I can find little which can truly compare to the fulfillment of one's life with so much which has brought about a completeness of meaning for a new and richer life—richer, in the sense that does not mean material wealth—but wealth of sharing and knowing that belief and trust and understanding of friends can be considered far above gold and jewels.

Sammy and I were talking a few days ago—we were in the recreation yard and I had taken one of the Varda collages to him—(I kept the one that had the dress design on the back) and we batted around the idea of what would happen to a place of this kind were each man, imprisoned here, to have a friend such as you—both of us felt that were this to happen these walls would simply crumble—there would be no one inside.

More adventures in *Miss MacIntosh, My Darling:* Marguerite reads to me over the telephone about "the blind portrait painter who painted us all."

About the musical compositions Mr. Spitzer concealed under his hat lining and which were blown away with the hat.

About the burial of Peron. They cannot find a tailor to fit his burial suit. He telephoned to himself, Peron the tailor.

Objects appear out to sea. A candelabrum. A carriage. Other objects are spewn out by the sea, a clock filled with barnacles, an umbrella, glasses.

Marguerite ponders the problem of being and nonbeing.

The character who always took the wrong train.

The character who bought coal so it would become diamonds.

Seldom did she meet anyone who did not suffer from some form of complex illusion. These illusions are never recorded as Marguerite does, yet they are the atmosphere in which we live constantly.

I visited Renate and she showed me a series of highly original, fantastic drawings by Peter. Someone wanted to make a filmstrip and needed narration for it, so I wrote the Snake Story to go with the drawings:

There was a gentle snake called Ophidia who hissed but did not bite. He carried no venom. But he became bored because the world and everything in it looked the same today as it did yesterday. He heard about a cactus plant which grew at the bottom of a purple bottle and which secreted a liquid which could transform the world and take one to places never seen before. So the snake embraced the sinuous contours of the purple bottle and drank of the cactus milk. The drops began to fly upward and scattered all around him like fireworks. Each drop carried a mouth, an eye, a lighted candle. As they fell to the ground from a giant mouth watched by a giant eye they became minnows on the ground, and then drops of blood which flew upward along a sword, up into the veins of an arm, into a hand with an index finger extended, holding a chain which held up the closed and smiling lips through which the drops of cactus milk had first slipped through. Another solitary hand was busy lighting the candles inside of the drops. Ophidia had disappeared as a snake but become particles, a more convenient costume for travel.

He was locked up in a capsule, his arms and legs swimming in space. Through a small periscope he followed the larger platform into space. It looked like the top of a drum torn from its base and carried by flying sea weeds, by tree roots and twin missiles. In the center was what seemed like a roulette table. As it turned, Ophidia by remote control could stop it for landing. They were accompanied by whirling tops, the acrobats of space. The landing field of the new planet looked like a chess board. Flat stones with tiny eyes showed the way, and large teardrops guided the landing.

An electronic centipede sent messages with vibrations of its wiry tentacles. Its face was like a colored top, and its body covered with purple velvet. The message read: Come into the land of metamorphosis. Nothing here is what you think it is. It is very restful.

Following the giant teardrops and the runway, Ophidia came into a world of flames, hissing snakes, revolving planets, flying burning candles, undulating, dancing, whirling. He became a wave among other waves. With a black cap, he became a planet with a tail. He became a snake bird, a snake cane, a spotted tree trunk. He became a snake mouth, a type of orchid, a snake stone, an ammonite.

Out of black striped waves of a symmetric ocean Ophidia emerged as a huge dragon with a crown on its head. His tongue was a red feather duster. He was at last in a different world. The tall houses were uninhabited as everyone was busy flying. The bats had butterfly wings. The sun was an octopus with fifteen heads. The fish stood on their tail fins. He was as tall as a tree, and at the tip of the tree emerged a man and contrary to the Bible story it was the man who was tempting the snake with an apple.

As soon as he ate of the apple the man was no longer a tree but a scaly purple-bodied dragon emerging from the rocks, with the green face of a man, the hair of a Medusa, the arms of an octopus. A fiery dragon challenged him, but he was not fighting his own battle. He carried a little man with a drawn sword at the top of his head.

Hands which are independent from the body can accomplish so much more. They can push a pelican between a flying crocodile and a flying sea serpent. They can sail in a flower vase, on a boat with sails of sliced heart. The bottle which was thrown out to sea contains fruit. Where is Ophidia now? He is a flying fish enclosed in a magnified sea drop. Two hands across the ocean touch, one with long nails which do not scratch, the other well manicured. The waves become plants. The bottle is now a giant pear carrying embryonic fruit about to be born. The snake has become a sunflower, a drop of dew.

The snake is now an eye. This eye is held up by two hands squeezing it. The snake is two dragon heads (and crowned, too, even though this is a kingdom without a ruler, for everyone is too busy becoming something else. There is no time for tyranny.) Out of the squeezed eye fall giant purple tears into a purple champagne cup. The huge tears fell from the sun, the trees, the skies, the dragons, the bats, the eyes, the moon. Everything changed and nothing was what it appeared to be. Tongues are waves, and waves are hair, hair are leaves, leaves are snakes, and snakes are waves, rocks are boats, and boats are bats. He was never bored, but as there was only one of each species he began to feel lonely. The big eye began to cry. So many tears caused a short circuit, so he became three snakes with electric eyeballs dancing on magnetic fields. He sprouted eyes like tops, batteries at the end of his feet, and flew back towards the bottle.

Sinfonia Erotica:

A friend in Los Angeles came to me for advice. She played in an orchestra conducted by a dynamic Italian with a powerful, dominant personality. She confided that the conductor was directing not only the playing of the women musicians but their lives as well. His baton was not only for the purpose of synchronizing the music, but it had its symbolic parallel in his conducting of the sensuous symphony of his players. As he waved his conductor's baton with a decisiveness, an *élan,* a hypnotic force which ruled the vibrations, drew forth brilliant sounds, he also waved his decisive, impulsive, hypnotic baton of desire over the women players and also the women patrons who helped to keep the orchestra afloat. My friend's conflict was her inability to become independent of the conductor. First he seduced, then he drafted his musicians, and then, like Svengali, he made zombies of them: "Play! Rehearse! Travel! Play! Rehearse! Travel! Carry my music! Clean my shoes! Take this note to my mistress!" My friend was possessed by the conductor and obeyed, but then somehow or other began to wish for freedom and ended at my door.

After many talks, she gradually gained in strength. A few months later she brought another girl, a second violinist, and then a cellist, and soon the harpist, the flutist, and in each case the slave slowly freed herself. Before I had met the entire women's section, the conductor sensed his authority was in danger, held an inquisitorial session and discovered who was conducting the life of his musicians.

He said: "I will solve this situation immediately. I will visit this woman. You say she is very feminine, very gentle. Good. I will seduce her. You will see what will become of her power."

And so, the conductor appeared at my house, and for a moment as he stood at the door I thought I was back in Russia in the days of Rasputin. The strong features, the piercing hypnotic eyes, the square chin, a skin like the texture of stone.

We began talking about music. He did not know my father was a pianist. He was willing to admit that the women in his orchestra were playing better. He was curious to know why this should be so;

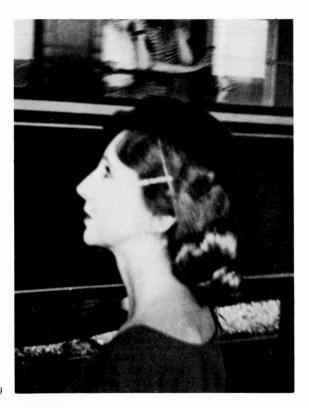

Anaïs Nin in Venice, 1959

Henry Miller visiting
Roger Bloom (left)
in prison, 1962

Copyright © 1975 by Joan Schwartz

Marguerite Young

Peter Hujar

Daisy Aldan

Still from Ian Hugo's film, *The Gondola Eye*

Christian du Bois Larson

Renate Druks

Two drawings by Peter Druks
for a story by Anaïs Nin

Peter Druks

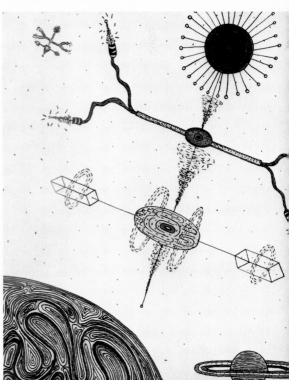

Marguerite Duras

Nobuko Venishi

Tracey Roberts

Bristlecone pines,
the oldest living
things on earth

John Pearson

Alan Swallow

Anaïs Nin autographing *The Diary* at the Gotham Book Mart;
Gunther and Barbara Stuhlmann at left

was it my love, my understanding of music? "Oh no," I said, "it is my love and my understanding of the need of freedom. Your women have become afraid of you; they feel tense and uneasy. They have lost their confidence."

"But without me they couldn't play at all!" And then he meditated a while. "And if you help them all, there will be almost no orchestra left. My strength is holding it together."

"There are two kinds of strength. One brings out the strength of the other, helps it to be born; the other kind imposes its own strength and weakens those who submit to it."

"I came here to fight you."

"Yes, I know."

"But now I feel like asking you to help me. This strength of mine—it is not only destroying the orchestra girls but me also. I am losing all my patronesses. I am in great trouble. Will you help me?"

It seems that whenever the orchestra needed funds to continue its performances, the conductor would set off on a fund-raising tour of all the wealthy women interested in music. He would be invited to stay on weekends at their homes.

"I could not resist seducing them, and, as most of them saw so little of their husbands, who were always very busy, they were helpless in the face of my technique. I must tell you I am prouder of my technique as a lover than of my technique as a conductor."

From the image of the conductor commanding the waves of sound rising from the lovely arms of the women players, it was easy to proceed to the image of his vehemence, his powerful gestures overwhelming the starved matrons.

"But this created jealousies and troubles. And now the orchestra is about to collapse."

The last one to succumb to his superb technique was Mrs. S., a handsome woman who looked like Emma Eames, the opera singer, statuesque, aristocratic, imposing. Yet she had yielded to the conductor with the pliability of a *jeune fille*. She had grown children. She was one of the patronesses of the orchestra. Added to the complexities of these multiple relationships, now a series of anonymous letters had been sent to Mrs. S. threatening to inform her husband and her children if she did not break with the conductor.

"Mrs. S. is hysterical, almost losing her mind, but she will not give me up. I wish you would help her. She is suffering so much. If this is going to wreck her life, I am ready to withdraw. I think the anonymous letters may be written by an old friend of hers with whom she often went on trips to Europe. She was jealous of me."

The orchestra was about to break up from intrigues, jealousies. The conductor appealed to my love of music.

For weeks I became almost a part of the orchestra. Mrs. S. came to see me. She is a noble woman, one who presents such an ideal figure to the world that everyone seeks unconsciously to maintain her in this role. She is condemned to behave as a mythological figure; the world is very insistent on people maintaining their roles and does not like confusion or paradoxes. Mrs. S. was noble; the conductor was the tempter, evil. Mrs. S. came to see me with a full box of Kleenex, and this practicality in the face of sorrow almost deprived me of my faith in this sorrow, for I never remembered having supplied myself with a box of Kleenex to face a love crisis. It seemed an act of premeditation. However she cried abundantly and the utilitarian advantage of Kleenex was not to be denied; but a spontaneous, unprepared sorrow would have touched me more. Before leaving she handed me the damp tissues to dispose of. It was my first encounter with efficiency in sorrow.

I saw Mrs. S. many times. The anonymous letters were of the utmost cruelty and could bring her misery and scandal. But she was weeping over the loss of the conductor. "Ah, you don't know, he was the only one, the only one who awakened me to love, who gave me pleasure. I have had three children and never knew pleasure!"

I felt more like Simenon than a confidante. After all, I was supposed to find out who had written the anonymous letters. I suggested that Mrs. S. and the conductor spend a night together at a hotel and *tell absolutely no one about it.*

All the time I had an uneasy feeling that it could only be the conductor himself. But why? Why should he torment Mrs. S.? What did he have to gain by informing her husband and children?

They followed my advice. Mrs. S. was radiant when she came to see me at the prospect of a night with the conductor. It was amazing to see this woman who was quiet and ponderous like a statue talk almost like a lyric poet about the conductor's gifts as a lover. I could imagine that just as he could call forth:

Sounds of Gaiety from the violins,
Sounds of Passion from the cellos,

Sounds of Melancholy from the English horn,
Sounds of Battle from the brass and cymbals,
Sounds of Buffoonery from the bassoon.

He could also evoke a symphony of erotic harmonies; he could or-
chestrate a symphony of pleasurable vibrations from all the parts of
the body: I could hear the hair, the neck, the blue eyes, the patri-
cian nose, the sumptuous shoulders, the Wagnerian bust, the legs
of Mrs. S. turned into a symphony—a *Sinfonia Erotica*—an erotic
fugue.

But—the conductor was not in the same mood.

A few days later Mrs. S. received another anonymous letter describing the events at the hotel, not as if the spy had been in the
room, but almost; and the threat: Break with the conductor,
NEVER SEE HIM AGAIN, was in much larger letters.

When I saw this letter I knew the writer must be the conductor
himself.

I questioned him alone and finally he broke down and confessed.
He had wanted to drive Mrs. S. to break with him. There was another patroness . . .

It was time for the orchestra's big concert. The conductor threatened to quit. The patronesses were hostile to each other, the musicians nervous. My friend asked me to help them. The conductor
asked me not to come to the concert. "I may walk off and leave
them sitting there. That will show them how much they need me,
how indispensable I am."

The night of the concert I appeared in the main box with the
highest of the patronesses. Then I went down to the reception room
and looking deeply into the conductor's eyes, I said quietly: "I
have come to hear you conduct. I have never heard you."

He came out, looked up at me, swung his head, swung his baton
and gave a magnificent performance.

[Fall, 1961]

There are some lovely mountains around Silver Lake in East Hollywood. I often walked there. From the steep mountains on the east side of the lake, one could look west at endless rows of purple mountains around the Griffith Park Observatory. One behind another. They looked like a Japanese screen. As the sun set, every evening presented a spectacle equal to a Russian ballet, all gold and trailing saris, or the Chinese opera, all red and smoky incense, or the opal coral islands of the South Seas, the flaming spill of Mexican sunsets. Every color shone like a jewel for a moment and then dissolved; and even the gray clouds, the smoky scarves, were iridescent. For a few instants, all the sunsets of the world, Nordic, tropical, exotic, condensed over Silver Lake, displaying their sumptuous spectacle.

There was a house being built on the side of a mountain facing the sunset and the lake. When the workmen left, I would sit on one of the walls and dream over it. There was a desert rose terrace, a garden being planted, a place carved in the garden for a pool overlooking the lake. There was a magnificent fireplace like that of a castle.

I discovered the architect was Eric Wright, the son of Lloyd Wright and grandson of Frank Lloyd Wright. I watched the roof take shape, not sitting squatly over the house but upheld by a "clear story" of glass windows, which seemed to make it float in space. I watched its graceful roof extending for shade like a hand over the brow. More and more, I felt I was inhabiting that house. I, who never wanted a house because it meant taking roots, was sitting there, and the growth of its beauty extended delicate tendrils, like those of a plant, around me. The roots of the house, so solidly planted in the ground, so strong of beam, so permanent of stone, were reaching to me. The stone, sand-blasted to give it a rough texture and the purple colors of the mountains, the wood, sand-blasted so it would look like sand on the beach (it reminded me of the first sand-blasted table top I bought at the *"Art Décoratif"* exhibition in Paris in 1935), the glass which would frame the garden, the lake, the mountains, the sky, all were growing around me. The roots were being planted in pure beauty. It was the house in which I wanted to live.

My wish came true. I moved into it. Everything in it was unlike other houses. The kitchen was all wood and Venetian glass mosaic tile, and did not look like a kitchen; it was part of the whole. The entire house was one large studio, no separate, small partitions. It had the sense of space of Japanese houses; it had the vista of a Japanese screen, all sky, mountains, lake, as if one lived out of doors. Yet the roof, held by its heavy beams, gave a feeling of protection while the big windows which separated the roof from the studio framed the flight of birds, the sailing of clouds. The clear story, the little windows just under the roof, brought your gaze upward and gave the impression that the house was filled with light.

The house conformed to the Wright tradition of living both within and out in nature, of bringing nature and hearth together. They were interrelated and fused. Both shelter and the freedom of a forest. The birds seem to be eating and flying within the house. The house seemed set exactly right to contemplate the sunset.

I had a little room to write in. If I sat in the studio facing the mountains, the lake, the sky, my attention wandered, as it did in Mexico. I became one with the natural scene. I needed the little room with its walls of books which did not let my wandering fantasies escape.

The house seemed to have a welcoming air for visitors. But it was hidden by another house from the street, so it also seemed to have an aura of secrecy.

The beauty of it was such that no matter where I came back from, Mexico, Paris, I never felt any loss, any break or letdown. The journey continued. The lights of the houses reflected in the lake could be the lights of Acapulco, of the Italian Riviera.

A new life began, a new cycle. Sun and air seemed so easy to invite, light penetrated the entire house, music rose to the high ceiling and spread into space. People never seemed crowded together. If one walked the garden at night and looked back at the lighted room, the scene, dresses, colors, poses, seemed like a play, like Antonioni's film, *La Notte*. Here I could make a film, giving the curious feeling I always sought, of entering the secret life of a house. The camera could watch from the darkness of the garden, a woman asleep in her bed on the right, walking or dancing or exercising in the center of the studio, serving drinks or brewing coffee in the kitchen on the left.

I thought a house would be a burden which would make traveling difficult. It never was. There was always someone willing to care for it, and it made my returns from travel joyous rather than regretful.

The pool smelled of pittosporum. The birds came to eat. The weeping willow lianas swayed in the jungle. Noises were muffled and neighbors invisible.

When earthquakes struck, the house barely trembled.

During the building of the house I made friends with the next-door neighbors, Louis and Edith Gross. Louis had built his own house of redwood, an attractive house set in a grove of eucalyptus trees. They were gentle and human, and their work interested me. Edith painted with both softness and strength. She paints abstractions but abstractions which stir the senses. One feels the wavering of leaves, the rustle of wind, the textures of nature, tree barks, clouds, the changes of season and the changes from night to day. A blue sky is distilled from one, an autumn sepia from another, a bluish snow scene from still another. The presence of nature is felt without the surface familiarity which obscures its effect upon our moods and our bodies. Her blending of colors is suave and balanced.

Louis in his wood sculptures gives a new vision of the body. By its concrete incarnation into wood, by various combinations of forms which suggest undulations, curves, valleys, fusions, weldings, he relates the body to nature, to mountains, valleys, slopes, mounds. The silk-smooth surface makes an appeal to the sense of touch, the flow of the wood's veins. Its river routes suggest harmonious connections, fluidity and sensuous motion. It is a celebration of the body as nature, origin of birth, growth, mating, uniting pleasure and beauty.

Louis was also a photographer, and he wove abstract tapestries which he framed.

We formed an enduring friendship.

Last letter from poet in prison:

Well, while you are reading this I should be free. I received your letter (original copy) a few days ago and received one from Edwin Fancher today. You are very kind. He gave me his phone numbers and wants me to call when I arrive in New York. This will be the 25th of October. One of the principal reasons for my going to New York will be to see Mr. Fancher. I'll only be out two days when I see him and will, no doubt, still have a dazed look about me. After ten years I'll probably be lost in New York. Chicago too, for that matter. Hmmm. Would probably even be lost in Boise, Idaho.

Damn! Only a few more days. I will write you the first day out. I will explain about that other address then. It will feel good to be alive again. You can write me at: 108 West Elm St., Streator, Illinois. Whatever I'm doing, wherever I'll be, mail will be forwarded to me. I don't know for certain where I'll be staying in Chicago. Yes, it will be fine to be able to write freely.

I hope to be able to see you during the holidays. It is best that I talk to Fancher first. After I talk to him a decision will have to be made. And, well . . . if I do return to the sewer I probably won't see you. You are a very, very wonderful person and have given so much of yourself to others and to art. No matter what decision I make, the writing will always come first. Pistol and typewriter can be compatible if they are not carried in the same case. I think too much of you and would not want you to know me if I did return to the sewer. You said in your letter that what is ugly in the world was always ugly and what was beautiful is always beautiful. Yes, you are right. But, also—the ugly has no right to associate with the beautiful. Yes, and as you also said—the world is split in two, one to be loved, one to be hated. What of those living in the middle of this split, not knowing which side is for them?

Please do not think I wanted financial help from you. Even if you had, I could never have accepted it. You have already given me much—so very much that it is I who should be concerned about doing things for you.

I stopped writing in the diary because an evening with people interested in Artaud gave me a shock and confronted me with the missing dimension in the diary. Jack Hirschman invited several friends who were studying Artaud, writing about him, doing their theses and Ph.D.'s on him. They had studied him as well as they could considering that the full body of his work, seven volumes, have not been translated. It was an academic study. They were not interested in my personal friendship with Artaud, my intimate knowledge of him. I suddenly felt terribly lonely with my special knowledge of him. They talked about theatre, and Jack's translations (he does not know French), and their greatest interest was in his drug addiction and his insanity.

But I felt suddenly that the very personal quality of the diary, which brought Artaud as a friend and would-be lover, was incomplete. They had a formal, academic knowledge of Artaud I never had. We did not even have time for my contribution, and in a way I was glad because the Artaud I knew was the suffering human being, intimate and confessional. I came home silent. I condemned my diary, my need of intimacy; to obtain this deep, personal knowledge of human beings, I had sacrificed objective knowledge. Would it be possible to encompass both? I suddenly wanted to see people from all angles. I began to look at Henry this way, outside of my personal intuitions.

I hope I have time to expand my vision. To record that Henry's great angers when I first met him have disappeared, ever since the world expressed its love. To record that when he went to a party he was outraged by the sullenness, indifference, absence of expansive talk. He insulted them: "I'm more alive at seventy than you are!"

But isn't the intimate knowledge the one we lacked? Henry was so happy to be listened to, to confide his life, so happy to know one woman intimately. Is it not the absence of this interest which makes us lonely, makes us talk to therapists, makes us seek groups and go to lectures?

I wrote a letter for Daisy Aldan to recommend her for the Guggenheim. I pointed out that she was not only an original poet in her own rights but how much she had done for poetry in general, for intercultural exchange between America and France by her translations, how little help she had received from the commercial publishers, how she had to print all her own books as well as the distinguished *Folder*, which introduced the best American poets and painters.

But Guggenheim is mystifying to me. They have turned down innumerable valuable writers and artists. Oliver Evans recently, who was highly recommended by Tennessee Williams, Marianne Moore, T. S. Eliot. Marguerite Young had high recommendations. The list of those who were turned down is more distinguished than the list of those who won the fellowship. There is also the ironic factor that they request letters of praise from many of the gifted people whose own requests they refuse. I have recommended many many writers and they always turned me down. How can they take the opinion of someone they do not respect enough to endow?

Letter to Frances Keene after her scathing review of *Spy:*

I don't know how to thank you for spending all that time on rereading my work, but I must ask you to forgive me for having completely misunderstood you and your attitude towards my work, or I would never have even vaguely suggested you give time to a work which meant so little to you. When I first met you, you had indicated great feeling for *Four-Chambered Heart,* a response to Djuna, even a certain identification with her role. Then you struggled to get *Spy in the House of Love* published. Why? Your total estimate is not only negative, it is distorted too, by most unobjective attitudes. First you generously admit I have influenced the young, and then you cancel out the effect of such a statement by mentioning the one writer whose writing has no trace of my influence, who is the very opposite of what I believe in, Gore Vidal, who represents all that I dislike in writing. Which either means you have not read Gore or that you do not understand what I mean by the poetic novel. Then you proceed to say something positive: "all the books . . . stem from a true searching inward eye. That's where the consistency lies." But a few paragraphs later your puritanism writes this extraordinary phrase worthy of the most illiterate, uncultivated, Middle West reviewer: "the story of Sabina, a would-be actress with all the instinct for miscellaneous coupling of an alley cat in heat . . . " Dear Frances, that is rather unbelievable of anyone who has read *Madame Bovary,* or Proust, or Simenon, or even of someone who reads English pure and simple. Sabina is the story of the dissociation of the personality (the breakdown of integrity) which motivates Don Juanism, it is an attempt to go deeper into the classical Don Juan, or Madame Bovary. It is written with seriousness and dignity, psychological depth and poetry. Was it deliberate that you insisted on the rightness of a glaring proof error? Sabina herself could not say "I have not loved yet," [it was said by Djuna] since that truth is what she is seeking throughout the book, and if she had known this the book would never have been written.

Also I think it is completely unethical, and a grave fault of subjective criticism, to imply that all these women I describe are me and that I have used the diary undisguised. In the first place let me remind you, dear Frances, that to say this you would have had to read the diary, and also no woman could be the gallery of women I have portrayed. It is malice to leave out the portrait of Stella, when you know whose portrait it is, the portrait of Lillian, or the portrait of Hedja . . . you mean I am also

a fat Syrian painter? Have you ever read Freud? There is a difference between individuality and ego. On the subject of the ego and the self you
sound absolutely moralistic and above all sociological. With our present-
day failure to prevent wars, it may be well to remember Freud and his
contribution to the understanding of the self not as an act of egocentricity but as a constructive, almost scientific attempt to get at the
source and a remedy for our collective neurosis, yours as well as mine.
Yours consists in being so obsessed with the Woman in my work that you
are able to make this astounding statement: that I have written about
myself to the exclusion of the rest of humanity. Do you deliberately exclude from humanity the servant in "The Mouse" story, the adolescent
Paul in *Children of the Albatross,* the one-legged captain, half-hobo, half-
drunk, in *Four-Chambered Heart,* the Indian revolutionary Rango in
Four-Chambered Heart, the modern painter Jay in *Ladders to Fire,* the
homosexual Donald, the movie actress Stella, the hoboes along the Seine,
the modern Christ in *House of Incest,* the entire French family in *Under
a Glass Bell,* the full-length portrait of a father in *Winter of Artifice,* and
an almost complete study of almost every kind of relationship possible
between human beings? The "self" in my work is merely an instrument
of awareness, the center of consciousness and experience, but it is like the
self in Proust, a mirror for many other personalities, it is the core from
which spring all kinds of relationships to others, studies of these relationships or of their failures. There is a constant, an organic preoccupation
with development and growth. If these various women (in which I have
studied the various stages of development in modern women) were all
myself, women would not recognize themselves in these characters. Ultimately what you mean by a broader canvas is merely the presence of the
immediate political drama. However that is not the only drama, and a
little more attention paid to our individual maturity might have its beneficial effect upon the political scene. Your broader canvas is not intimate
relationships, but Cecil B. De Mille productions, crowds, hundreds of
characters playing bit parts as in the movies. A canvas is not judged by its
size but by its depth.

With this self, this ego, as you call it, I have contributed to woman's
knowledge of herself. To make a few human beings deeply known to
others is more important than to write about a hundred in the shallow,
blurred manner of so many novels today. What is important in my work
is not the self but the seeing power of this consciousness, what it encompasses in its search for truth, what new awareness it unearths, what it
penetrates and reveals. The distortions in our present-day world are not
caused by self-absorption but by lack of self, lack of centrality, the integrated individualism which should lie at the core, be the structure of the

personality, because it is the lack of knowledge of self, of understanding of self which we project onto the outer world, just as you projected onto my work your own ambivalences in values, your own embarrassment at truths. I have used myself only in a thread of awareness in all the various types of women, as a scientist uses himself to try out a dangerous medicine. I belong to the age of Freud, and what you should have been able to seize upon is the contribution I have made to our knowledge of woman, instead of continuing the nihilistic and negative, petty fault-finding of another neurotic reviewer.

Vogue magazine accepted *Old Man and the Seals* and changed the title without my permission.

A letter from an English fan:

I was amused to meet recently a very British gentleman, an ex-army officer, who had known Durrell in Alexandria during the war: "A writer chap, you know, and the way he treated his women! . . . appalling!" Why should Durrell's women crumble under forces mostly external to themselves and *not* act principally because of their own natures? I am glad that Durrell has had the recognition he deserves, the more so as his success obtained primarily in England where the critics do not take kindly to fantastic manipulations of the English language.

Letter to Alan Swallow:

I rewrote and improved a section of the *Minotaur* but as I am not sure that your copy is numbered exactly like mine, would you be so kind as to insert it after the section on Sabina ending with the last line
                    wave, its heaving restlessness, its mobility.
After this line there is a space, and a section beginning with: "Pierre was a playwright who had resurrected the theatre," etc. (the introduction of a new character here was not very good). The whole section replaces the entire section which ends with "exploration and discovery," ends the Sabina section before I take up Djuna. In my manuscript this section is on page 242.
Now there is a question here, as this is a continuation of the novels and closely knit to *Solar Barque,* whether you would like for the sake of greater unity to include *Solar Barque,* which is short and out of print as a separate book, to give a background (as most of it is centered on Lillian). It might make a more substantial book. Think this over. It is merely a suggestion.
As Gunther is writing you about details, I am only mentioning this

and also whether you would like to have a cover for the book in character with the other books, which would not cost you anything but the off-setting: either a photomontage by Val Talberg, who did the *House of Incest,* or the reproduction of a painting by Janko Varda which I own and which would be most appropriate. Does this appeal to you? These are mere suggestions. You may have your own definite feeling about these things and I will naturally respect them. My best to you.

Review of Antonioni's *La Notte:*

In this film the artistry of the director suffers from being allied to a writer without distinction, to Antonioni the screenwriter. All that the camera seeks to create, an atmosphere of inevitability of doom, of isolation, separateness, futility, the writing destroys with clichés. There is a reduction of quality, a change of level from subtlety to flatness, which finally dispels the power of the film. Once aware of the disparity between the quality of expression of the dialogue and that of image, the image ceases to be spellbinding. Antonioni has a beautiful sense of rhythm, the images flow into one another, the movements of crowds, the opening up of vistas, alleys, rooms, the use of reflections in glass, the entire range of the evocation of mood is poetic and spellbinding. By the very use of rhythm slowed down slower than life, he conveys a passivity, a subjection to external forces, a drifting. In *La Notte* Antonioni takes up the same theme as in *L'Avventura*. Human beings have no power to create their destiny, they are prey to their moods, to the moods of others, to whims, flights, blind pursuits, mirages. They await to be acted upon. This passivity causes withering and death and isolation. It is a cliché theme, and in this case no added insight is brought to show a hidden, unexplored aspect of this death in life. Desire is not the cure. Solitude and anguish are subtly portrayed by the image, and banalized by the words exchanged. The camera seeks further dimensions, which the expressionless faces of Jean Moreau and Marcello Mastroianni, lingered too long upon, to convey emptiness, finally transpose into boredom. One ceases to be interested in the personages who have not been severed from the flow of life by any tragedy, sensitivity, but by their own emptiness. Absence of passion, of livingness is not in itself a passionately enticing theme. The camera lingers too long over inanimate matter, over the static elements of character, and does not travel inwardly or behind the scenes. The spectator feels only the contagion of indifference. The lovemaking at the end, far from stirring up sensuous interest, seems like the lovemaking of zombies.

Billy Kluver, a young Swedish scientist who worked for Bell Laboratories, and his wife drove me to their home in New Jersey. There I met Jean Tinguely and heard about his motion sculptures. They were constructed of objects from the junk yards of Paris where Tinguely loves to live. Their activities are animated by cast-off electric motors. The ultimate effect is one of chaos, humor, perversity. How might they be made to do the opposite of what they are expected to do? It is a mockery of the machine. The one which is designed to make bottles, breaks them. The roll of drawing paper on which artists are to draw and sign their names, instead of unrolling, rolls up again and disappears. Some of the machines look so threatening and dangerous that when he dragged them through the streets of Paris to the gallery he was arrested on suspicion of possessing death-dealing instruments.

For Americans, who believe in and admire the efficiency of machines, these machines which fell apart, jumped, exploded, shook with Dadaist humor, produced a startling shock and often gave them a feeling of sacrilege.

Before the opening of a show in Düsseldorf, Tinguely flew over the city dropping one hundred and fifty thousand leaflets (not one landed in the city) with his manifesto, "For Statics":

Everything moves continuously. Immobility does not exist. Don't be subject to the influence of out-of-date concepts. Forget hours, seconds, and minutes. Accept instability. Live in time. Be static—with movement. For a static of the present moment. Resist the anxious wish to fix the instantaneous, to kill that which is living.

Stop insisting on "values" which cannot but break down. Be free, live. Stop painting time. Stop evoking movement and gesture. You *are* movement and gesture. Stop building cathedrals and pyramids which are doomed to fall into ruin. Live in the present; live once more in Time and by Time—for a wonderful and absolute reality.

Billy Kluver was taking Tinguely to the New Jersey dumps. They brought back balloons, bassinets, baby carriages, bicycle wheels, an old piano. Billy was working day and night at the wiring. They were preparing "The Machine that Destroys Itself" for the Museum of Modern Art in New York.

Came the night in the courtyard of the museum; a winter night; the snow had already fallen; a blue mist came up from the pavement as if it were breathing.

In the courtyard of the museum stood a floodlighted pile of objects one could not at first identify, a pile of objects such as one might find in a junkyard: an old piano, a broken bicycle, a child's carriage with only three wheels, a broken ladder with only half its rungs, punctured tires, soap boxes, old bottles, odd pieces of machinery like those of an automobile cemetery.

The entire pile was painted chalk white; it looked like a mound of debris covered by snow. Hung on the scaffolding were large bottles of colored chemicals. A giant roll of paper hung ready to unroll, like a newspaper going through a printing press. A giant brush hung poised over it to write on it as on a ticker tape.

The entire structure was wired and several men were still testing the connections which would set it in motion. A huge balloon topped the edifice, and a torn umbrella opened over a fire extinguisher.

The public began to wander in, to stumble over the TV wires, to be blinded by flash bulbs.

In the icicle blue night the floodlights looked orange. Smoke came from everyone's mouths as they talked.

There was a tussle between a museum guard and a cameraman who had climbed on one of the valuable statues and rested his camera bag on a valuable naked arm. Faces were violently lighted, cameras whirred, the wired structure seemed about to totter, the snow melted.

The fire chief in his uniform looked solemn and concerned.

There was a rumble as of an advancing earthquake. Clattering, steaming, hiccoughing, vibrating, puffing, hissing, juggling, dislocating, trembling, the entire structure went into a spasm which opened the bottles of chemicals, and they exploded into colored smoke which filled the balloon with air, set the roll of paper unrolling and the brush painting erratically the names of the artists like stock market quotations. But before the list was finished, the roll of paper rolled backwards, perversely, and swallowed the names in desperate inversion.

The child's carriage detached itself from the mass of shaking, sputtering, burning structure, as if it wished to escape destruction. It rolled towards one of the spectators as if looking for a child in the audience. It carried a drum which played automatically. And then it returned, as if hypnotized by electronic umbilical cords, resigned to its fate, unable to escape. It made one more sortie towards the spectator, one more appeal from its drum, an appeal for life, and inevitably rolled back into the pyre.

The piano started to burn slowly, and as it burned the notes played wistfully, out of tune, unreal, like a pianola. The flames consumed the wood but not the notes and not the wires. The notes played like the cry of trapped music, hollow, expiring.

The whole structure rattled erratically, in counter-rhythms, steaming senselessly, all motions in reverse, each interfering with another, negating it, inverted activity, bending and twisting and tearing at itself, introverted activity ending sometimes in a deadlock so that the fire was allowed to spread more quickly. The ladder trembled, lost a few rungs, fell. The balloon at the very tip of the structure, a huge orange balloon, gasped and burst. The chemicals smoked green, orange and blue.

The paper with the names of artists unrolled again, a few more names were added, and then it swallowed them all again, finally catching fire.

It seemed at times like an infernal factory in which every operation had gone mad, in which the levers and buttons did the opposite of what they were designed to do, all the mechanisms reversed.

The fire devoured one more note of the piano, and only three notes were left playing. Then two. Then one which would not die.

The fire chief stood by, preoccupied, wondering at which moment the suicide of the machine would become an attempt to overthrow the government.

Smoke and winter's breath met in mid-air. The snow melted at the edges, but the white paint did not.

The piano played the last will and testament of a dying piano. The public pressed closer to hear its last melody. The fire chief picked up the fire extinguisher.

At this point the artist protested against the interrupted climax. The public hissed the fire chief. The artist said everything was under control, but the fire chief did not believe him. He began to extinguish the fire.

One more explosion of an orange chemical, one more balloon bursting, one more umbrella closing mournfully, one more piece of wood falling to the ground, one more tire rolling out of the pulsing machine, epilepsy of tin, turmoil, one more gasp, one more twist of metal, one more hiccough.

The fire chief interfered with the drama. He retarded the process. If the ladder had not burned he would have climbed on it to rescue the piano, the baby carriage. Suicide is illegal.

The skeleton of the mischievous dinosaur of the dump heap did not collapse; its suicide was about to fail. The artist gave a quick, discreet kick to the last supporting beam and then it collapsed, and the public moved closer to the smoking remains, picking up fragments for souvenirs, dismantling.

What the photographers caught was the kick.

Letter to Professor Vowles:

I am very glad you sent me your article on Swedish poetry. I am very interested in what you had to say, and I feel it is accurate. I was in Stockholm for a week, they love my work there, and I met Lundkvist and became interested in the poetry you study. I tried to understand why they were not better known and brought back translations, an anthology which I tried to get published and failed. Lundkvist said the insulation came from them, but I felt sure no poet, no artist, would choose to be little known by the rest of the world. These things are interactive, don't you think? Of course, America would not be attracted to the Swedish poets for the very reason that you stress in your work. Anguish. Sweden acknowledged its anxiety. America is busy denying it, even when all its writers are reflecting it, America says: that is not our anguish, it is the writers who are "sick." But the mood of anguish is so strong in Sweden. Just saw the last Bergman film, a somber study of a girl going insane. Every time I see an equally tragic theme here, in plays by Albee, or others, the critics seem to say: this is the artist's own nightmare, not ours. Lindegren is marvelous. And I enjoyed your summing up of *Anguish In Search of a Form*. I liked your saying: "I do think the poet has to find an absolute and robust harmony of parts." You say the theme of anguish has run its course, but you read Swedish and I can't, so I hope it is true. I would like to read your article on the fiction of Pär Lagerkvist. If you know anyone who would publish some poems translated from the Swedish do let me know. I will read Erik Lindegren in French as you suggest. Have you been back to Sweden? I feel such affinity with them. It may be due to ancestry, as my grandfather was Danish. I am sending you books of mine you have not read.

It all started with a letter from William Kozlenko on Hollywood studio stationery expressing interest in filming *Spy in the House of Love*. He wrote that he had someone ready to invest in producing it.

We met for dinner, found much to talk about. He was a musician as well as a writer. He had an understanding of *Spy in the House of Love.* He brought me *Masterplots of 1954,* an anthology of the best plots, and *Spy* was included in it.

A few months later the backer-producer had decided to invest in a string of movie houses, and that mirage vanished.

Kozlenko invited me to his home and played the piano. It was here that I met Tracey Roberts. She was beautiful, expressive, magnetic. Her voice was rich and seductive. She talked emotionally, exuberantly about *Spy.* She felt that she *was* Sabina. She was so changeable, fluid, and many-faceted that I could well imagine her as all the women in my novels. I had been reading many Russian novels and I could also imagine her as Anna Karenina, with her large blue eyes, fair skin and reddish-brown hair. I could see her in a fur bonnet riding a troika.

We became friends. She began to bring people who might produce or might write scripts. Then I began to see a series of Sabinas I did not recognize. Basically, the men judged her, described her either as a nymphomaniac or a vulgar adventuress. Not one accepted her emotions, her illusions, her romantic experiences, her pains and her conflicts.

Letter to one of the script writers:

I hear from Tracey that Djuna has caught your fancy. I do hope it will be a passing fancy. For I feel strongly that the romance of Djuna is romantic, less contemporary than Sabina. Sabina has found more response in women, has appealed to more people. Sabina's story is more universal. She walks among us. She belongs to our time of anxiety. There is more tension in her story, more active relationships than Djuna's absorption in one love. The dramatization of a cripple such as Zora would not be nearly as appealing. I would like to remind you that the story of Sabina was already tested. It was sold in Avon pocketbooks. It was chosen by all the foreign publishers. It was selected by *Masterplots of 1954.* These I know are external factors but the letters I receive about Sabina prove that there are more Sabinas in women than Djunas. The structure of *Spy* is tighter, easier to dramatize. It falls into scenes, each relationship is almost a story in itself. We also need love stories, not so much the particular and very special story of Djuna and Rango, but the story of fragmented loves which is happening all around us. Djuna's story still belongs to the romantic tradition, it is centered upon one love until its ultimate destruction. But Sabina is a phenomenon of our time. There is also the factor that Tracey and I feel more enthusiasm for Sabina. I was hoping you would add to her the dimensions which I discarded in order to expose the inner workings. I only abstract to intensify the inner drama. I concentrated on the essence, you can give the full-bodied presence.

I decided to try a film treatment myself.

Tracey came last night, two hours late, tired, without make-up, in an old skirt. She had been rehearsing all day. Her batteries had given out. I had to feed her first. Then she sat down to read the treatment. She was moved, but made some criticism. Not enough of the lie detector. Not enough of Alan, need of more knowledge as to why Sabina moves forward and then retreats.

She kicked off her shoes, removed her earrings and necklace and sat down to read. She pushes her hair away from her face.

Tracey should be a famous, successful actress. She has every quali- fication. I saw her act. She not only was a good actress, but she pro- jected vitality and magnetism. I began to wonder why she had not succeeded. Our friendship became a telephone friendship. We talked for long periods, confiding, trusting. She always began her talk with: "I don't want to be negative, but . . . " Then would follow a story of why she could not accept this role, or that role, a list of impedi- ments, obstacles. She was too intelligent not to give perfect ration- alizations for the failure. I could never truly find the error, the act of self-destruction, yet I sensed that the pattern of self-destruction was there.

I have never been able to resist challenging self-destruction, to seek for its cause, to spend energy and time on combating it. I wasted time giving Tracey my "recipes," for work, for relationships, for constructing, for discipline. It was absurd and I should have been cured long ago, for the *"fatalité intérieure,"* as Allendy called it, cannot be defeated by friendship, only by therapy.

I began to see that all the people I met through Tracey were great time-wasters. Endless talks, and no creation.

One was ready to compose a "theme song" for Sabina. Another made an architectural drawing of the scenes. No one approximated the meaning of Sabina. And meanwhile I was receiving letters from women telling me that *they* were Sabina, and even Tracey referred to this often when speaking of her life.

Self-destructive patterns cause as much suffering as outer catas- trophes. I felt great compassion for Tracey.

I could see the potential Tracey, I could imagine her directed by a European director, who would know how to bring out her sensuous qualities, her luminous beauty.

I always had a feeling that we had, in America, people as imaginative and as gifted as foreign directors, but who were controlled, dominated and repressed by commercial organizations. But now that I was looking for them I could not find them. I only heard formulas, clichés. They were puzzled by the success of foreign films, but they clung to their one-dimensional stuff. What worried them most was my not using colloquial language. One of them asked insistently: "Is Sabina a hippy? She wears a cape."

It is true that I gave no element of time to the novel. It covered ten years. But as I did not state this, they talked about Sabina as a nymphomaniac. Tracey said playfully: "A lost weekend of sex."

When I was most discouraged, I saw a film, *The Girl with the Golden Eyes*. It was from a story taken from Balzac's *Histoire des Treize*.

It is a film which proves that realism is not reality, that the majority of films we are shown which insist on a flat, one-dimensional realism do not move us. When the poet moves in (and Albicocco, the director, is certainly a poet of the camera) we are at last taken into reality. Any story, any experience, any place, any world, is then opened to us by the magnetic effect of emotion, the hypnotic effect of poetry. The experience portrayed can be shared as if by transfusion. Such a miracle of empathy can only be attained by art. In this story, there is a respect for mystery, for the shadows, for suggestion, for exact emphasis, timing, rhythm. Although it deals with the present, the world of fashion, photographers, Paris, everything in it becomes enhanced, heightened, by the intensity of the focus on meaningful detail. The poetry of each scene is the medium for charming, for casting a spell. How is this done? Only the poet and the artist know how to illumine a realistic scene (lighting, emphasis, rhythm) so that it suggests other dimensions. Even the cliché scene of a fashion show, treated by Albicocco, becomes an animated painting. One is outside of realism, even when all external realism is there, cars, walls, traffic, airports. A telephone in the center of a room, on the floor, becomes a suspenseful dramatic object. He infuses everything with an echo, a shadow, an atmosphere. Rhythm, for instance, the variations in rhythm between a girl who is dreaming enveloped in fantasies is slower than that of the young man who is nervously alert to the pace of modern living. When an object becomes dramatically important, as when a crisis is reached, and the continuation of a love depends on whether an illusion will be shattered by a telephone call, a lie exposed, then the telephone becomes the center of focus. It is placed in such a way as to become a personage. The girl and the lover are far from it, almost offstage, frightened, paralyzed. The silence of the girl who does not answer the call, the development of the drama is strong. There is a scene in which he calls her by all the names of women, all women, because she is a mystery to him, she is intact, flawless, mysterious. All through, the inner fantasy plays as strong a role as the outer drama. To imbue a story with such emotional intensity is what lifts this film above the majority and makes it a haunting, indelible experience.

Tracey had not seen *The Girl with the Golden Eyes,* but she knew Norbert Auerbach, the producer. He was an American who had been raised in France and had a partiality towards European directors. He left our meeting saying: "Show me a treatment and a budget. I will be back for the premiere of *Girl with the Golden Eyes.*" Evidently Albicocco had come to him with a complete treatment, a budget, and a beautiful actress, Marie Laforet, and he accepted it.

I made the treatment, Tracey made a budget, but Mr. Auerbach neither came back nor answered letters.

My French publisher invited me to come to Paris. I felt it was an opportunity to see Albicocco. I went.

The Hôtel de Crillon is filled with French Africans, the President of Tchad and his entourage. There is a conference going on. Paris is full of flags. The King of Saudi Arabia is here too, with his harem. There are guards on each floor of the hotel.

The men from Tchad are seven feet tall, astonishingly handsome, branded on the face like cattle. Some are dressed in tuxedos, so stiff, so clean, so well pressed that they look like mannequins. Others wear flowing robes sumptuously embroidered, and little round caps covered with pearls and rubies. The women are dressed in the latest Paris fashions. They are exceptionally beautiful, tall and statuesque. Erect stance, a noble aspect, royal manners.

At the Louvre there was an exhibit of Tchad art.

There was also the largest and most complete exhibit of Mexican art. They had to enlarge the doors of the museum to move the huge blocks of tombs and giant statues.

The Crillon no longer the color of engravings, but cream-white. A new Paris. More like the pictures of ancient Rome. Gayer. The touching, moving quality about the French is that no matter how black the political scene, art goes on, exhibits, inventions, creations, all forms of solace and nourishment of the spirit so that the human being does not collapse with despair.

Meeting with Albicocco. Very Italian-looking, short, black eyes, black hair, a moon-shaped face. But when he talks about films he is illuminated. Marie Laforet joined him, as beautiful as in the film, with her long black hair and immense green eyes. Unfortunately I had only a rough translation of *Spy in the House of Love,* done hastily by Jean Fanchette, but Marie Laforet reads English, had loved the book and kept translating it for Albicocco. He was about to go to South America, to film an adventure story by Jacques Lanzman, somewhat like a Western. But after that he would be free to do the treatment. The money for the script was raised by friends. I was so happy at the mere idea they would film *Spy* that I could hardly eat or sleep.

How well he talked about the poetry of films. How amusing his story of wanting a flight of many doves in the young girl's room, and how the backers, already worrying about expenses, began to limit the number of doves, and he had to use a camera trick to film over and over again the same few doves to create the illusion of a flock.

Calder's film of his "Circus" enchanting. Created out of wires, tin, straw. The belly dancer moved in a hilarious way. The lion, the acrobat, made out of pipe cleaners, were comical. When the acrobat unrolled a moth-eaten green rug for the performance I was laughing to the point of tears. It was filmed in his studio on Long Island. His wife sat by the record player putting on the right circus music. Calder has a jolly red face. His face alone made everyone laugh.

Dinner chez André Bay, my editor. Met his wife and children. A simple family dinner. André paints, and writes. Later, Anne Metzger came, who translated *Ladders to Fire* out of love. We had corresponded. She lives in a house similar to my house in Louveciennes. Her husband is an archeologist, so she takes interesting trips to out-of-the-way places. She was very lively and charming.

Jean Fanchette, drunk, shouting as I was leaving across the street: "I met you too late. You could have been my first mistress, the mistress one never forgets!"

Dinner with Stuart Gilbert. Talk about all the expectations people had from a writer becoming Minister of Art. So far the only visible change was the whitening of Paris buildings. But he did not forbid cold neon-lighted lanterns on the Place de l'Opéra. The cold, dead light invented by America. All atmosphere killed. Fortunately the street lanterns of Place de la Concorde were declared historical and so the candle-gold glow is there and the magic atmosphere of a dream out of history preserved.

We thought the collection of Cinématèque by Henri Langlois would be the first thing attended to, as it is unique, and the film cans are lying piled up in an open garage, gathering dampness and rust.

Stuart Gilbert in his nineties remains as lively and witty and time does not change him. He was the first to write a review of *House of Incest* in the thirties proclaiming me a witch of words, entering realms until now forbidden.

I visited Mrs. Bradley, the widow of the best known of the American literary agents I knew in the thirties (when Henry and I disagreed with his opinions). She is herself a powerful literary agent. I sat on a sofa and as my head touched the wall Mrs. Bradley said: "On the other side of that wall lie Proust's notebooks. The niece of Proust lives there. She is fond of money. She wanted to sell Proust's manuscripts to an oil man in Texas where French students will never be able to see them. Malraux stopped the sale of the notebooks. But the law can only control the property while the heir is alive. At her death property may be dispersed, sold at auction. She sold the film rights."

I pressed my head against the wall, as if I could touch Proust's notebooks.

There was an exhibit of objects made by painters for the home. It was a playful one, like pop art, like Hollywood furniture, or objects one kept in the attic. A bed for eight people. Half were Daliesque jokes, very comical, half were beautiful innovations. A light box similar to Wilfred's "Lumia," but covering a whole wall with constant smoky changes. Objects made with clear plastic illumined from within, a door lit from within, door knobs lit from within. A sculptured dressing table like the dressing table of a fairy princess. A fountain made of semi-precious stones, simply piled up, with the water running down, also lit from within.

Dinner at the Jockey Club, the most élite of all clubs, described by Proust.

A private room. Red damask walls. Chandeliers with a thousand candles. A fire in the fireplace. A servant for each guest. Comte Jacques de Phalandre and his wife. A Syrian banker and his wife. An American lady millionaire and her husband. Jacques Chambrun and his wife. The Syrian banker had a beautiful collection of paintings and had been all over the world. His wife said: "The most beautiful, the most modern thing I saw in America was the Wayfarers Glass Chapel by the sea near Los Angeles, designed by Lloyd Wright. Fabulous! Incredible! Unforgettable!"

The bank of red roses on the table exhaled their perfume.

The Chambruns had a story to tell about American hospitality. They met a Texas millionaire on the plane. He invited them to his home in Texas. He had talked so much about Thanksgiving that the Chambruns expressed regret not to be able to time their visit for Thanksgiving. The millionaire said: "Come. You'll see." He went home and bribed the entire small town to put on a Thanksgiving festivity for the French visitors.

The soufflé was so light it was like eating a cloud. The conversation was so witty and delightful it was like living in a special world untainted by war, hostility, misery. Muted sounds. Even the dishes seemed made of velvet and the wine like liquid silk.

I returned to Los Angeles, lighthearted at the thought of filming *Spy*. Then Tracey began to worry about the fact that I had raised the down payment in France and that this would deprive her of control. That Albicocco might give the role to his wife. I reminded her that Marie Laforet had met her in San Francisco and had said she would be just right for Sabina. But her neurosis persisted. She wanted to pay for the treatment out of some savings she had which had never been mentioned before.

Meanwhile I waited for Albicocco's treatment and reassured Tracey daily over the telephone. The truth is she was frightened to step out of her element, of Hollywood, into a foreign country, a foreign production, and she feared that her need to control might not work with a language barrier. I felt I could overcome all those obstacles.

We waited. The deadline was long past. I had a letter from Albicocco from South America. The filming took much longer than expected. Lanzman was working on the treatment. This alarmed me for I knew Lanzman was no poet.

A month later a treatment came which was pure trash. Albicocco must have given it to a hack writer. It was totally unfaithful to the book, and banal, and flat, a cliché. It was worthless. He had betrayed my confidence.

[Spring, 1962]

Letter from Jim Herlihy in Key West:

This is the first day in ages that I've felt like myself—whoever that is! Anyway, thank heaven for all the miracle drugs. I had flu for over a month, not serious enough to go to bed with; then finally I got fed up and went to the doctor and got medicine. I was so convinced it was psychosomatic that I felt like celebrating when he told me I had a virus!

I was surprised to get your card from Paris! And to hear that you've broken through in France. It always seemed curious that you hadn't been published in French all these years. Also, pleased to hear that mine sold well. I hadn't known that it had come out yet, as they didn't send me copies. Do you think if I wrote to Bay, he would have a couple of them sent to me?

And how wonderful that your film is going forward, and that you're happy about the writer-director. Please let me know more. I had only heard about the actress in Hollywood being interested, and didn't know it had reached this stage. I hope there'll be money in it for you, too.

Last night in bed I was reading biographical notes on the Swedish writer, Stig Dagerman, who killed himself at thirty-one because he couldn't write anymore; and experienced a moment of terrible identification with him. Then, inexplicably, I woke up this morning rather elated! I've been having a difficult time understanding the fluctuations of my spirits, and am still uncertain whether to attribute it to the flu, or vice-versa.

Anaïs, about photos of the *All Fall Down* film for Bay: I don't have any, but have written to MGM suggesting they send him some. I'm not sure to what extent I want to be identified with the film—not having seen it yet. But I still have the gnawing suspicion that it is going to be just violence for the hell of it, and that I won't like it at all. It's playing in Miami now. They wanted me to take a bow at the local premiere; but I ran like the wind from such a situation. It'd be quite different if I'd written it, or felt that it accurately represented the book in tone and meaning.

Have you read James Purdy's "63 Dream Palace," in a collection called *Color of Darkness;* published in $1.65 edition (paperback) by Lippincott? Brilliant, beautiful, terrifying. He does a splendid, illuminated realism that comes out surrealistic. There is also a splendid novel called *Revolutionary Road* (an unappetizing, inappropriate title that would probably keep you from touching it), a tragedy of American marriage that is as hair-raisingly true as anything I've ever read on the subject. By Richard Yates.

This has been a difficult period, Anaïs. The main compensation has been the opportunity to discover my own strengths, or some of them, but I am not out of the woods yet, and am not getting any writing done. I did some stories when I first got back here in October, but nothing since. I am pretty completely convinced that this is a normal thing, a winter of the heart, so to speak; but there is always the terrifying question hovering over me: will I ever, ever again? A good deal of energy is spent reminding myself of similar and even worse periods in the past, periods from which I emerged triumphantly productive; and I have managed to allay any real panic. Now I know I'll be leaving here soon, either to be in New York or California or god-knows-where. There is still a profound connection with —— inside of me, which I have come to think of as a permanent part of me. Once you have been inhabited by someone, there remains the question of whether they ever truly move out. I am learning about a kind of alone-ness that I hadn't experienced so deeply ever before. Not the sentimental popular song version of "lonesomeness," but the kind that seems to be at the very root of all human existence, the kind that is usually, in most people I think, covered so completely with so many illusions and romantic phantasies that they only sniff its presence occasionally, perhaps in nightmares or moments of grief. I've been thinking lately that if one could simply accept it and press on, that its nightmare quality might not only be mitigated and removed, but perhaps even transmuted into something true and life-giving. If I had to make a guess about what the hell is going on here lately, I would say that this is probably what I am trying to do: trying to grow up and away and beyond the fairy tale, the medieval legends of one-true-love, etc. You and I have talked about this many times over the years, and I understand it oh so well, except that understanding has very little to do with actually rooting it out; the legend is seated in the soul itself. And then, too, there's this: the danger of becoming free of that legend by adapting its even more deadly antithesis: that love does not exist, etc. . . . And so, dear Anaïs, to bring you up to date on my doings, I suppose it is fairly accurate to say I'm trying to maintain some balance between these poles; and I wouldn't be a bit surprised to discover that there has been some headway. But it is a long process for me, and God knows where it is leading to. . . . I hope it won't seem strange to you that I go from not writing any letters at all to speak of—and then suddenly plunging to these matters of the soul: I have to assume that I can always speak to you on these levels without initial waltzes, prefaces, attitudes, shenanigans, etc. And that my silences will be accepted and understood; or forgiven. There is never a time when I don't think of you a great deal, and always with so much love.

———

I heard that the Kinsey Institute bought some of the erotic pages I wrote (for 1 dollar a page) for a collector when we needed money. But what distressed me was that they bought them under the false information that it was my diary. So I wrote them a letter to clarify this and began a correspondence with Mr. Pomeroy. He expressed much interest in the diary, regretted they could not afford the original, and I regretted not being able to place it there because they had achieved a complete freedom from censorship. The government had promised not to tamper with their collection, which became a part of their research. I let Mr. Pomeroy read a few volumes. He wondered if they could buy a copy of the diary and promised everything I asked: temporary sealing, no one to read it until a certain date. We met in New York. Even a copy was beyond their means. This incited me to condense and edit the diary. But while I was working Kinsey died, the research was stopped, and for some reason I cannot understand, the collection, which would have been the rarest in the world, unique, in fact, came to an end. I never knew what happened. But meanwhile I was started on editing. I became deeply interested in the problems of editing, how to avoid hurting or damaging people, how to reveal in such a subtle way that no explicit statement could be deduced, no facts. How to complete sketchy parts, how to eliminate weak or foggy parts. It was a complex problem of ethics and humanism. How to enrich others and reveal without the destructive aspects of revelations. How to extract the essence of the life without damage.

I have typed, edited and revised 175 pages. I seem to know at last how to handle the diary. After the diary is written roughly like a sketchbook, there has to be a craft like that of the fiction writer in the choice and cutting. For example in a sketchbook, you may sketch the same person twenty-five times, looking for new angles, for changes, for a new vision. The repetitions have to be eliminated from the diary when they are almost exact. People do change, and changes should be noted, but there is an element of art in the selection, in the observation of missing bridges, etc.

Like Rimbaud, I am walking out of my poetic world, so definitely unwanted. I am starting now as a diary writer and realist. For the rest of my life I will be at work on this. The poetry and the fairytales (Oliver Evans called *Collages* The Arabian Nights) have isolated and alienated me too much.

Letter to Oliver:

The question about how much is autobiographical in my novels is a delicate one. I feel that the act of writing a novel is an immediate transposition, and a composite which bears no relation to personal experience. Every writer has felt that. You remember Proust, how much he resented the friends who asserted they were the "models"! It would take a whole book to separate the imaginative from the experienced. I do not think this is a matter which should be analyzed, do you? If I had wanted to publish an autobiography, I would have published the diary directly, but I felt the need to separate my personal life from fiction, and created a work of art which is to be judged entirely separately. I do hope you will agree with me. I have always felt the request to be a violation. If you were here, talking with me, I would not hesitate to tell you there is *something* of my father in *Winter of Artifice,* but actually, it is not my father, it is not me, or my life. I would be immensely grateful to you if you avoided this. I do not think it is relevant to a study, do you? If you were writing my autobiography, then such research would be natural. I don't want you to feel I am being evasive, or secretive. Yes, I know all the distorted legends which surround me, and are talked about. All this will be clarified the day the diary is published. And then those who took liberties and make statements that so-and-so was so-and-so in the novel, will be distressed. Please help me protect my personal life. It is the laboratory in which poetry is produced. I will answer what I *can* answer. The diary started when I was eleven and on my way to America. It was the adventurer's log. It has continued ever since. It has reached its 103rd volume. It has served as a notebook, sketchbook, and *some* extracts from it have served directly as material for stories: "Birth" story, for example, in *Under a Glass Bell* collection. But most of its *contents are entirely different from the novels.* The novels are a kind of mythology. The diary is the untransformed, untransposed, untransmuted material. I would like the novels to be considered as poetry. Not autobiographies. I think the origin and roots of the characters, sources of invention, etc., should be for later studies. Not for present evaluation of the work.

I hope someday we can talk about this at length.

I did write to the Gotham Book Mart for the booklet *On Writing.* If she has not sent it, it means she does not have any. Most of it, I assure you, was recast in a more objective form, in the manuscript you have now.

Whatever questions you want to ask me personally, as a friend, I will gladly answer, but not for publication. Do you ever come to New York? Will we have a talk one day?

Do you read French? I have a report on *Ladders to Fire* in French which may interest you. Forgive me for not wishing to dissect the novels in several volumes, to separate reality from surreality, which I am always trying to fuse instead.

Letter to Oliver:

What I like about your article on my work is the balance and solidity of it, the integration of so many elements. I will send a copy to my French editor André Bay of Editions Stock, who reads English and is a writer, to see if he would like it as a preface. You may achieve what you offered to do in your telegram, to reverse the negative verdict during my lifetime. I'm always amazed to be an enigma to anyone. It seems to me I have confessed indirectly so much. It is true I avoid publicity and live for my loves and friendships. It is painful for me to appear in public. As you avoided personal references in your article, I feel you are a friend. I found you a copy of *On Writing*. I am preparing a talk for Los Angeles State College Writers' Conference. I liked what you wrote about your first impression of the stories: a sense of illimitable space.

[Summer, 1962]

Letter from Roger Bloom:

Henry has been here—just left about an hour ago after almost 3 hours of discussion of many things—as he came in, this morning, our Director of the Corrections Department was here to welcome him and we three retired to an office and talked for about a half-hour—then after the Director left we had about an hour and a half to ourselves and then spent the rest of his visit with several fellows of the Newspaper staff who are friends of mine. Yesterday, he came in about nine o'clock and we were together about the same amount of time—an open visit with nothing between us but clothing—no bars, as would there have been had we been in the visiting-room—about an hour of this first visit was spent in the Dormitory where I live—he was amazed at the many books I have and spent quite some time reviewing my mountain of correspondence—and he was most especially interested in your letters—he exclaimed over your handwriting, and spoke of the many beautiful letters he had of yours—too, he spoke for awhile about your Diary and of the impact it will make one day—

As we approached my cell he went at once to your pictures—picked them up and as though talking to himself said: "Ah, yes, this is Anaïs, my, how beautiful she is—yes, this is Anaïs—how young she looks—it has been so long since I have seen her, ah yes, this is she." And as he turned from placing it on the table he made a swipe at his eyes—truly, dear Anaïs, it was a momentous moment for me—for it had so much significance for me —you see, I know a little of your past associations to know that in the be-ginning you had a vast and very impressive place in his mind—you were the influence which brought him to the place where he could cast the chains off and write—he expressed only the nicest and kindest remarks about you—he said it has been some 14 years since he last saw you—he enlarged about you and your Diary—and said that someday it will become the greatest contribution to literature which will remain in the limelight, so to speak, for the next hundred years—from its inception—(as he bid me goodbye today the last thing he said was—I will write Anaïs just as soon as I can and when I return to Los Angeles will go see her—we both had tears in our eyes at parting—several times during our talks I could not keep the tears from my eyes—I simply wept—partly, for joy).

Another wonderful thing about this most generous gift of his visit was that I have come to know so much better—he gave me *The Cosmological Eye* which contains two distinct articles about you—one, your Diary and the other a play or scenario of the *House of Incest*—have not read either but after I have put aside this machine I will read these—as he scanned through my books he opened the book of reproductions of watercolors which came from Germany a few weeks ago, and as he leafed through it he described the photos shown in several of the pictures which show him at home, and in his studio—gleefully he remarked as he pointed to one— "there she is, there's Anaïs—isn't she beautiful"—so much expression in his voice—and Moricand—and Katsimbalis, his friend of Greece—these he pointed out to me—all, of course, which made all this more meaningful.

A dear friend here, a Doctor and Pathologist of mid-Missouri, met Henry at the airport and spent the evening with him—last night he took him to a small town and had dinner at a Germanhouse—today he wants to make contact with the parole board Chairman if possible—tonite he will dine with our Chaplain and his wife—he leaves tomorrow for Europe where he will spend about a month in Spain at some conference—then return via Minneapolis and Chicago.

This is all for now—just wanted to let you know he was here—am in "orbit." I love both you and Henry, so very much—the scales are off my eyes—

Letter from Roger Bloom:

And now, dear Anaïs, comes a matter which requires the assistance of someone whom I can trust—I really have a problem and it is large—

First of all, on the 31st of May I met the Board Secretary in the hall and told him of Henry's impending visit—the next day he sent for me and handed me a letter from the Office of the Board stating that my case had been continued until May, 1963—I cannot begin to tell you of how I felt —I became ill, both mentally and physically—I am ashamed to admit that I cried, as well—I just could not begin to vision three men simply agreeing that I was not deserving of a parole—I asked the Secretary if there were any comments—he told me that there had been nothing offered in the way of a solution—and so, I asked him if the Board felt that the only way a man could prove to them that he was sincere was to commit suicide —for I have done everything within my means to convince them that I am as honest and sincere in what I feel about my future life as it is humanly possible—I offered to give them all my correspondence over the past several years to read, and, if they could find a single sentence which concerns deceit, lies or dishonesty then they have the right to put me in solitary confinement—I cannot recall just all I might have said but I am quite sure that I surprised the Secretary, no end—

I am not bitter, dear Anaïs, I am hurt—and not simply because I did not receive a parole—I am hurt because of the total ignoring of all those who wrote and offered assistance—what can I tell these people, I asked—what must I tell Henry Miller and Anaïs Nin, two of the finest people I have ever known—must I tell them that they don't know what they are talking about, that they are completely mistaken in their belief in some-one—(he just sat there and shook his head). They did not have the common courtesy to write and thank any of you for your interest in this case—they did not acknowledge Doctor Fink's offer of a home and a job—and do you know why—they have become Gods—I, and all like myself are animals—lower than the lowest animals as far as they are concerned—

At the last I asked if perhaps they had in mind for me to sever all relationship with Henry, you, Dibbern and the few others who have made some effort in my behalf—did they feel that I was not worthy of these friendships—(still no answer at all, except that I should not hurt myself by doing this). I returned to the shop and about six-thirty that evening, the Warden called me up to the Control Center and asked for a haircut—he had been told about my interview with the Secretary—I merely repeated what had taken place that morning—he told me not to discontinue these friendships—and offered the thought that perhaps the Board had something in mind when they gave me this continuance—and not to allow it to affect my friends—it is good advice, dear Anaïs, but I feel that there is a lot more to it than that—I have to consider, first of all, these wonderful people who have shared their lives with me—and in doing so have given me something I have never had—a desire to live a normal useful life—

And I feel that to allow them to continue on in an endeavor to help me to gain my freedom is nothing but an imposition on my part—in a sense I feel that Henry has a tiger by the tail and, even though he wishes to turn it loose he feels that he shouldn't—and so, it is not only right but proper that I should ask him to just go back to California and forget Roger—just to consider it a part of his "world life"—just another human he happened to stumble into on his way to his hotel—if I do this then I can make whatever effort it is in my power to make for an eventual parole—next year, or ten years from now—

Letter to Roger Bloom:

I was very upset for you when I got your letter, but do not give up, dear Roger. I feel I should have followed my first intuition, the time I suggested you copy all your letters. You see, the fact that your friends are writers, artists, does not as you think impress the Parole Board. Ordinary men do not understand the artist, the writer, or value his judgment. What we should have done, and I think we should try now, is to collect copies of all your letters, to me, to Henry, to George, etc., and I will take them to a psychiatrist. I will try to get a professional opinion on your character. The kind of men on the Parole Board will be more impressed by that. I wish I had done that. I was optimistic about George's efforts, and your Dr. offer of a job, and friend's offer of transportation cost, etc. Talk this over with Henry. He may know a psychiatrist who would be more important than the ones I know. Also he is able to pay for the consultation and I am going through a bad time financially. He may not agree with me. If he does not, then I will pursue this, as I felt from the beginning, in my bones, that being befriended by us was not the best thing in the world for hard-boiled and professional men. Do not lose hope. Our letters crossed. I had already decided to concentrate on helping you and nothing else. I know how you feel. I would tell Henry the truth. Do not fear to burden him. He has taken this on because all through his life he was helped by others. He is trying to return all that he was given. This is his way. He was always receiving, and the last years he wanted to turn into a giver. Let him help you. He has power now. He is at the height of his fame. Do not withdraw. I know that is natural when one is hurt.

Do they not have a psychiatrist in the prison? Could you talk with him. Say the shock of not getting parole has made you need counsel (which is true). The psychiatrist's job is to be able to judge a man's true nature. He is supposed to be objective, and has many ways of telling. I do know several people in New York. But I have to find the one whose weight will most impress the Board. Edwin Fancher, editor of *The Village Voice*, who is most of the time a practicing psychiatrist for young drug addicts. I will discuss it with him. Meanwhile, have hope, and copy your letters, as many as you can get . . . get them from Henry, from George . . . I will collect yours. Don't lose hope.

Telegram from Roger Bloom: "Received word that George [Dibbern] passed away suddenly last Tuesday. Deeply grieved. Will write."

Such tragic timing. George Dibbern, the courageous adventurer, who sailed around the world alone, who was staying in New Zealand and who started a request for Roger Bloom to be paroled to New Zealand. Several persons would be responsible for him there. His parole board seemed to approve the idea. We all worked at assembling an impressive file. We all corresponded. We found that Dibbern's book about his journey, *Quest*, was out of print and worked to have it reprinted. George was in his seventies but already preparing for another trip. Just when things seemed to be coordinated, he dies. It was the end of Roger's hope for New Zealand. The parole board was suspicious of all these activities. Dr. Fink, the scientist, to compensate, offered him a job at a good salary in his laboratory. This too was suspect. And all these writers, themselves not solid citizens. They suddenly decided to deny parole. Roger was crushed.

[The correspondence became so bulky that I cannot include all of it.]

While Henry contacted a lawyer he knew, Elmer Gertz, and made all efforts possible to have Roger Bloom paroled, the correspondence revealed a man who by his own efforts, by reading and studying, was reconstructing his character and life. He had none of what I call the criminal attitudes, vengefulness, resentment, impotence, blaming others, society for his own behavior. He read voraciously, studied, did some writing and was considered an "honor" prisoner. He was the barber of the prison. At Christmas he was allowed out with guards, dressed in civilian clothes, to distribute toys made by the men in jail to orphan asylums. He gave lectures against crime. So we all worked towards his parole. The ironic factor was that at the same time I was receiving letters from a young actor-poet who had resorted to violence, whose letters were full of anger, vengefulness, who asserted violence was the only way, who had no regrets for past acts, and the contrast between the two was sharp. I knew the young poet would revert to violence as soon as he was let out. He was freed after ten years. It seemed irrational to me, for anyone could have known that the young poet was dangerous and Roger Bloom was not. When this absurd contrast was discussed, I was told that Bloom had committed the most terrible of all crimes: to attack a sacred BANK, and this was a far more serious offense than violence exerted on a human being.

The exchange of books, of news continued. Roger Bloom hand-tooled a leather bag for me, and sent me a radio he had built himself. I sent recordings which were not delivered. Our correspondence was examined and stamped each time. The fight for parole continued. Henry Miller went to visit Roger Bloom. During the visit Bloom showed Miller his scrapbook of letters and photographs and newsclippings he had been keeping. It was Henry Miller who made the comment that "they were worth a lot of money," which shocked me. Bloom was utterly without thought of using our friendship. In fact, during the publication of *Tropic of Cancer* by Grove Press, when there was talk of a trial, because I knew what the media could make of such a case, I asked Roger Bloom to send me back all my letters temporarily while there was danger of scandal splattering all of us. He did.

[Fall, 1962]

Visit with Henry Miller in Los Angeles. Our mutual interest in Roger Bloom renewed our friendship. Henry gave me a present of the copyright on his letters to me.

He had lived most of these years in Big Sur. I had not seen him since my visit to him in 1947. Now he lived in his own house with his children. I had heard he was not well and that made me want to see him. I wanted to preserve the good sides of the friendship.

He looked more than ever like a Buddhist monk, with the same jolliness. He had a picture of a Buddha on his wall as if this were his model. He was the same Henry with the scrutinizing eyes and the mellow voice.

He talked about his children. He loved them more than anyone (as Eve wrote me). He had not slept the night before because Val, his sixteen-year-old daughter, still had not come home at four A.M. He was about to call the police when he found her asleep on the living room couch—she had not wanted to wake him. He complained they did not notice his watercolors, even when he placed them where they could not fail to see them. His son had broken his ankle surf-boarding. They both came in. They looked like a million other teen-agers. I could not have said: these are Henry's children.

"Success, oh Anaïs, success does not mean anything. The only thing which means anything are the few special letters one gets a year, a personal response."

He was unchanged, modest, unaffected, naïve, no ego showing. The Henry who wants to be thought a saint. I asked about his health. He had had the flu in Mallorca and the doctor had said his heart was in a bad state. But when he came back to America, the tests showed no heart trouble.

"But I'm not afraid of death. I believe in reincarnation. I believe I will have a great deal of time somewhere else."

He fell in love with a woman in Germany, a publisher. He would have stayed in Europe, but he missed his children. "They make me feel young. When I hear them talk, play games, live, I feel their age. Jesus, I get all stimulated. Did you know Eve got married?"

We talked about *Odd Obsession*, the Japanese film he voted for at the Cannes Film Festival. I admired it. He gave me the book (*The Key*). He told me an opera was being written from *The Smile at the Foot of the Ladder*.

In Germany, he wrote a play, *Just Wild About Harry*. "The French found it too sentimental. They thought I was getting old, I the ruthless one becoming soft."

He always had a soft side not many people know, a childlike side which shows in his watercolors and in *The Smile at the Foot of the Ladder* or *To Paint Is to Love Again*. His compassion was irrational. It would go to someone like Roger Bloom, but not to his wives. He does not believe in protection. He related a story told by the Indians: "A child watched a butterfly breaking out of its chrysalis. He was told not to help it. He watched it struggle. He helped it and bruised its wings forever." He told me this because he said I was overprotective.

We talked about Roger Bloom in jail.

He said he was not done with writing, but that the world did not give him time now. He was on his way to a writers' conference at Edinburgh, then to Paris, Germany, etc. Would be back in November.

"Tony dresses better than I do," said Henry admiringly. "And my daughter came home the other day with a poem by Rimbaud to translate. I never thought my children would be reading and translating Rimbaud."

Henry cannot understand my shunning publicity. He has always lived his life publicly.

I do not think of him as a lonely man. His relationship to the world was always more important to him than his intimate relationships. He never loved anyone more than himself. He would never die of a broken heart.

Story of Raven:

When Renate was a child she felt she had been born in the world to rescue all the animals. She was concerned with the bondage and slavery of animals, the donkeys on the treadmills in Egypt, the cattle traveling in the trains, the chickens tied together by the legs, the rabbit being shot in the forest, dogs on leashes, kittens left starving on the sidewalks. She made several attempts to rescue them. She cut the strings around the chickens' legs and they scattered all over the market place. She opened all the cages she could find and let the birds fly out. She opened field gates and let the cattle wander.

It was only when she reached the age of twenty that she realized the hopelessness of her task. Cruelty extended too far. She could never hope to extinguish it. It stretched from the peaks of Peru and the jungles of Africa to Arcadia, California, where the inhabitants protested against the wild peacocks who were wandering in the neighborhood and had them arrested. So she began to paint the friendship of women and animals. She painted a luminous woman lying peacefully beside a panther, a woman floating on the opened wings of a swan, her flesh blue-tinted from the night's sky, a woman with eyes exactly like the eyes of a Siamese cat, a woman tenderly holding a turtle. This turtle was so small that Renate had to use a magnifying glass to study its eyes. She was quite startled when she found herself facing the turtle's cold malevolent glance. Renate did not believe in the malevolence of animals. She had thought only of achieving harmony with them. She had thought first of imprisoned animals; then of free animals; and finally of women and animals living in harmony.

Raven was a girl with very long black hair and a pale skin. When she saw Renate's mythological paintings she told her about her raven. Her wish for a raven had been born so early in her life that she could not remember how it was born, whether from Edgar Allan Poe's poem, or from a small engraving she still carried about as others carry photographs of their children. She had always considered herself too gentle, too pliant. This dream of a raven seemed to balance her being. "His black wings, his sharp beak, his strong claws completed me, added something I lacked, added the elements of night." She searched for a raven and grew concerned when she heard that in the United States they had been nearly exterminated.

She went to visit ravens at the Zoo. She read that they had once been an object of veneration and superstition. Symbols of the night, of the dark side of our being? She noticed too that they were intelligent and mischievous. They learned to articulate words in a hoarse, cracked bass voice.

Once in San Francisco she picked up a newspaper and there was an advertisement by a rich eccentric old lady who had collected birds and animals and was forced to move back to Europe. She had a raven for sale. Raven rushed to see her and met her raven there. She made a down payment and asked the old lady to hold him for her until she found a home for it. But before she was quite ready she received a telegram: "Raven arriving by TWA, Flight 8, at eight P.M."

The image of her raven flying in a box from San Francisco startled Raven. She had somehow expected he would fly on his own power.

When she found him in his box at the airport he seemed crestfallen and humiliated. His wings were held close to his body as if the flight had handicapped him forever. He looked angrily at the plane as an unworthy rival. He cackled and made harsh sounds. Raven took him home.

She had to buy a huge cage. But she was happy. She felt she had fulfilled a long dream; felt completed in herself. In the raven she liked some mute, unflying part of herself which would now be visible and in flight. His wings, so wide when open, became hers. His blackness was hers. And strangely, the child in Raven who had been too gentle, too docile, now felt liberated of this meek image, felt that the raven became a part of her she wanted to express; a stronger, darker, and more independent self. His irony, his mockery, his fierceness suited her. They were extensions of a Raven who might have become selfless, self-effacing. So Raven sat on her dark red couch, and her raven wandered through the room, the raven of legends—raper, ravenous, ravishing, rapacious. But Raven loved him.

His black feathers were full of dark blue luster, his eyes so sharp, his claws curling twice around the bars of his cage, he stared at Renate, a black, rayless stare. Raven loosened the chains. Renate expected him to perch on Raven's hair or shoulders. She wanted to see hair and wings entangled. But Raven and the bird displayed no intimacy. He pecked with his long beak at Raven's toes. With hoarse vague sounds, like a man clearing his throat after smoking, he flew from his perch with a rushing sound.

The men who came felt he was threatening them, that he was staring at their eyes, meditating an attack. Like a lion tamer, Raven controlled him, shook a folded newspaper to drive him back into his cage, but Renate could see she enjoyed his angry retreats.

The young men who visited her considered him a menace, a

challenge, a rival, a test of their courage and masculinity. They could not court her, dream of her in front of him, they wanted to challenge him and drive him away, as if in some obscure way he guarded Raven from intimacy with them. He was an obstacle, an alien part of her, ruling a realm they did not want to know. Too immense he loomed, too forbidding.

Raven said: "After I tamed him, I let him run free in the apartment. I wanted to know if he really loved me, if he would stay with me. So I opened the window and he flew out to the roof of the house next door. He explored the gutter, pecked at some stray leaves, and flew back to me. From then on I knew I was as necessary to him as he was to me."

He walked gingerly between delicate furniture, vases, statuettes and brocades. But when he spread his wings and shook them, tremulous with rhythms and vibrations, one could hear the wind from the mountains where ravens like to live, and one marveled that he submitted to captivity. How intently he looked at Raven, her hair, eyebrows and eyes matching his blackness, but seeming blacker by contrast with her moonlit skin.

Raven often contemplated Renate's painting of "Our Lady of the Beast." In the late afternoon light a luminous naked woman reclines beside a panther sitting on his haunches. The faces of the panther and the woman are the same size. But the eyes of the panther shine more brightly with all the visions of night, while the flesh of the woman shines with all the lights of the flesh. They are Beauty and the Beast after a long marriage; both equally beautiful. But later when it grows dark, it is the body of the woman which begins to shine with all the gold phosphorescence of the animal, and the panther disappears into the night. They have exchanged souls. The woman has incorporated the panther into herself.

Renate painted Raven standing nude in front of a mirror. Her back was covered with undulating black hair. Her reflection was smaller, the skin a shade paler, her eyebrows and hair and eyelashes touched with coal dust. The raven had become diminutive. His wings were closed. He pecked at the tip of a lace scarf. The girl had become more powerful than the raven. She had absorbed the quality of night, of mystery, of hidden violence. His wings had become her hair, his eyes the pupils of hers.

And thus the raven she had carried, tended, offered to the eyes of others as if saying: love the raven night in me, see it in me—once it had revealed Raven to the world, vanished into the night.

Visited Renate. She had her sewing machine on the table next to her paintbrushes. On the couch lay a piece of black fabric. On the back of the chair a black jersey jumper dress. On the dining table yards of black lace wrapped around yards of tissue paper. "John and I are getting a divorce. That's why I am sewing. I'm making a black wardrobe for the occasion."

I could see Renate all in black lace like a Goya woman, giving a party I could not attend, to which she had invited two potential lovers.

John had insisted so much in separating the mother from the mistress that he had left the house, and they tried a game to revive the relationship: John would give Renate money and make her a kept woman. This fantasy appeared over and over again in his short stories. He was always writing the same story. His last work was a play in which the prostitute was chosen in preference to the girl who loved him. Marriage was described as having the smell of diapers.

When she came back, Renate's reaction to breaks, to the end of a relationship, was to sew a new dress, fix up her hair carefully, don her Mexican earrings and a bright Mexican shawl and start a new courtship dance. Instead of withdrawing, she sallies forth, audacious, provocative. I love brave women.

Oliver Evans came to teach at San Fernando State College. Because the house is hard to find, we met at the supermarket. Strange meeting. He has no friends here so I set about introducing him to Christopher Isherwood, and others.

He is doing a study of Carson McCullers. After his essay on me appeared in *The Prairie Schooner,* he was asked if he wanted to do a study of my work. He accepted.

He is a refined and skillful cook, so his dinners were quite a feast.

But he had difficulty fusing academic people with his writer friends. At one evening the professors all sat on one couch in a row, and the writers on another couch (Christopher Isherwood, Don Bachardy, Gavin Lambert, etc.). There was a comical barrier, almost visible. They were not impressed with his long friendship with Tennessee Williams.

Oliver was a gourmet cook. The day before an important dinner, he found some snails at a market. They had traveled from Norway on ice, not dead but frozen. He was advised to take them home, place them in shallow water, and the next day they would be defrosted and alive, ready to cook. Oliver followed instructions. He placed them in shallow water in the washstand of his kitchen and went to sleep. The next morning he found the snails not only defrosted and alive but galloping about (at a snail's pace)! They had crawled out of the kitchen sink, climbed up the curtains, the windows, along the icebox, over the stove, on the linoleum, over the tiles, the toaster, the pans, the dishes. In the sun they looked iridescent and festive. Watching them enjoying themselves, he did not have the heart to cook them. I thought to myself that such a compassionate man would write a sensitive study of my work. And from that moment, I trusted him.

He came very often with his tape recorder. I objected somewhat to doing my own interpretation of *House of Incest*. It seemed to me that it should be his. Gide repeated always that the interpretation belongs to others.

It took a long time. Oliver has to teach; he has to finish the book on Carson. Once I took a list of questions to ask Carson McCullers by telephone from New York. She was somewhere in the country. Her voice was so plaintive, she sounded so lonely; she asked me to come and see her but I could not at the time and I regretted it later when she died. I always remember how *Reflections in a Golden Eye* impressed us in the forties. She was only twenty-eight. Even though the influence of D. H. Lawrence was apparent, it was a haunting book.

There was another element in Oliver which made me expect great understanding from him: he was a poet. He wrote a charming book on New Orleans. He had lived with writers and was not ostensibly academic.

When Henry's mother died and Henry went to New York, he went to see June. The story I heard made me very sad. June suffered from deforming arthritis. She set a sumptuous table to welcome Henry, good wine and plenty of food, remembering his enjoyment of them. He had a shock at her appearance. She talked as profusely as before, a compulsive talk. Henry was so disturbed that he wanted to leave. Then he realized that June expected him to stay. She pointed to the bed. He began to weep and left hurriedly.

I often asked for news of her. Henry wrote me: "June is always in bad shape. I send her a little something monthly. I don't see how she can possibly live longer. Eve writes to her fairly regularly. She's quite a wreck, physically, but full of spirit and lots of complexes too. We are on good terms. But I got a terrible shock when I visited her a year ago in New York."

Letter to Dr. Bogner:

First I want to wish you a fulfilled New Year.

You know I always wanted to bring you a change, progress, an evolution, a gift, symbolically, for all your persistence, courage, and for this hard work of yours. It always seemed a fitting fulfillment. This time I can do this, for your new year, which actually you have given me, so that I was able to start the new year changed. All your work came to this: After the keen disappointment with the French script, I came here and immediately made several important decisions. I know these things are not sudden, but the subterranean work does suddenly seem to catalyze. I felt and acted firm, direct, confident. I decided that I knew enough about Tracey over a year and a half to know she could not be a producer or raise money. I convinced her to give that up. She only wanted the power, to assure herself of the role. I began to see people myself. No shyness. No fears. I met two very important producers, sensitive and intelligent, also successful businessmen. I told them the truth. I committed myself to a writer, made Tracey raise the advance (she never had come through with any money, sacrifice or commitment). As I moved forward naturally I also inspired confidence. Tracey began to trust me and to listen to me. It is the way I handle these situations which has changed.

Also I was put through a very unpleasant experience which would have wounded me before. Two friends invited me to a committee of a film society to advise on films I had seen. The rest of the group, young, tensed up, became very hostile, said they didn't want famous or well-known figures to advise them, thought I wanted to be a member, and I had to listen to the arguments, but instead of feeling personally offended I remained objective, realized their fears (authority on films), talked, helped them, withdrew (with understanding of the symbol I represented). I even made a joke. I said I didn't know I was that famous!

I am not giving you too many details. The main thing is that I feel strong and confident. I will have a conflict of human versus the practical if the big agents take me on as professional fund raisers, for then Tracey runs the risk of losing the part; I will do all I can to protect her (and this can be done by getting a name director and then they won't need a star). Also they do give me a vote on script and casting. But the advice I was given was: do not lock up (in film language it means do not be too rigid about Tracey, too intransigent; keep your fighting power to get a good film done).

I will be in New York around January 20 and so will have time to discuss this with you. The feeling of strength and cohesion also shows in my writing. I did some short stories.

The change is in the directness, I say what I feel, and think in a new way. To all. This firmness, or activity, is what was inhibited by my fear of "aggressivity." I can act. Call up. Talk. Nothing *frightens* me.

The main change was also in seeing Tracey clearly. I have always had sympathy for Tracey, who is chaotic, self-destructive, and always in trouble, always in debt, always in a mess, always two hours late to important meetings, always dispersed and in a panic at every meeting, every test, every decision or culmination. Her relationships are disastrous.

For a long time, I never knew why, I couldn't write you. But there we are. It is a New Year.

I do not remember how I met Jerry Bick. But he had literary taste, we both loved D. H. Lawrence, he was very sensitive and determined. Unfortunately, after the disappointment with Albicocco, in my usual way I jumped into a new project. Gunther Stuhlmann had introduced me to a professor of English. I entertained him, as he had recently arrived in Los Angeles.

That evening he gave me a perfect synopsis analysis of *Spy in the House of Love*. I made the mistake of thinking interpreting a book was the same as writing a script. He was very eager to try his hand at a scenario. I committed myself to a down payment which Tracey agreed to cover as I had given her a free option. When I met Jerry Bick I was entangled with both the professor and Tracey. He said: "If I were a big, rich producer able to offer you fifty thousand dollars for your book, I would buy the book and feel free to work as I please, but since I am offering a partnership and have to raise the money, and I have a respect for you, we will work with the professor. We'll try him out."

Tracey's check bounced. She was against the project. By the time she covered it it was too late, the professor had paid debts and I had to pay him. He said: "You are empathizing with the self-destructive."

Letter to the professor:

Nothing to be sad about, really. The talk was good and cleared up fumes of poetry to get at the skeleton of the drama. I understand your intents. And I know you have to be able to finish your interpretation. I came away thinking more clearly than I could at the time. Naturally, I did want faithfulness to the book, every writer wants that. I was ready to concede whatever changes had to be made for cinematic reasons (what could not be transposed). But I cannot accept character changes such as Sabina being sexually aggressive and masculine in the scene with Philip, which is totally untrue to her, and to the way I built up the character: it is a psychological activity but not a real masculine element, only an impersonation of the father to the extent of being the active lover in selection, in daring, no more. And of course, there are debatable questions. Cinematically I think the haunting lie detector is far more tense and suspenseful than an ex-lover. But all this I feel is something we can work out together in goodwill and collaboration. I have always felt films were not faithful enough, that the marriage of Grillet and Resnais was right. That the basic idea of what is filmic is wrong, as the basic idea of what a novel is . . . I had another idea: when a relationship fails to come off, as with Philip, could we suppress it and concentrate on the one which does, as with the flyer (does in cinematic terms)? But all this later. I also did not want to hear Sabina talk realistically. This is a stylization. It does not have a folkloric familiarity . . . I realize how hard it must be for a writer with as strong an individuality as yours, a style of your own, to adapt. But I put my whole confidence in your exact interpretation the first time we talked. Above all, finish your version, untroubled. Then let's work together, may we? I wanted to preserve an atmosphere . . . mostly poetic. If we are to remove motivations from the scenes, then we can't supply different ones . . . we talked together too soon. Let's go on. Neither you nor I has ever worked *with* anyone before. The writer's world, as poet and novelist, is autocratic, eh?

An intuition: I feel that the danger in the treatment was in taking a position outside instead of inside of Sabina, which is the book, accepting her world, not trying to make it clear to others.

With the professor's script I realized what was wrong. Each person thought they had to rewrite the book, re-create Sabina, so that each time the tone, the atmosphere, the language, the situation was different. It was dissonant, like a false piece of music. It was a caricature. Sabina would become too masculine, too aggressive, or too kittenish. It was a different story and a different woman. The writer projected his own vulgarizations.

Jerry Bick and I were distressed. Jerry thought it could be revised. But the professor wanted more money. He thought Jerry, Tracey and I had money. I tried to explain to him. I said every writer wanted faithfulness, that there were changes demanded by the film media, but for example there was no reason to make Sabina sexually aggressive and masculine in the scene with Philip. I also felt the lie detector was a more subtle, haunting figure than a vengeful ex-lover. Sabina never talked "tough." The scenes are too blatant, and direct.

That was the end of the script. I learned from it that those who talk well about the book, lucidly, are not those who can handle it as an artist.

In 1961 Ian Hugo made his film, *Venice, Étude Number One.* In 1963 he made a longer version, which he entitled *Gondola Eye.* Lotte Eisner, the best of film critics, who works for the Cinématèque in Paris, wrote: "This time you feel in a curious way the decay of the watertown, the suffering, the turmoil, the toil. One notices more the leprous walls of old palaces. You feel work going on, there is a social consciousness, problems of poverty, and there is something melancholic in the great longing to find *le temps perdu* and the grandeur of the past."

In *Gondola Eye* there is more of Venice at night, fluid, golden, all lights and reflections of lights and ghostly houses made of precious stones. He captures the intricate laciness of the buildings, the voluptuous modeling, trellises of shadows and white colonnades, the music of the water washing stairways and walls, boats and boat landings, lapping at the hem of houses as if seeking to engulf them.

Hugo's Venice is a city striving to rise out of the sea each day, with the magic that only water can create, for it cradles emotions and the senses, lulls them, enchants them, hypnotizes them. It is not a city but a drug.

Hugo has described how the sun tints the chalky colors with gold, the rocking of tides which sway the houses and gondolas. It is the canals and sleep of the womb. The gondola, noiseless, silky black, carries you into a current of passivity and contemplation.

In the sun it is an orgy for the eyes, a fiesta, a shimmering and tinkling of light. Between the ochres and sepia, gray engravings, smoke colors, faded corals and silky turquoise. Then suddenly a dark alleyway, mildewed, coal-dusted, pockmarked, a death alley. Steps worn by the encroaching waves, houses leaning towards each other, spanned by laundry lines on which clothes furl and unfurl like flags, deserted houses withering, crumbling, melting, half-swallowed by the sea. A constant friction, an eternal wearing caress binds city and sea, struggling to engulf each other. Then a window filled with exuberant flowerpots, a window open upon a chandelier and tapestries, or gaping into darkness. Some doorways in the film suppurating with age, others yielding their last rays of declining colors, the dying golds. Damp barnacles and green mildew become rich brocades in the setting sun. Venice changes its costume like a favorite pampered courtesan with many lovers to please, but all of them, gay or sad, tragic or frivolous, all of them one wants to touch because they have the texture of skin, velvet or fruit. Ian Hugo makes one aware of textures, of color patterns, of changes, variations, and at times he abstracts a patch of intense blue from the street which produced it, so that we are immersed in blue, the sensation of blue. On the black stones the rain creates snowy rivulets and capricious sculptures which the camera registers. Some roofs are peaked, and some are flat, with crumbling edges. Some windows are boarded, some wide open. The balconies give all the houses an expression, like fans, or masks, or veils.

The wooden poles are painted like candy sticks, planted into the sea to tie the gondolas at rest. Ian Hugo registers how they dance in unison when the motorboats pass.

The waters from which the houses emerge give them an ephemeral beauty, for they seem to lack moorings, they seem to heave and breathe restlessly like the gondolas, as if they might float away at any moment. The intricacies of ornaments have to be learned like a scroll, and their variations are elusive. Gondolas are all black with silver tips, like black swans gliding on the surface of the water with their heads stretched out. Some carry aristocrats to the opera, and some coffins to the cemetery. The silver tips are carved like a warrior's helmet, sharp-profiled, made to cut a passageway. The nobles sit on brocades, like effigies. They look at no one, they are created to be looked at. Ian Hugo placed his camera on the gondola, so that one feels the rhythm, the turns, the voyage. And one almost touches the couple to be wedded, the child to be christened. You brush against the boats which carry wine caskets, garbage, cement, statues. Ian Hugo uses the statues as the inhabitants of Venice. They are everywhere. They watch all the events from their nooks. They speak of eternity.

Some are the canals of poverty, they are narrow and stagnant. The laundry receives no sun. Some are the canals of work, and the gondola glides through houses filled with the pounding of printing presses, or glass blowing, or carpentry done in the courtyards. Some are the canals of passion, carrying memories of indefatigable lovers.

The film gives at the end the feeling that Venice is sunk in reflections, that perhaps it lies already at the bottom of the sea.

From the diary, 1935: "I believe now in the intensification of our personal experience to the point of overflow into the universal. A rich personal experience, a rich personal intensity breaks its own shell and its own obsessions and reaches the whole."

I have decided to retire as the major character of this diary. From now on the diary will be called *Journal des Autres* (Diary of Others).

New York.
Marguerite Young calls me to tell me what she is writing about: Fantastic athletes and their psychological difficulties. Theft of the great carbuncle offered to Mr. Spitzer in the street. He left home because woodpeckers pecked his house away.

"You're running on your negative, Miss Young," said the typewriter repair man to her. "Rollers are worn to pieces."

"You know," said Marguerite, "I feel he made this comment on my book itself. I wish I could make a character."

"But you are making characters, what they contain. *La Vida Es Sueño*. I know Mr. Spitzer very well, in fact, I can never forget him. Our character is what we dream, imagine."

"I would like to be a Stendhal."

"Oh, a bore, Marguerite, external."

"I would like to become external. I feel I get lost."

"But your gift is to let yourself be carried away by waves. You have to complete the motion—it is spiral and organic, like cells."

"My book is too long. I have seven hundred more pages to do."

"Length is organic. It will have its proper size when you are through."

"When I was a child I wanted to knit the longest cross stitch ever knitted. An endless one. I did do one which stretched for three blocks. Now put that down in your diary."

"I will," I said, thinking I didn't want to tell her that the diary had died while I made a transition away from myself, shed myself, but that I would write this down because it was so symbolical of her work. Perhaps I am able to write the Diary of Others now.

Marguerite likes red. She wears red dresses, and her curtains are red, and her cushions are red. Her hair weeps, her eyelids weep, but when her voice takes up the rhythmic spirals of her writing it is the female soul of Joyce, Joyce without the male ego, the intellectual juggler with language, it is the waves, the ocean of myths, the American myth, in fact the only dream ever invented by America. The first time I saw her at Bill Kennedy's, the adventurer-mythomane, her flow of talk like a tidal wave frightened me. Once or twice we telephoned. Her voice was sweetness. Then I read a fragment of her book in *New World Writing* and was seduced. I visited her. She then had a small apartment in the Village which was crowded with objects like a museum, all of them from other periods, not today. The world of her mother and of her grandmother. The world of her childhood. She was dressed as if the body did not matter, as if the body were a coat for warmth, a shawl, a bathrobe, something one takes down from a rack or a hanger and dons for the day. She was in a sense a womb, enclosing and garnering with tenderness. She had love and humor, and the only folklore one could love, one already transmuted by her into a myth. Everything she touches, lawyer, suffragette, bus driver, etc., becomes a myth. Over the telephone I heard about the passenger pigeon, the butterflies, the fishing net bringing back black tennis balls to Mr. Spitzer, and one tennis racket, and if it ever brought back two tennis rackets he would die. We talked about our families.

I met her friends, Mari Sandoz, Elizabeth Bowen, Gene Baro, Norman Zierold, Leon Edel, Ruth Stephan, etc. She met mine, Sylvia Spencer, Daisy Aldan, Nobuko, Caresse Crosby. I talked to her novel class at the New School, and our theories were so similar her students thought there had been collusion, yet we had never discussed methods or ideologies.

Sylvia promised her that if she stopped teaching she could get her a fellowship, a grant. But after three refusals from Dorothy Norman, Jimmy Merrill, and the Mary Roberts Rinehart Foundation she gave up. So I had to continue. I wrote to Tennessee Williams, who responded warmly but negatively. He was in the process of setting up a fund in the name of his sister to function only after his death.

Marguerite's voice is often like a somnambulist's. It trails off . . . "Hold onto the phone a while longer . . ." And I can see the phone's multiple copper-wire connections, as I can see in her work, as in Proust, an unbroken web, a man of connected cells, organic, and proliferating. She and Proust are both against the separation of cells. I see her as a dreaming womb, fecund with images. Everything she touches comes to a symbolic life, and expands. Her first book was a book of poems, and her second *Angel in the Forest*.

She is obsessed with dreams of peace, and writes letters to the President against the bomb. Her students love her. She is tolerant and liberating. She is sometimes tyrannical and sometimes a monologuist, self-engrossed but rarely unkind in her vision or interpretation of others. She can be jealous, as when Dr. Hammerschlag married recently. He was one of her lifelong friends (lover?). I cannot imagine her sensual (this theme never appears in her book or in her talk). She gives no indications. At certain times she appears like Genêt, a hermaphrodite, but there is nothing masculine in her work, rather asexual. At times mother, woman in her hatred of destruction, masculine in her epic monumental proportions, scope. I see a child, now and then, mischievous, able to play with Truman Capote. There is no ugliness there such as appears in

Henry's work, in Norman Mailer, in Albee (shoot to kill). She does not kill your appetite for life. The big book she has been working on for seventeen years *(Miss MacIntosh, My Darling)* and which no one believes she will ever finish has offspring (three hundred pages of a murder story, which makes a separate book). She is generous. She shares her friends. She creates a warm and human world. The dreamer is never dehumanized by her dreams.

"Nothing ever happens to me."

Perhaps because less has happened to her she has learned to magnify, develop, to become a hothouse to small plants. She created a world.

"A twin house. Everything in it had to be double. Every painting, every room, every decoration."

We talk about expansion, and condensation. We are sitting at the Figaro, too near the door. It is cold outside; people keep going in and out, but I see no one, notice no one; I am absorbed by her words. I look into her brown eyes. The eyelids fall towards the edge of her eyes, they begin round at the center, then become Oriental.

"My life was tragic."

She does not mean empty. She has a gift for friendship. Truman Capote called her up every night in secret from his mother. And now Norman Zierold, on the staff of *Show* magazine.

After so many years of practicing on my own inner plainchant I can render those of others. I can tell what passes through her mind. I can see the alchemy which transforms all she sees.

"How can people ever say they don't know what to write about," we say in unison, laughing. All we lack is time. There's a story everywhere.

Examples: Story 1. Sitting in the lobby of the Shelton Hotel, several times I sat next to an old lady who looked like an ancient, worn Greta Garbo, long, shoulder-length hair, man's hat, smoking and looking at people passing by.

"What time is it?"

"A quarter to six."

"What day of the year?"

"February 3, 1963."

After a while she repeated the questions and forgot what I had said. She had cataracts but feared an operation. She asked again:

"What time is it? What day of the year?" I answered. Then she said: "My trouble with my eyes affects my memory."

Story 2. The taxi driver who had been in France during the war, talking about his French mistress. "She asked for so little, she needed a winter coat. All I could give her was an army blanket. She dyed it, cut a pattern out of her old coat, and made herself a beautiful winter coat. When her sister got married I bought a silk parachute (at that time they were made of silk, not nylon). They all sat down and out of the parachute they made a beautiful wedding dress, veil and all, and panties, and a nightgown for the bride."

Story 3. Meanwhile Capitol Records calls Daisy (who was once on the *Let's Pretend* show) to come down. They have made a record of *The Wizard of Oz* with Ethel Merman. But she can't laugh like the witch, she can't render the laughter of the witch. So, all by herself in the sound room, Daisy has to laugh the witch's laugh as Ethel Merman would do it if she could.

Was the opium lady your mother? I asked Marguerite.

"In a way. She was first of all an 'opiumane' I met in Chicago. I knew her well over a number of years. She lived in sordid surroundings. I was living in a drab room where nothing worked, heat or hot water. So I thought of placing my 'opiumane' in a beautiful house, so wonderful to be writing about a beautiful house. And then I chose the sea nearby, and I surrounded her with crazy characters. Mr. Spitzer began then. He is one side of Dr. Hammerschlag, the musician side. The other day I told him over the telephone that Mr. Spitzer was coming to an end, and he cried: 'My God, I feel as if I were dead!' We had a very intimate relationship for ten years which died a natural death. He was never wholly devoted to me, always had a need of this other woman, something vulgar and hip-swinging, but I never believed he would marry one of them."

[Spring, 1963]

While we drove to Ruth Stephan's house in Greenwich, Connecticut, Marguerite carried a manila envelope with her last batch of pages to leave with Ruth for safekeeping away from the bomb's target. We arrived after seeing trees in flower which evoked Japan, and many lakes, and a dying day which always caused me melancholy. A woman was playing the harp. A maid took the coats. A man parked the car.

We had brought Nobuko with us. A Japanese dream. An exquisite being. Small, dainty. Glistening black hair piled high on her moon face. A golden skin, absolutely flawless. A chanting, childlike voice. Classical print gestures, stance, way of standing and sitting. A tender sensibility. The line of her neck, from the shoulder, from the middle of the back, to the roots of the hair curved like the lines of their finest brush drawing. It is no wonder it is considered one of the erotic zones of Japanese sensual guides. She is perhaps four feet tall, the rest is hair. Her eyes are tiny, almost closed, her nose has almost no bone at its beginning, between the eyes, and then spreads in a way which would not be beautiful in a non-Oriental, but which in her sums up a balance of child, woman, sprite, wit, poetry and exoticism. It is the face of the moon become woman. Her talk is breathless, with a tone of voice which is composed of songs, wind-chimes, doves, and schoolgirls laughing in forbidden places.

"Oh Anaïs, in my country I was considered a very advanced girl. But when I went to Paris I met two handsome and charming twins, the sons of a widow who brought them up alone. They invited me for a weekend at their country home. The young people had a guest-house all their own, *La Maison des Oiseaux* (when Nobuko says *"Oiseaux"* it sounds like the Z of feathers through foliage, ZZZ of bees, of breeze) and then I discovered how ignorant I was, how conventional, how afraid. And Christian was sweet about my fear." She does not know the meaning of promiscuous, so she says, speaking of Westerns, "they shoot promiscuously."

When I first met her I found her dressed in her native clothes. She told me that in ancient Japan, ladies owned as many kimonos as days in the year, and she excused herself for wearing in March a kimono embroidered with a flower which only blooms in June. So that they literally wear a design corresponding to a seasonal design in nature. Chrysanthemums in the ninth month. When we went to Ruth Stephan's party she wore one kimono of white cotton embroidered with eyelets, *"fils tirés,"* and covering that a black transparent one (organdie) so the white was like the pearly glaze of pottery or like a bride seen through a widow's veil. The obi was red, and on the black coat appeared a large red flower similar to the flat opened flowers of the American painter Georgia O'Keeffe. She again apologized for her costume not matching the season. It was twilight as we drove through Greenwich, Connecticut, passing several small lakes and many trees in flower, but Nobuko laughed at our respect for cherry blossoms "because they are so silly and bloom so briefly and the rest of the time the trees drop worms on our hairdos."

"I loved Italy most of all, because they are so natural and in Japan everything is unnatural." With her two fingers she held up the corners of her lips in a wide grin, "we must smile," then dropped her lips and mimicked with her hands a flow of tears falling from the eyes. "Even when we feel like weeping."

She keeps a diary.

"Anaïs, how did you stay so gentle and delicate?"

Ancient Japan is dying. The new Japan is formless. To emancipate themselves the young Japanese have to leave Japan. They are too oppressed by tradition. When Nobuko tells me something intimate (the struggle with Christian) she bows her head, closes her eyes, seems to be contemplating, meditating, asking forgiveness. When she opens her pillholder containing Sugaril it is the smallest pillholder in the world. Today she wears a yellow dress, yellow silk, and carries a small basket, and with her black hair in a big bun at the top of her head she looks like those giant sunflowers with black cores that bend over the fences in the fields.

"Anaïs, I love your voice very much," she writes me. "It is just beyond words, beyond imagination how much I appreciated and was encouraged by your sweetest letter. To have a sensitive, understanding friend, or not to, makes all the difference in the world, I now think. When you are cared for and loved by someone else, suddenly you find yourself so precious and worthy of being alive."

An evening at Tennessee Williams'. He wears a beard to conceal his face swelling from mononucleosis. He wears glasses. He is full of warmth and laughter. It is his *pied à terre*, his *garçonnière* for *garçons*. It has a balcony with trailing plants, an empty birdcage, a painting by Larry Rivers, a marvelous round copper lamp from a whorehouse (stage, or New Orleans antique) with four red bulbs, a Spanish rug, a Spanish bed cover in vivid colors, a haphazard assortment in which the mother's and the grandmother's setting predominates.

On the table with some recordings is an estimate of manuscripts by Lew Feldman. A manuscript of *The Milk Train*. As we settle down, the cast of *The Milk Train* arrives, and then Geraldine Page, who is acting in O'Neill's play on Bleecker Street, Geraldine and her haloed gold hair and pale face, with a handbag bursting with fan mail. An old record is being played. Tennessee dances. A young actor dances with me. Tennessee wonders if he should visit his sister with such a beard. It might frighten her. In Japan he had a great success: "I am neurotic, they are neurotic, we understand each other." I say: "Come back well!" (from Taormina) and he answers: "I have never been well."

He brought out a photograph of himself in 1943, when Robert Symmes (later called Robert Duncan) brought him to me in Provincetown saying he was someone who had written marvelous short stories. The contact or friendship did not take place. We were both shy, and we both needed encouragement and warmth. I have only a vague remembrance of his effaced and inarticulate presence. I saw him again at parties, at the Circle in the Square poetry readings, at Ninth Street, where he once came with Oliver Evans and we had a quiet talk.

Most of the time he was a public figure. He made interesting statements to the press on being psychoanalyzed, his reasons for quitting. I heard stories from Jim Herlihy and Stanley Haggart: his mother was senile. A woman journalist came to her and ghosted a book about her son, a destructive book. She had a lobotomy performed on her daughter, Tennessee's sister, now hopelessly crippled. Drinks. Chinese hors d'oeuvres. Theatre talk. Sydney Lanier, Tennessee's friend, bringing out a book of poems. His ex-friend dying of cancer. I was told: "He drinks too much, takes sleeping pills, then waking pills, and it affects his work. His memory. Sometimes he does not touch his mail for weeks. He writes fewer and fewer letters."

He answered personally my letter for Marguerite Young, an appeal to his foundation for writers, a lovely letter. I feel both the sweetness and the corruption, the living out of the neurosis, and his insight when he says: "You touch upon their illness and so they turn on you." He has the compassion Albee does not have, but schizophrenic America demands more and more violence, as each day it feels less, is more desensitized, numbed, and so they want louder and stronger spectacles, for they feel nothing, only horror and sadism.

He brought in a diary he wrote when he was young. It was a Xerox. The person who copied it (a biographer) asserted he had found it in his mother's house, but Tennessee is sure he never left it there, that it was taken from him. His love letters were sold. And a relentless biographer was found one day reaching into his closet in Key West, exonerated in his own eyes by whatever and whoever titled him official biographer for a university. Tennessee said any adaptation of my work is bound to be a disappointment, that my work is beautiful, etc.

Marguerite says: "When I was sixteen I was fascinated with Anatole France. He taught me to write. My grandmother died shortly after he did and I thought she would tell him how much I liked him. I am writing about the twin house. John Crowe Ransom said a poem is imagery you love accompanied by an argument you approve. I believe in the pursuit of the logic of an obsession. You have a strong sense of imagery, Anaïs, but you must develop, expand, fill out. You can follow an obsession, like the spiral of a sea shell, so far, and then you reach the shores of normalcy."

The shores of normalcy!

"I knew very early that I would one day write an all-consuming book, one big book, but I also know that I might have postponed it forever because my father (who was Mr. Spitzer too) always deferred all his activities. He dreamed them. But for that crazy incident at Grand Central Station, when a publisher I met at a party gave me champagne and I signed a contract for my first book and he gave me a check, and there it started. It was pure chance, and once I have signed a contract my nature is to respect it."

So Mr. Spitzer is her father, and also Dr. Hammerschlag. She read me a long passage over the telephone. For the first time I understood her all-inclusiveness, her earthy catalogue, books in the bookcase, canceled checks, letters from a dead lady asking Mr. Spitzer to tea, etc. Not like others I object to in realistic novels (Thomas Wolfe) but objects to which she confers a meaning and life. *The whole world.* From reading about Liberace she gets a description of his having placed a piano on the roof of his house for a Christmas decoration instead of Santa Claus or a reindeer, and this becomes a poetic image of Mr. Spitzer walking on giant piano notes. A candelabrum on the beach evokes surrealist paintings.

A tragic life. Desertion by the parents. Very little happening. One trip to Italy. Teaching year after year. Editorship at *Tiger's Eye* (when she accepted a story of mine). And ends talk with: "Anaïs, I feel you are on the verge of a great new development with what you call the Diary of Others. I become so interested in your stories (I never have in other people's) that I write them or rather extend them from where you left off. I am most obsessed by the story of the machine" [Tinguely's].

"You should have seen it with me."

"Oh, I would not have seen what you saw. I get my ideas in other ways. From what you saw in it, for instance. It's what you saw in it that sets me off. I read a book on the legalities of whale fishing, an old book. It inspired the passage: 'The first one who sinks his iron into the whale is not the one who owns it. A whale may receive fifteen irons, and swim like a bull covered with banderillas, and not belong to anyone until he is truly captured.' You see, I get my ideas anywhere. Write the story about Joaquin and the old Spanish house, and the lady who looks like your mother. You have told me a million stories. I don't really like poetry any more than you do. It is so small . . . There is poetry in character, in relationships."

We incite each other. She has been my inspiration this year.

Once when I went to Smith College, a professor came to my reading. Later this professor wrote an article for *Harper's Bazaar* on "Romantic Realism in Writing." He did not mention me. I felt he should have, and I sent him *House of Incest* and *Under a Glass Bell* with a letter. He replied curtly and returned the books (one of a million incidents).

Marguerite now tells me somehow or other his private papers fell into the hands of the FBI, his intimate diaries, and correspondence. They revealed what the law calls "moral turpitude." The professor committed suicide.

Glenway Wescott. He is at Monroe Wheeler's apartment. Paintings and well-polished furniture. He is helping Monroe Wheeler to leave for Europe, sorting papers. Monroe calls librarians and dealers Culture Vultures. This is the world we are in now. Texas University trying to build a BIG collection by outbidding all the other universities. Library of Congress seeking a law that libraries have copyrights so they can control publication of manuscripts or letters deposited there. Greed in the air, stronger than smog. Glenway tells me the story of the book he is working on, *The Stallions*. A mythological pattern on which he embroiders other erotic incidents, themes. Tells me how tiring lecture tours are, and how few books he sold in spite of good reviews. Six or seven thousand dollars from one lecture tour and the writer makes a few thousand for years of work.

"You're an aristocrat," I say. "We're in the '*voyou*' (hoodlum) age."

At my mention of LSD he flinches. "I have seen too many drug addicts. Paris was full of them. I met Cocteau and saw him deathly ill. At one moment he was so drugged it looked like the end of his career. He didn't write. He was mixed up with an American boxer. Then came Jean Marais. A beautiful boy. He forced Cocteau to create, to write, to stop the opium, all for him. But once, I remember, Cocteau was in a hotel, and he could not be awakened. A doctor was sent for who said drug addiction was not in the realm of medical practice, and left. They could not get hold of me. Jean Marais did not know what to do. They all knew it might be a fatal sleep. If he could have awakened enough to smoke one pipe he could be saved. But he couldn't. So Jean Marais took the pipe, lit it, inhaled the smoke and then he breathed the opium smoke into Cocteau's lungs, like mouth to mouth respiration for the drowned. And this saved him."

Glenway has a winning Irish smile and Irish temper. But he was shocked at the savagery of Albee's play. But he thinks the "Vulgar Brigade" made breaches in the wall, broke down puritanism, changed laws, asserted freedom, performed a valuable feat of arms.

Dynamism. The key word. The new Barbarians, Americans and overcivilized Europeans, love them, as Japan likes Miller. They want naturalness at the cost of aesthetics. Glenway does not understand the popularity of Durrell. He laughed when I said Durrell came like Loti in his own period. When America tired of their plain, homely writing, "social consciousness writing," moralistic tensions, they needed sex, but exotic, far away, excused by foreignness of situations, Loti. *Justine* is a painter's book, a poet's book, beautiful, a lure, a promise, charm. Durrell is a skillful writer, a fine craftsman using a rich language.

Marguerite (over the telephone): "I am writing, now, about Mr. Spitzer giving away his mother's clothes, and the suffragette who had only forty bridal gowns in her estate when she died. Mr. Spitzer says that without his great Inverness flapping around him he would not be the dead man walking on water as if it were land."

Later: Marguerite saw Isabel Bolton. "She is writing about her twin sister who was drowned, and as I am writing about Mr. Spitzer who had a twin, we have twins in common. She loves you, Anaïs. I told her you mentioned her to Pierre Brodin for his history of American literature."

[Summer, 1963]

I met Timothy Leary and Richard Alpert at an evening at the Chues, who live in a glass house at the very top of a Hollywood mountain. We had been there before. They were artists and entertained artists. Leary and Alpert had been preceded by vague stories: that they had been researching drugs at Harvard with the university's lukewarm approbation, but that when the research gained momentum and the students participated in the experiments, Harvard became strict and made a condition that no undergraduates would be permitted to experiment (to take LSD). Already Huxley's book (*Doors of Perception*) had aroused interest. That a cool, scientific intellectual should describe a drug which gave dreams, fantasies, hallucinations, disclosed aspects of reality not observed before, intensified vision and observation and released the imagination, impressed Americans far more than the visions of Blake or the "sur-reality" of the surrealists. Huxley was a scientist. These visions came from chemicals. They were controlled. There was no danger of a Rimbaud walking out of his poetic world. The interest spread. To one familiar with surrealism and with the lives of Baudelaire and De Quincey, this was not a startling novelty. What Leary described was another vision of reality—what we called "sur-reality" or beyond reality. What he described was a break with artificial patterns, values, with the persona, with the dogmas and conventions which imprisoned us. Transparence. What I had experienced taking LSD with Dr. Janiger was a waking dream very close to the states I reached by writing. I did not realize that America with its pragmatic culture had no access to this inner world; it was blocked both by puritanism and by materialism. No one I knew had read the *Tibetan Book of the Dead.* No one had tried automatic writing. No one but neurotics and psychoanalysts had paid any attention to dreams. Symbolist writers were not even taught. Students did not understand the symbolism in D. H. Lawrence's work. I had read the reports of those who had taken LSD with Dr. Janiger. Alan Watts' first report stated the visions of LSD were not as mystical as religious states. But old religions did use drugs. Leary made perfect sense to me. Alpert was more fluid and lyrical.

Leary was tall and dark, an Irish face; Alpert was blond and more elusive.

We went to several parties. Most of them at Virginia and Henry Denison's, another beautiful house on the side of a mountain looking down on Lake Hollywood and a wooded valley. Huxley was there; Alan Watts, James Macy.

I talked with Huxley but we never connected. But with Alpert, I did feel warmth and freedom. He started to talk euphorically about *Seduction of the Minotaur*. He said that it was only after taking LSD that he saw the infinite meaning of it, its endless perspective. At first I felt distress. Did that mean my work could only be understood when the veil was torn by chemicals and the drug-taker's own transcendental vision of experience was revealed? The Barrons had said the same thing. Before taking LSD, they often asked me: "Are the stories in *Under a Glass Bell* true? Are you pulling our leg? They are not credible." Then, when the Barrons came to my house to take LSD, Bebe picked up the number of *Vogue* with the "Seal" story and read it with amazement. "Did you write this? I see all kinds of meaning I never saw before."

At first, discouragement! Would I have to pack LSD with each book? Then, understanding. No one had taught them to dream, to transcend outer events and read their meaning. They had been deprived of all such spiritual disciplines. It was a scientific culture, a technological culture. It was logical that they would believe in drugs, drugs of all kinds: curative, tranquilizing, stimulating and (logically) dream-inducing drugs. They were now discovering the *Tibetan Book of the Dead* which had so affected me in the thirties when I myself realized the esoteric meaning of "Bardo states" as not necessarily experienced only after death, and when my stories began to take flights which alarmed those who loved me. So, they were going in their own scientific way into their other reality.

At one party, Leary discussed a statement he had made, that there was no language, no way to describe the LSD experience. I did not agree. I mentioned the poets; I mentioned Michaux; I mentioned the surrealists. All unknown to them. They were scientists, not poets. Huxley's plain, precise, methodical report was more trustworthy. They were making links with ancient religions but not with literature, I felt. For a while, it seemed confined to serious, dedicated, intensely scholarly people. It was like the small group around

André Breton. Our parties were meaningful and very special. We shared our esoteric experiences. These experiences should have remained esoteric. All the ancient beliefs, religions, philosophies were at first esoteric. This was not an expression of superiority; it meant that to enter certain realms of knowledge and experience one needed initiations.

But this is an anti-democratic concept. Slowly, I saw the media infiltrate. Anyone could get possession of LSD. It became a fad, a game, with disastrous results. I begged Leary not to go to Zihuatanejo to form a commune. I know Mexico's small towns; even Acapulco at one time was puritan Catholic. They were offended by the behavior of the tourists. Instead of seclusion in idyllic surroundings, the commune would draw attention to themselves. I was invited to go but sensed the error. Journalists followed. The village was appalled by the naked figures on the beach, by the opiumized behavior of the visitors. There were complaints. The government expelled the commune.

STATEMENT OF PURPOSES, International Federation for Internal Freedom (established by Timothy Leary, Ph.D.):

BECAUSE the past several decades have brought an imbalance in the basic equilibrium of human life, a far-out pendulum-swing toward control, humorless contradiction, stereotypy, automated intellectuality; and,

BECAUSE we witness an increasing alienation from the natural rhythms and messages of organic life, of the body, and of the nervous system; and,

IN ORDER TO counterbalance society's inevitable tendency to destroy ecstatic forms of life which do not fit its structural ambitions, and to exploit those which do; and,

BECAUSE each generation of men must continue the ancient and holy dialogue between the material-secular-artificial-ethnocentric, on the one hand, and on the other the spiritual-ecstatic-natural-experiential:

THEREFORE, IFIF proposes to reintroduce old social forms and communication methods which will augment the understanding and experiencing of such venerable and neglected human potentials as:

AWE for the natural life process, the evolutionary drama, the complexity of the energy dance;

BODY AWARENESS: reverence for the universe within;

CONSCIOUSNESS EXPANSION, by methods which are both natural (vegetable or chemical), and artificial (verbal, cultural, behavioral). Up-to-date information on the available means for consciousness expansion will be regularly passed on;

DIRECT EXPERIENCE: "How are you going to explain anything to anyone who hasn't ever?";

ECSTASY-FUN;

FREEDOM, internal and external;

GAME FLEXIBILITY, the ability to move in and out of routines—space, time, game, role, ego—at will;

HUMOR;

INDIVIDUAL as well as social modes of experience and communication; and J, K, L, M, N, O, P, Q, R, S, T, U, V, W, X, Y, to:

ZEN appreciation of the artifactual nature of "problems" and of the ecstatic possibility of the "here-and-now" moment.

From the San Francisco *News-Call Bulletin,* July 2, 1963:

Paradise Lost by Mexico LSD Colony, by George Dusheck

Life was lovely, casual, and open at Zihuatanejo, the disbanded LSD colony on the west coast of Mexico, a detached observer reported here Monday.

Dr. J. J. (Jack) Downing, a top San Mateo County psychiatrist and LSD experimenter, was among 20 Americans expelled from Zihuatanejo by Mexican authorities June 16.

Dr. Downing himself has treated about 40 alcoholics with the mind-joggling drug at San Mateo County General Hospital, with "hopeful" results, as the *News-Call Bulletin* reported last January.

He was not, however, a member of the International Federation for Internal Freedom, sponsors of the Zihuatanejo LSD colony. Dr. Downing was there, in his own words, "as an observer and investigator of the group treatment situation. . . ."

The colonists were sedate, professional people, he reported. "There were no beatniks among them," he said. "The majority of them were successful people, who seemed to have a religious or self-improvement motivation in being there."

"Zihuatanejo is a middle-class Acapulco," said Dr. Downing. "The very rich go to Acapulco, those moderately well off go up the coast . . . about 120 miles north . . . to Zihuatanejo."

There Dr. Timothy Leary and Dr. Richard Alpert, both former Harvard psychologists, set up a Mexican branch of IFIF, headquartered in Boston.

The colonists, screened from thousands of applicants, paid $200 a month for food and lodging, lived in one of several bungalows above a beautiful white beach, dotted with palm trees and cabanas.

"There was an open-air dining room," Dr. Downing observed. "The funicular, a little railroad going down to the beach, didn't run, so we had to walk. There was lots of fresh fish, caught in the bay by Zihuatanejo fishermen. The staff was friendly and casual. The setting is lovely."

There are four rooms to a bungalow, he said. One of these was set aside for group LSD sessions. Every morning two to five persons would gather in this room, with Hindu prints on the wall, and Hindu woven prints on two double mattresses and boxsprings on the floor. The LSD companions, including one member of the IFIF staff, would swallow liquid LSD and plunge into the dream world of visions, mind-expansion, self-awareness, and mystical ecstasy.

The Staff consisted of Dr. Leary, who was busy most of the time screening applications—more than 5000 were received from all over North America—and fending off the curious officials of the Mexican immigration service; Ralph Metzner, a pharmacologist, and his wife, Susan, 22.

One of these sat with the LSD group, taking the drug also, so as to be simpatico. Those who take LSD and "sail," as the saying goes, believe that only users can understand those who are taking it.

The dosage was heavy: 100 to 500 micrograms. More than 300 micrograms is considered an overwhelming dose by most experienced pharmacologists and psychiatrists. There are 22 grams to an ounce, and a million micrograms to a gram. Thus, enough LSD to cover the head of a pin can send one off like an Atlas rocket.

As the hours wore on, the group . . . possibly consisting of an actress, a magazine writer, an alcoholic businessman, and Mrs. Metzner . . . would exchange visions, cry out at sudden insights of omnipotence and glory, listen to a motley collection of records. Gradually, toward 4 or 5 o'clock in the afternoon, the effect of the drug would wear off, and the group therapees would emerge one by one into the bright Mexican evening.

For those not taking LSD, the day was relaxed and endless: Breakfast at 11 a.m., lunch at 3 p.m., dinner at 9 p.m.

"The atmosphere was highly unusual," Dr. Downing reports. "People accepted one another without suspicion or anxiety. They seemed very open, very relaxed."

Even when immigration officials, embarrassed by stories of the LSD paradise in the Mexican press, moved in to close the IFIF colony on June 12, nobody was upset.

"Dr. Leary was very calm. He went to Mexico City to seek a modification of the order, but when he failed, took defeat without bitterness," said Dr. Downing.

They all left for Mexico City on Sunday, June 16, on a special DC-3 chartered by immigration officers. The Zihuatanejo experiment had begun on May 1.

"Six weeks is too short a period to measure any results," said Dr. Downing. "It must be regarded as a ruined experiment. My own view is that Leary and Alpert have developed techniques of potential value. But I do not agree with them that LSD should be available to all who want it. It is a potent, potentially dangerous drug, and should be used on an experimental basis only, by qualified professional researchers."

By this time LSD was a public affair. Unbalanced people committed suicide. Neurotics became psychotics. Unprepared, uninitiated, they floundered in a world unfamiliar and nightmarish. Didn't I myself, so familiar with dreams, ask my LSD guide anxiously whether I would return safely to shore? The separation from the self was far more distant than in dreams.

Leary accepted the role of leader of the drug cult; he invented ritual and combined it with meditation. Books and articles came out. I helped Tom Payne put together a book of essays on LSD, but when the book appeared, my essay offering substitutes for the drug was left out. In a few months, it seemed to me, LSD had become public property. The wisdom of esoteric knowledge became clear to me. I felt whatever beauty the drug could bring to those who had never dreamed was vulgarized. People like Varda, who did not need it, finally succumbed to it. The intuition I had, that a passive, externally and artificially induced reverie would not awaken our power to impose this reality upon our drab daily existence and cause a metamorphosis, was justified. The newborn dreamers were born without will, confused drifters. It did not give birth to a Varda, to a Michaux, to a new form of life. It was born of the laboratory, not born of our own efforts.

Meanwhile, we listened to Leary talking to thousands. The password was *"La Vie Onirique"* (Nightlife). I was suspicious of science trying to uncover our unconscious, subterranean life. There were other ways and the organic ways were permanent, seeds planted, by way of the arts: music, language, painting, the awakening of the senses, the combining of dreams and action. I feared for the dreamer born of artificial insemination.

Michaux was translated by Louise Varèse but nobody wanted to publish it.

We studied yoga with Virginia Denison. We lay on colored mats on the porch of her house looking out over the Hollywood mountains. She is pretty and slender and beautifully molded. In our ballet tights, we tried to mold ourselves, to breathe deeply.

Virginia gave parties where I met Leary and Alpert, Alan Watts and Aldous Huxley. Alan Watts sat silent at the parties. His disciples sat on the floor around him, silent also. Perhaps under the influence of marijuana. The lovely novelty was they had learned a living silence, not inarticulateness but meditation, traveling inward. Alan had an infectious grin, and I always remember him as he walked out with us, standing under an umbrella tree and manifesting the euphoria he had, just staring at the sky through the leaves. He brought a group of friends to my house one Sunday afternoon. The mood was gloomy. Everyone was hungover from a big party Saturday night. Suddenly in the stormy El Greco sky, Alan Watts spotted a double rainbow. All conversation ceased, and everyone watched the rainbow grow until it stretched across the entire sky. "It is a magnificent portent," said Watts, and everyone's mood brightened. Christopher Isherwood said the house appeared to have been built on a turntable and then turned back and forth until it achieved just the right aspect.

I did not feel drawn to Huxley. He was beautiful physically but again without vibrations or sensory antennae. I could never imagine him as a friend of D. H. Lawrence. He talked to me about the grave problem of overpopulation. I saw him in the white house designed by Laura in the Hollywood mountains above Beachwood Canyon, all white so he could see better, and I had a painful impression of a psychic blindness. With all his science and knowledge, in the mystic world he blundered. It was understandable that he should be the one giving the example of reliance on chemicals. He reminded me that drugs are beneficial if they provide the only access to our nightlife. I realized that the expression "blow my mind" was born of the fact that America had cemented access to imagination and fantasy and that it would take *dynamite* to remove this block! I believed Leary's emphasis on the fact that we use only one per cent of our mind or potential, that everything in our education conspires to restrict and constrict us. I only wished people had had time to study drugs as they studied religion or philosophy and to adapt to this chemical alteration of our bodies.

My own definition of LSD is the taking of a chemical which makes no permanent alteration of the personality but which enables one to shut out the outer world, the conscious, the strict forms and frozen molds of our conventional thinking, which temporarily puts to sleep the will, inhibitions and all formal habits of looking at the world, at others and at our own inner selves. There is no danger in it. It is like dreaming. One returns to everyday reality any time one wishes. Its value is in being a shortcut to the unconscious, so that one enters the realm of intuition unhampered, pure as it is in children, of direct emotional reaction to nature, to other human beings. In a sense it is the return to the spontaneity and freshness of childhood vision which makes every child able to paint or sing. One is not victimized by it, or possessed by it, nor does one lose memory or awareness as in heavy drinking. A super-awareness, a heightened understanding takes place. If there is a nightmare instead of a fantasy, or a beautiful experience with color, music, etc., it can be dissipated instantly by yourself or a word from the person one confides in. The word "expansion" should not cause fear. As we mature, duties, responsibilities, the daily grind of jobs, the friction, competition, the constant routine of everyday life does cause an atrophy of the power to *see* around and further than our preoccupations; it creates certain rigidities. Realms of thought, of religious experience, of creative experiences we may once have entered spontaneously, grow inaccessible and dim. We shut them out. They might disturb the order, the discipline, the demands of our established pattern. The beauty of the LSD experience is that it is a voyage such as one might make suddenly, freed of all binding, rigid habits and responsibilities. For this reason the word "freedom," inner freedom, has been associated with it. Its results are very much like an accelerated, condensed psychoanalysis. The real self, as it were, is freed from the molds life sets around it. Society exerts great pressure to standardize us, to make us a useful cog in the machine, a robot in the organization. This does not mean that after LSD we cannot return to our former ways, or patterns. It simply means that we have taken a voyage into inner space instead of outer space, become more familiar with the self we have lost contact with. In self-defense people naturally create a "social" self. The real denial of it creates fatigue and boredom.

LSD

For

The chemical is a shortcut to the unconscious and is used now in psychotherapy. Reports from "normal" people's use of it demonstrate what Dr. Leary and Alpert call *expanded consciousness,* or a greater awareness of the unconscious self such as children have, or artists. It is useful for the people who have become too much out of contact with their deepest self.

Our over-practical, over-rational, over-controlled daily life puts a barrier to spontaneous, imaginative and creative life. Chemical was found to have same effect as inspiration described by poets, painters, or musicians or religious mystics.

Huxley has written enough about its use in old religions. Its use today could be to restore the creative power, the openness to experience, which have been damaged by education's restrictive conventions. For example, children learn languages easily. Grownups develop blocks. Under influence of chemicals, a woman learned a new language in a few days. A sense of free-

Against

I am against the indiscriminate use of it, without a doctor's presence and protection. The careless use of it by people in search of "kicks" has given it a bad name. It should not be used by psychotics without medical care. It should not be available to all. Research should not be impeded, but it should be made clear that it can be dangerous to the mentally unbalanced (without therapy), to those with heart trouble or liver trouble. A person under its influence (like the influence of alcohol) may believe he is capable of starting a new way of life, and this may prove to be illusory. The chemical causes no change of the personality except such as might come from travel, experience, associations with others, a rich, broad life.

As the chemical brings on heightened awareness and insight, it is unsettling to people not trained in the arts or in religion, and these insights should be interpreted by a professional.
During the absorption of LSD one should not be left alone, or allowed to drive, or to swim, or to go to one's job.

dom can be experienced, a sense of liberation. It has given uneducated people insights and a facility for expression they did not have before. It is not habit forming. It could be used occasionally and far more beneficially than alcohol to expand the consciousness of those who feel too hemmed in, events closing in on them, in short, the claustrophobia of our mechanized life.

[Fall, 1963]

More notes on Leary, LSD, etc.:

First impressions of Leary: He has an inexpressive face which is like a closed window. He speaks little. He does not evince response to others. His public speaking is colorless, academic. Alpert was outgoing, alive. I could talk with him.

But Leary changed, and this interested me. In the short time I knew him, his whole personality changed. From seeming immured from people (at the first meeting), he learned to talk in a desultory, relaxed, free-associative way of his reactions, his experiences, of changing our vision of the world. What captivated me was that X-ray vision I had known alone, that penetration beyond appearance which enables one to see the false selves, the roles, to detect the inner core of people in spite of their disguises. And Leary's talk about the *games,* the disguises, the false life, made perfect sense to me. Once more, I was faced with someone I understood who could neither read me, nor see me, nor perceive me.

Another thing that attracted me to the use of LSD was that people who had not understood my work before, suddenly did under its influence. I felt perhaps this was the key to the stone wall between Americans and my work. Their unconscious, their senses, had been closed (much as I imagine Leary's was); and if LSD could open them, then it was a blessing. I was facing an instant opening of the unconscious in place of my painstaking explorations via analysis. Analysis simply gives the method and the skill for going deeper, for releasing its content, for confidence in the reception of it. What would happen to those who suddenly found and opened Pandora's box?

Huxley once said to me: "Of course, you are lucky; you had access to this world naturally. One can see that by your work. But others are not as fortunate."

A jolt, a shock, a violent tearing away from the earth, and now they could see transcendental elements, focus with all senses on the beauty of a flower. Until the advent of LSD, I never knew how closed people's vision was, how blocked their receptivity, their antennae, how dull their senses, how impotent they were to dream, to feel, to see. At first, I was grateful to the drug. Suddenly, they understood Hesse and Artaud.

But what I did not like and could not understand was that Leary could not believe such states could be achieved without drugs. These states had been known to the German romantics, to the mystics. Also, he did not believe that there was a language to describe these states. He did not know the literature: the poets, Michaux, Artaud, the German mystics. It was simple; he did not know there was a language for every experience, the language of the poet. He was a scientist. He adopted the language of Eastern religions and mixed it with scientific or psychological terms. He tried to prove Hesse was under the influence of drugs. Why this need of attributing to chemicals the creation of the human brain? He could not prove that about Hesse any more than Moricand could prove that drugs enabled me to write *House of Incest* (at first, he was convinced I took drugs). Naturally there are chemicals in our bodies, and a chemistry and balance of one or another can make one human being more visionary than another, can facilitate his escape from the daily world, from contingencies, the web of factual, actual slaveries survival subjects us to, the concerns for food, shelter, job, etc., or for the world we live in. But the power of imagination, invention, creation, cannot be chemically analyzed. And what happened to those who had not become familiar with the meaning of the unconscious, of the dream, of creation through poetry, myths, psychology? They were frightened, confused; they were passive under the shock of dreams, visions, hallucinations. They could not integrate the visions with the art of living or the art of language. They were thrown into the great ocean of the unconscious, unprepared, uninitiated. The old religions which used drugs initiated one. The mystics and poets initiated us. The uninitiated fell headlong into chaos.

My dreams altered the house I lived in, altered my relationships, enhanced my reading, my dressing, my travels. What happened around me? The discovery of color, of motion, of the explosive nature of feeling did alter our consciousness. There was a revolt against the grayness of American dress and house. There was a revolt against staid fashions, lack of imagination. The sense of smell, reawakened, demanded incense and perfumes. The dreams brought imaginative dress. Some ideas were not original; the young borrowed costumes from the past or from other countries. They adopted ready-made religions. They demanded the magic of lights—candles, light shows. They wrote poetry. They revolted. There were good and bad consequences. Some lost their minds, their health; some were passive and lost their bearings. Leary appeared as a priest of a new religion. The films and the happenings were absurd at times, no art, no invention, a bastard mass from Eastern rituals. But at least the unconscious was freed, though in a dangerous way. Would they recognize it now in its beautiful aspects, in painting, poetry, architecture? Was the instant "blowing of the mind" as benefic as an organic, disciplined search for the keys to our subterranean life? They risked floods and short circuits. Nature was not meant to be violated, accelerated, induced.

The first time I sensed danger was when Leary and Alpert went to Mexico. The dangers came from the Mexican puritanism and the permitting of publicity. I knew the destructive force of publicity, the inherent caricature, the malicious effect of the press. Publicity destroyed the Mexican experience. From a symbol of the liberation of the imagination, Leary became the symbol of dropping out, of disaffection from the culture, of separation from so-called American values (work, survival).

Leary became the victim of the blind justice which never persecutes the real culprit, of a culture which made drugs necessary, a culture of false values, slavery to commerce, taboos in the dream, aesthetics and the senses, taboos on imagination and freedom of the individual.

Delightful story of Leary: He was spending the night with a very beautiful devotee. He wears a hearing aid (because of a war wound), which he takes off to sleep. At dawn, the woman's current lover arrived, and finding Leary in bed with her, he began to tear up the furniture, break mirrors and pottery, to rage and scream. But without his hearing aid, Leary slept blissfully through the whole scene.

When I met Ginsberg in the lobby of The Living Theatre I tried to discuss with him the misleading statement being made to the young, that the drug experience could not be described. "Poetry can do it. Michaux can do it, but that is because, as he explained to me, he takes the drug rarely and will work two years at the poetic rendition. Isn't the poet's role to struggle with the indescribable, the inexpressible?"

Ginsberg's answer was: "Oh, I don't believe that. I take it for kicks."

Words which deeply disappointed me, coming from a poet.

I do not remember exactly when Gunther Stuhlmann and I decided to edit Henry Miller's many letters to me, but I do know that it turned out to be a much bigger task than we had envisaged. Most of the letters were not dated. Miller had a habit of picking up writing paper from different cafés but writing on them at another time, from another place, so the headings of the letters did not help. Gunther had to consult bibliographies, other books on Miller, and I had to consult the diary often. Then there was Gunther's editing from a general point of view, my particular concern with not hurting people, and finally Henry's own new concern for the consequences of his frankness.

It took a great deal of work. I found myself terribly tired from working on the Miller letters and also on the *Collages* stories.

My friend, the forest ranger, decided I had been working too hard and needed diversion. "I'm going to take you to visit the oldest living things on this planet." As we drove north from Los Angeles, I assumed we were going to the redwoods. On our right was the great California desert; on our left the Sierra Nevadas (living up to their name, "Snowy Mountains"), capped with an endless mantle of blinding white snow, rising vertically fifteen thousand feet from the floor of Death Valley, one of the lowest places in the world. Suddenly the black highway disappeared in a great cloud of sand. Just as suddenly, the ranger pulled off the highway and stopped. "It's too dangerous to drive in a sandstorm." The sandstorm ended abruptly and we drove on through the desert past dry lakes. Chemicals in the earth give the dry lakes soft, pastel colors, gray, oxide red, a green like copper dipped in acid.

At Big Pine, instead of turning left into the Sierras, we turned right into the desert. "Isn't this too hot and dry for redwoods?" I asked. The forester just looked mysterious. Then we began to climb into the White Mountains through juniper and piñon pines. The

Piute Indians still come here in the fall to gather piñon nuts. Up through red oxide mountains, black calcinated mountains, pink, gray, covered with many colors of lichen. We seemed to be going straight up; the road signs said 5000, 6000, 7000 feet. The radiator boiled over and we had to stop to let it cool. Finally at eleven thousand feet we reached the top of the ridge. The ranger lowered the car top. It seemed as though we had landed in a spaceship on another planet, the planet Mars. Out of great expanses of bare, white, bone-colored rock grew a few scattered trees, nothing else. The trees were short, stunted, twisted and gnarled, only a few green needles, a symbol of strength and defiance. The forester said they were bristlecone pines, the oldest known living things. Methuselah, the eldest, is 4,600 years old. Many were growing here when the Egyptians were building the Pyramids. He explained these trees are the only plants that can survive here, exposed to high winds, growing on very poor rocky soil with very little rainfall. They have been able to survive by allowing most of the tree to die so that a small part may live on in equilibrium with the harsh environment. They grow incredibly slowly, in one hundred years only one inch. Their twisted roots have been almost completely exposed by four thousand years of erosion. Many of the pines had been sculptured into objects of powerful beauty by wind-blown sand, by ice and by fire.

A huge wind almost blew us off the mountain. It began to snow. The ranger raised the car top and we left the mountain abruptly. Perhaps the Gods were angry at our invasion of the world of these strange, noble trees, living here for thousands of years with no companions but a few animals and the Piute Indians, who worshipped them and climbed the mountain to commune with their spirits.

A doctor's story: A woman complained her husband made love too often, never had enough and had finally caused her distress and soreness. This was a recent development after a fairly neutral marriage. The doctor suspected a form of syphilis which causes priapism. He sent for the husband and tested him but found no abnormality. The wife observed that the nocturnal excesses synchronized with warm nights when the smell of night-blooming jasmine invaded their room. She discussed this with her husband, and one night both of them went out with clippers and cut the bush down. He never bothered her again.

At the airport a child says: "Oh, there is a general on the plane with us. Nothing can happen to us now."

[Winter, 1963–1964]

Lecture at Carbondale, Illinois University. Bruce Harkness, tall, dark, courteous, reserved, tactful. Harry Moore (author of *The Intelligent Heart,* a book on D. H. Lawrence) gray-haired, stocky, Irish-looking, big blue eyes, humorous, dreamy, serious. His wife Beatrice, noble vintage, a beautiful and lovely woman. Harry's library impressive, two rooms with shelves up to the ceiling, big desk, piles of manuscripts, books on tables, on chairs. Scholarly. Collections of Proust, Aldington, *Roman Nouveau,* Shakespeare, Milton, modern writers. He is writing a History of European literature. He is editor of *Crosscurrents in Literature.* He contracted with Oliver Evans to do a study of my work. When required to be tactful he will mischievously upset expectations. There was an important meeting arranged during the war, much dependent on good contact with a general. They had both been born in the same town in California. Harry Moore tells him this, but he adds: "Do you remember the Arab who sold matches on little trays suspended from his neck?" No, the general did not remember. "Do you remember that in the winter when the animals had no food in the mountains, they came down to eat in our backyards?" General did not remember that, he turned away, shrugged his shoulders as if saying: this fellow is mad. Diplomatic expectations shattered. At the restaurant he flares up at the blank look on the waitress's face: "Trained never to see you or notice anyone!"

The librarian who was supposed to be interested in purchasing my diary originals is Pinocchio in person, short, fat, with thyroid eyes popping with surprise, friendly, warm, expansive, drinking martinis by the dozen. He was gay and playful, though he is in charge of collecting rare books, in control of manuscripts and collections, the one in possession of many secrets, the one who slides open file drawers and shows you letters from James Joyce, Glenway Wescott, D. H. Lawrence, Henry Miller, Crevel, Aldington, diaries, first editions, treasures, indiscretions, betrayals sold for gold. He had just purchased Caresse Crosby's papers. He opened the drawer containing correspondence between Caresse and Kay Boyle. I asked him if Caresse had not sealed these letters. He said: "Oh, yes! They are sealed. But showing them to you is not treachery." "I don't want to read them," I said, having already experienced the shock of seeing all my letters to Caresse under glass. Harry Moore, himself a victim, his letters to someone sold, lying there, with students, researchers, assistant librarians, biographers all over the library. Was this a cemetery, or a Manufacturer of Immortality? It chilled me. Biographers. D. H. Lawrence's contracts with publishers. What race of men feeds on other's lives. And will I be one of them in the unlocked files, with Pinocchio offering a visitor a look into the diaries? "Goodies," says Pinocchio, commenting on these treasures in the files. It all gave me a ghostly feeling. I see Miller's letters to Caresse, watercolors, Cartier-Bresson photographs, snapshots, a painting of the Mill, portraits of Caresse and Harry, Harry's diaries in red leather bindings, letters of Glenway Wescott, Tennessee Williams.

A strange world, suddenly discovered. Mr. Kaplan sold my letters concerning the sale of Miller's paintings when I was in need of money. Everything sold, recorded. Yes, I understand later biographers will rummage through these treasures to immortalize so-and-so. Caresse, over seventy, no longer cares about secrets, sacred trusts. But because they have just bought her collection, the library has no funds for my diaries. And in a way, I feel relieved. To be just, am I not also recording secrets, and the secrets of Caresse's life are here in the diaries. But the activity of the librarians is now affecting writers: they write fewer letters. Beckett's intimate letters were sold at auction in London. A very honorable collector I know, who was a friend of Beckett's, bought the letters and gifted them back to him. All of us so occupied in living, not aware of records. But letters will be reduced by the use of the telephone, cables. Frightening to see one's friends becoming history, and what was personal and intimate made public. In the past people waited for the death of writers, and then set out to find letters and diaries. They were not so easy to find. They were hidden in attics, in trunks, in relatives' homes. It was an arduous search, slow, and when biographies came out time had erased the damage it might do to human lives. But today the young poets manufacture documents, sell letters and manuscripts when barely written. Today amorality, absence of ethics, greed, impatience, acceleration of life precipitates the young, not yet famous, the commercial, to sell everything to these huge and numerous libraries eager to be filled. Under glass, the story of the days when Gonzalo and I worked for Caresse printing a book and found her an exacting, capricious taskmaster, as I recorded in the diary.

If I look honestly into the present I should remember how I love to read about Proust, not only his work but every book which enables me to feel his presence, to know him intimately, his family, homes, friends, Paris, his period. Historians. It is hard for me to see Pinocchio as a historian. Many lies will be told, many inventions, distortions, in spite of documentation, as are told in fiction (read the conflicting versions of Chopin's life, George Sand's life, De Musset's life, three contradictory versions, depending on the biographer, depending on which one he is in love with, identifies with, has affinities with).

It was a visit to tombs, mausoleums, pyramids, to the past, relics, vestiges.

And on the plane to St. Louis I was reading *Le Temps Retrouvé*.

Harry Moore was co-editor of Caresse Crosby's *Portfolio*. It was his idea. One for each country. It was he who incited her to write her autobiography, her *Passionate Years*.

I tried to interest him in Marguerite Young, in poetic prose. He once said America did not love poetry. Edith Sitwell protested: "Look how they love me!"

Bruce Harkness wants to write about Conrad. A Polish writer told him the style of Conrad was not original. He translated expressions which were clichés in Polish but which sounded original in English. Harry Moore tells me the plot of a Henry James story, praising his subtleties. He is the only critic who felt Durrell's plots were melodramatic, and that he was not concerned with deep exploration of character, psychological exactitudes. Harry Moore defended *Tropic of Cancer*. Academic scholarship is totally different from mine, alas, and for the first time I measured the abyss between the study of history, biography, archeology, and my approach to the intimate knowledge of a character.

The Web. I introduce Tana de Gamez to Daisy for our poetry-reading program at F.M. station. Tana reads Spanish poetry magnificently. I see Kim Stanley, who was married to Alfred Ryder, who visited me in Los Angeles and introduced me to Jacobina de Caro, who then invites me to a dinner with Jeanne Rainer and Serge Bourguignon, whose film, *Sundays and Cybele,* I loved. He is charming, intelligent, genuine, and he disserts on the lyricism of Henry Miller. I meet Pola Chapelle with the lovely voice, lovely face, and she makes her way into the New York life. I see a lot of Billy Kluver, who flew with me to Sweden and introduced me to all the artists there. When Billy and Hill Kluver first arrived from Sweden there were two writers they wanted to see, Henry Miller and Anaïs Nin. Billy was at the Museum of Modern Art the night of the Tinguely exhibit of the machine that destroyed itself. He was helping with wiring and controls, and in the floodlights his long narrow face reminded me of Bergman's actor, Max von Sydow. That night at the Museum Dr. Max Jacobson was there, standing next to me. He had injected himself with so much B12 that he smelled of it in the snow and in the cold.

How marvelous Kim Stanley was in Colette's story *Cheri,* and Colette would have loved her, voluptuous, luminous, earthy, warm. She was wonderful in *Freud,* intense, with her husky voice, and even more wonderful in *A Clearing in the Wood* of Arthur Laurents. Kim could be violent. She sees herself in my women. How perfect she was in this dramatization of several selves, the child, teen-ager, woman, older woman. Laurents found the technique for dramatizing multiple states. He was on the track of mastering the inner drama when he gave up because the play failed. He came too soon.

Maya Deren, a few years before she died, felt isolated from the community and tried to reintegrate her life in the most naïve way imaginable by giving Bebe Barron a "shower" for her expected baby, a traditional shower like the housewives of the West give, with pink decorations, pink pastry, pink-wrapped gifts. Because we loved Bebe we all joined in this celebration. But Maya Deren could not permit this afternoon to remain innocent, bourgeois, and the witch in her reappeared when she asked Bebe when she was expecting her child. Bebe told Maya in a few weeks, then Maya said: "You are wrong, it is coming much sooner, I can tell by the constellations and the formation of the clouds." Suggestible Bebe began to have her child on her way down Maya's stairs.

The pink shower party could not neutralize the studio, which was like a voodoo shack, filled with masks, drums, necklaces, shells,

African baskets, textiles, pillows, and filled with friends provincial mothers would not have wanted around their babies, musicians, filmmakers, writers, electronic engineers, science-fiction writers, all such dangerous influences from a bourgeois's point of view!

Adam was born premature and feet first, leaving his head longer to enjoy darkness and sleep in his mother's womb. I started a diary for him, with the story of his birth.

Maya had gone to Haiti with a Guggenheim Fellowship to film the voodoo ceremonies. She lived with a voodoo priest, danced, prayed, wrote and filmed, but when I met him at a party and asked him if it was true that Maya had been declared a "priestess" of the Haitian religion, he answered in a most precise, psychological, archeological tone: "But of course we all know that Maya is a psychotic hysteric," using an even more medical term than I remember. Maya took her early films to colleges. Often she preceded me, and I would hear the complaints of the students who felt that she had lectured to them in a dogmatic way about what they should see in the films rather than allow them to discover it for themselves. Her obsession was to employ symbolic acts but to deny that they had symbolic significance. "A flower," she said, "is a flower, a mirror is a mirror, a knife is a knife." But the flower appeared over the vulva, the mirror was covered, and the knife was dug into the table as if thrown by a knife thrower. How could she say there was no symbolic meaning when the woman crawls over a long banquet table? I always felt that it was because her father was a psychiatrist, and that Maya must deny him and his language and his interpretations over and over again. Maya the gypsy, the Ukrainian gypsy, with wild, frizzy hair like a halo around her face. Sasha Hammid placed her face behind glass and in that softened image she appeared like a Botticelli. The camera can be a lover, or a hater, or a sadist, or a defamer, as the press cameramen well know. It lies. Photography lies. When they filmed an old New England attic in one of my friend's films they used filters to make the colors new. That is how Paris looks in Hollywood films. Everything must be glossy and new. The poetic diffuseness which dissolves the sharpness of the eyes is now tabooed, an anachronism. Today the camera lies by crudity, the freckles become coffee stains, the birth marks a volcano, the wrinkles a map of rivers, the necks barbed-wire fences.

The first time I saw Maya was at Amagansett. It was on the beach.

As we approached, we found she was filming the scene of her being tossed on the sand by the waves, and she had to repeat this many times to give the feeling of flotsam thrown gently by the sea on shores of dreams (no meaning please), and saltbrined, washed, rolled; I saw her finally rise and walk away with Sasha and another person. That was during the summer of 1945, when many nationalities found themselves in Amagansett, Syrian, Japanese, Mexican, Scots, French, Russian, South American, French. The German-Jewish philosopher Jean Wahl came to the beach dressed in a formal black suit, with collar, dark tie. He looked widowed, a mourner, allergic to the sun, the sea's glitter, the swimmers, branded by his race's sorrow, the ghost of concentration camps.

In Hollywood, in 1948, young filmmakers, Curtis Harrington and Kenneth Anger, looked up to Maya as the pioneer, the American equivalent of Buñuel, Cocteau, Dali. She was older, bolder, fiercer than they were.

When I went to Hollywood Curtis and Kenneth were my guides to films, history of films, homes of the stars. I had been taken to see Kenneth Anger's *Fireworks* in San Francisco, and although the sadism repulsed me, I recognized a talent. Kenneth Anger, who looked gentle, Latin, tender, spent all he had made in a week dishwashing in restaurants to take me to dinner at a luxurious Russian restaurant. In Hollywood Kenneth and Curtis took me to the original stars' homes, behind Franklin Boulevard, in the hills. The houses of Valentino, Harold Lloyd, Theda Bara, which may in their time have seemed magnificent but which today looked small, pathetic imitations of Spanish ranches, castles, haciendas. We sat in Harold Lloyd's deserted house by an empty pool, on a broken-down swing covered by a tattered umbrella, and they told me the history of Hollywood, their birthplace.

Kenneth today expresses the Beats' atmosphere, leather coats, motorcycles, sadism. The French poets lacerated themselves, destroyed themselves. The American poets destroy others.

Maya chose her actors from my group of friends, appropriated Frank the dancer, the beautiful girl who lived with a Negro musician, the South American painter and his mistress, others. She called up early in the morning and we reported for work, at Riverside, at Central Park, on Wall Street, or in her studio.

We went to New Jersey, to a park filled with statues, a hothouse, a formal garden. We danced. There were sadistic scenes. But Maya giving a pink baby shower was impossible to superimpose over Maya the gypsy, dancing African dances or setting her camera in front of the cat who was expecting kittens.

She wanted to make improvised films, she expected that, undirected, things would "happen," but the era of happenings had not yet developed. When she expected to catch accidentally a scene, a relationship, her amateurs froze. As soon as the camera stopped clicking they resumed the life she had wanted to capture. She did not know how to create the happening. There has to be a suggestion, a theme, as in a charade. If she set up a Maypole and gave us ribbons, it became a Maypole scene. In her studio, once, after hours of vague, chaotic absence of direction we reached a hysteria of fatigue, and then it almost happened.

The quest for ugliness is one I never understood. Was it because Americans were for the most part born in ugliness, familiar with it, and had grown to love it, or because they associated beauty with the undemocratic upper class, art, the past, Europe, and repudiated it? The American definition of realism was ugliness. To avoid being accused of creating illusion, they always showed the same ugly view of everything. Maya magnified the skin blemishes, the knotted nerves, the large ears; she stressed the oily surfaces, the thyroid white of the eyes, the baldness or the pimple. Maya's actors happened to be beautiful. She uglified them. I had never seen as clearly as in Maya, the power to uglify in the eye behind the camera.

Daisy, with a charm of voice and laughter, and a youthful animation. We went to dinner in the Village, and talked like two shocked idealists outraged by the callous behavior of people, and Daisy listed those hostile to her work, and I mine, and our bond was made in this wistful recognition of evil in the world. There is also the astrologic web. Daisy continues the sign of Virgo, my father's and my brother's, but her criticism is tempered by love.

Should I stop to compare Moricand and Sydney Omarr? Compare their language, the levels of expression, the same science on utterly different levels.

Much of this extraordinarily rich material I did not fully encompass, delve into. I was living too feverishly, a lover's life, and all that I sensed and perceived intuitively (like the understanding of

Artaud) I did not take time to expand. I did not have the care, the patience, the craftsmanship, the thoroughness I have now. It is no accident that I found Artaud's letters in the vault, that I read them with new eyes, rediscovered them and will be able to complete his portrait. As I wrote to Henry, I am enjoying these relationships now more than in the past, because my hypersensitivity made them painful at the time, and I am free of that today.

Mary Caroline Richards translated Artaud's *Le Théâtre et son Double*. There is a growing interest in Artaud. But so little of his work is translated into English that what is known about him is the sensational aspect of his periods of madness and his drug addiction. Today re-creating and rediscovering them, Pierre Jean Jouve, Suarez, Giraudoux's novels, I felt a painful nostalgia for my life in France. It is rare in me, for I live in the present. Marguerite is a great poet, but she feeds only on native food, what nourished me does not interest her, so I can't share the writers I love with her.

During this month I dreamed the words: *Apologia pro Vita Sua*. I am not even sure of the spelling. Was that the name of Oscar Wilde's confession written in jail? Bogner opened a new pocket of guilt. My Proustian world is my only joy, tracing webs and correlations.

Pinocchio is stunned by the condensed, edited diary. Sat in his chair one hour without speaking or moving. Could not write me. Cursed silence. I had to call him up and then he told me. But the university cannot afford the original. My French editor, André Bay, awakens and writes me: *"Je vous embrasse pour ce que vous êtes."*

The first time I saw Varèse, the lightning eyes, wild hair, vehemence, awed me. Gentle Louise beside him. *Grande dame.* The room of their house tinted green from the trees in the backyard, more like a European house. Thickly furnished, cumulative, books, records, settees, small tables, Louise's small desk on which she translates Michaux, Rimbaud, Simenon. Downstairs, on street level, is Varèse's den. Music scores pinned to the wall, big Chinese gongs, instruments whose names I do not know, the piano, recorder, records, a cluttered desk, chaos. One has to see him at work to know the joy he takes in it. Every sound a miracle! He listens to the very last echo. He plays the tapes as loudly as possible. It was like being inside the steeple next to the bells, as in Chartres, a loudness which is a form of torture. Varèse's laughter, his play on words ("You suffer from Proustatite"), his descriptive *jeux d'esprit*. He is ready to mock, rebellious, explosive. He intimidated me until I grew tougher and he mellower. Women were always impressed with his vigor. In Brussels he was on the film jury, and Baroness Lambert was charmed by him.

[Spring, 1964]

The Odyssey of *Spy in the House of Love* continues. Jerry Bick interested Robert Wise, who always wanted to make an art film with his own money.

He admires Marguerite Duras. I started a quest to reach her. I knew her French literary agent. Marguerite Duras was interested. Cables and long-distance telephone calls. She is afraid to fly. She is willing to meet Robert Wise wherever he is filming *The Sound of Music*. Robert Wise invited Jerry Bick and me to meet him in Salzburg.

André Bay, my publisher, gave her the wrong book, *Ladders to Fire,* instead of *Spy in the House of Love*. I felt I had to see her to reorient her. I expected a great deal from her own subtlety in relationships, her elusive dialogues, her indirect approach to situations, her suggestiveness, extraordinary poetry. I thought of *Moderato Cantabile*. I could already see Sabina emerging from her intelligent, skillful hands.

Meeting with Marguerite Duras in Paris warm and spontaneous. We embraced like old friends. She is small, Oriental-looking, with short dark hair and very brilliant black eyes. First meeting alone. She loves *Spy in the House of Love,* said it was a beautiful book and she was willing to adapt it for the screen. Then we had a meeting with Jerry Bick. Jerry thought at first it was not necessary for me to come, to spend money on a gamble, but when we found how little English Marguerite spoke, he was glad. His time was short so we kidnapped her and the three of us took the train to Salzburg to meet Robert Wise, who was filming *The Sound of Music*. We were to meet at dinner. Wise was on location during the day.

Salzburg so beautiful. A wide river, old town, flowers, mountains. Amusing touch: every café, every bakery is called Café Mozart, Patisserie Mozart, Cinema Mozart.

Jerry is courteous and thoughtful as a manager. He and Marguerite went shopping together. Marguerite is straightforward, earthy. Says Jerry is *"gentil."* I write while waiting for Wise to return from work.

So far I have been very malleable, watching my children (characters in my books) grow and change before my eyes and becoming Duras' children, or Jerry's children, without a murmur.

What impresses Americans are Duras' flat-heeled shoes, colorless shirt, soiled pullover, brown leather jacket, her naturalness and directness, boyishness. She is really simple and lovable.

Robert Wise is refined, has sensitive hands, looks like a businessman but with keen observant eyes, and gentle manners. Duras made a hit by saying that what she had done (slow rhythm) she did not want to do again. That she liked the quicker pulse of my work and American films. Much exhausting talk. Jerry always establishes a sensible balance. But Duras, though far out and not sensible, won out. It might turn out to be a good marriage after all. All I did was to encourage, sustain, translate. Dinner was relaxed and pleasant. Mrs. Wise returned from a concert later. Rain prevented me from visiting the city. I was happy, and even if the film is not *Spy* it is a breakthrough for other works.

Duras is very small, maybe four feet, tiny. Born in Indochina. Peasant stock. The *Sea Wall* novel was her story. I saw the film long ago. She is earthy and enjoys everything. Wise liked her.

We returned to Paris.

I arrived at eleven P.M. at the Hôtel d'Angleterre, which I like, with its bathroom in the closet. Found a bouquet of red roses from André Bay and a pile of *Spy in the House of Love* in French. I was tired and went to sleep, watched over by giant daisies and roses dancing on the walls and bedspreads, and giant pine cones on the curtains. The French love nature. I had my traditional breakfast in bed.

Television program, radio program, and meet the press. Sunday I will see Duras.

Photographs from Tracey. Cable from Antonioni asking to see Jerry. Jerry is in London seeing Joseph Losey (Duras likes him). When Jerry came we went together to visit Malraux. Jerry wants to film *La Condition Humaine*. He knows it by heart, can talk about the characters with intimate knowledge of them. Malraux had said he did not speak English but I could see he understood what Jerry said and did not need a translator. An Empire-style room, all mirrors and gold, a lackey in red with a stick. More doors. From the window of Malraux's office one can see across the courtyard, the balcony of Colette's room before her death. As a special honor she was allowed to remove one of the balcony's supports to be able to lie in bed and see the garden. I, who remembered the thin, passionate Malraux of the Spanish war days when Gonzalo and I went to hear him speak and incite us against fascism, could not reconcile this image with the man before me, a well-fed, cozy-looking businessman. He looks like a comfortable bourgeois with thyroid eyes, and nervous tics (he had them in his youth). We had a good talk. He liked the idea of the film now that France was on speaking terms with China. The French like Jerry because he is bright and well read.

Sunday I sat quietly in a little café in front of Saint-Germain-des-Près, talking with Duras. Her last book is a best seller and is in all the windows. She gave me photographs of herself. This was our last talk because she leaves for the country.

Visited Paule Thevenin, who is editing all of Artaud's works. She showed me drawings by Artaud. I saw his letters and notes. A note by him on the back of a picture of Heliogabalus: *"Mon amour pour vous, Anaïs, prend la forme d'une sorte de religion."*

Worked with Jean Le Gall-Trocmé on proofs of *House of Incest* to be published by *La Table Ronde.*

Basic difference between American and French films is pace. The French films are slow, brooding. American films active and fast-paced. Americans always want humor, not tragedy. I like the quick pace, but there are themes one cannot treat humorously when feeling is deep. So here we are trying an international alliance.

This morning an interview with *Art.*
City soft and beautiful, Malraux has increased lighting. Saint-Germain-des-Près Church, the light comes through the trees, the whole church is dappled with moving shadows. I was photographed walking along the Seine looking for my houseboat. The thing I always find human in Paris and which touches me are tiny houses, tiny windows, tiny restaurants, people sitting at small tables with small

red lamps, something of the doll house. Even the policemen are small, not big and fat as in New York.

Duras lives around the corner from my hotel. Three flights up, dark, dirty stairs but a big apartment overlooking the most picturesque tiny French courtyard with small medieval houses. Lots of books. Uncrowded. Big desk in her bedroom. A sixteen-year-old son, sullen, tough-mannered, indifferent, like any standard American teen-ager. I like her tousled short hair, her big warm eyes, her laugh. She is warm, alive. She shows no ego. Wants badly to work in America.

Was on TV with Du Mallet. Asked me why do they always link my name with Miller and Durrell. "You have nothing in common with them. You are closer to Marguerite Duras and more genuine, more human."

Saw a flower show stressing that ninety per cent of flowers are poisonous to human beings. Someday they might prove that ninety per cent of human beings are poisonous to other human beings.

I am not made for public life. Even when I am treated lovingly as the French do. I suffer from stage fright. I feel nervous and tense all the time.

Met the dean of critics, Maurice Nadeau. He made Miller and Durrell famous.

Interviews. One for Lausanne *Express*.

As television was live, everyone discovered I was in Paris and friends began to call.

For my spirit it has been good, after so much neglect in America. This acceptance makes me feel less lonely.

Radio Canada one hour.

At Musée Moderne a depressing show. Painting gone mad. Hideous. Old valise full of old dolls. A shelf of cooking spices. A black womb filled with broken dolls. A headless woman on a motorcycle.

Marguerite took me walking through the Marais, once a dirty, unkempt, sloppy quarter nobody went to. Malraux went to work, classified all historic buildings, restored, cleaned and illumined some jewels of architecture from the fourteenth, fifteenth and sixteenth centuries. Really beautiful. He had the gardens restored as they were. These were once the homes of aristocrats, and many famous people. Some of the gardens are used for open-air concerts, plays. When one sees the whole scene now, illumined, one understands the spirit of the French who wanted order, symmetry, serenity in design. By night they re-create the past with scenes from French classical plays.

Lunch with Lotte Eisner, who writes on film and knows the history of films thoroughly. She is the heart of Cinématèque.

Long interview with *Le Figaro*.

French homes are filled to the brim with good books, the talks are marvelous, the aliveness, mental alertness, the knowledge, the atmosphere, the sparkle.

This morning more journalists.

Spirits high. I don't have to worry about inadequate clothes, as America has made informal clothes fashionable.

Burroughs, Mary McCarthy and my books all in shop windows together.

Varèse's score for *House of Incest* will be played at Berlin Festival next year. I am so euphoric to have reconnected with France.

The journalists write nonsense: I have the face of a feminine Pharaoh (Pharaonne in French); I wear a red dress; I ask for hot coffee . . . How amazing!

[Summer, 1964]

And now home!

Waiting. Waiting. Waiting. The script arrives. It is a Marguerite Duras story. It is not Sabina. I translated it, distressed by the altered, changed, unrecognizable story. It was not my decision. Robert Wise did not like it.

At times I could see the humor of it: the combination of my misty writing and Duras' oblique style was bound to produce pure fog.

Another deep disappointment, when I least expected it.

Alan Swallow came to Los Angeles for the Publisher's Conference, invited by Leo Hamalian. I was shocked to see him on crutches, and with absolutely white hair when he is only forty-nine. He was, as I knew he would be, natural and warm and genuine. He was the only panelist who did not talk about money. He talked about the writers he had loved and published because he loved them, how he had managed to start with a printing press in a garage printing poets and now had a long list of writers. The other publishers I felt were misleading the students, talking about Norman Mailer's fifty-thousand-dollar advance, making a novelist's life seem lucrative, when so few reach such best-seller status. Alan Swallow talked about the pleasure of discovering writers, the "mavericks," as he said, and stressed the love of publishing, and the kind of writers who loved their work. He was vigorous and made important points.

We gathered afterwards for an evening of talk to which he had invited the writers he publishes. It is striking that he published Maude Hutchins when no one knew about her. He published Allen Tate, Vardis Fisher, Natalie Robbins, Glenn Clairmonte, Frank Waters. And how I dislike the snobbish attitude of the East about a "little publisher out West."

At dinner he talked about his wish to move to California. The climate would be kinder to him and the problem of storage was becoming acute in Denver.

In his talk he did not say the commercial publishers should not exist, he merely felt that they needed to be complemented by independent small publishers. "A small publisher can assert his taste and judgment. He need not compromise so much. He may bring to light some excellent work."

Very often a book he had launched would end on the list of bigger publishers.

He was a writer himself, a poet and an essayist.

He published a valuable book, Wallace Fowlie's book on *The Art of Surrealism*.

Writers could not survive without small publishers, just as small magazines had given space to so many writers who would never have become known otherwise. Small publishers correspond to the research workers, pioneers, paid by big industries.

I was invited to the housewarming of Dr. Raymond Weston and Lynn Weston. I became interested in her because she was a painter and her paintings were hung all through the house, and in him because I heard he was a brilliant doctor, and I have always had (perhaps because of my need of them) a strong attraction towards talented doctors. We became friends. They had two sons. One was very fragile-looking, with enormous green eyes, reminded me of Proust; he could have been my own son.

Lynn often telephoned me when the events of the world crushed her and impeded her painting. I suggested she start the day painting before reading the papers, as I do with my writing.

When she had an exhibit she asked me to write about her painting, which I was glad to do.

Lynn Weston depicts human figures with boldness and dynamism but not with the static surface faithfulness of representational art. In her work they are integrated with a total and very modern condensed vision of the world. Her work has both a vigorous and emotional appeal and yet is able to suggest the mythological overtones of human life. She can render the poetry of light and motion. She has a skill for breaking up monotonous surfaces into radiant fragments which give mobility and liveliness. In her human figures she portrays drama, joy, pain, loneliness, injustice, but they bathe in the atmosphere of unwithered nature. Her human beings are whole but condensed by a modern selection of essential details. Abstraction in painting has represented the forms revealed by science. It is a development which runs parallel to science. Lynn Weston uses it in the way it is used by the new novelists in France, a distillation of human experience into a form which suits the speeded-up rhythm of our life and our heightened consciousness of its meaning. In Lynn Weston, abstraction means a selection of meaningful traits to achieve what one might call the mathematics of emotion.

Her human figures have a core, an individuality moving in a brilliant air of heightened consciousness. She is able to portray, without ever resorting to banality, the theme of man's inhumanity to man, as in "Give Me Utterance." With montages, she dramatizes the plight of the black man. She is able to draw figures which arouse compassion without sentimentality of color or form. In her gouaches she expresses reveries and sensitivity. The tones melt and become transparent but the lines remain delicately accurate, integrated while imaginative and poetic. There is a care for detail which in the end explodes in a light, transparent, lyrical world. She appeals both to the mind and to the senses. She is a painter of intelligence. The human quality of her work includes a knowledge of mutation and metamorphosis, growth and expression. It welds two elements rarely found in unison today, the human with the abstract, insight with lyrical ebullience, lucidity and reverie.

I can hardly keep up with the activities around me, and the bulky correspondence.

Oliver Evans begins his study of my work for Harry Moore's collection of criticism, *Crosscurrents,* published by the Southern Illinois University Press. This means frequent meetings with him, answering his questions, which he tapes.

Marguerite Young's *Miss MacIntosh, My Darling* is accepted by Scribner's. Which means we are collecting statements, planning reviews and informing all her friends.

Robert Wise gives up on *Spy in the House of Love.* This means starting new correspondence with other possible producers. Marguerite Duras likes Losey and starts discussing the project. He was interested until he read the script.

Ever since I had done the editing for Kinsey's collection I began to see how I could solve the problems of editing the diary. When the Kinsey project fell through because of his death, I was already involved in the editing, and I began to show it to Alan Swallow, and to Gunther. Their reaction was encouraging. Swallow liked the diary immensely but felt it might be too big a burden for him. The first volume was already a big book, and there would be others, with photographs. We began to discuss the possibility of a shared publication. He gave me the names of publishers he had worked with who might collaborate with him. I would rather have worked with him alone because we work so harmoniously together, he is so devoted to his writers, works so hard for them. I did detect in his letters a growing fatigue. He could not find a helper. The young men who might have been interested were afraid to be drafted and did not want to exploit his training and then leave him.

[Fall, 1964]

I had edited one thousand pages and could now go back and edit more tightly, more severely.

Gunther began to show it to publishers.

I worked very hard on obtaining permissions from the main personages in the diary, which meant showing them the manuscript and starting a correspondence. The objections were always minor details. The essence of the portraits no one objected to.

Every other day I receive a letter from a librarian asking if I would not give the originals of the diary and letters to their library. They are not aware that because they did so little to contribute to my reputation as a writer, because they were passive spectators to my difficulties, the diaries are my only capital.

Collages was published by Alan Swallow with a reproduction of one of Varda's collages on the cover. It received good reviews, one by William Goyen in *The New York Times,* and a much more perceptive one by Deena Metzger in *The Free Press.*

The English edition, published by Peter Owen Ltd., also gathered good reviews, very unusual in England, where my work is not understood. If the diary is ever published, I worry about its reception there because of the English horror and hypocrisy about the personal. It is from England that America inherited its taboo on the personal. To be interested in self-development, in self-growth, in self-education and improvement is inevitably a symptom of neurosis, narcissism, egocentricity.

Never has the word "ego" been so misinterpreted as in America. The dictionary definition is: "The self that feels, thinks, wills and acts." It is always confused with egocentricity, or egomania, which is altogether another thing. The only virtuous state in America is selflessness, and the illusion by which America lives is that it has a collective spirit. Humanism should be the result of such virtue, but it is totally absent. And what can a nonexistent self contribute to the universal? This great American persecution of the self does not recognize the egomania of competition, of ambition and greed. And this so-called nonself has resulted in a people who can be brainwashed more easily than any other because without the self there is no power of discrimination or evaluation.

After an enormous labor I finished my part in the dating and editing of the Miller Letters. A big book. I had to consult the diary, reread my own letters, question friends. Henry was working too, and Gunther and I had to study his comments, his opinions. He has entered a period of concern about the consequences of his frankness. Henry was not sure that such a concentration on his work would interest people, but everyone who looks at the letters is fascinated with the story of his development as a writer, the books he liked, his preoccupations and meditations.

Three novelists had a determining influence on my novel writing (aside from Proust and D. H. Lawrence). They were Jean Giraudoux, Pierre Jean Jouve and Djuna Barnes. The reading of *Nightwood* finally crystallized my aspirations towards poetic prose in the novel. I read it in the thirties and wrote Djuna Barnes a letter which she did not answer. I admired her from afar when she sat at the Dôme. She looked handsome in her tailored suit and red hair, but I never dared approach her. The effect of her not answering influenced me in another way: I have never left a letter unanswered because I remember my own disappointment.

I have always mentioned *Nightwood* in lectures, written about Djuna Barnes, praised her work whenever the occasion arose. I still think it is a perfect example of the poetic novel, a classic.

In the forties I was concerned that no one seemed to follow the direction indicated by D. H. Lawrence, James Joyce, Djuna Barnes.

I read the section, "Watchman, What of the Night," many times at lectures. I repeated that I owed my formative roots to Djuna Barnes among others. It did not seem to me that America had given her the recognition she deserved, did not give her the general respect they gave to Isak Dinesen. I classified her among the nocturnal writers.

Albert Guerard classified her as effete. There is nothing effete in *Nightwood*. Djuna Barnes deals with the anguish of love instead of the horrors of destruction and sadism.

I am glad to pay tribute to the depth, the power and vision of *Nightwood*.

Beatrice Wood is a very beautiful woman who wears saris and American Indian jewelry. Her ceramics are luminous, pearly, bejeweled against the light in her studio. They are so remarkable that the State Department sent her to India to exhibit and to teach her art. She wrote a book about her colorful life, travels, adventures in New York as an art student. She knew Marcel Duchamp and had a copy of the famous unfinished book, the first of the Dadaist pranks. Inside of a box, he had thrown sketches, slips of papers with notes for intended books, fragments of projects, quotations he liked, a scrapbook, and offered it as it was.

She had been in love with Reginald, and in witty letters teased him for his English reserve. Reginald was at once fascinated with her and cautious, and would not commit himself, but when she married someone else he complained, and often came like a reproachful visitor to her house in Ojai.

We visited her and watched her work. The clay, the ovens, the paints were interesting to see as a prelude to the ceramics she exhibited in a glass studio, where the light could illumine them. They had the quality of ancient Egyptian pottery, as if kneaded out of pearls and colored by rainbows.

I wrote a review of her exhibition:

People sometimes look wistfully at pieces of ancient ceramics in museums, as if such beauty were a part of a lost and buried past. But Beatrice Wood is a modern ceramist who is creating today objects which would enhance our life. As Erik Satie the composer said: "The artist has a vision of beauty, but the critic only looks at it through eyeglasses." The colors, textures and forms of Beatrice Wood are both vivid and subtle. But more important perhaps because of her training as an actress, Beatrice Wood is able to portray a sculptor's range of dramatic presences, from tragedy to comedy. The decorative ability is extended into portrayals of humor, euphoria, or contemplation. She constructs a vase of the purest aesthetics and then carves around it a string of witty abstract clowns on a trapeze. Her colors are molded with light. Some pieces have dignity and grace, some are homely and fat and contented. Others are mellow, yielding, suave, or mobile and alive. They are both ornamental and entertaining. They fill an empty space with the same individual presence as a piece of sculpture. Some have tiny craters, as if formed by the evolutions, contractions and expansions of the earth itself. Some seems made of bubbling gas-filled lava. Some are jewelled like crushed sea shells or pearls, others are iridescent and smoky like the trailways left by satellites. The warmth and range of her moods would bring relief to our harsh cubistic architecture. The Japanese say it is the irregularity of the potter's clay by which the sculptor reveals his humanity. Beatrice Wood combines her colors like a painter, makes them vibrate like a musician. They have strength even while iridescent and transparent. They have the rhythm and the lustre both of jewels and of human eyes. Water poured from one of her jars would taste like wine.

When Nobuko went to Japan she aroused the interest of a Japanese publisher, Kawade, in my work. When I was in New York, they both came to see me. Nobuko acted as translator. Kawade came with a basket full of the delicate, small gifts that I love. The result of the visit is that he will publish *Spy in the House of Love.*

Lincoln Center, New York, has the most remarkable features: TWO rolls of toilet paper, for example, to make sure you don't run out; then, to notify you it is time to enter the pretentious hall with its sky of cheap-restaurant portholes, there is the pleasant, charming sound of a wartime alert signal; leading to the taxi stand, in perfect harmony with stone, steel, marble and glass, is an Old-Ladies-Home Trellised Canopy to save you from rain, a frivolous, flimsy, tea-garden trellis with climbing ivy; as an afterthought, they try to warm up the Cool World, to add charm by scattering a few pathetic tables with umbrellas to remind you of Piazza San Marco . . . but even the pigeons stay away, they are not taken in.

[Winter, 1964–1965]

In New York the women wear boots and have heavily made-up eyes. We are all afraid to take the subway because of so many attacks by hoodlums. They write graffiti on all the subway windows, slash the seats and hold up people. The city is obliged to let policemen travel in the subway and patrol the cars.

It was while I was in New York that I heard of Peter's suicide. Renate's voice over the telephone was so desperate, so terrible to hear, the wails, the weeping, the lamentations. I could only suffer with her. I could not ask questions. I would have liked to be there to console her. But John behaved so humanly, stayed at her side day and night, fearing for her reason.

Peter's story: Because Peter's father was not there (Renate had divorced years ago), we all felt Peter was in part our child. This was emphasized by the fact that he was a dreamer, an artist, a sensitive child. When Dr. Janiger asked if any one of us knew a child whose parent would be willing to let him try LSD, I thought of Peter because I felt he had been exposed to dreams, to fantasies, to the artists' work around him, and that he would be more prepared for visions and dreams than any child I knew. But I found that Renate had a horror of drugs, and that she expressed her disapproval of drugs so vehemently that this was later to influence events and prevent Peter from admitting that he took drugs at college from his drug-pusher roommate.

But before college, from the age of seven, he was always drawing, with vivid imagination. He drew mythical drawings, imaginative drawings and also science fiction, automobiles, airplanes. He was truly a modern child. He was used to being the only child among grownups, and Renate's young lovers treated him more like a playmate than a child. At parties and masquerades he invented his own stories and costumes. During the filming of *The Pleasure Dome* by Kenneth Anger he played a role and was a part of the fantasy.

He made some very strong drawings which reminded me of a modern version of the sculptures on Mayan architecture. I used them to illustrate the first version of *Seduction of the Minotaur* [first titled *Solar Barque*]. The little book looked beautiful.

He was a dreamer. When he went to school for the first time he heard a distinction made between Jew and Gentile. He questioned his mother. His grandmother was Jewish.

He also discovered that he preferred his mother to all the little girls in school. He told his mother he would much prefer to sleep with her.

He had pale blue eyes. Gentle manners. But he was reticent. When Renate went traveling with John on the sailboat, Peter had no way to come and see me. The one time he did come, he was so disturbed by his mother's absence that he did not talk very much. I would see him at the beach. Perhaps because I was his mother's friend he did not confide in me. He was then in trouble. He had difficulty adjusting to college. He consulted a psychiatrist. He did not confide in his mother. As he had always had a dreamy manner, no one noticed a change in him. He was more secretive perhaps, that was all.

When his mother went to Europe with John he was left in the care of a very conventional family. He was not used to fixed meal hours, fixed hours for coming home, a structured orderly life. There were clashes. He was lonely, he missed his mother's free bohemian life, with the playfulness, the laughter, the openness. When he came to see me, I could not reach him. He was wrapped in a cocoon of reverie which carried him far away from people, and no one could fill the need for his mother.

No one was aware of the change in him because he had always been pale, and distant. Very little of his feelings showed on the surface. He was outdistancing all of us. He had often heard his mother say she did not believe in drugs, that there were other ways to attain high moods, illuminations and reveries. He took her words as a judgment.

We all failed to hold him, to pierce his reserve, his elusiveness.

He was depressed, and went to Mexico with his roommate to buy drugs. He came back and visited Synanon. They told him if he wanted help he had to move in. Again he was afraid of his mother finding out.

He came to live with Renate. While she was out, he took an overdose of drugs and died in her house.

Renate went through an agony which was as terrible as the death itself. It was a nightmare from which she could not awaken. John stayed by her side. It was a period of insane grief. She wailed, and wept and lamented. I was not there but her voice over the telephone was a long cry of pain. This was a bitterer sorrow than the ordinary death of a child. It was an unbearable burden on a mother's sense of responsibility for her child. A mother was there to help, to comfort, to rescue, and Renate was capable of all the mother roles, she was essentially maternal. Why had he not turned to her, not reached for her? Why had he gone alone into his final solitude? Why had he died mute and unconfiding, with so much love around him? Why did all connections with others break so that he floated into the void? All of us felt the same way, as if we had failed to hold him. It was too ironic that a son of Renate, who was eminently created for maternity, who was protective, nurturing, full of empathy and devotion, should die by his own will.

Were there signs we did not read? How near did he feel to life and people? Was he not already remote, detached, and the drugs merely a confirmation of that remoteness? A confirmation of a solitary journey. For if a drug awakens the dreaming man, it does not bring the man nearer to other human beings. It may extend his journey into the unconscious but does not point to the return to human life. How much did he care for the sea, for the sun, for women, for pleasure, for communion with others, for tenderness? Was he gone from all of us long before the final parting?

If one is not comfortable in human life, one dreams. But these dreams can be fulfilled and create a world that is endurable. His mother's solution. The artist's solution.

The rippling, the free, the contagious laughter of Renate was never the same again. She has her humor and her ironies, and her tendency to convert every experience into comedy. But underlying it all, there is a part of herself which died with Peter.

All we could do was to exorcise a guilt she should not have. He had been well loved, protected, and understood. But guilt is not rational. Every suicide raises the question of our responsibility. We question our attentiveness, our care of each other, our communal duties. Were we observant enough, clairvoyant enough, did we listen for the cry of the nightmare, the lament? Did we observe the quiet ones, the remote ones, the silent ones, the mysterious ones?

Do we feel we have to keep everyone in life, alive? Rescue each other, dispel each other's phantoms, watch over each other's sleep? Lest one of us sink and vanish beyond help or rescue.

Diary writing is reduced to a minimum by the bulk of my correspondence. Many letters exchanged with Daisy Aldan, with Gunther on publication matters, more and more publication problems, books being translated into Catalan and Spanish, published in England, in France, all requiring discussions. Correspondence with reviewers, with Alan Swallow, with Nobuko, with Ruth Witt Diamant, who, after being the most popular hostess to all the poets in San Francisco, retired from teaching and embarked bravely on a new career. She took all the tapes of poets' readings to Japan and taught American literature. She wrote expansive letters on life in Japan. There was much correspondence and many visits with Henry Miller over the editing of his Letters and of my Diary. There were many meetings and correspondence with Oliver Evans over his critical study of my work. So much outward activity prevented me from describing, from meditating, from analyzing events. The publication of Henry Miller's letters to me caused a stir and brought reviews and letters. I sat on a panel at San Fernando State College and discovered I was ineffectual on panels. I withdraw from arguments. I can only perform alone. I was trying to get a perfectly edited diary, which gave me a lot of work. Eliminating repetitions. Joaquin read the diary and rectified errors in family history.

The problem of not hurting others' feelings caused me much distress. Henry was offended by certain statements, and as I said, I wanted to do him justice, not injustice. The discussions ended peacefully, and he gave me a Varda collage. He himself has begun to be concerned at the consequences of his frankness. He fears a libel suit from his first wife and from June. He writes me: "June was in an asylum for two or three years. Out sometime, now, and holds a civil service job for the City of New York. I help her when I can."

His days of poverty will be over when Grove Press publishes five of his books all at once.

———

Alan Swallow has trouble with his leg, an infection of the bone which intermittently responds to antibiotics, and often causes him much pain.

I have the greatest admiration for Simenon. I read every one of his books. I think he knows more about human nature than any writer I know, he is subtle and a wonderful psychologist. He has the greatest quality of all for a writer, that of not passing judgment on his characters.

[Spring, 1965]

A big crowd came to see the new Varda collages at the Brand Library, Glendale. It is a library where they have art shows, art books, recordings and music, the gift of a rich woman. It is an imitation of the Taj Mahal in India. By a coincidence, because we are all supporting an Indian student through college by buying saris made by his father, about six of us were in saris, quite lovely. Harry Partch was there. Varda, white-haired and rosy-skinned, was happy. I read his portrait from *Collages,* and students showed a film they had made of Varda constructing collages on his houseboat in Sausalito. Afterwards we all went for a snack at Dr. Bob Macy's (Jim Macy's brother). I have not had time to describe Dr. Jim Macy, an immensely skilled eye surgeon who, outside of his science, is interested in drugs, in Zen, in Miller. We call him the hippy doctor. He once brought me an eye in a little box. As we all demonstrated our abilities, he wanted to demonstrate his. He has a Varda gold collage in his office. The gold collages are those I longed to have but could not afford. He is full of humor, pranks, and uses Miller's language freely.

Friends wanted to publish a magazine devoted to Varda but could not get him to write an autobiography. We know so little about him. Finally he wrote me:

Facts: Born out of a woman, weight at birth 9 pounds and a half. My head so bulky I had to be pulled into this world with forceps. Immediately out of the womb I started playing with laces on the bed from which my mother inferred that I would be forever irresistibly attracted to women and concerned with their apparel. These are God's truth. More prosaic ones: Studied in Paris. Loathed and despised all my teachers so I changed constantly from one academy to another. At 29 I had my first one man show in London which was a great success. Since then I have lived from my paintings and never more through crime (only very periodically). I have had exhibitions in all the major towns of the U.S.A and in Europe, including London, Paris and Marseilles. Lately the tempo of the exhibitions has increased in speed to the ratio of 3 a year. The FBI is watching me as a crypto-exhibitionist.

No museum will have any of my work. I am only represented in every home where taste, intelligence and all the refinements of the spiritual and physical voluptuousness are enthroned. But above all I am proud of Rexroth's title for me: a boudoir painter. The most beautiful eyes of America loaded with infinite bliss are feasting on my pictures while museums gather works scientifically and electronically devised by computers previously aerodynamically psychoanalyzed to give the public a pain in the neck. I don't teach anymore. My last class composed mostly of women had an abrupt and violent ending. I dismissed the whole bunch, and without white gloves as is my innate courtesy when dealing with the fair sex. Two or three of the pupils uttered an obscenity so gross and revolting, although all these ladies were of good birth and breeding, that I hesitate to commit it to writing (I have at different times of my life been connected with arrant ruffians and the rabble of the evil quarters of the Mediterranean harbors so it takes a lot to shock me). Nevertheless what I heard from these soft-spoken socialites was topping all profanity. These charming dolls confessed that they still derived pleasure (here I still hesitate to commit to paper this monstrous obscenity), they confessed that they derived pleasure from Rouault and Rembrandt.

At a musician's house I met Deena Metzger, who looked like the most beautiful of the Biblical women, with her dark hair, suntanned skin, and keen black eyes. We became friends immediately. She and her husband, Dr. Metzger, took me out on their sailing boat. She was writing in a very original way, sometimes mysterious. While writing novels she wrote reviews for the *Los Angeles Free Press*.

After reading her first novel, *Skin-Shadows/Silence,* I wrote Deena:

I like what you have done. I expected to. But I was not sure how skillfully you could weave this sensory perception of events, with realism, with the unconscious dialogue and the documentary, because it is the problem of writers today which all of us are struggling with. I think you did marvelous things with silences, with images, some almost like a film, the physical world and its taste. I can see why you understood the perception of the senses so well. You have a respect for the image, for sensation, for a receptivity and awareness which seeks to develop other ways of experiencing. The story is strong. At times almost exaggerated as experience is when lived through emotion. You make no pretense at objectivity and detachment, as so many novelists do. In that sense you work as a poet. There is much poetry in the writing. The sea, the animals, the trees, all play a role. They are not backdrops. I like the way it is all woven together, one organically affecting the other, words, people, sounds, images, places . . . You would make a good filmwriter. Dialogue both outward and inward.

But words *not overused* or the will or the mind in the D. H. Lawrence definition of modern crime. Go on. And show me more. I think the writing is individual, personal, and original. And today, when we are swamped in mechanical standardized writing, I can't say more. Go on and dare all of it. All the way. In your own way.

At Dr. Robert Haas' house I meet an editor from *Partisan Review*, who looks immensely surprised at my appearance and says: "Nature is certainly kind to you."

I answered: "To make up for the unkindness of *Partisan Review*."

So many new friends I have no time to describe. I like Dr. Haas, who is head of U.C.L.A. Extension, Department of Humanities. He is warm and passionate about art. He is married to a charming Japanese woman, Tomi, and has two adorable little girls. He is enthusiastic about his projects, programs, books, and was a devotee of Gertrude Stein when he was a very young student. This devotion was sustained all through his life.

Today Oliver Evans is coming with his tape recorder and a list of questions. He is now working on *House of Incest* to which he is giving as much care and meticulousness as if it were Rimbaud or Mallarmé. He is a very conscious analytical critic. He asks me if it was intended, the return motif of the quena, the flute made out of human bones, and later the mention of bones cracking under weight of lovemaking. It is hard to explain how I work unconsciously, trusting, flying blind by some other sense not conscious, and how these accidental coincidences of images happen. Before he began the study of my work I pleaded with him to study the sources of which he knew nothing: surrealism, psychoanalysis.

[Summer, 1965]

One of Proust's firmest beliefs was that a writer and his work should not be made to fit together. "A book is the product of a different self from the self we manifest in our habits, in our social life, in our vices. It is not very agreeable to think that when I am dead anyone who chooses will be able to study my manuscripts, compare them with the definitive text, and infer suppositions which will always be false as to my method of work and the evolution of my thought."

This is what I felt as I read chapters from Oliver's book. I finally wrote to him:

I may be wrong, but I had the feeling that you had shifted your ground in the last chapter, from the first inspired concept of my other dimensions to a rather literal base. You are now judging the novels from a conventional, realistic point of view. Everything I say, I mean symbolically as Lawrence did. When I speak of emotional connection with woman, elation, I do not necessarily mean lesbianism. For the first time you apply definitive category, explicit interpretations: lesbian, nymphomaniac, incest. For the first time you have used your reading of the diary to affirm: Djuna is Anaïs Nin. If you are going to relate the novels to the diary you will get involved in errors as the diary unfolds and develops and proves the fiction is not biography. If one writes fiction there are alterations and transpositions. Another thing which distressed me is comparisons with Henry Miller. Miller is a comic writer, not a romantic writer. *Winter of Artifice* is a tragic book and one does not look for humor in a tragic book. You don't look for Miller comedy in Djuna Barnes or in Kafka. This seeking of humor and caricature was made by critics looking for the wrong thing in my work. I did do a humorous book, *Collages*, when the themes were light. You once gave me high praise for the poetic passage on dreams. But you can't have surrealism, and then suddenly analyze the plots of the novels by standards of conventional novels. You started by considering the novels as poems. You first approached me as a poet. You cannot apply standards of conventional structure to someone who never worked by those standards. I know what the basic difficulty is: that my roots and influences are not familiar to you, you judge by American literature, native influences. Then you also make personal judgments. You decide that I repudiated my father's salon world because I did not want to share him, but

377

both in the novel and in the diary I made it absolutely clear that the conflict was between bourgeois and bohemian life. I think from now on I should not read chapter by chapter and leave you free to pursue your own interpretations.

Having done the editing of the diary for the Kinsey Institute and then been faced with the disintegration of the Institute, the impulse to continue editing "for the future" kept me at work. Gradually I began to see how I could edit it for the present. I let others read the pages I had done, first hoping to find a home for the original diaries, then confiding in Swallow and Gunther. One activity would lead to another. The reactions encouraged me. But before I let Gunther show it to publishers there was a crisis.

It began with a nightmare: I opened my front door and was struck by mortal radiation.

I grew fearful, anxious. I went to talk with Dr. Bogner. We discussed each fear separately. The main fear was my concern with hurting others through my revelations. Having written the diary always with the conviction that no one would read it, I never censored myself. I wrote spontaneously. The only fragments I showed others were selected (I let Henry read his and June's portraits because he was anxious about what I was writing). So, there was the problem of the frankness of the portraits.

There was another dream: My mother (no longer alive) was reading the diary and was as shocked as she was when I wrote a book about D. H. Lawrence.

Another fear. As most critics had treated my novels so maliciously, what would they do with the diary?

Bogner pointed out that most of my fears were related to *past* experiences.

There was also the old guilt about sensual experiences. This taboo was my own.

Meanwhile, as if to confirm the old fears, several publishers wrote negative letters.

Joaquin was tolerant and understanding, noting only the different versions of the past which arise in every family. He reacted against my father's tendency to enhance and color his past. I employed legends and rumors which I never sought to confirm;

Joaquin was cautious: "This was neither proved nor disproved." I, the fiction writer, opted for my father's embellishments. We reached a compromise.

Bogner stressed how all of us were deeply marked by events in the past in which parents or teachers appeared as *judges*. Childhood sexual games punished left a deep scar.

Suddenly it seemed to me I was exposing myself to the maliciousness of the world.

No. I would not publish it.

But another force, far stronger, was pushing me on—I had faith in the diary. I had put my most natural, most truthful writing in it. I was weary of secrecy, of showing only a small portion of my work. I felt the strongest and best of my work was there. I felt a maturity in the editing. I felt able to solve the problems. There was plenty of material so that what I could not publish would not be missed. I could avoid the blank spaces.

A driving faith urged me on. It was the vulnerable human being who trembled. But had I not always made these audacious leaps in spite of my fears? When I wrote the preface to *Tropic of Cancer* I risked losing everything, everyone who loved or protected me. It was an act of defiance and rebellion against the very world which sheltered me.

Dr. Bogner watched the struggle. She took the fears one by one and we considered them. What would be left if I took out the few phrases which distressed Henry? So much more! Those who asked not to be in the diary. I could not violate their wish. Some people have a horror of exposure. One by one we struggled with the human problems, the ethical problems. For example, I could not write about what was confessed to me during the five months that I acted as a therapist under Rank's supervision. Henry had never considered all this when he was working in Paris. His life was the theme of his work. He mocked my concerns. Yet today he is concerned about June and about his first wife. And in his letter to me, he protected his first daughter.

After each talk, the fact remained that there was so much richness of experience that the excisions did not matter. And people would read between the lines. It was not in my nature to be explicit in sexual matters because for me they were welded to feeling, to love, to all other intimacies. Explicitness destroyed the atmosphere, the secret beauty, the moonlight in which sensuality took place.

The ambivalent condition was painful. I wanted to give, to share. I could give and share myself, but as my life was entangled with others, I could not *give* their lives. They did not belong to me.

One main theme emerged: I had to act according to my own nature or else the diary itself would be destroyed. Others trusted me with their intimate life. If I betrayed this, I would no longer be Anaïs and the diary would end. It was in my nature anyway to bypass the destructive aspect of others and to relate to their creative or numinous aspects. That was my world.

Soon I began to see the fears as born out of the past—the eye over your shoulder, parent, teacher, therapist—as, for example, when Allendy forgot the therapist does not judge and he judged my artist life from the point of view of a bourgeois and a Marxist—I may not have listened to him but the judgment left its mark. America's puritanism, even though I did not believe in it, was expressed in all its criticism of writers. And the standard applied to women was truly a double standard, twice as strong!

So, Dr. Bogner, the world appears as a vast jungle full of dangers to one's vulnerability. I have to venture, not with a work of art separate from myself, but with myself, my body, my voice, my thoughts, all exposed.

Already, I had had to suffer from the concept that all diaries are narcissistic, that introspection is neurotic, when I knew that I overflowed with love of others and that introspection was the only way to accomplish the inner journey of self-creation.

Help me, Dr. Bogner. She is aware that I am reverting to the Catholic confession. Give me absolution. That would give me peace.

But she is too wise to re-enact a childhood conditioning. Her role is to show me there is no sin, no wrongdoing, just an artist obsessed with her portrayal of experience. Ever since I left Europe and the marvelous confessional talks (such as Henry and I had in Louveciennes), I felt the loneliness of Americans locked in their fear of intimacy with their secret self and therefore with others. I felt the need to publish the diary as strongly as the snake pushing out of its old skin, the crab desperately pushing out of his old shell grown too tight, too small. All evolution had this impulse. The impulse to give and the impulse to hide fought a mighty battle in this quiet office overlooking a garden. I would call it a battle between the woman and the creator. The woman, protective, secretive, placing the needs of others before her own, accustomed to her mysteries which man has feared; and the creator, no longer able to contain her discoveries, her knowledge, her experiences, her lucidities, her compiling of the hidden aspects of people so ardently pursued. Dr. Bogner, you won't just give me absolution in the old way and tell me that I have committed no crime. You want me to see that the fears are created by the past, that there is a possibility that this work is beyond such petty judgments, that it is beyond the personal. You, Anaïs, have to be as courageous now as you were while writing it. While writing it, no one looked over your shoulder; while writing it, your mother did not read it; or your father, who said D. H. Lawrence was all chaos and clumsy writing; the Irish priest who forbade your reading Zola and Gide was not reading it. You admired Henry for not having such concerns about the family reunion in Brooklyn he depicted so savagely. Your diary is mostly a work of love. You were primarily a lover. Let the woman lose her small personal fears. Let her dare to offer her creation and if necessary suffer the consequences. After all, the fear of being judged is a very minor one. Every artist had taken that risk.

Dr. Bogner sits so calm, so serene, so wise. The small, timorous concerns fall away. The main, mature objective becomes clear. I believed every word I wrote. They were written by another self. So let this self, the creator, face the world.

As I worked to bring all the fears to the surface, the mature writer accepted the challenge. I solved the problems of editing according to my own standards, my own ethics.

I feel like Proust, that I must get the diary done before I die, and even though I have no organic illness, each time I have been to the hospital it has been a near-death affair, like double pneumonia, so I don't expect to survive the next crisis. But I don't mind any more, since I have known the joy of being accepted in France, which mattered deeply to me. Good reviews, correspondence, friendliness of critics. It compensates for America's indifference.

Gunther was showing the edited diary (eight hundred pages) to publishers. Their reaction was hardly encouraging. Random House, after reading only 150 pages, felt the diaries would not be interesting to enough readers to make possible the scale of publication I had proposed.

Peter Israel of Putnam writes me:

The main thing I want to tell you is how fascinated I am with the diaries. I had no idea what was in them except by reputation and no idea that I would become so utterly engrossed in the pages. Surely they stand as one signal example of the confessional genre. Perhaps I expected depth of self-revelation and it is certainly there, but I never anticipated that people about whom I knew little and didn't particularly care, Allendy, your father etc. would come so vibrantly alive, like characters in some great Proustian novel. I have not quite finished these 800 pages but I am most of the way through them, and I find myself hoping that they never end. In sum, I don't know whether these pages are commercial or not, or what the answers are to the commercial questions. By which I mean that I don't know how a reader who knows nothing about Anaïs Nin, will react. Personally and unprofessionally I think they are terrific, a great personal expression—and somehow I wanted you to know that right off.

No faith in their personal reactions. Always the Sphinx: is it commercial? He will now try it on the salesmen, on the doorman, the elevator man, the night watchman, the cleaning woman, the delivery boy, the telephone girl, and then he will ask me to make it more like *Candy,* or more like Simone de Beauvoir, or more like Mary McCarthy, and yet keep it clean for the *Ladies' Home Journal,* and perhaps rewrite it in the third person, make Allendy a black physician, my father a taxi driver, for human interest, and instead of a stillbirth describe nine healthy children, and my life in Harlem, in Indochina as a missionary (for the social angle) and throw in a few famous names. Also I might perhaps have one of the characters have an alcoholic problem, make Joaquin a dope addict, to be in the trend. Everything to make it like other best sellers.

Letter from William Morrow to Gunther Stuhlmann:

I'm sorry that we have taken so long to reach a decision concerning the Anaïs Nin Diary, but in truth it has not been an easy project to assess. There have been several readings of the first volume, and a good deal of thought.

And now I must tell you that we have come reluctantly to the conclusion that we are not the proper publishers for the Diary. To be perfectly frank, we found this first section disappointing from a purely editorial point of view, though perhaps one reason for this is that we are not sufficiently tuned in to Anaïs Nin's over-all point of view and style. Nonetheless, we did not find in this section the forthrightness and the sense of contact with real people that one expects from a journal. It was all as if it were half-fictionalized even as it was first being set down, and the form into which it has been edited strengthens this impression. It reads almost like a loosely constructed novel. In short, we could not see that this would appeal to more than Anaïs Nin's present devoted but—we think—rather small audience and that, accordingly, the project represents a disproportionate investment, even with Alan Swallow's help.

I am returning the manuscript to you herewith. We are all sorry indeed that we could not enter into this enthusiastically.

In New York I spent much time with the Open Theatre, a group of young actors with extraordinary talent. Improvising, experimenting in a loft below Houston Street.

Cannot catch up with events. Edgar Varèse writes a score for *House of Incest.* So mystifying that he who made fun of any talk about the unconscious, did enter this realm by way of *House of Incest.* The music is a strange wail, from a sorrow never described before in music.

Bruce Tsuchida was not allowed to do his Ph.D. on my work by the English Department of Amherst College. "She is an eccentric writer." We corresponded, as he could not resign himself to the decision, and I had to encourage him not to quit his college for that reason.

No reviews in *Los Angeles Times.* No review of Miller *Letters* in *Time* magazine, which makes it a practice to assassinate Henry and to ignore me.

After the negative letters from Random House, Putnam, and Morrow, Alan Swallow spoke to Hiram Haydn of Harcourt Brace. I was in New York, and Gunther gave a cocktail party. It was at this party that Peter Israel definitely turned down the diary and Hiram Haydn said to me: "I love it. I will do it." How I loved his directness and conviction. We talked. We had met before. He had me talk to his students at the New School. He has a daughter and he said something about the father-daughter relationship moving him deeply in the diary.

[Winter, 1965–1966]

Writing to a Belgian poet I admitted knowing the states he describes, the anxieties, missing heartbeats, failing intuitions, deserts, disconnection from other human beings, but I added that I had waged a constant and stubborn war against my neurosis. I never believed that creativity came from such seasons in hell as the romantics did. I gave my faith to psychoanalysis, and after many years the energy I wasted on anxieties ceased and I was able to work better, to live better, to commune with others, to be relaxed in the world. I had more intuitions, more states of illumination, more awareness, more inspiration and fertility than before. I truly believe that a perpetual season in hell can be exorcised. The poet does not have to live in hell. The life of Kafka is the best example of the corrosive effect of neurosis. Everything that he wanted, a wife, a family, heirs, he destroyed. It would have interfered with the writing. And yet the writing itself was painful and harmful to the human being.

Just read in *Art* magazine that France has at last recognized Pierre Jean Jouve as a great poet and possibly the inventor of the anti-novel. Planted the seed for the poem novel to which I responded in 1931. He was ignored until now. When I first read his novels I became aware of what I wanted to do with the novel. I cannot forgive France, which has such a tradition of poetic novels. America could not help judging everything by Hemingway journalism. But France! And on the same day I had another shock. A whole book to prove that Jean Giraudoux was schizophrenic, too far from reality! France, the capital of symbolism, surrealism, metaphors.

Marguerite's book [*Miss MacIntosh, My Darling*] is out, published by Scribner's. Much will be written about this book; but I feel the portrait of her as a person, of the woman who wrote it, is a key to the work.

She is a down-to-earth Middlewesterner whose conversation soars into the infinite. She is, herself, one of her own most fascinating characters. She has a native sense of comedy with a recognition of American imagination. She studied philosophy, is articulate, eloquent, fecund, at ease in the daily world. She has the power of an epic writer, nothing of the minuteness we consider feminine. She has the wide span of America, its vast epic vistas. Her apartment is filled with objects which pay their respect to the past. She loves her roots.

Friends know she loves antiques and help her collect them. She may receive you barefoot, in a loose mumu dress, but while participating in daily, homely life, she dreams as Don Quixote did for Spain, as Thurber did for America, but *Miss MacIntosh* is America's most literary dream.

One of the keys to the book lies in the acceptance of Proust's vast cellular expansion, the vast web she weaves. The human basis of this laborious structure lies in the scarf story (as a child she wanted to knit the longest scarf ever knitted). This beehive, this organic cell-like proliferation, is an effort made to unify all experience, rather than the fragmented life so often presented by writers today. Her scarf wish enabled her to sustain the mood and unity of this work. She knitted the unbroken chain, the work with a disappearing shoreline.

Her characters are native, the old maid, the prizefighter, the suffragette; but her hero is illusion. Where else but in the quest for illusion or the stripping of illusion could she have found an Esther Longtree, everlastingly pregnant, who could not remember all the fathers of her still-unborn child? She could not remember the featherweight champion who wanted his son to be a heavyweight. She could not remember anything about him, though he was the father of a child he had never seen. "He was not the peak of her existence. He wanted to be cherished by Esther Longtree, he wanted her to remember this night with him, the turning point, a triumph over death if she had known the date."

Stillbirth of dreams.

"Nature does not care if we are born or not."

She interpreted differently when she said to me: "I just tried to put down every pebble on the road so that no one could get lost." Her feeling was that if one were to follow the full expansion of a flight of imagination, it was necessary to complete the cycle, to bring the wave which carried one away, back to shore.

She fulfills the image of maternity, to bear, to carry, to sustain one through the most abstract dimensions, far-off voyages, but also to carry one back to be redeposited on earth.

She said, once: Joyce was not her ideal; America was her ideal. As Adlai Stevenson defined it: "An America, aristocratic in its expression and proclaiming itself a realist while dreaming the boldest dreams."

"Modern writing (with the exception of great poets) lies in prose," said Marguerite.

She wanted to tell all she knew of illusion and reality. It took her seventeen years. Many of her friends did not believe she would ever finish the book.

As I wrote my review, I kept hearing her voice reading passages to me over the phone, reading with the poetic intonations of Dylan Thomas, with the hypnotic wave sounds of the rolling, spreading, tidal movements of the sea.

Review of *Miss MacIntosh, My Darling:*

When a writer decides to give us a complete universe, all that he has explored and discovered, it is necessarily vast. No one ever questions the expanse of the ocean, nor the size of a mountain. The key to the enjoyment of this amazing book is to abandon one's self to the detours, wanderings, elliptical and tangential journeys, accepting in return miraculous surprises. This is a search for reality through a maze of illusions and fantasy and dreams, ultimately asserting in the words of Calderón: "Life is a dream."

The necessity for the cellular expansion of the book lies in Marguerite Young's own words: "I just tried to leave pebbles along the road so that no one could get lost." For the perilous exploration of illusion and reality, the author's feeling is that if one is to follow the full swelling of the wave of imagination one must bring back to the shore the wave which carried you. It is in the fullness and completeness of the motion that one achieves understanding.

That is why she is able to sustain all through both the rich deep tone and powerful rhythm of the book. This is a feat of patience, accomplished by weaving of each connecting cell, with unbroken bridges, from word to word, image to image, phrase to phrase. She is an acrobat of space and symbol but she gives her readers a safety net.

This tremendous edifice is not as abstract as it might seem because it is cemented throughout by her individual vision which is fundamentally human, compassionate and humorous.

The furling and unfurling of her lyrical phrases are at times like a slow-moving camera which is able to catch not only the plain, homely, familiar gestures but the levitations of fantasy, the fluidity of emotional quick changes achieved only by magicians of language.

Although she accomplishes for native American folklore the same immortality of the myth that Joyce accomplished for Ireland, Joyce was not her inspiration. Her inspiration was America, her Middlewestern, down-to-earth America with its powerful orbital dreamers, so rarely portrayed, born on native soil, American as Joyce's characters were Irish, with the American high sense of comedy, extravagance and vividness: the bus driver, the suffragette, the old maid, the composer of unwritten music, the clamdigger, the dead gambler, the waitress, the featherweight champion, the hangman, the detective, the stonebreaker, the passenger pigeon, the frog, the moose.

The power of imagery suggests paintings (she admits she would have married Chagall). But what she is past master at is the description of subtle, ambiguous events which never become explicit. One of the characters, for example, is Esther Longtree, who is perpetually pregnant in fantasy only and who is the mother of us all in the end because she is the mother of stillbirth fantasies. Another is the featherweight champion who falls in love with the only child he never had. There are other shadow-boxers. "Nature does not care if we are born or not."

The work has a disappearing shore line. It is a submarine world, geographically situated in the unconscious and in the night. "The sea is not harmful if you sleep under it, not over it, best place for keeping pearls," says one of her characters. Parallel with science, we are taken as far up into space and as deep below as it is possible for a man to explore.

The numerous characters enter one's own stream of consciousness and cannot be erased because they are part of the American psyche, a psyche, as Marguerite Young says, capable of the wildest fantasy. They are listed only in the Blue Book of the Uncommon. Marguerite Young is an aristocrat among writers, perhaps the precursor of a new era in American literature.

The book is also a canto to obsession. Life is filled with repetitions culminating in variations which indicate the subtlety of man's reactions to experience. "To get hold of a character I may have expanded it too much but if I shortened it it would not be an obsession, and obsession is what possesses people. If I removed the repetitions I would remove one of the motifs of life itself."

The characters are tangible, accessible, familiar. But it is the nature of their experience which Marguerite Young questions, its sediments, its echoes and reflections. What is reality? Deep within us it is as elusive as a dream and we are not sure of anything that happened.

Nobuko visits me. She wears white lace stockings, a pea-green shift dress, giant daisies tied around her loose black hair which falls divided, one daisy behind each ear.

She offers me a bouquet of spring flowers, with her face buried in it, as if she were offering her face and smile with it.

When she laughs, she hides her face behind her hands.

She leans over, whispering in a conspiratorial tone: "Anaïs, I will tell you everything."

Her talk is like the whispering of leaves; if you are tempted to ask an explicit question her words fly off like a flock of migratory birds. Impressionism. Allusions. Suggestions. Diffuseness. I who thought myself adept at capturing elusiveness, could not tell whom she loved, deserted, traveled with, ignored, collaborated with. When she left I realized I knew no more about her feelings, her thoughts, her actual experiences than when I first met her.

I found the same elements in Japanese novels. I would have to find a word opposite to explicitness. In the novels there was so much of the nebulous, moonlight, poetic imprecision.

Her letters were delightful, full of inventions, a language of her own which I encouraged, waiting always for the novel she was writing, while others were concerned with phrasing it in proper English. How much originality can spring from the misuse of English.

Samples:

I was simply murdered by work.

Much has stampeded over me.

You must have gone through such a murky ordeal inside you (of my hospitalization).

Hurts me to see Japan so out of her mind.

I am made fundamentally very nostalgic.

I am like a bird with seven wings, I just flutter, can't collect my thoughts.

New York lets you remain unnoticed, unanimous conspirator . . . but out of wishy-washy self-pity I must and want very much to rise.

My reading your diary manuscript supplied me with the Super Quality petro. I feel I can take off. Like a Caravelle!

We all celebrated the success of Marguerite's *Miss MacIntosh, My Darling*. At last a work of literature, forty thousand copies sold, appreciation from intelligent readers.

The ignorant reviewers, from *Time* magazine down to *The Village Voice,* demonstrated what I call their poison-pen style, comparable to spitting in the subway. They could not read the book. They looked at its thousand pages and read that it took seventeen years to write. They attacked the giant because it exposed their illiteracy. I always held the editor responsible for allowing an untrained, obviously illiterate person to review a book, which meant spitting venom uncontrollably. It reflected on the magazine or newspaper.

William Goyen wrote a beautiful review in *The New York Times.* I wrote in the *Los Angeles Times.* Scholars wrote essays. French students at the Sorbonne struggled through with their limited knowledge of English, to write Ph.D.'s about the book.

It seemed to herald the end of the Four-Letter-Word School of Writing. It renewed one's faith in the early literary distinction of Melville, Poe, Emerson, Whitman. Ireland had its Joyce, Spain had its Cervantes, and America has Marguerite Young.

It was accepted in England immediately. Marguerite was invited to visit England.

Ruth Stephan gave a magnificent party at her home in Connecticut. A bus took the guests there. The garden was lighted with lanterns. The crowd was glamorous.

I met two remarkable women, Anita Faatz and Virginia Robinson. They were retired from the Philadelphia School for Social Research where Otto Rank lectured so often. They decided to devote their lives to Otto Rank's work, to see that the books which were out of print were reprinted, to translate material his widow gave to Columbia University, his diaries, correspondence with Freud, poems, plays. They established the *Journal of the Otto Rank Association.* All of Rank's admirers began to contribute articles. The *Journal* became a focus for all activities related to him.

Anita Faatz came to see me. They wanted to reprint my portrait of Rank in the *Journal,* but Harcourt Brace only allowed them ten pages at no cost. They would have been charged for more. A friendship was established. These were the women who came all the way to Paris to the Rank Seminars at the Cité Universitaire. I was too immature to appreciate them at that time, but today their lives touched me and impressed me and we collaborated lovingly and loyally. Wherever I went I made the *Journal* known. They in turn published everything I had of Rank's, his prefaces to the *House of Incest* and to my childhood diary. They had yearly meetings which I attended and lectured for. Once I came back from Europe at one o'clock at night, the plane was late, and I persuaded the doorman to drive me in time for the session, which meant starting out at six A.M., and I talked at ten A.M. They were extraordinarily brilliant women, who contributed much to the social sciences.

There was so much activity in preparation for the publication of the diary. To find photographs and have them duplicated. I designed constellations of friendships, like the design of horoscope charts, only the planets were cities and people.

When I tried to map out the characters which appear in the diary it occurred to me that the relationships formed a constellation similar to the planets. There were the centers or core of activities represented by cities instead of large planets! New York, Paris, London, Los Angeles, Sweden, Mexico, etc. People radiated around these major planets. Smaller constellations of friendships revolved around personalities. These in turn were linked by interrelations and their activities so they formed smaller clusters. The revolutions of friendships, their displacements, their voyages, could only be recorded by this vast web. And so I came to the drawing of planets, and each one surrounded by names of friends and the central core of their activities.

New York has an electronic heart. California a sun heart. Mexico is a nebula. Paris another form of nebula.

The animals too are in orbit.

I had hoped my publisher would use them as endpapers, as they do in travel books, or geographies. It would have meant much to the readers. But they decided to have them printed and sent to reviewers who did not care about them and never mentioned them.

There were permissions to obtain for my portraits. The lawyers at

Harcourt were very concerned with libel. As I could not communicate directly with June, Henry gave me the name of her psychiatrist, Dr. Baxter, who had helped June, and was sensitive and full of insight. I visited him and his wife, Annette Baxter, a talented teacher of literature who had written a study of Henry Miller to prove that Americans never truly uproot themselves. They were tactful and sincerely helpful, and thanks to them the portrait of June was made possible.

In the middle of all the activity, I was rushed to the hospital again. This time it was more serious. I was barely recovered when Mrs. Lindley sent me the jacket of Volume I of the Diary. I remember thinking that if I had not survived surgery I would have died believing myself a failure. But now it seemed as if everyone were interested, there was excitement, curiosity and goodwill.

During my stay at the hospital, Edgar Varèse died, and no one would tell me, knowing I would mourn him.

He did not want to die, Louise told me later. He was not ready to die. He protested to the very end. This caused much pain. There was so much vitality in him, yet he succumbed in surgery.

The first thing I did as soon as I recovered my energy was to write about him for *Perspectives of New Music*, Princeton Press.

To recognize the unique value of a man and an artist most people wait for the perspective of distance and time. But those friends of Edgar Varèse who were aware of how strikingly the personality of the man and his music matched each other, had a more immediate clue to his true stature and unique place in the history of music. He was a man who lived in a vast universe, and because of the height of his antennae he could encompass both past, present and future. I could feel this each time I rang the bell of his home and he opened the door, for if he received me with the warmth he showed to all his friends, at the same time I could hear all around him and flowing out of the house an ocean of sound not created for one person, one room, one house, one street, one city or one country, but for the cosmos. His large, vivid blue-green eyes flashed not only with pleasure of recognition but with a signal welcoming me into a universe of new vibrations, new tones, new effects, new ranges, in which he himself was completely immersed. He led me into his workroom. The piano took most of the space, and on the music stand there was always a piece of musical notations. They were in a state of revision resembling a collage:

all fragments which he had arranged and rearranged and displaced until they achieved a towering construction. I always looked with delight at these fragments which were also tacked on the board above his work-table, and on the walls, because they expressed the very essence of his work and character: they were in a state of flux, mobility, flexibility, always ready to fly into a new metamorphosis, free, obeying no monotonous sequence or order except his own. The tape recorder would be on high volume for open spaces. He wanted one possessed by, absorbed into its oceanic waves and rhythms. Edgar Varèse would demonstrate a new bell, a new object capable of giving forth a new tonality, new nuance. He was in love with his materials, with an indefatigable curiosity. In his workroom one became another instrument, a container, enclosed in his orbital flights into sound.

When we climbed the small stairway to the living room and dining room to join other friends, greeted by his gentle and gracious wife Louise, Varèse the composer became Varèse the conversationalist. He radiated in company, he was eloquent, satirical, and witty. There was a harmony between his work and his talk. He had contempt only for clichés in music or in thought. His revolt against the cliché never ceased. He used vivid, pungent language. He retained the revolutionary boldness of youth but always directed by his intelligence and discrimination, never blind or inaccurate. He never destroyed anything but mediocrity, hypocrisy, and false values. He attacked only what deserved to be attacked, never in personal, petty or blind anger as is practiced by some artists today.

Speaking once of an unsavory political character he said: *"A faire vomir une boîte a ordure."*

His wars were on a high level; they were waged against the men who always stood in the way of vast original projects because they could neither perceive them or control them.

The last talk we had together was about the irony of the Foundations and Universities not giving him a complete electronic workshop to work with. He was filled with concepts he could not carry out for lack of the necessary electronic facilities. He needed the machines which were so easily entrusted to young, unformed musicians. He needed a laboratory for exploration into future sounds. Most of these young men could not feed the machines, only run them, and Varèse could have fed them with endless volcanic richness.

Many musical experts will write about what Varèse composed. I would like to stress what he was not allowed to create, because every artist dreams of being emptied of all his riches before he dies, and when he leaves us, carrying into oblivion untapped treasures, it should arouse our sense of guilt. Varèse knew the blindness which besets most people in the presence of creative giants. I told him the story of a dinner I had attended for members of a famous corporation set up to produce new inventions. After molding their men to standard forms, disciplining them, inhibiting them, they were trying to find a way to get spontaneous, creative ideas out of them. The men, reduced to automatons, sat at a conference table and someone shouted at them: "Don't think, say the first thing which comes to your mind, anything," and this grotesque effort even had a technical name. Naturally, nothing could come from men who had long ago lost their power to create. I suggested they call in the artists I knew who were overfull of ideas, designs, etc. There was a silence. "Oh, yes, we know," they said, "you mean those mad geniuses who will not wear a clean shirt and a tie, will not come in time and *cannot be controlled.*" Controlled was the revealing word. In music too, everyone turned to the men who could be controlled, disciples, imitators, derivatives. They never dared to consult the source from which creation and invention issued like some great phenomenon of nature, the highest waterfalls, the highest mountains, the deepest canyons, the bottomless lakes. Every artist has known this isolation in which giants are left as if they were dangerous creatures. A more familiar, homelier connection could be made with the innocuous; the hack painter was easier to deal with than the original painter. It would have required a critic, a listener, a conductor or a Foundation director of equal stature to approach the artist who is, by natural rights of the creator, the dictator in his own province. How frightened we are of a revolutionary force in full eruption.

Varèse was merciless towards the timid, the flabby and the impotent. He would say: "They have handed the whole business to mechanics. The new machines need composers who can nourish them." This was the substance of our last talk. It was the first time I noticed that at 81 he stooped, but it was from illness. He was wise enough to know men's fears. He knew they would approach him when they were no longer in danger of being swept into the resonant coils of his sound flights. He is now an archetype, whose potentials were not exploited by the world, but what he left belongs to the same vast cosmology which science is seeking to charter. For every new discovery we need new sounds, and Varèse heard them before the undiscovered spaces were reached. He said gently once: "There is no avant-garde. There are only people who are a little late."

If light travels faster than sound, in the case of Varèse sound traveled much faster.

[Spring, 1966]

My convalescence was spent proofreading Volume I. Convalescence in Los Angeles was helped by the garden, the sun, the mockingbirds, the pool.

Finally I was ready to talk and read from Henry Miller's *Letters* on a television program, with Alfred Ryder reading most of the letters and Turnley Walker and I talking about them.

The Rank *Journal* will publish part of my portrait of Rank.

I began editing Volume II.

I received an invitation to visit Japan.

I reviewed the plays of D. H. Lawrence for *The New York Times.* The editor, Christopher Lehmann-Haupt, wanted to rewrite it because it was "feminine writing." I said I would withdraw it if it was rewritten. His idea of altering the femininity was to use a *passé* expression like "kitchen sink realism" à propos of Lawrence.

Private showing of Genêt's film, *Un Chant d'Amour,* at U.C.L.A. I was so moved I wrote a review for our underground newspaper, the *Los Angeles Free Press:*

Jean Genêt's film *Un Chant d'Amour* proves that true morality lies in aesthetics, not in the nature of the experience. The beauty and power of this film of homosexual love captures the very essence of love through its sincerity and absence of vulgarity. Genêt is a poet of the erotic and has created a canto to love with so much pride and style that it expresses ultimately the beauty of all desire. The only morality is that of the great artist who can arouse pride in sensual expression. He never offends the senses as many other films have done by their repellent weakness or humiliating ugliness. Genêt's film is a film of virility. That is the important theme. The prisoners could be any men—and the prison the cells which society erects between men to the detriment of their love. The men in prison are vital, filled with love; and ironically the guard is the only perverted figure: he does not love or desire, he is the voyeur—jealous, envious, impotent. He can only punish what he does not possess. This is the most unrestrained film I have ever seen, but Genêt's vigor, naturalness, and great sense of beauty give it a ritualistic, classical nobility. It converts experience into a symbolic action. By the choice of men of quality, vitality, intensity, he is saying we imprison what is alive because it is dangerous to those who are not.

There is poetry and sensitiveness in the exchange of symbolic acts: pushing a straw through the prison wall, breathing the smoke of a cigarette as a carrier of the breath of desire, swinging flowers from window to window just beyond the reach of thirsty hands. What casts a shadow of ugliness in other films results from the attitude and vision of the film maker. Puritanism paints in ugly colors. Here the Negro's priapic dance in his cell untainted by hypocrisy assumes the stature of a pagan ritual. The contrast between the destructive, sadistic impulses of the guard and the primitive, lyrical outbursts of the prisoners indicates that fine shading between impotence and virility, life and disease. When stated by a poet who accepts the full expression of desire as an act of life, it becomes as naked as nature—and as innocent. If all experience could pass through the censorship of art, it would achieve what the law has been unable to do. It would assert the need of beauty. It would teach that the only vice is ugliness, and it would automatically rid us of the caricatures of sex which have been passing for eroticism and restore to sensuality its nobility, which lies in the quality and refinement of its expression, the refinement of wholeness.

The cells become a tragic enclosure, separating man from life, from joy. At the film's most sadistic moment, a prisoner being whipped by a guard dreams of woodlands, sunlight, and pagan fulfillment. It is the guard who, unable to attain this, can only wield a gun as a symbol of virility, can only destroy because he is incapable of desire.

Volume I of the Diary is published!

April, May and June were months which erased all the past disappointments. I received wonderful reviews from Karl Shapiro, Jean Garrigue in *The New York Times,* Harry Moore, Marion Simon in the *National Observer,* Deena Metzger in *The Free Press,* and others.

I gave a talk at Barnard College to an overflowing room.

I appeared on Camera Three with lifesize sets of Louveciennes, reading from the diary.

I had a book-signing party at the Gotham Book Mart. The crowd was so big that many people stayed on the stairs, in the bookshop downstairs, and even on the sidewalk.

My mail was described by one of my correspondents not as fan mail but as love letters. Suddenly there was joy, celebration, praise, invitations to lecture, flowers, interviews, In Berkeley at Cody's

Book Shop, Ferlinghetti, one of my favorite poets, threw rose petals over my head.

The deepest and most understanding review came from Robert Kirsch in the *Los Angeles Times:*

"A sorrow made me create a protective cave, the journal. And now I am preparing to abandon this sorrow, this cave," Anaïs Nin wrote in November, 1933, at a time when she was in analysis with Dr. Otto Rank. He saw in it a "last defense against analysis. It is like a traffic island you want to stand on . . . I do not want you to analyze the analysis."

Fortunately for literature, Anaïs Nin returned after the analysis to that diary, one of the most remarkable in the history of letters. A portion of it now appears in *The Diary of Anaïs Nin, 1931–1934* (Swallow Press– Harcourt, Brace & World: $6.95; illustrated) edited with an introduction by Gunther Stuhlmann.

Dr. Rank had said that she was "being kept" by the diary, that it was the "compulsion" of the diary he fought. But the artist within Anaïs Nin sensed that the diary, begun for personal reasons as a child, had evolved as a work in itself, differing in degree and even in style from her novels and stories, satisfying another need in herself, reflecting a special set of truths about herself: "A great passion for accuracy because I know what is lost by the perspective or objectivity of art. My desire to be true to the immediate moment, the immediate mood."

It is a theme which occurs over and over again. "If what Proust says is true, that happiness is the absence of fever, then I will never know happiness. For I am possessed by a fever for knowledge, experience, and creation," Miss Nin writes.

"I think I have an immediate awareness in living which is far more terrible and more painful. There is no time lapse, no distance between me and the present. Instantaneous awareness."

Others talked about the diary, noted the striking difference in style, in intensity, in language. One of those who saw the difference was her good and close friend Henry Miller. "Elaborate! That is the only way out of these watertight abstractions of yours. Break through them, divest them of their mystery and allow them to flow . . . I think that one of the reasons you have lodged yourself so firmly in the diary is because you fear to test your tangible self with the world. You are producing gems."

Again, Anaïs Nin followed her own intuition. "I think Henry is right about elaborating. But I think he does not understand that it is because I have a natural flow in the diary: what I produce outside in a distillation, the myth, the poem."

No one, not even Miller himself, has produced as discerning and living a portrait of Miller, of Antonin Artaud, of Miller's strangely troubled second wife, June, of dozens of other characters of that period in Paris. "Kill the diary, they say; write novels; but when they look at their portrait, they say: 'That is wonderful.' "

And these portraits are uncompromising; perhaps most uncompromising is the self-portrait. Weakness and strength equally are recorded in a prose so poetic and supple that all comes alive in terror, awe and beauty. After her second analysis (the first with Dr. René Allendy turned into an analysis of the analyst), Miss Nin considered becoming an analyst herself. She rejected it. "Just when I have learned not to clutch at the perfume of flowers, not to touch the breath of the dew, not to tear the curtains off, not to extract essences from petals, to let exaltation and dew rise, sweep by, vanish. The perfume of hours distilled only in silence, the heavy perfume of mysteries untouched by human fingers . . . To formulate without destroying with the mind, without tampering, without killing, without withering. That is what I have learned, that delicacy and awe of the senses, that respect for the perfume. It will become my law in writing."

The diary in this portion becomes an odyssey, more powerful than a novel, though possessed of the same elements, beginnings, a middle, a climax, but not an end for we can expect that the remaining volumes will be published. This volume stands on its own. When the rest come along, if they possess the same qualities of insight and perception, the whole will certainly be one of the enduring works of the diary form.

It has been said that each life if traced through its labyrinth of experience contains the elements of a revelation. But, as we see here, there are other elements involved. There must be one who sees in detail, who penetrates below the surface, who connects individual experience to universal truths. ". . . Living is the constant motion toward unraveling, a dynamic movement from mystery to mystery."

There is the mystery of femininity and the mystery of identity, the mystery of poetry and the mystery of reality, the mystery of things, places and events. "I want to be the writer who reminds others that these moments exist; I want to prove that there is infinite space, infinite meaning, infinite dimension."

The ultimate test of this diary as a literary accomplishment is this: subtract the well-known names and you will still be interested in the characters and events which remain. For a long time, publication of these diaries has been anticipated. Miss Nin lived through the years which produced a great spasm of creativity. She knew writers, painters, musicians, dancers and actors. She was herself one of the central talents of this period. But unlike other memoirs—those of Sylvia Beach, for example—the interest in this volume does not depend on incidents and anecdotes. It is self-sufficient as a chronicle of a life lived with extraordinary intensity and sensitivity, recorded with great empathy and luminous understanding.

She began to write this diary as a child, to record for her father, the Spanish musician Joaquin Nin, who had deserted his family, their journey to America. She sought through this to win him back. (Some of the most touching scenes in the book deal with her relationship with her father in the years covered.) The journal became an island, a refuge. If it remained solely that, it would be of less interest than it is.

But it began to change. As she emerged into life, attempting to find herself, it gradually became something more than a protection against the world. In it she was able to discern in retrospect the thousand fragmented selves which make up a deep and sensitive person. Her face for the world to see was that of a beautiful woman, one of the most beautiful of her time. In these pages we see her despair, her shyness, her uncertainty, her enslavement to a past. But as the diary goes on, the identities become fused, meaningful and accepting of truths. Yet, even at the end of 1934, as she is about to leave for America, after three crucial and exciting years, mysteries still remain. We live with her through relationships and friendships, analysis and the desperate experience of losing her prematurely born infant.

Of special interest is what she has to say to women. Few women diarists since the 18th century have so eloquently expressed the core of femininity. "We love best those who are, or act for us, a self we do not wish to be or act out," she writes near the end. She brings out in others not merely an extension of herself but, through a kind of catalysis, illumination. Even the tortured Artaud, haunted, driven by a sense of persecution, expresses this: "With most people you can only talk about ideas, not the channel through which these ideas pass, the atmosphere in which they bathe, the subtle essence which escapes as one clothes them."

All this is done without the loss of femininity no more than the lens loses its substance when the light passes through it. With this initial publication, Miss Nin, already assured of a place in contemporary literature, makes this doubly secure.

Robert Kirsch confirmed my belief that if one goes deeply enough into the personal, one transcends it and reaches beyond the personal.

I will no longer be vulnerable to the old cliché that I am only interested in the personal.

At the end of this diary I feel I have accomplished what I hoped to accomplish: to reveal how personal errors influence the whole of history and that our real objective is to create a human being who will not go to war.

I am not indifferent to the greater dramas hanging over us, but drama is everywhere the same, microcosm or macrocosm. It is not my destiny to live the drama of Spain, war, death, agony, hunger. It is my destiny to live the drama of feeling and imagination, reality and unreality, the drama underlying the others, a drama without guns, dynamite, explosions. But it is the same one, it is from this one that the other is born: conflict, cruelty, revenge, jealousy, envy. In me it all happens in another world, in myself, and myself as an artist who remembers each day more what each day of my life touches in the past. I do not live beyond war, the drama that hastens death, accelerates the end. I live the personal drama responsible for the larger one, seeking a cure. Perhaps it is a greater agony to live this life in which my awareness makes a thousand revolutions while others make only one. My span may seem smaller but it is really larger because it covers all the obscure routes of the soul and body seeking truth, seeking the antiserum against hate and war, never receiving medals for its courage. It is my thousand years of womanhood I am recording, a thousand women. It would be simpler, shorter, swifter not to seek this deepening perspective to my life and lose myself in the simple world of war, hunger, death.

Index